Pearson Edexcel GCSE
French
Foundation

Clive Bell, Eleanor Mayes, Michael Wardle,
Tom Hockaday, Sandrine Chein

Published by Pearson Education Limited, 80 Strand, London, WC2R ORL.
www.pearsonschoolsandfecolleges.co.uk

Copies of official specifications for all Pearson qualifications may be found on the website: qualifications.pearson.com

Text © Pearson Education Limited 2024
Edited by Pearson and Newgen
Designed and typeset by Kamae Design
Original illustrations © Pearson Education Limited 2024
Illustrated by Beehive Illustrations (Adam Linley, Joseph Wilkins and Andrew Pagram) and Andrew Hennessey
Cover design by Kamae Design
Cover photo © Getty Images/FilippoBacci

Audio recorded at Chatterbox Studios, London, with thanks to Rowan Laxton, Lilian Lorain Broca, Elea Lorain Broca, Ryan Ghoussainy, Jean-Baptiste Fillon, Katherine Pageon, Tamara Moreau, William Ghoussainy and Giselle Begley

Written by Clive Bell, Sandrine Chein, Karine Harrington, Tom Hockaday, Eleanor Mayes and Michael Wardle

The rights of Clive Bell, Sandrine Chein, Karine Harrington, Tom Hockaday, Eleanor Mayes and Michael Wardle to be identified as authors of this work have been asserted by them in accordance with the Copyright, Designs and Patents Act 1988.

This publication is protected by copyright, and permission should be obtained from the publisher prior to any prohibited reproduction, storage in a retrieval system, or transmission in any form or by any means, electronic, mechanical, photocopying, recording, or otherwise.

For information regarding permissions, request forms and the appropriate contacts, please visit https://www.pearson.com/us/contact-us/permissions.html Pearson Education Limited Rights and Permissions Department.

Pearson Education Limited is an exclusive trademark owned by Pearson Education Limited and/or Pearson or its affiliates in the United Kingdom and/or other countries.

Unless otherwise indicated herein, any third party trademarks that may appear in this work are the property of their respective owners and any references to third party trademarks, logos or other trade dress are for demonstrative or descriptive purposes only. Such references are not intended to imply any sponsorship, endorsement, authorisation, or promotion of Pearson Education Limited products by the owners of such marks, or any relationship between the owner and Pearson Education Limited or its affiliates, authors, licensees or distributors.

First published 2024

28 27 26 25 24
10 9 8 7 6 5 4 3 2 1

British Library Cataloguing in Publication Data
A catalogue record for this book is available from the British Library
ISBN 978 1 292 466590

Copyright notice
All rights reserved. No part of this publication may be reproduced in any form or by any means (including photocopying or storing it in any medium by electronic means and whether or not transiently or incidentally to some other use of this publication) without the written permission of the copyright owner, except in accordance with the provisions of the Copyright, Designs and Patents Act 1988 or under the terms of a licence issued by the Copyright Licensing Agency, 5th Floor, Shackleton House, 4 Battle Bridge Lane, London, SE1 2HX (www.cla.co.uk). Applications for the copyright owner's written permission should be addressed to the publisher.

Printed in the UK by Bell & Bain Ltd, Glasgow

Acknowledgements
We would like to thank Polita Anderson, Sarah Bleyer, Florence Bonneau, Jonathan Caudle and Kenzie and Corey Wardle, Pascale Collier, Naomi Crookston, Céline Durassier, Gillian Eades, Gemma Etienne, Bill Finegan, Missy Finegan, Seth Finegan, Jérôme Garnier, Shirley Hockaday, Louise Leportoux, Chris Lillington, Liliane Nénot, Sheena Newland, Mario Rogic, Fabienne Tartarin, Jo Heaton and the central team at Northern Lights Learning Trust, and everyone else who has helped in the development of this course.

The authors and publisher would like to thank the following individuals and organisations for permission to reproduce photographs:

123RF: valiza 21, Iakov Filimonov 27, doodkoalex 36, Noriko Cooper 38, Cathy Yeulet 39, cladanifer 42, Cathy Yeulet 59, RUTCHAPOOM MUANGKAEW 82, Sergii Koval 82, milkos 98, stylephotographs 101, Olena Kachmar 108, zurijeta 109, Valerii Honcharuk 110, kazmierczak 110, Cebas 122, Tbralnina 123, Ihorsw 139, Cathy Yeulet 140, arnoaltix 141, amisb 147, Frugo 159, Bloodua 160, Piyawat Nandeenopparit 164, Stockee 164, Iakov Filimonov 182, Gelpi 186, Stockyimages 189, Cathy Yeulet 216, Stockbroker 221, Rido 224; **10jourssansecrans:** Association 10 JOURS SANS ECRANS 6, 10; **Alamy Images:** Sergi Reboredo 14, Associated Press 32, UrbanImages 32, Pacific Press Media Production Corp. 38, STANCA SANDA 42, Ulrich Doering 58, Boaz Rottem 66, Cavan Images 99, FORGET Patrick/SAGAPHOTO.COM 106, Antonio Guillem Fernández 107, JOHN KELLERMAN 108, Christophe Boisvieux 110, Eskimo 110, Avalon/World Pictures 112, Elena Bobrova 112, Guichaoua 112, Johner Images 116, Wavebreak Media Premium 121, Nature Picture Library 134, Thornton Cohen 138, Abaca Press 141, Aleksei Isachenko 159, Jonathan Larsen/Diadem Images 189; **Brussels - Jean-Paul Remy:** CREDIT (c) visit.brussels - Jean- Paul Remy - 2017 14; **Camping Le Haut Village:** Camping Le Haut Village 106; **Céleste De Kervenoaël:** Céleste De Kervenoaël 41; **CIJF:** ©CIJF 6; **GAELLE VANESSA PRUDENCIO E.I:** Gaelle Prudencio 32; **Getty Images:** Simon002/iStock Editorial/Getty Images Plus 6, SDI Productions/iStock/Getty Images Plus 12, skynesher/E+ 13, Mark Leech/Offside 15, Alistair Berg/Photodisc 16, Rawpixel/iStock/Getty Images Plus 16, RichLegg/ E+ 18, Andreas Rentz/Staff/Getty Images Entertainment 32, Stephane Cardinale - Corbis/Corbis Entertainment 33, Pascal Le Segretain/Staff/Getty Images Entertainment 33, cesarrospoho/iStock/Getty Images Plus 34, Mark Hunt/DisabilityImages 34, RobertDodge/iStock/Getty Images Plus 34, Pascal Le Segretain/Staff/Getty Images Entertainment 38, John Berry/Contributor/Getty Images Sport 38, FRANCOIS GUILLOT/Contributor/AFP 38, Edward Berthelot/Getty Images Entertainment 40, Dominique Charriau/Contributor/WireImage 40, KAMPUS/iStock/Getty Images Plus 42, miodrag ignjatovic/E+ 42, kali9/E+ 43, Tony Anderson/DigitalVision 48, aldomurillo/E+ 48, Tony Anderson/Stone 61, Stuart Fox/Gallo Images ROOTS RF collection 63, Vladimir Godnik/fStop 64, Golser/E+ 66, Juanmonino/E+ 68, ChiccoDodiFC/iStock 82, bhofack2/iStock 82, Cook Shoots Food/iStock 82, golero/E+ 84, blackCAT/E+ 85, Westend61 90, TatyanaGl/iStock/Getty Images Plus 90, Evrymmnt/iStock 90, Pablo Rasero/iStock/Getty Images Plus 90, adamkaz/E+ 90, DGLimages/iStock 90, Rockaa/E+ 92, BERTRAND GUAY/Contributor/AFP 93, Julien Hekimian/Contributor/French Select 93, ALLEKO/iStock 94, sbossert/iStock 94, DianeBentleyRaymond/E+ 96, Andreas Kindler/Johner Images Royalty-Free 108, LeoPatrizi/E+ 108, Pavliha/iStock 108, Maremagnum/Corbis Documentary 108, SDI Productions/E+ 109, Johner Images/Johner Images Royalty-Free 110, Balate Dorin/iStock/Getty Images Plus 110, Nick David/Photodisc 117, Westend61 117, VikramRaghuvanshi/E+ 117, Stas_V/iStock/Getty Images Plus 138, yongyuan/E+ 138, Cavan Images/Cavan 141, Mgreen2007/iStock/Getty Images Plus 158, SrdjanPav/E+ 159, Walter Bibikow/Stone 161, Laurent/iStock Unreleased 161, SDI Productions/E+ 163, Westend61 163, Catherine Ledner/Stone 163, Crispin la valiente/Moment 164, Phynart Studio/E+ 168, Murat Taner/The Image Bank 169, Giraudou Laurent/Moment 169, AlexKozlov/iStock Editorial/Getty Images Plus 169, FatCamera/E+ 174, ajijchan/iStock/Getty Images Plus 174, kali9/E+ 182, Imgorthand/E+ 183, pixelfit/E+ 184, ozgurdonmaz/iStock/Getty Images Plus 185, FG Trade/E+ 185, Jasmin Merdan/Moment 186, FG Trade/E+ 189, iStock/Getty Images Plus 189, boonchai wedmakawand/Moment 191, Hill Street Studios/DigitalVision 191, Catherine Delahaye/Stone 200, SolStock/E+ 214, miniseries/E+ 217; **Gite La Troglo à Plumes:** Troglo a plumes, ©Gîtes de France Anjou 106; **MANGERBOUGER:** Mangerbouger.fr 83; **NICOLAS LEBLANC:** Nicolas Leblanc 141; **Pearson Education Ltd:** Jon Barlow 59, Studio 8 77, Handan Erek 86, Gareth Boden 98, Gareth Boden 113, Miguel Dominguez Muñoz 171; **Samaya Production:** Samaya production/Luxe Photographie 17; **Shutterstock:** Adriaticfoto 11, Olga_Kuzmina 11, Nipa74 14, Christopher Chambers 15, Brocreative 15, Donna Ellen Coleman 24, Jorge Argazkiak 25, BAZA Production 28, Iakov Filimonov 28, 10topvector 29, Spotmatik 39, Brostock 39, Tinka Mach 42, Iryna Zhezher 42, Shutterstock 51, 10topvector 53, Pyzata 58, dan.nikonov 56, Shutterstock 59, Daisy Daisy 64, Prostock-studio 65, Angelika Jakob/imageBROKER 66, Prostock-studio 68, Aniwhite 69, Anna Kraynova 72, Fotosparrow 74, 10topvector 79, Casper1774 Studio 85, Zurijeta 86, StevenK 90, Wazzkii 92, Ph.FAB 93, Joe Gough 94, Zurijeta 98, 10topvector 103, Mila Supinskaya Glashchenko 108, Wavebreakmedia 108, David Hughes 108, Gonzalo Buzonni 108, Fasttailwind 108, Holbox 108, Olrat 108, CrispyPork 108, Gkuna 108, Viacheslav Lopatin 108, Gautier Willaume 109, VH-studio 109, Samuel Borges Photography 110, VladKK 110, T photography 113, T photography 113, BIRYUKOVA EKATERINA 116, Ina Meer Sommer 116, AndriyShevchuk 118, APIWAN BORRIKONRATCHATA 125, 10topvector 127, Saiko3p 136, Slavik_ua 136, T.Schofield 136, 2009fotofriends 137, PhotocechCZ 137, Rich Carey 138, Spwidoff 138, LanaElcova 138, chanasorn jele 138, efka 138, FocusDzign 138, AYO Production 138, Julia Tsokur 138, Julia Kuznetsova 140, Serenity Images23 142, Bist 143, kelvn 144, R_Tee 150, Dusan Petkovic 153, Valmedia 154, 10topvector 155, Enrika Samulionyte 158, LuckyPhoto 158, Alexgo.photography 159, ASashka 159, Leonid Andronov 160, AJR_photo 160, Jacob Lund 160, Krakenimages.com 163, SHARIFUL RIFAT 164, Marko Plevnjak 164, Tracy Whiteside 167, Ekaterina Pokrovsky 169, SB Arts Media 174, Kevin Eaves 174, Daniel M Ernst 177, 10topvector 179, Bensliman hassan 183, Zoltan Katona 183, Prostock-studio 187, Insta_photos 189, Blend Images 189, Lucky Business 189, Shutterstock 189, SRStudio 196, GagoDesign 197, Michaeljung 199, 10topvector 201, Pressmaster 210, Jacob Lund 213, GaudiLab 218, Prostock-studio 219, JP WALLET 223, fizkes 230, Ground Picture 233, Prostock-stock 233; **Village Flottant Pressac:** #levillageflottantpressac 106; **Yannis Richardt:** Yannis Richardt 40.

Text extracts reproduced with permission from:
Collège Alpin Beau Soleil: 58; **eurail.com/interrail.eu:** 183

Notes from the publisher
Pearson has robust editorial processes, including answer and fact checks, to ensure the accuracy of the content in this publication, and every effort is made to ensure this publication is free of errors. We are, however, only human, and occasionally errors do occur. Pearson is not liable for any misunderstandings that arise as a result of errors in this publication, but it is our priority to ensure that the content is accurate. If you spot an error, please do contact us at resourcescorrections@pearson.com so we can make sure it is corrected.

Table des matières

Module 1 Tu as du temps à perdre?
Thematic contexts: Media and technology, My personal world

Zone de culture Fêtes et jeux — 6
- Exploring events in the francophone world
- Using *aimer* + noun and *aimer* + infinitive

Unité 1 Ma vie en ligne — 8
- Talking about what you do online
- Using the present tense of regular *-er* verbs
- Discussing pros and cons

Unité 2 Tu as une vie active? — 10
- Saying what you do to stay active
- Using the present tense of irregular verbs
- Listening and transcribing in French

Unité 3 Qu'est-ce que tu regardes? — 12
- Talking about what you watch
- Forming and answering questions
- Preparing a role play

Unité 4 Qu'est-ce qu'on va faire? — 14
- Making plans to go out
- Using the near future tense
- Understanding and making invitations

Unité 5 Qu'est-ce que tu as fait? — 16
- Saying what you did last weekend
- Using the perfect tense
- Pronouncing é, er, ez correctly

Unité 6 J'ai participé aux Jeux de la Francophonie! — 18
- Taking part in an interview
- Understanding questions in the perfect tense
- Using two tenses together (present and perfect)

Grammaire 1 — 20
Grammaire 2 — 22
Contrôle de lecture et d'écoute — 24
Contrôle oral — 26
Contrôle écrit — 28
Vocabulaire — 30

Module 2 Mon clan, ma tribu
Thematic context: My personal world

Zone de culture Libre d'être moi — 32
- Talking about your identity
- Using emphatic pronouns

Unité 1 Un week-end en famille — 34
- Talking about your weekend routine
- Using reflexive verbs in the present tense
- Extending sentences using sequencers and connectives

Unité 2 L'amitié est la clé du bonheur — 36
- Discussing friends and friendship
- Making adjectives agree
- Translating a passage into French

Unité 3 Couleur famille — 38
- Talking about what people look like
- Understanding the position of adjectives
- Describing a photo

Unité 4 La place des idoles — 40
- Talking about positive role models
- Using direct object pronouns
- Using the present and perfect tenses

Unité 5 Famille, amour, gâteau — 42
- Talking about celebrations
- Using the perfect, present and near future tenses
- Recognising adverbs

Grammaire 1 — 44
Grammaire 2 — 46
Contrôle de lecture et d'écoute — 48
Contrôle oral — 50
Contrôle écrit — 52
Vocabulaire — 54
Révisions de grammaire: Modules 1–2 — 56

Module 3 Ma vie scolaire
Thematic context: Studying and my future

Zone de culture Au collège chez nous — 58
- Learning about school life in francophone countries
- Describing photos

Unité 1 Quelle est ta matière préférée? — 60
- Talking about school subjects and school life
- Using comparative adjectives
- Giving opinions with reasons

Unité 2 C'est injuste! — 62
- Discussing school rules
- Using *il faut* + infinitive
- Expressing opinions, agreeing and disagreeing

Unité 3 As-tu fait des progrès? — 64
- Talking about what has happened at school
- Using irregular verbs in the perfect tense
- Pronouncing *oi* and *oy*

Unité 4 Souvenirs d'école — 66
- Talking about what school used to be like when you were younger
- Using verbs in the imperfect tense
- Translating into French

Unité 5 Les langues et l'avenir — 68
- Talking about learning languages
- Using the imperfect, present and near future tenses
- Using negatives in different timeframes

Grammaire 1 — 70
Grammaire 2 — 72
Contrôle de lecture et d'écoute — 74
Contrôle oral — 76
Contrôle écrit — 78
Vocabulaire — 80

trois 3

Table des matières

Module 4 — En pleine forme
Thematic context: Lifestyle and wellbeing

Zone de culture *Sain ou malsain?* — 82
- Describing and giving opinions about dishes
- Understanding advice in the *vous*-form imperative

Unité 1 *Bon appétit!* — 84
- Talking about meals and mealtimes
- Using the partitive article (*du, de la, de l', des*)
- Using present and perfect tenses in translations

Unité 2 *Bien dans ma peau* — 86
- Talking about good mental health
- Using modal verbs (*devoir, vouloir, pouvoir*)
- Giving advice

Unité 3 *Ça ne va pas?* — 88
- Describing illness and accidents
- Using the perfect tense (with both *avoir* and *être*)
- Booking a doctor's appointment

Unité 4 *Je change ma vie* — 90
- Saying what you are going to do to improve your life
- Using the near future tense
- Using *plus* and *moins*

Unité 5 *Mieux vivre* — 92
- Talking about lifestyle changes
- Using the imperfect, present and near future tenses
- Distinguishing between tenses when listening

Grammaire 1 — 94
Grammaire 2 — 96
Contrôle de lecture et d'écoute — 98
Contrôle oral — 100
Contrôle écrit — 102
Vocabulaire — 104

Module 5 — Numéro vacances
Thematic context: Travel and tourism

Zone de culture *Voudrais-tu voyager?* — 106
- Talking about holidays and accommodation
- Using *pour* + infinitive

Unité 1 *Des vacances de rêve* — 108
- Talking about your ideal holiday
- Using the conditional of *vouloir*
- Giving reasons for your preferences

Unité 2 *On part pour la Corse* — 110
- Discussing what you can see and do on holiday
- Forming different types of questions
- Giving advice with *il faut*, *on doit* and *on peut*

Unité 3 *Le monde en fête* — 112
- Talking about festivals
- Using the perfect and imperfect tenses together
- Understanding more complex sentences using *qui*

Unité 4 *Guide de voyage* — 114
- Reviewing and booking holiday accommodation
- Using negatives in the imperfect and perfect tenses
- Identifying positive and negative opinions

Unité 5 *Vive les vacances!* — 116
- Talking about staycation activities
- Using a range of tenses
- Using *si* + the present tense + the near future tense

Grammaire 1 — 118
Grammaire 2 — 120
Contrôle de lecture et d'écoute — 122
Contrôle oral — 124
Contrôle écrit — 126
Vocabulaire — 128
Révisions de grammaire: Modules 1–5 — 130

Module 6 — Notre planète
Thematic context: My neighbourhood

Zone de culture *Madagascar: miroir du monde?* — 134
- Understanding infographics about the environment
- Practising numbers and percentages

Unité 1 *Notre monde est beau* — 136
- Talking about geography and the climate
- Using comparative adjectives
- Learning about francophone countries

Unité 2 *Planète en danger* — 138
- Talking about environmental problems
- Talking about future weather
- Pronouncing the 'open o'

Unité 3 *Des grands gestes* — 140
- Discussing what we can do together to protect the environment
- Using the present and perfect tenses
- Describing a photo taken outside in nature

Unité 4 *Des petits gestes* — 142
- Talking about day-to-day actions to protect the environment
- Using the imperfect tense to describe what you used to do
- Extending spoken and written answers

Unité 5 *Innovation verte* — 144
- Discussing school environmental projects
- Using the present, perfect, imperfect and near future tenses
- Practising answering questions featuring a variety of tenses

Grammaire 1 — 146
Grammaire 2 — 148
Contrôle de lecture et d'écoute — 150
Contrôle oral — 152
Contrôle écrit — 154
Vocabulaire — 156

Module 7 Mon petit monde à moi
Thematic contexts: My personal world, My neighbourhood

Zone de culture À louer, à vendre **158**
- Understanding adverts
- Using demonstrative adjectives (*ce, cet, cette, ces*)

Unité 1 *Là où j'habite* **160**
- Describing your town or village
- Using indefinite adjectives *chaque, tous, tout(e)(s)*
- Using the correct preposition for 'in'

Unité 2 *Sur la bonne route* **162**
- Asking for and understanding directions
- Using *à* and *de* with the definite article
- Using negatives to talk about your town

Unité 3 *Tendances et shopping* **164**
- Talking about shopping for clothes
- Using *de* to indicate possession
- Practising shopping role plays

Unité 4 *La maison de mes rêves* **166**
- Describing your ideal home
- Working out if adjectives go before or after the noun
- Using *si* clauses

Unité 5 *As-tu déjà visité Paris?* **168**
- Talking about visiting another town or city
- Translating questions in different tenses
- Spotting different tenses from verb endings

Grammaire 1 **170**
Grammaire 2 **172**
Contrôle de lecture et d'écoute **174**
Contrôle oral **176**
Contrôle écrit **178**
Vocabulaire **180**

Module 8 Mes projets d'avenir
Thematic context: Studying and my future

Zone de culture Mon été de rêve **182**
- Talking about summer plans
- Using two different tenses to express the future

Unité 1 *Mes passions et mon avenir* **184**
- Talking about future plans and hopes
- Using a range of structures followed by the infinitive
- Using sequencers

Unité 2 *Express Mondial* **186**
- Talking about travelling and earning money
- Using verbs that take *être* in the perfect tense
- Buying tickets at a station

Unité 3 *Quelles sont tes compétences?* **188**
- Talking about possible future career paths
- Forming feminine nouns
- Looking up words for possible future jobs

Unité 4 *Bien payé, mais fatigant!* **190**
- Talking about different jobs
- Using verbs followed by *à* or *de*
- Translating into French using a range of timeframes

Grammaire 1 **192**
Grammaire 2 **194**
Contrôle de lecture et d'écoute **196**
Contrôle oral **198**
Contrôle écrit **200**
Vocabulaire **202**
Révisions de grammaire: Modules 1–8 **204**

Révisions

Module 1	*Tu as du temps à perdre?*	210	Module 5 *Numéro vacances*	218
Module 2	*Mon clan, ma tribu*	212	Module 6 *Notre planète*	220
Module 3	*Ma vie scolaire*	214	Module 7 *Mon petit monde à moi*	222
Module 4	*En pleine forme*	216	Module 8 *Mes projets d'avenir*	224

Speaking support

Speaking exam revision: Conversation questions **226**
Speaking exam revision: French phonics **228**
Speaking exam revision: Role-play skills **230**
Speaking exam revision: Picture task **232**
Derivational morphology and useful verb tables **234**

Module 1: Tu as du temps à perdre? Fêtes et jeux

- Exploring events in the francophone world
- Using *aimer* + noun and *aimer* + infinitive

A. 10 jours sans écrans

Qu'est-ce que c'est, les dix jours sans écrans?

Les jeunes passent dix jours sans télévision, sans portable, sans jeux vidéo et sans ordinateur!

Les parents, les professeurs et les associations locales organisent d'autres activités:

- du sport 
- de la danse 
- du théâtre 
- de la cuisine 
- de la musique

sans	without
l'écran (m)	screen

B. Tous les ans, c'est la Fête de la Musique le 21 juin

Plus de 120 pays participent à la fête.
Il y a des concerts dans plus de 1 000 villes.

♪ On peut écouter toutes sortes de musique.
♪ On peut voir toutes sortes d'instruments.
♪ On peut voir toutes sortes de groupes!

C'est vraiment génial!

le pays	country
participer à	to participate in, to take part in

C. Les Jeux de la FRANCOPHONIE

Tous les quatre ans, c'est les Jeux de la Francophonie.

Plus de 3 000 jeunes de 88 pays francophones participent aux Jeux de la Francophonie.

C'est le seul événement sportif et culturel international, en langue française, pour les jeunes.

les jeux (m)	games
la Francophonie	group of countries that have French as their main language
seul(e)	only, alone
l'événement (m)	event

D. Programme des Jeux de la Francophonie

Concours culturels
- la chanson
- la danse (hip-hop)
- la littérature
- la peinture
- la photographie

Compétitions sportives
- le basket
- le cyclisme
- le football
- le judo
- le tennis de table

■ pays participants

le concours	competition
la peinture	painting

Zone de culture

Module 1

1 Écouter
Listen and repeat these words. Pay special attention to the pronunciation of **é**.

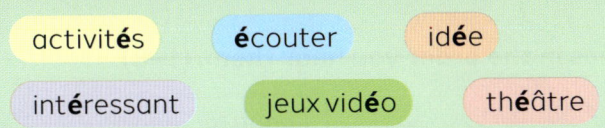

activit**é**s   **é**couter   id**é**e   int**é**ressant   jeux vid**é**o   th**é**âtre

> The letter **é** is a shorter sound than 'ay' in English. To pronounce it correctly, try grinning widely as you say it!

2 Écouter
Read text A. Then listen. Is each person positive (P) or negative (N) about the *dix jours sans écrans* initiative? (1–3)

Les dix jours sans écrans. À ton avis, c'est une bonne idée ou une mauvaise idée?

À mon avis, c'est …	🙂	une bonne idée. amusant. intéressant.
	☹️	une mauvaise idée. ennuyeux. nul.

je suis d'accord — I agree

> In French words, the final consonants **-n, -s, -t** and **-x** are usually silent. However, if the next word begins with a vowel, the final consonant is pronounced. This is called a **liaison**.
>
> Listen and repeat the phrases:
> dix jours san**s é**crans
> à mo**n a**vis
> C'es**t u**ne bonne idée.

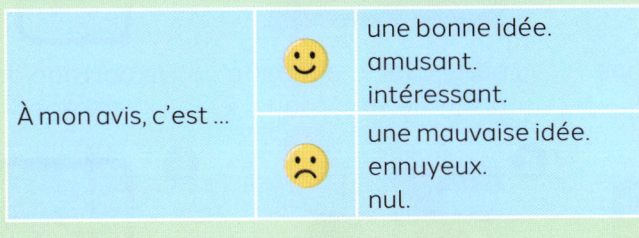

3 Parler
In pairs, give your opinion in French about *les dix jours sans écrans*. Pay attention to the sound é and the liaison.

- Dix jours sans écrans! À ton avis, c'est une bonne idée?
- À mon avis, c'est … Tu es d'accord?
- Oui, je suis d'accord. / Non, je ne suis pas d'accord. À mon avis, c'est …

4 Lire
Read text B. Copy and complete these sentences in English about la *Fête de la Musique*.

1 The *Fête de la Musique* is every ▭ on the ▭.
2 More than 120 ▭ take part.
3 There are ▭ in more than 1 000 ▭.
4 You can ▭ to all kinds of ▭.
5 You can see all kinds of ▭ and ▭.

5 Écouter
Listen to and read text C. Note down in English <u>four</u> key facts about *les Jeux de la Francophonie*.

6 Lire
Read text D. Look up any unknown words. Copy and complete the grid in French with your own likes and dislikes from text D. Make sure you use the correct definite article (*le/la/l'*).

Example:

J'adore … ❤️❤️	J'aime … ❤️	Je n'aime pas … ❌	Je déteste … ❌❌
la danse	**le** tennis de table		

7 Écrire
Translate these sentences into French.

1 I love basketball.
2 I like playing football.
3 I don't like dancing.
4 I hate sport.

G

To express likes or dislikes, use *aimer* (to like), *adorer* (to love), or *détester* (to hate), followed by:

- a definite article + noun
  J'aime **le** basket.   I like basketball.
  J'aime **la** danse.   I like dancing.

- a verb in the <u>infinitive</u>
  Je n'aime pas <u>jouer</u> au basket.   I don't like playing basketball.
  Je n'aime pas <u>faire</u> de la natation.   I don't like swimming.

sept

1 Ma vie en ligne

- Talking about what you do online
- Using the present tense of regular -er verbs
- Discussing pros and cons

Écouter 1
Listen and write down the letters of the activities in the order you hear them. (1–8)

Qu'est-ce que tu fais en ligne?

l'appli (f) app

a Je télécharge des applis sur ma tablette.

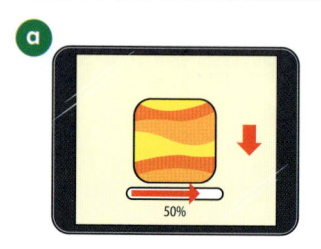

b J'écoute des chansons sur mon portable.

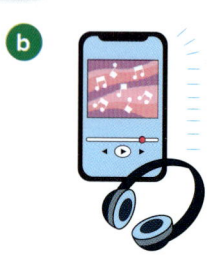

c Je parle avec ma famille en Tunisie, en Afrique.

d Je partage des photos.

e Je cherche des idées pour des activités.

f J'achète des vêtements.

g Je joue à des jeux contre ma meilleure amie.

h Je regarde des vidéos amusantes.

Lire 2
Find and write down the eight regular -er verbs used in exercise 1. List them like this:

je télécharge → télécharger
(I download)   (to download)

Écouter 3
Listen. For each speaker (1–4), note down in English:
- what they do online
- how often they do it.

tout le temps	all the time
tous les jours	every day
souvent	often
quelquefois	sometimes
de temps en temps	from time to time

G
There are many regular -er verbs in French. They work like this in the present tense:

jouer (to play)	
je joue	I play
tu joues	you (singular) play
il/elle/on joue	he/she/one plays / we play
nous jouons	we play
vous jouez	you (plural or polite) play
ils/elles jouent	they play

envoyer (to send) changes **y** to **ie** in these forms:
j'envo**ie** tu envo**ies** il/elle/on envo**ie** ils/elles envo**ient**

Page 20

Parler 4
Read the dialogue with your partner, then create two new dialogues by changing the underlined details.

- Qu'est-ce que tu fais en ligne?
- <u>Je regarde des clips sur TikTok</u>.
- Est-ce que tu fais ça souvent?
- Oui, je fais ça <u>tous les soirs</u>. Et toi? Qu'est-ce que tu fais en ligne?
- <u>J'écoute des chansons sur Spotify</u>. Je fais ça <u>souvent</u>. C'est <u>génial</u>!

Listen and repeat the words. Say these as though they were one word.
Est-ce que (tu) ... ? (sounds like *eska*) = **Do** (you) ... ?
Qu'est-ce que (tu) ... ? (sounds like *keska*) = **What** (do you) ... ?

Use **c'est** + a masculine adjective to give simple opinions:
C'est ... 👍 amusant / génial / super!
           👎 dangereux / mauvais pour la santé.

8 huit

5 Écouter — Listen and read. Is each statement below true or false?

Internet: pour ou contre? La parole aux jeunes Québécois

Le pour 👍

Malik
Internet, c'est génial, il y a des applis pour tout, pour la musique, pour les jeux, j'adore ça!

Hugo
Pour les jeunes, Internet, c'est essentiel. On parle avec des amis, on écrit des e-mails, on envoie des messages.

Noémie
J'adore les réseaux sociaux comme TikTok et Instagram. Par contre, il y a des problèmes de sécurité.

Le contre 👎

Alexia
Au Québec, les jeunes aiment passer du temps devant un ordinateur ou sur un portable, mais c'est mauvais pour la santé.

Omar
À mon avis, Internet, c'est dangereux. Il y a de fausses informations et de mauvaises images.

Karima
Je n'aime pas utiliser ma propre identité en ligne car il y a des risques.

on envoie (envoyer)	we send (to send)
passer du temps	to spend time
la santé	health
la propre identité	real identity

1 Malik doesn't like using the internet.
2 Hugo thinks the internet is very important for young people.
3 Noémie thinks social networks can be unsafe.
4 Alexia thinks spending time online is good for you.
5 Omar thinks information online can be trusted.
6 Karima uses a different identity online.

6 Lire — Re-read the text in exercise 5. Find the French for the phrases below.

1 there are risks
2 apps for everything
3 social media
4 it's dangerous
5 fake news
6 it's bad for your health

> The following are often used to express contrasting points of view:
> *mais* — but
> *par contre* — however

7 Parler — In pairs, take turns to read the sentences out. Give feedback on each other's pronunciation. Then listen and check.

1 À mon avis, Internet, c'est une bonne chose.
2 J'adore jouer à des jeux en ligne.
3 Par contre, les jeunes passent souvent trop de temps devant un portable.
4 Il y a aussi des risques de sécurité.

- Watch out for silent final **-e** (e.g. chos**e**) and silent final consonants like **-s**, **-t** and **-x** (e.g. jeu**x**). The verb endings **-e**, **-es** and **-ent** are also silent.
  One exception is *Internet*, where the final **-t** is pronounced.
- Words that are similar to English are usually pronounced differently in French, e.g. *Internet, risque, portable*.

8 Écrire — Write a post about your online life for the web forum in exercise 5. Include the following bullet points:

- what you do online
- how often you do it
- opinions
- good and bad points of the internet.

Je joue à des jeux contre mon ami.	
J'écoute de la musique sur mon portable.	
J'envoie des messages.	
Je partage	des photos sur Instagram.
Je regarde	des clips sur TikTok.
Je fais ça	souvent / quelquefois.
	tous les jours / tout le temps.
À mon avis, Internet est	génial / essentiel.
	dangereux / mauvais pour la santé.
Il y a	des risques de sécurité.
	de fausses informations.
	des applis pour tout.
	des réseaux sociaux géniaux.

neuf 9

2 Tu as une vie active?

- Saying what you do to stay active
- Using the present tense of irregular verbs
- Listening and transcribing in French

Écouter 1

Listen and read. Write down the letters of the **two** activities mentioned in each text. Then translate the phrases in **bold** into English.

bientôt	soon
être en ligne	to be online
s'il ne fait pas beau	if the weather isn't good
être membre de	to be a member of

C'est bientôt les 10 jours sans écrans

Qu'est-ce que tu fais comme activités, si tu n'es pas en ligne?

1 Manon
Normalement, **je fais du vélo** avec mon frère. S'il ne fait pas beau, on va à la piscine et **on fait de la natation**.

2 Enzo
Je suis très actif! **Je suis membre de l'équipe de handball** au collège et on a un match tous les week-ends. Je joue aussi au tennis avec mes amis.

3 Ahmed
Toutes les semaines, **j'ai un cours de musique**. Je joue du violon et mon meilleur ami joue de la guitare. Souvent, **on va à des concerts**.

Lire 2

Read the texts again. Note down in English with whom each person does an activity.

G

The following key verbs are irregular in the present tense.

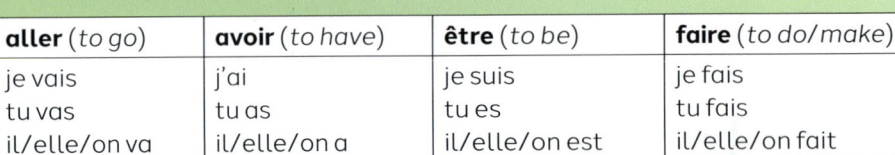

aller (to go)	avoir (to have)	être (to be)	faire (to do/make)
je vais	j'ai	je suis	je fais
tu vas	tu as	tu es	tu fais
il/elle/on va	il/elle/on a	il/elle/on est	il/elle/on fait

On means 'one', but can also mean 'we'. It takes the same part of the verb as *il/elle*.

Some French expressions use *faire* (to do/make) where 'to go' is used in English:

faire **du** vélo — to go cycling
faire **de la** natation — to go swimming

Page 21

Écouter 3

Listen to Sarah talk about what she does to stay active. Note down in English (1–4):
- the activities she does
- when she does them
- how often she does them.

Parler 4

In pairs, imagine you have a no-screen day once a month. Make up your own conversation.

- *Qu'est-ce que tu fais comme activités, si tu n'es pas en ligne?*
- *Normalement, je vais au centre sportif avec mes amis et on joue au basket. Et toi, qu'est-ce que tu fais?*
- *Normalement, je lis un livre mais quelquefois, je vais à la piscine avec ma sœur.*

Je joue	**au** basket / football / rugby	dans	l'équipe du collège.
	du piano / violon		un groupe de musique.
	de la guitare / flûte		
Je fais	**du** sport / vélo	avec	mon ami(e).
	de la cuisine / danse		ma famille.
Je vais	**au** centre sportif / théâtre		mes amis/amies.
	à la piscine / plage		
J'écoute	**de la** musique.		

10 dix

Module 1

5 **Lire** In pairs, look at the gapped sentences. Predict what sort of word could go in each gap.

Look at the verb in each case. Does it tell you what they play or do, or where they go?

1 Je vais à la ____ avec mon ____.
2 Je fais du ____ avec mes ____.
3 Je joue au ____ dans une ____.

What do these words tell you? Is the missing word a person or a place?

What clue do these give you? Is the missing word something masculine, feminine, singular or plural?

6 **Écouter** Listen and fill in the gaps in the sentences in exercise 5.

Remember, the final **-e**, **-s** or **-t** on French words is silent (unless the next word starts with a vowel), but it must be there when you write it!

7 **Lire** Read the texts and answer the questions in English.

Est-ce que tu as une vie active?

Je ne suis pas très actif. Normalement, le soir, ma sœur et moi jouons à des jeux en ligne. Mais, comme c'est les dix jours sans écrans, je fais un effort et on va à la piscine. Après, je bois un coca avec ma sœur et on mange quelque chose ensemble. **Manu**

Généralement, le dimanche, je regarde des séries. Mais, pendant les dix jours sans écrans, je vais au parc avec mon chien. J'écoute aussi toutes sortes de musique et je lis un bon livre. **Coralie**

faire un effort — to make an effort
toutes sortes de musique — all sorts of music

Who …
1 goes to the park?
2 usually plays games online?
3 is going to the swimming pool?
4 normally watches series on Sundays?

G Negatives go around the verb:
Je **ne** suis **pas** actif/active.   I am **not** active.
Page 21

G These two verbs are irregular in the present tense:
boire (to drink)   *je **bois*** (I drink)
lire (to read)   *je **lis*** (I read)

8 **Lire** Translate Coralie's text into English.

onze 11

3 Qu'est-ce que tu regardes?

- Talking about what you watch
- Forming and answering questions
- Preparing a role play

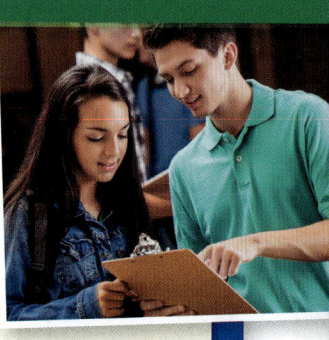

Écouter 1 Read the questionnaire. Listen and note down the answers that Marie gives to the survey. (1–5)

Example: 1 b

1 Qu'est-ce que tu aimes regarder?
J'aime regarder …
- a des séries ou des comédies.
- b des émissions de sport.
- c un peu de tout.

2 Quel type de vidéos est-ce que tu regardes?
Je regarde …
- a des clips de musique ou de danse.
- b des vidéos de cuisine.
- c des vidéos amusantes d'animaux.

3 Quand est-ce que tu regardes des vidéos?
Normalement, je regarde des vidéos …
- a le matin, avant le collège.
- b le soir, après les cours.
- c quand j'ai du temps libre.

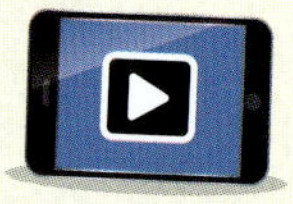

4 Comment est-ce que tu préfères regarder des films?
Je préfère regarder des films …
- a chez moi, à la télé, ou en streaming.
- b au cinéma.
- c sur mon portable.

5 Avec qui est-ce que tu aimes regarder des films?
J'aime regarder des films …
- a avec les membres de ma famille.
- b avec mon meilleur ami / ma meilleure amie.
- c tout(e) seul(e), dans ma chambre.

l'émission (f) de sport	sports programme
un peu de tout	a bit of everything
le temps libre	free time
chez moi	at home, at my place

G

To form questions, you can use a question word + *est-ce que* …
Qu'est-ce que tu aimes regarder? — What do you like watching?
Comment est-ce que tu préfères regarder des films? — How do you prefer to watch films?
Avec qui est-ce que tu aimes regarder des films? — With whom do you like watching films?

quel/quelle/quels/quelles + noun means 'which …?' or 'what … ?'.
It is an adjective and has to agree with the noun it refers to.

masculine singular	feminine singular	masculine plural	feminine plural
quel cinéma?	**quelle** vidéo?	**quels** films?	**quelles** émissions?

Quel type de vidéos est-ce que tu regardes? — What type of videos do you watch?

Page 21

Parler 2 In pairs, do the survey.
- Qu'est-ce que tu aimes regarder?
- J'aime regarder <u>des émissions de sport</u>. Et toi?
- Moi, j'aime regarder <u>un peu de tout</u>.

qu is always pronounced 'k'.
c is also pronounced 'k' in front of the letters *a*, *o* and *u*.

Listen and repeat the words.
quand, **qu**e, **qu**i, **qu**el, **c**ombien, **c**omédie

Écrire 3 Copy and complete the French translations.
1 With whom do you like going to the cinema? ▢ ▢ est-ce que tu aimes aller au ▢ ?
2 When do you prefer to watch TV? ▢ est-ce que tu préfères ▢ la ▢ ?
3 Which programmes do you watch? ▢ émissions ▢ tu regardes?

12 *douze*

4 Read the text. Find the French for the phrases below, choosing from the bold phrases in the text.

J'aime regarder un peu de tout, mais **je regarde souvent** des émissions de télé-réalité. **Je finis** les cours à cinq heures, donc je regarde la télé le soir ou le week-end. **Je ne regarde jamais** de vidéos de cuisine parce que c'est complètement nul!

Je préfère regarder des films toute seule, sur mon ordinateur. Par contre, **je vais** au cinéma tous les mois avec ma meilleure amie. **On choisit** un film d'action ou un film de science-fiction parce que c'est passionnant!

Amina

G Regular -*ir* verbs like *finir* (to finish) and *choisir* (to choose) work like this in the present tense:
je fin**is**
tu fin**is**
il/elle/on fin**it**

nul	bad, rubbish
par contre	however
passionnant(e)	exciting

1 We choose
2 I go
3 I prefer to watch
4 I often watch
5 I finish
6 I never watch

5 Re-read the text in exercise 4. Copy and complete the sentences below in English.

1 Amina often watches ___.
2 She finishes ___, so she watches TV ___.
3 She never watches ___.
4 She prefers watching films ___ on her ___.
5 Amina and her best friend go to the cinema every ___.
6 They choose ___ or ___, because ___.

6 Listen and read, paying attention to how the underlined words are pronounced. Then read the dialogue with your partner.

- Vous voulez voir quel type de film?
- Un film d'<u>action</u>.
- À quelle heure?
- Le film de dix heures.
- Vous voulez combien de <u>billets</u>?
- Trois billets, s'il vous plaît.

- Pour des <u>adultes</u> ou des <u>enfants</u>?
- Un adulte et deux enfants.
- Très bien.
- Le film finit à quelle heure?
- À midi.
- Merci!

7 Re-read the dialogue in exercise 6 and find the type of film, the number of tickets and the start and finish times.

8 Listen to the conversations. For each dialogue (1–2), find:
- the type of film
- the number of tickets
- the finish time.

9 Prepare your answers to this role-play card. Then listen and respond to the teacher.

You are at a cinema in France and you are buying tickets.
The cinema employee will speak first.

1 Say what type of film you want to see.
2 Say at what time you want to see it.
3 Say how many tickets you want.
4 Say whether the tickets are for adults or children and how many of each.
5 Ask a question about the finishing time.

Use *je voudrais* … to say 'I would like …'.

Be polite! Use *s'il vous plaît* and *merci*.

Remember how the words for 'adults' and 'children' are pronounced.

Use a simple time, e.g. *à huit heures*, but avoid one-word answers.

Make your question sound like a question. Lift your voice slightly at the end.

treize 13

4 Qu'est-ce qu'on va faire?

- Making plans to go out
- Using the near future tense
- Understanding and making invitations

Écouter 1
Listen and read the times on the clocks.

- à neuf heures
- à neuf heures vingt-cinq
- à dix heures moins le quart
- à neuf heures dix
- à neuf heures et demie
- à dix heures moins dix
- à neuf heures et quart
- à dix heures moins vingt
- à midi / à minuit

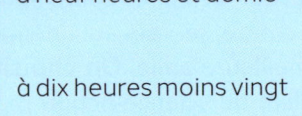

Écouter 2
Listen to the voicemails (1–4). For each one, write:
- the letter of the correct advert
- when they are going to do it (e.g. tomorrow morning, nine o'clock).

aujourd'hui	demain
ce matin	demain matin
cet après-midi	demain après-midi
ce soir	demain soir

Que faire en Belgique, pendant les vacances de la Toussaint?

A Château de Vêves
Adultes: 9,00€
Enfants: 6,00€

B Parc Georges Henri
Ouvert tous les jours

C Musée des Sciences Naturelles
Entrée libre
Fermé le lundi

D Marché du Midi
le dimanche, 6h00–14h00

les vacances de la Toussaint — autumn half-term holiday (usually at the end of October)

Lire 3
Read the two text messages. Translate one of them into English.

1 Aujourd'hui, je vais aller au centre commercial avec mon frère. On va faire les magasins. On va prendre le bus à deux heures et quart. Tu viens?

2 Demain après-midi, ma famille et moi, nous allons voir un spectacle de musique au parc. Tu viens avec nous? Nous allons partir à midi.

Tu viens? Are you coming? / Do you want to come?

G
You can use the present tense of *aller* (to go) + an **infinitive** to refer to the future. This is called the **near future tense**.

je vais	**aller** au parc
tu vas	**prendre** le bus
il/elle/on va	**jouer** au football
nous allons	**visiter** le musée
vous allez	**voir** un spectacle
ils/elles vont	**partir** vers midi

Page 22

Parler 4
In pairs, turn the exercise 3 text messages into two voicemails. Read them aloud. Then create a new voicemail by changing the underlined details.

14 quatorze

Module 1

5 Read the chat. Fill in the gaps with the correct word from the box. There are two words you don't need. Then listen and check.

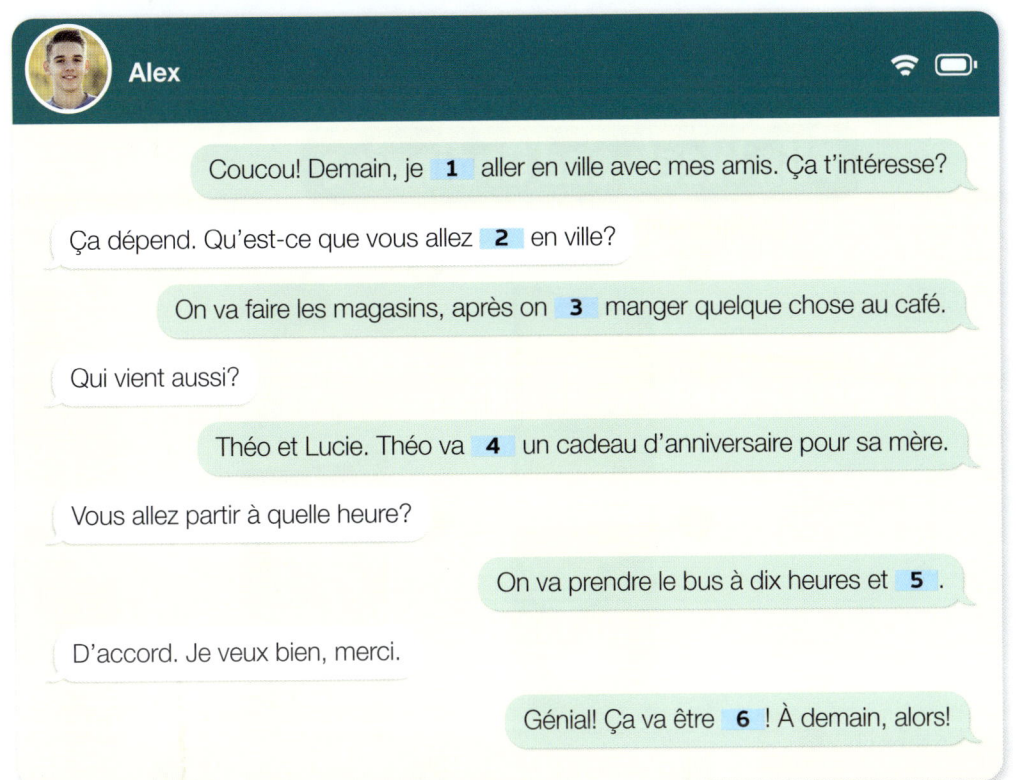

Alex

Coucou! Demain, je **1** aller en ville avec mes amis. Ça t'intéresse?

Ça dépend. Qu'est-ce que vous allez **2** en ville?

On va faire les magasins, après on **3** manger quelque chose au café.

Qui vient aussi?

Théo et Lucie. Théo va **4** un cadeau d'anniversaire pour sa mère.

Vous allez partir à quelle heure?

On va prendre le bus à dix heures et **5** .

D'accord. Je veux bien, merci.

Génial! Ça va être **6** ! À demain, alors!

acheter
allons
amusant
faire
matin
quart
va
vais

6 Listen. Copy and complete the grid in English. (1–2)

	Place / Activity	When	Time	Accepts? ✓ ✗
1				

pas de problème! no problem!

Ça t'intéresse?   Tu es libre?   Tu viens?

👍
Oui, je suis libre.
Ça m'intéresse.
Je veux bien, merci.
D'accord.

👎
Non, désolé(e), je ne peux pas.
Je ne suis pas libre.

Le stade Roi Baudouin à Bruxelles

Le parc d'attractions Walibi près de Bruxelles

7 Imagine it's the start of the half-term holiday! Write a message to your friend about your plans for today and tomorrow. Include the following bullet points:
- where you will go (*je vais aller en ville*)
- what you will do and when (*ma famille et moi allons voir un film à 15h*)
- which transport you will use (*on va prendre le bus à dix heures*)
- an invitation to your friend (*Ça t'intéresse?*).

	aller	au musée	
Je vais	faire	les magasins	aujourd'hui.
On va	jouer	au foot / au tennis	demain.
Nous allons	acheter	un cadeau / un tee-shirt	ce soir.
	partir		cet après-midi.

quinze 15

5 Qu'est-ce que tu as fait?

- Saying what you did last weekend
- Using the perfect tense
- Pronouncing é, er, ez correctly

Lire 1 Look at the pictures (a–i) and match each one to the correct caption (1–9).

#Un Week-end Ordinaire

Qu'est-ce que tu as fait, le week-end dernier?

1 J'ai joué au foot sur la plage.
2 J'ai marché à la campagne.
3 J'ai bu un coca avec mes amis.
4 J'ai pris des photos.
5 Je suis allée au café avec ma famille.
6 On a mangé du couscous.
7 Je suis resté à la maison.
8 On a lu un peu.
9 On a regardé la télé.

On is sometimes used in French to say 'we'. *On* takes the same form of the verb as *il/elle*.

Lire 2 Re-read the sentences in exercise 1. Then find <u>nine</u> different verbs in the perfect tense and translate them into English.

G You use the perfect tense to refer to the past. It is formed of two parts:
1 the auxiliary verb (part of **avoir** or **être**)
2 the past participle.

You form the past participle of regular **-er** verbs like this:
chanter (to sing) → chant**é**
j'**ai** chant**é** (I sang)   il/elle/on **a** chant**é** (he/she/we sang)

The following verbs have an irregular past participle:
boire (to drink) → j'ai **bu** (I drank)
faire (to do/make) → j'ai **fait** (I did/made)

For verbs that take **être**, e.g. *aller* (to go) and *rester* (to stay), the past participle must agree with the subject:
elle **est** all**ée** (she went)   on **est** all**és** (we went)

Page 22

Écouter 3 Listen and note down the letters (a–i) of the activities each person did. Listen again and note in English when they did them. (1–4)

samedi	matin
dimanche	après-midi
	soir

Parler 4 Read the tongue-twisters aloud. Pay attention to the pronunciation of the key sound in the tip box. Then listen and check.

1 Mon footballeur pr**é**f**é**r**é** est Kylian Mbapp**é**.
2 Elle est all**ée** mang**er** au café.
3 Samedi derni**er**, je suis rest**ée** ch**ez** Chlo**é** et on a pass**é** une bonne journ**ée**.

é is pronounced the same as **er** and **ez**.

Listen and repeat the words.
mang**é**   mang**er**   mang**ez**

16 *seize*

5 Listen and read what Mariama did over the weekend. Complete each sentence starter by writing the letter of the correct activity. Make sure that you put the activities in the order in which Mariama did them.

Un week-end extraordinaire au Burkina Faso

Samedi dernier, c'était la Fête de la Musique dans notre capitale.

Il y avait un programme fantastique avec des concerts gratuits. C'était extraordinaire!

Pour commencer, je suis allée à un concert de Marko, un jeune chanteur de rap. J'ai adoré sa musique et on a chanté et dansé.

Ensuite, j'ai vu un concert d'Élue 111, qui est ma chanteuse préférée. Pendant le concert, elle a chanté toutes sortes de chansons. C'était vraiment génial!

Après, il y avait un concert de Teriya, un groupe africain, mais on n'a pas vu le groupe parce que c'était complet!

Finalement, j'ai acheté un poster, mais je n'ai pas acheté de tee-shirt car c'était trop cher.

J'ai passé un week-end parfait!

Mariama

Élue 111

gratuit(e)(s)	free (no cost)
extraordinaire	extraordinary
complet (complète)(s)	full

G
c'est	it is
c'était	it was
il y a	there is/are
il y avait	there was/were

1 First, …   a she bought a souvenir of the occasion.
2 Then …   b she saw her favourite singer.
3 Afterwards, …   c she missed seeing a band because the concert was full.
4 Finally, …   d she went to a concert where everyone sang and danced.

6 Listen and, for each speaker (1–3), make notes on each point below:
a what they did last weekend
b what they didn't do
c whether a positive or negative opinion.

C'était	amusant / cher / complet extraordinaire / génial passionnant / sympa / nul.

G In the perfect tense, negatives go around the part of *avoir* or *être*:
je **n'ai rien** acheté — I haven't bought anything
on **n'a rien** vu — we haven't seen anything
je **ne** suis **pas** resté(e) — I didn't stay
il **n'est pas** allé — he didn't go

Page 21

7 In pairs, make up a conversation about last weekend.
- *Qu'est-ce que tu as fait, le week-end dernier?*
- *Samedi matin, pour commencer … Ensuite, / Après, / Finalement, …*
- *Et dimanche?*
- *Dimanche, …*
- *C'était comment?*
- …

To create extended sentences, use:
- time expressions   *samedi soir, dimanche matin*
- sequencers   *pour commencer, ensuite, après, finalement*

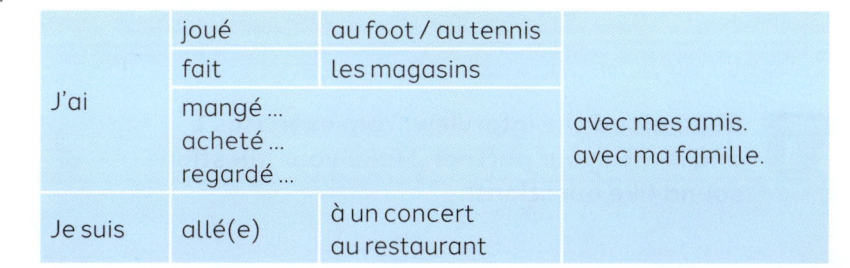

J'ai	joué	au foot / au tennis	
	fait	les magasins	
	mangé … acheté … regardé …		avec mes amis. avec ma famille.
Je suis	allé(e)	à un concert au restaurant	

8 Write a blog entry about a busy weekend. Include opinions and at least one negative.

dix-sept 17

6 J'ai participé aux Jeux de la Francophonie!

- Taking part in an interview
- Understanding questions in the perfect tense
- Using two tenses together (present and perfect)

Lire 1
Read the interview questions. Copy and complete the English translation of each one.

1 **À quel âge** as-tu commencé à jouer au tennis de table?
   ▒ did you start playing table tennis?

2 **Quand** as-tu participé aux Jeux de la Francophonie?
   ▒ did you take part in the Francophone Games?

3 **Qu'est-ce que** tu as fait pour être bien préparée pour les Jeux?
   ▒ did you do to be prepared for the Games?

4 **Est-ce que** tu as gagné aux Jeux de la Francophonie?
   ▒ you win at the Francophone Games?

préparé(e)   prepared

Lire 2
Read the answers below. Write the letter of the correct answer for each question in exercise 1. Then translate all the answers into English.

Un grand succès aux Jeux de la Francophonie!

a J'ai participé aux Jeux de la Francophonie pour la première fois l'année dernière.

b J'ai fini en première position – j'ai gagné la compétition!

c Pour être bien préparée, j'ai joué trois ou quatre heures chaque jour au centre sportif.

d J'ai commencé à jouer au tennis de table à l'âge de quinze ans.

j'ai participé	I participated
la première fois	the first time
à l'âge de	at the age of

Écouter 3
Listen and check.

> **G**
> Questions in the perfect tense often use inversion.
> The subject swaps places with the first verb, with a hyphen in between.
> *Tu as participé aux Jeux de la Francophonie.* → *As-tu participé aux Jeux de la Francophonie?*
>
> When there is a question word, it comes at the start of the question:
> **Quand** as-tu participé aux Jeux de la Francophonie?
>
> Inversion is **not** used with questions that start with *Est-ce que...?* or *Qu'est-ce que...?*
>
> Page 23

Parler 4
Read aloud the interview from exercises 1 and 2 with your partner. Make your questions sound like questions!

> Use **rising intonation** when you ask a question. Make your voice go up at the end.
>
> Listen and repeat the question.
> *Est-ce que tu as gagné aux Jeux de la Francophonie?*

18 dix-huit

Module 1

5 Lire Read the text about the JDLF (*Jeux de la Francophonie*). Copy and complete the profile in English.

Les JDLF, ce n'est pas seulement une compétition sportive, c'est aussi un concours culturel!

Je m'appelle Lucas et mon pays, c'est le Mali, en Afrique. Je suis chanteur et musicien.

J'ai commencé à jouer du piano à l'âge de huit ans. J'adore faire de la musique et j'écris tout le temps des chansons!

Tous les jours, je passe sept heures à mon piano, pour être bien préparé pour les Jeux de la Francophonie.

J'ai déjà participé aux Jeux, c'était il y a deux ans – j'ai chanté une chanson. Je n'ai pas gagné, mais j'étais content.

L'important n'est pas de gagner mais de participer!

Name: Lucas
Country:
Talent(s):
Started when?:
Preparation for contest:
Took part in JDLF when?
Success at JDLF?

le concours	competition
passer	to spend (time)
L'important n'est pas de gagner mais de participer!	saying that means 'It's not the winning but the taking part that counts'.

il y a has two meanings:
1 there is/are — *il y a un centre sportif*
2 ago — *il y a deux ans* (two years ago)

6 Lire Read the text again. Find at least <u>six</u> verbs in the present tense and <u>four</u> verbs in the perfect tense.

7 Écouter Listen to the podcast and answer the questions in English.
1 What country is Thomas from?
2 What sport does Thomas play?
3 At what age did he start playing?
4 When does he play?
5 When did he participate in the *Jeux de la Francophonie*?
6 Did he win?

8 Parler In pairs, create a podcast interview with a participant at the JDLF. Use details from one of the boxes below.

Nadia – Belgium
basketball – started age 12
plays every day – sports centre
JDLF – last year – won

Ahmed – Senegal
hip-hop dance – started age 7
dances in the evenings – school
JDLF – 3 years ago – 2nd place

Présent

Tu es de quel pays?	Je suis	du Sénégal. de Belgique.
Qu'est-ce que tu fais comme activité?	Je joue	au basket.
	Je fais	de la danse hip-hop.
Quand est-ce que tu fais ça?	Je joue	au centre sportif — tous les jours.
	Je fais de la danse	à l'école — le soir.

Passé

À quel âge as-tu commencé à pratiquer ça?	J'ai commencé	à l'âge de … ans.
Quand as-tu participé aux Jeux de la Francophonie?	J'ai participé aux Jeux	l'année dernière. il y a trois ans.
Est-ce que tu as gagné aux Jeux de la Francophonie?	J'ai gagné / J'ai fini en deuxième position	aux Jeux.

dix-neuf 19

Grammaire 1

The present tense of regular verbs (Unit 1, page 8)

Regular -er, -ir and -re verbs form the present tense like this:

parler (to speak/talk) → parl-	finir (to finish) → fin-	attendre (to wait for) → attend-
je parle	je finis	j'attends
tu parles	tu finis	tu attends
il/elle/on parle	il/elle/on finit	il/elle/on attend (no added ending)
nous parlons	nous finissons	nous attendons
vous parlez	vous finissez	vous attendez
ils/elles parlent	ils/elles finissent	ils/elles attendent

💡 The endings on the underlined verbs are silent, so these forms of each verb are pronounced the same.

Écrire 1
Copy and complete the sentences with the correct form of the regular -er verb in brackets.

Example: 1 Je parle avec ma famille en France.
1. Je **(parler)** avec ma famille en France.
2. J' **(acheter)** des choses sur Vinted.
3. Est-ce que tu **(regarder)** souvent des vidéos?
4. Elle **(jouer)** à des jeux avec sa meilleure amie.
5. Ils **(écouter)** de la musique en streaming.
6. Vous **(chercher)** des idées en ligne.
7. Nous **(partager)** des photos sur Snapchat.

Lire 2
Translate the sentences into English.
1. Tu regardes des photos sur ton portable?
2. Il passe trop de temps en ligne.
3. Est-ce que vous parlez avec ma sœur?
4. Nous regardons des vidéos sur TikTok.
5. Elles écoutent souvent de la musique.
6. Je finis les cours à cinq heures.

Parler 3
In pairs, read out the sentences from exercise 2. Pay attention to the pronunciation of the subject pronouns (*je, nous* etc.) and the verb endings (which ones are silent?). Then listen and check.

Écouter 4
Listen to the sentences with the subject pronouns missing. (1–6) Can you work out from the sound of each verb what the missing pronoun is? Choose from the pronouns listed. Then listen and check.

1. je / nous / ils
2. elle / nous / vous
3. je / on / ils
4. tu / vous / elles
5. je / nous / vous
6. tu / elle / nous

💡 **Watch out for:**
- *je* shortens to *j'* in front of a vowel, e.g. *je + écoute = j'écoute*. Pronounce *j'* plus the verb as a single word
- verbs that end in *-ger*, like *manger, partager*: the '*nous*' form is *mangeons*
- verbs like *acheter*: the *je/tu/il(s)/elle(s)* forms add a grave accent: *j'achète / ils achètent*.

💡 In French, there is only one present tense. So, *je parle* means 'I speak' and 'I am speaking'. Time phrases often give you a clue about which of the two English meanings applies.

Pronouncing subject pronouns
- *je* (or *j'*): *j* is a soft sound. like a fast car whizzing by: "jjjuuuhhh!"
- *tu*: *u* sounds similar to 'ew' in 'few'.
- *nous* and *vous*: *ou* sounds like an 'oooh!' of surprise.
- *il* and *ils*: *i* sounds like 'e' in 'evil'.
- *elle* and *elles*: *e* sounds like 'e' in 'bed'.

💡 Remember, the final **-s** is silent (unless the next word starts with a vowel), so *il* and *ils* are pronounced the same and so are *elle* and *elles*.

💡 Remember that the pronunciation of regular *-er* verbs in the plural of the present tense (ending in **-ent**) is the same as the singular (ending in **-e/-es**).

The present tense of irregular verbs (Unit 2, page 10)

The following key verbs are irregular in the present tense:

aller (*to go*)	avoir (*to have*)	être (*to be*)	faire (*to do/make*)
je vais	j'ai	je suis	je fais
tu vas	tu as	tu es	tu fais
il/elle/on va	il/elle/on a	il/elle/on est	il/elle/on fait
nous allons	nous avons	nous sommes	nous faisons
vous allez	vous avez	vous êtes	vous faites
ils/elles vont	ils/elles ont	ils/elles sont	ils/elles font

> If there is no subject pronoun, think about which part of the verb to use:
> *mon équipe et moi* = *nous* (we)
> *mes amis* = *ils* (they)

Écrire 5 Copy and complete the sentence for each day in French, using the correct form of the verb in brackets.

Example: 1 *Le lundi, on fait du vélo.*

1. Le lundi, on **(faire)** du vélo.
2. Le mardi, j'**(avoir)** un cours de guitare.
3. Le mercredi, nous **(aller)** au centre sportif.
4. Le jeudi, tu **(faire)** de la cuisine.
5. Le vendredi, on **(aller)** au théâtre.
6. Le samedi, mon équipe et moi **(avoir)** un match de foot.
7. Le dimanche, mes amis **(aller)** au parc.

Negatives (Unit 2, page 11)

Parler 6 In pairs, one person asks the questions, the other plays Norman Négatif who always answers in the negative! Try to use all three negatives from the grammar box.

- *Est-ce que tu es sportif?* ■ *Non, je **ne** suis **pas** sportif.*

1. Est-ce que tu es sportif?
2. Est-ce que tu joues de la guitare?
3. Est-ce que tu fais du vélo?
4. Est-ce que tu vas au cinéma?
5. Qu'est-ce que tu fais, le soir ou le week-end?
6. Est-ce que tu utilises ton portable après vingt heures?

Norman Négatif

> Negatives are usually in two parts:
> *ne ... pas* (not)
> *ne ... rien* (nothing/not anything)
> *ne ... jamais* (never)
>
> In the present tense, they make a 'sandwich' around the verb:
> *Je **ne** joue **pas** au tennis.*
> I don't play tennis.
> *Je **ne** fais **rien**.*
> I don't do anything./I do nothing.
>
> After a negative, *du*, *de la* and *des* usually change to *de*:
> *Je ne fais jamais **de** cuisine.*
> I never cook.

Forming questions (Unit 3, page 12)

Lire 7 Read the answers (1–5). What were the questions (a–e)? Match the answers to the questions.

1. J'aime regarder des comédies avec mes amis.
2. Je regarde des vidéos amusantes d'animaux.
3. Je préfère regarder des films en ligne.
4. Je regarde des films avec ma famille.
5. Le film finit à douze heures.

a. Le film finit à quelle heure?
b. Qu'est-ce que tu aimes regarder avec tes amis?
c. Avec qui est-ce que tu regardes des films?
d. Comment est-ce que tu préfères regarder des films?
e. Quel type de vidéos est-ce que tu regardes?

Grammaire 2

The near future tense (Unit 4, page 14)

Parler 1 Read the grammar box on page 14. Imagine this is your diary for today and tomorrow. In pairs, take turns to describe what you are going to do. Try to use a variety of verb forms (*je, on, nous*).

- *Ce matin, je vais aller au centre commercial avec … On va faire …*
- *Cet après-midi, nous allons jouer …*

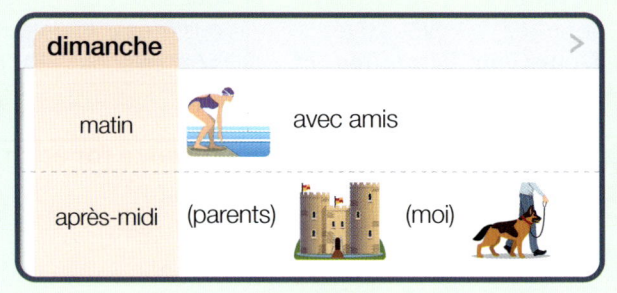

samedi	
matin	centre commercial avec Clara
après-midi	

dimanche	
matin	avec amis
après-midi	(parents) (moi)

The perfect tense (Unit 5, page 16)

You use the perfect tense to refer to things that happened in the past. It is formed of two parts:
1. the auxiliary verb (part of **avoir** or **être**)
2. the past participle.

You form the past participle of **regular -er** verbs like this:

dans**er** (to dance) → dans**é**

j'**ai** dansé	I danced
tu **as** dansé	you (singular) danced
il/elle/on **a** dansé	he/she/we danced
nous **avons** dansé	we danced
vous **avez** dansé	you (plural or polite) danced
ils/elles **ont** dansé	they danced

The following verbs have an **irregular** past participle:
boire (to drink) → *j'ai bu* (I drank)
lire (to read) → *j'ai lu* (I read)
faire (to do/make) → *j'ai fait* (I did/made)
prendre (to take) → *j'ai pris* (I took)

Some verbs take **être** (not *avoir*), e.g.
aller (to go) → *je suis allé* (I went)
rester (to stay) → *je suis resté* (I stayed)

The past participle must <u>agree</u> with the subject:
il est resté (he stayed *(m)*)
*elle est resté**e*** (she stayed *(f)*)
*ils sont resté**s*** (they stayed *(m pl)*)
*elles sont resté**es*** (they stayed *(f pl)*)

Écrire 2 Copy out the sentences, putting the verbs in brackets into the perfect tense.

Example: 1 *Je suis allé/allée au centre commercial et …*

1. Je **(aller)** au centre commercial et j' **(acheter)** un bracelet.
2. Est-ce que tu **(regarder)** la télé?
3. Mon frère **(rester)** à la maison.
4. On **(faire)** de la natation.
5. Nous **(écouter)** de la musique.
6. Qu'est-ce que vous **(manger)** au restaurant?
7. Mes amis **(danser)** et **(chanter)**.
8. Les filles **(aller)** au centre sportif.

💡 Don't forget, the perfect tense is formed of <u>two</u> parts!

💡 Remember, *je* shortens to *j'* in front of a vowel: *je + ai = j'ai*.

vingt-deux

Module 1

3. Translate the sentences into French.

Example: 1 *Samedi dernier, mes amis et moi sommes allés à un concert.*

1 Last Saturday, my friends and I went to a concert.
2 I danced, but I didn't sing.
3 We saw our favourite group.
4 My friend Thomas bought a tee-shirt.
5 We took lots of photos.

> In the perfect tense, negatives go around the auxiliary verb (the part of *avoir* or *être*):
> Je **ne suis pas** allé(e) au concert.
>
> Remember that *ne* shortens to **n'** in front of a vowel:
> Je **n'**ai **pas** chanté.
> Nous **n'**avons **rien** acheté.

Questions in the perfect tense (Unit 6, page 18)

4. Complete the questions using the verb in brackets and the pronoun *tu*. Remember to use inversion. Copy out the questions and translate them.

Example: 1 À quel âge as-tu commencé à jouer au handball?

1 À quel âge (**commencer**) à jouer au handball?
2 Quand (**participer**) à la compétition?
3 Quand (**jouer**) au tennis de table pour la première fois?
4 L'année dernière, (**gagner**) aux Jeux de la Francophonie?
5 Quel film (**regarder**) hier soir à la télé?

> When you use inversion, put a hyphen between the verb and the subject:
> *Comment as-tu …?*

Using the present tense and the perfect tense together (Unit 6, page 19)

5. In pairs, play 'tenses tennis'. Take turns to change each sentence from the present tense to the perfect tense or vice versa.

- *Je joue de la guitare.*
- *J'ai joué de la guitare. J'ai fait …*

1 Je joue de la guitare. → (*perfect*)
2 J'ai fait de la natation. → (*present*)
3 J'écoute de la musique. → (*perfect*)
4 J'ai regardé une comédie. → (*present*)
5 Je vais au cinéma. → (*perfect*)
6 Je suis allé(e) à la piscine. → (*present*)

> Make sure you pronounce *je* and *j'ai* as different sounds. The letter **e** should sound a bit like 'uh'.
> The letters **ai** should sound a bit like 'ey'.
> Remember that *j* is a <u>soft</u> sound in French.

C'est parti!

6. Listen and note down the missing word or words. Remember, some endings are silent in French!

J'aime faire du sport. **1** membre d'une équipe de foot et nous **2** un match tous les week-ends. Le dimanche, je **3** fais **4** de sport.

Samedi dernier, je **5** au centre commercial. J'ai acheté un tee-shirt. Ensuite, j' **6** quelque chose au café. Et toi, qu'est-ce que tu **7** samedi dernier? Demain, je **8** le château. Tu viens?

vingt-trois 23

Module 1 — Contrôle de lecture et d'écoute

Reading

Lire 1 — *Watching TV.* Read these comments from an internet forum. Answer each question with the name of the correct person.

Manon ▸ Je ne regarde pas souvent la télé mais de temps en temps, je regarde des émissions de **télé-réalité*** avec mes amies.

Jules ▸ Le soir, je regarde la chaîne de musique avec ma sœur mais je préfère regarder des vidéos de musique seul sur mon portable.

Eva ▸ J'adore les comédies et j'aime bien les émissions de sport. La télé, c'est bien, mais Internet, c'est génial!

*****la télé-réalité**   reality TV

Who …
a prefers to watch on their phone?
b doesn't often watch TV?
c prefers the internet?
d watches with their friends?
e loves comedy programmes?
f watches a music channel?

Lire 2 — *My hobbies.* Read Rachid's entry to a forum about hobbies. Write the letter (A–F) for each of the **three** correct statements.

#Rachid#

Salut!

Je suis actif. Je m'intéresse à la télé et au sport, mais la musique classique, c'est ma passion. Souvent je vais à des concerts. Je joue de deux instruments. Je joue tous les soirs.

Jouer d'un instrument est difficile. Toutes les semaines, j'ai un cours de musique. Ça prend beaucoup de temps mais ce n'est jamais ennuyeux.

> In reading tasks, you may come across words that are not familiar to you but some of them will be cognates. Cognates are words that look very similar to English words. Can you find any cognates in this text?

> Watch out for negatives either in the text or the questions, as these can completely change the meaning.

Rachid …

A isn't very active.	D thinks playing an instrument is difficult.
B is interested in TV.	E thinks an instrument takes up a lot of time.
C plays in the morning.	F thinks playing an instrument can be boring.

24 *vingt-quatre*

Module 1

Lire 3
Celebrating cinema in France. Translate the following sentences **into English**.

- You don't need an English word here. → **a** J'adore les films d'action.
- What tense is it? → **c** J'achète les billets en ligne.
- Think carefully about the timeframe. It is no longer the same as in the previous sentence. → **d** L'année dernière, j'ai regardé cinq comédies.
- **b** En France il y a un festival du cinéma en juillet. ← Think carefully about the word order here.
- **e** Quand je vais au cinéma, je mange quelque chose. ← This will be translated as one word in English.

Listening

Écouter 4
Free time. Yasmina is being interviewed about her free time. What does she say? Listen to the recording and make notes **in English** under the following headings. You do not need to write in full sentences.

a Her favourite activity
b How she celebrates a friend's birthday
c When she reads

> In this task, think of French words that might help you to spot where the relevant information is given (e.g. *activité, anniversaire*).

Écouter 5
A new TV series. Listen to this advert about a new series. What is mentioned? Write the letter (A–F) for each of the <u>three</u> correct options.

A	name of the programme
B	type of programme
C	time it's on TV
D	month it starts
E	singers
F	actors

> You may hear words that are linked to each option but you should focus on what is actually mentioned.

Écouter 6
Dictation. You are going to hear someone talking about music.

a Sentences 1–3: write down the missing words. For each gap, you will write one word **in French**.

1 Demain, on ___ au ___.
2 J'___ la musique ___.
3 Ma ___ préfère la ___.

> Listen carefully to these words as you may not have heard them before.

b Sentences 4–6: write down the full sentences that you hear, **in French**.

vingt-cinq 25

Module 1 — Contrôle oral

Read aloud

Parler 1 Look at this task card. With a partner, take turns to read out the five sentences, paying attention to the underlined letters and the highlighted liaisons.

> Mathis, your French friend, has emailed you to tell you about music in France.
>
> Read out the text below to your teacher.
>
> J'adore la musique.
> En France, il y a beaucoup de spectacles et de fêtes.
> À mon avis, c'est une bonne idée.
> J'aime écouter des artistes et des chansons francophones.
> Demain, je vais aller à un concert de musique classique.

Take extra care with how you pronounce the underlined sounds.
- The final *e* and/or *s* are silent on these words.
- Make sure you pronounce *é* correctly.
- *qu* is pronounced the same way as a 'k'.

Remember to make the liaison between the highlighted sounds.

Écouter 2 Listen and check your pronunciation.

Parler 3 Listen to the teacher asking the two follow-up questions. Translate each question **into English** and prepare your own answers **in French**. Then listen again and respond to the teacher.

Remember to use different opinion phrases.

Role play

Parler 4 Look at the role-play card and prepare what you are going to say.

> **Setting:** At the leisure centre
>
> **Scenario:**
> - You are at a leisure centre in Belgium.
> - The teacher will play the part of the leisure centre employee and will speak first.
> - The teacher will ask questions **in French** and you must answer **in French**.
> - Say a few words or a short phrase/sentence for each prompt. One-word answers are not sufficient to gain full marks.
>
> **Task:**
> 1 Say what sport you'd like to do.
> 2 Say how many people it is for.
> 3 Say at what time you want to do the sport.
> 4 Give your opinion on sport.
> 5 Ask a question about food at the leisure centre.

Start with *Je voudrais*.

You could start with *Est-ce qu'il y a …?* or *Où est …?*

Parler 5 Practise what you have prepared. Then, using your notes, listen and respond to the teacher.

Écouter 6 Now listen to Lola doing the role-play task. **In English**, note down (a) how she **answers** the questions for task prompts 1, 2, 3 and 4 and (b) what question she **asks** for task prompt 5.

Picture task

Écouter 7 Look at the exam card below and read the **first part** of the task. Then listen to Enzo describing the picture. Answer the questions **in English**.

a What does Enzo say about the people?
b Where are the people according to Enzo? Do you agree?
c What does Enzo say the people are doing?

Describe this picture.
Your description must cover:
- people
- location
- activity

When you have finished your description, you will be asked **two questions** relating to the picture. Say a short phrase/sentence in response to each question. One-word answers will not be sufficient to gain full marks.

You will then move on to a **conversation** on the broader thematic context of **Media and technology**.

During the conversation, you will be asked questions in the present, past and future tenses. Your responses should be as **full and detailed** as possible.

To talk about what someone <u>is doing</u>, use the **present tense**. Remember, 'they are watching' is the same as 'they watch' in French.

Parler 8 Prepare your own description of the picture, mentioning **people**, **location** and **activity**. Then, with a partner, take turns to describe the picture.

> Sur la photo, il y a ...

Parler 9 Read the **second part** of the task. Then listen to the two follow-up questions and respond to the teacher. Remember: you only need to give a short answer to each one.

Écouter 10 Read the **third part** of the task. The teacher asks Enzo: *Quels sont les dangers d'Internet?* Listen and write the letters of the activities in the order you hear them.

a last weekend
b without a phone
c videos
d using social media
e sport
f health

Écouter 11 Listen to Enzo answering the question: *Qu'est-ce que tu vas faire en ligne le week-end prochain?* Write down <u>two</u> things he is going to do.

Parler 12 Prepare your own answers to the Module 1 questions on page 226. Your responses should be as **full and detailed** as possible. Then practise with a partner.

Remember to use opinion phrases, time phrases and connectives, and a range of verbs in present, past and near future tenses.

vingt-sept 27

Module 1 Contrôle écrit

Photo description

1 Look at this writing exam task. Spend one minute looking at the photo and thinking of useful vocabulary and structures you could use. Share and compare your ideas with a partner.

> Describe the photo. Write four short sentences **in French**.

2 Read Diane's response to the task. Summarise **in English** what she says about the photo.

> Il y a un groupe de jeunes.
> Ils sont au cinéma.
> Ils regardent un film.
> Ils sont amis.

3 Now write your own answer to the following task.

> Describe the photo. Write four short sentences **in French**.

When describing a photo, use the present tense. There are several people in the photo, so you will need the *ils* and *elles* part of the verb.

40–50 word writing task

4 Look at this writing exam task and then, **for each bullet point**:

1. think about what vocabulary you have learned which you could use in your answer. For example:
   - **nouns** and **verbs** to talk about a sports centre
   - **verbs of opinion** and **adjectives** to give your opinion
   - how to say when you will next go to the sports centre.
2. write down two or three ideas for what you could write about.
3. write down which tense(s) you will need to use in your answer.

> Write a review of a sports centre for a website.
>
> You **must** include the following points:
> - where the sports centre is
> - your opinion of the activities
> - when you will next visit the sports centre.
>
> Write your answer **in French**. You should aim to write between 40 and 50 words.

Use only language that you know. For example, if the sports centre is next to the bus station but you don't know the French for it, use a different way to describe where it is.

vingt-huit

5 Read Sofiane's answer to the exam task. Answer questions 1–4 in the coloured shapes.

1 These different opinion words show a **variety of vocabulary**. What do they mean? Find <u>four</u> examples of adjectives that give his opinion.

2 What does this **connective** mean? What other connectives does he use?

3 These are examples of a **variety of grammatical structures**. What do they mean?

4 Which **tense** is this? What time expression does he use with it and what does it mean?

Le centre sportif est à la campagne.
J'aime les activités au centre sportif.
Je préfère le basket car c'est amusant mais je n'aime pas la piscine. À mon avis c'est trop petit et ennuyeux.
Je vais aller au centre sportif demain soir après l'école. Ça va être génial.

6 Read Sofiane's answer again. Copy and complete the sentences below.
  a The sports centre is ▬.
  b Sofiane likes ▬.
  c He prefers ▬ because it's ▬ but he doesn't like ▬.
  d In his opinion, it's ▬.
  e Tomorrow evening after school, he is going to ▬.

7 Prepare your own answer to the 40–50 word writing task in exercise 4.
  • Think about how you can develop your answer for each bullet point.
  • Look back at your notes from exercises 4 and 5.
  • Look at the 'Challenge checklist' and think about how you can show off your French!
  • Write a **brief** plan and organise your answer into paragraphs.
  • Write your answer and then carefully check the accuracy of what you have written.

Challenge checklist	
🌶	✓ Present and future timeframes ✓ Connectives, time phrases and sequencers ✓ Different opinion phrases (e.g. *c'est génial*)
🌶🌶	✓ The present and near future tenses ✓ Different persons of the verb ✓ A variety of opinions ✓ Negatives (e.g. *ne … pas*) ✓ A wide range of interesting vocabulary
🌶🌶🌶	✓ A variety of grammatical structures (e.g. *à mon avis*) ✓ A variety of language (e.g. *ennuyeux, amusant …*) ✓ Positive/negative phrases ✓ A variety of connectives

vingt-neuf 29

Module 1 — Vocabulaire

Key:
bold = this word will appear in higher exams only
* = this word is not on the vocabulary list but you may use it in your own sentences

Fêtes et jeux (pages 6–7)

Les opinions	Opinions	J'adore / J'aime …	I love / I like …
Les dix jours sans **écrans**. À ton avis, c'est une bonne idée ou une mauvaise idée?	Ten days without screens. In your opinion, is it a good idea or a bad idea?	Je n'aime pas …	I don't like …
		Je déteste …	I hate …
À mon avis, c'est …	In my opinion, it is …	Le sport	Sport
une bonne / mauvaise idée.	a good / bad idea.	le basket / le football	basketball / football
amusant / intéressant.	fun / interesting.	la danse / la natation	dancing / swimming
ennuyeux / nul.	boring / rubbish.	le tennis de table	table tennis
		faire de la danse	dancing
Tu es d'accord?	Do you agree?	faire du sport	doing sport
Oui, je suis d'accord.	Yes, I agree?	jouer au tennis de table	playing table tennis
Non, je ne suis pas d'accord.	No, I don't agree.		

Ma vie en ligne (pages 8–9)

Qu'est-ce que tu fais en ligne?	What do you do online?	Je fais ça …	I do it …
Je télécharge des applis sur ma tablette.	I download apps on my tablet.	souvent / quelquefois.	often / sometimes.
		tout le temps.	all the time.
J'écoute des chansons / de la musique.	I listen to songs / music.	tous les jours.	every day.
		de temps en temps.	from time to time.
Je parle avec ma famille en *Tunisie.	I speak with my family in Tunisia.	À mon avis, Internet est …	In my opinion, the internet is …
Je partage des photos.	I share photos.	C'est …	It is …
Je cherche des idées pour des activités.	I search for ideas for activities.	amusant / essentiel.	fun / essential.
		dangereux.	dangerous.
J'achète des vêtements.	I buy clothes.	génial / *super.	great.
Je joue à des jeux contre ma meilleure amie / mon ami.	I play games against my best friend / my friend.	mauvais pour la santé.	bad for your health.
		mais / par contre	but / however
Je regarde des vidéos amusantes / *clips sur TikTok.	I watch funny videos / clips on TikTok.	Il y a …	There is / are …
		des applis pour tout.	apps for everything.
J'envoie des messages.	I send messages.	des **risques** de sécurité.	security risks.
devant un **écran**	in front of a screen	de fausses informations.	false information.
		des réseaux sociaux géniaux.	great social media networks.
Est-ce que tu fais ça souvent?	Do you do that often?		

Tu as une vie active? (pages 10–11)

Qu'est-ce que tu fais?	What do you do?	Je vais …	I go …
Qu'est-ce que tu fais comme activités, si tu n'es pas en ligne?	What activities do you do, if you are not online?	au centre sportif / à la piscine.	to the sports centre / to the swimming pool.
		J'écoute de la musique.	I listen to music.
Je joue …	I play …	avec mon frère / mon ami(e) / ma famille / mes ami(e)s	with my brother / my friend / my family / my friends
au basket / au football.	basketball / football.		
au *rugby.	rugby.	normalement	normally
du *piano / du *violon.	piano / violin.	Est-ce que tu as une vie active?	Do you have an active life?
de la *guitare / de la *flûte.	guitar / flute.	Je suis (très) actif/active.	I am (very) active.
dans l'équipe du collège / dans un groupe de musique.	in a team at school / in a music group.	Je ne suis pas actif/active.	I am not active.
Je fais …			
du vélo. / de la cuisine.	I cycle. / I cook.		

Qu'est-ce que tu regardes? (pages 12–13)

Qu'est-ce que tu aimes regarder?	What do you like to watch?	Quel type de vidéos est-ce que tu regardes / préfères regarder?	What type of videos do you watch / prefer watching?
J'aime regarder …	I like to watch …	Je regarde …	I watch …
des comédies / des séries.	comedies / series.	des *clips de musique ou de danse.	music or dance clips.
des émissions de sport.	sports programmes.		
un peu de tout.	a bit of everything.	des vidéos amusantes d'animaux.	funny animal videos.

trente

Modul 1

Quand est-ce que tu regardes des vidéos?	When do you watch videos?	Je préfère regarder des films …	I prefer watching films …
Normalement, je regarde des vidéos …	Normally, I watch videos …	chez moi, à la télé, ou en streaming.	at home, on TV, or streaming.
le matin, avant le collège.	in the morning, before school.	sur mon portable.	on my phone.
le soir, après les cours.	in the evening, after school.	Avec qui est-ce que tu aimes regarder des films / aller au cinéma?	Who do you like to watch films / go to the cinema with?
quand j'ai du temps libre.	when I have free time.	J'aime regarder des films …	I like watching films …
Comment est-ce que tu préfères regarder des films?	How do you prefer to watch films?	avec les membres de ma famille.	with members of my family.
		tout(e) seul(e) dans ma chambre.	alone in my bedroom.

Qu'est-ce qu'on va faire? (pages 14–15)

aujourd'hui	today	Je vais …	I am going …
demain	tomorrow	On va … / Nous allons …	We are going …
ce matin / demain matin	this morning / tomorrow morning	acheter un cadeau / un *tee-shirt.	to buy a present / a t-shirt.
cet après-midi / demain après-midi	this afternoon / tomorrow afternoon	aller au musée.	to go to the museum.
ce soir / demain soir	this evening / tomorrow evening	faire les magasins.	to go shopping.
		jouer au foot / au tennis.	to play football / tennis.
		partir …	to leave …
		voir un spectacle.	to see a show.
à …	at …		
neuf heures	nine o'clock	Ça t'intéresse?	Are you interested?
neuf heures et demie	half past nine	Tu es libre?	Are you free?
dix heures moins vingt	twenty to ten	Tu viens?	Are you coming?
dix heures moins le quart	quarter to ten	Je veux bien, merci.	I'd like to, thanks.
midi / minuit	midday / midnight	Non, désolé(e), je ne peux pas.	No, sorry, I can't.

Qu'est-ce que tu as fait? (pages 16–17)

Qu'est-ce que tu as fait, le week-end dernier?	What did you do last weekend?	je suis allé(e) au café / au restaurant / à un concert.	I went to a café / restaurant / concert.
Samedi matin / après-midi / soir …	On Saturday morning / afternoon / evening …	je suis resté(e) à la maison / chez Chloé.	I stayed at home / at Chloé's house.
Pour commencer, …	To start with, …	on a lu un peu.	we read a bit.
Ensuite, / Après, …	Next, / After, …	on a mangé (du *couscous).	we ate (couscous).
Finalement, …	Finally, …	on a regardé la télé.	we watched TV.
j'ai acheté (un *poster).	I bought (a poster).		
j'ai bu (un *coca).	I drank (a cola).	C'était comment?	How was it?
j'ai fait les magasins.	I went shopping.	C'était …	It was …
j'ai joué au tennis / foot sur la plage.	I played tennis / football on the beach.	amusant / nul.	fun / rubbish.
j'ai marché à la campagne.	I walked in the countryside.	(trop) cher / complet.	(too) expensive / full.
j'ai pris des photos.	I took some photos.	passionnant / sympa.	exciting / nice.
j'ai vu mon *footballeur préféré.	I saw my favourite footballer.	un week-end ordinaire / extraordinaire.	an ordinary / extraordinary weekend.
		Samedi dernier, nous avons passé une bonne journée.	Last Saturday, we had a good day.

J'ai participé aux Jeux de la Francophonie! (pages 18–19)

Tu es de quel pays?	Which country are you from?	À quel âge as-tu commencé à …	At what age did you start to …
Je suis du *Sénégal / de *Belgique.	I am from Senegal / Belgium.	pratiquer ça?	practise that?
		jouer au tennis de table?	play table tennis?
Qu'est-ce que tu fais comme activité?	Which activity do you do?	J'ai commencé à l'âge de (dix) ans.	I started at (ten) years old.
Je joue au basket.	I play basketball.	Quand as-tu participé aux Jeux?	When did you participate in the Games?
Je fais de la danse *hip-hop.	I do hip-hop dancing.	J'ai participé aux Jeux l'année dernière / il y a (trois) ans.	I participated in the Games last year / (three) years ago.
Où est-ce que tu fais ça?	Where do you do that?	Est-ce que tu as gagné aux Jeux?	Did you win at the Games?
Je fais de la danse …	I do dancing …		
au centre sportif.	at the sports centre.	J'ai gagné (aux Jeux).	I won (at the Games).
à l'école.	at school.	J'ai fini en première / deuxième *position.	I finished in first / second position.
Quand est-ce que tu fais ça?	When do you do that?		
Je joue …	I play …		
tous les jours / le soir.	every day / in the evenings.		

trente-et-un 31

Module 2: Mon clan, ma tribu

Libre d'être moi
- Talking about your identity
- Using emphatic pronouns

Gaëlle Prudencio
Carrière/travail: Gaëlle est blogueuse.
Pays d'origine: Elle vient du Sénégal. Maintenant, elle habite en France.
Famille: Elle a un frère. Elle avait une sœur mais sa sœur est morte.
Temps libre: Elle aime la mode.
Langue: Elle parle français et wolof.

elle avait	she had
mort(e)	dead
la mode	fashion

Many francophone countries are multilingual. While the 'official language' of Senegal is French, Wolof and Pulaar are classed as 'national languages'. There are also many other national languages spoken in Senegal.

Marinette Pichon
Carrière/travail: Marinette est joueuse de foot international.
Pays d'origine: Elle vient de France et maintenant elle habite au Québec.
Famille: Elle a une sœur.
Temps libre: Elle aime lutter contre la discrimination.
Langue: Elle parle français et anglais.

As in English, French speakers are free to choose their pronouns to talk about themselves. The most commonly used non-binary pronoun is **iel**, which is a mixture of **il** and **elle**.

Omar Sy
Carrière/travail: Omar est acteur.
Pays d'origine: Il est né en France. Maintenant, il habite en Amérique.
Famille: Il a sept frères et sœurs. Sa mère vient de Mauritanie et son père vient du Sénégal.
Temps libre: Il aime le football. Il est fan de l'Olympique de Marseille.
Langue: Il parle français, pulaar et anglais.

If you'd like to talk about your gender identity and sexuality, you can say: *je suis* (I am) … / *je me définis comme* (I define myself as) …

masculin	gay
féminine	hétéro(sexuel(le))
non-binaire	lesbienne
transgenre	bisexuel(le)

Liberté, Égalité, Fraternité
'Liberté, Égalité, Fraternité' est la devise nationale de la France et de la république d'Haïti.
La devise est importante pour beaucoup de personnes.

la devise	motto

The values *Liberté* (Freedom), *Égalité* (Equality) and *Fraternité* (Brotherhood) are found on coins, buildings and government documents in both France and Haiti.

Some think that **fraternité** is too masculine. What do you think?

trente-deux

Zone de culture

Module 2

1 Lire
Read the profiles of Gaëlle Prudencio, Marinette Pichon and Omar Sy. Then, according to their profiles, find …

one person who:
1 is an international footballer
2 speaks three languages
3 likes fashion

and two people who:
4 come from France
5 live outside France
6 have brothers.

2 Écouter
Copy the profile card, then listen and complete it in English for each celebrity. (1–2)

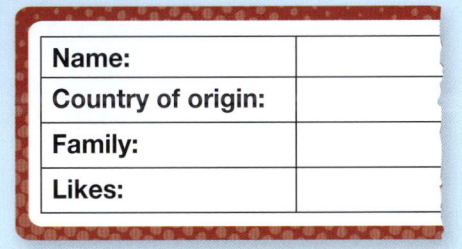

Name:	
Country of origin:	
Family:	
Likes:	

Redcar

Angèle

3 Lire
Read the sentences. Write the correct letter to match each heading to a sentence.

1 Je parle français, wolof et anglais.
2 Je suis indépendante et patiente. Ça, c'est moi!
3 J'adore ma sœur! Elle est toujours là pour moi.
4 Je suis croyante. C'est important pour toi aussi?
5 Moi, je suis non-binaire.
6 Mon groupe d'amis passe beaucoup de temps avec moi.

Ce qui fait mon identité, c'est …

a ma religion
b ma langue
c mon groupe d'amis
d ma personnalité
e ma famille
f mon genre

toujours always
là there
croyant(e) religious

G Emphatic pronouns are used after prepositions such as **pour** and **avec**.
avec moi — with me
pour toi — for you

G There are three different ways to say 'my' in French. The word for 'my' has to agree with the gender and number of the noun that follows it.
masculine: **mon**
feminine: **ma**
plural: **mes**

Page 44

4 Écouter
Listen and write down in English what defines each person. (1–6)

Qu'est-ce qui fait ton identité? — What defines your identity?
Ce qui fait mon identité, c'est … — What defines my identity is …

5 Parler
In pairs, talk about what defines your identity.
- Qu'est-ce qui fait ton identité?
- Ce qui fait mon identité, c'est … et …Tu es d'accord?
- Oui, je suis d'accord. / Non, je ne suis pas d'accord. À mon avis, ce qui fait mon identité, c'est … et …

6 Lire
Read the text about 'Liberté, Égalité, Fraternité' on page 32. Copy and complete the English translation.

1 Liberté, Égalité, Fraternité is the national motto of ▢ and ▢.
2 It is important for ▢.
3 It means Freedom, ▢ and Brotherhood.

trente-trois 33

1 Un week-end en famille

- Talking about your weekend routine
- Using reflexive verbs in the present tense
- Extending sentences using sequencers and connectives

Écouter 1
Listen and read. Then write down each person's family members in English.

Il y a combien de personnes dans ta famille?

Qu'est-ce que tu fais le week-end, en famille?

Yanis: Dans ma famille, il y a trois personnes: ma mère, ma sœur et moi. Le week-end, je me lève tôt, à huit heures. Le soir, on s'amuse bien ensemble!

Chloé: J'habite avec ma belle-mère et mon frère. Le samedi matin, je travaille dans un magasin de vêtements, donc le dimanche on se lève tard, à midi. L'après-midi, je mange et après je me repose.

Dorian: J'habite avec mes pères et mes demi-sœurs. Le dimanche, je m'habille tôt et ensuite, je m'amuse chez moi. L'après-midi, je fais du vélo. Plus tard, à 22 heures, je vais au lit.

tôt — early
tard — late

Lire 2
Re-read the texts from exercise 1. Find the French for the verbs below, choosing from the underlined verbs in the text.

1 I get up
2 I get dressed
3 I enjoy myself
4 I rest
5 we enjoy ourselves
6 we get up

In French, you don't need a word for 'at', 'in' or 'on' when talking about when you do something.
at the weekend = *le week-end*
in the evening = *le soir*
on Sundays = *le dimanche*

Lire 3
Re-read the texts from exercise 1. Then answer the questions in English.

1 Who goes to bed at ten o'clock?
2 Who works on Saturdays?
3 Who gets up at eight o'clock?
4 Who eats in the afternoon?

Lots of daily-routine verbs are reflexive. They have a **reflexive pronoun** before the verb.

se lever (to get up)	
je **me** lève	I get up
tu **te** lèves	you get up
il **se** lève	he gets up
elle **se** lève	she gets up
on **se** lève	we get up

Page 44

Parler 4
In pairs, choose a text from exercise 1 and take turns to read it aloud.

Take care with the pronunciation of these two sounds:

1 è ai ê
Listen and repeat the words. Open your mouth widely as you say: p*è*re / j'*ai*me / v*ê*tements

2 œu open eu
Listen and repeat the words. With your lips in a more rounded shape and your jaw lower: s*œu*r / h*eu*re

34 trente-quatre

Module 2

5 Écouter
Listen. Then copy and complete the grid in English. (1–2)

	How many people are in their family?	What do they do on Saturday mornings?	What do they do in the afternoons and evenings?
Fatima			
Lucas			

6 Parler
In pairs, choose a set of pictures each and take turns to talk about your weekend.

- Qu'est-ce que tu fais le week-end, en famille?
- Le samedi, je me lève à sept heures. Ensuite, je …

> Use **sequencers** to link the activities together:
> ensuite — then
> après — after, afterwards
> plus tard — later

A

B

7 Lire
Read the text. Copy and complete the sentences below in English.

> Clément habite en Guadeloupe avec sa sœur, sa mère, son beau-père et ses grands-parents. Le week-end, Clément se lève tôt car il aide sa mère à la cuisine. Il adore le sport, donc il joue au foot avec ses amis. Le soir, toute la famille mange dans le jardin. Ensuite, la famille se repose ensemble.

> Use **connectives** to create extended sentences:
> et — and
> donc — therefore, so
> car — because

1 Clément lives in ▇ with his ▇, his mother, ▇ and ▇.
2 He gets up ▇ because he helps ▇ in the kitchen.
3 He loves ▇, so he ▇.
4 His family ▇ in the garden and then they ▇.

8 Écrire
Write a paragraph about your real, or an imagined, family routine at the weekend. Say what you and other people do. Extend your sentences using sequencers and connectives.

Dans ma famille, il y a (deux / trois / quatre …) personnes.		
Il y a	mon (beau-)père / mon (beau-)frère.	
J'habite avec	ma (belle-)mère / ma (belle-)sœur.	
Le samedi matin, Le dimanche après-midi, Le dimanche soir, Après, Ensuite, Plus tard,	je me lève je me repose je m'habille je m'amuse	
	mon frère se lève mon grand-père se repose ma sœur s'habille on s'amuse	à … heures.
	je vais au lit	

G Possessive adjectives are words such as 'my', 'your', 'his' and 'her'.

	masculine	feminine	plural
my	**mon**	**ma**	**mes**
your	**ton**	**ta**	**tes**
his/her	**son**	**sa**	**ses**

mon grand-père — my grandfather
ta grand-mère — your grandmother
son frère — his/her brother
sa demi-sœur — his/her step(half)-sister

Page 44

trente-cinq 35

2 L'amitié est la clé du bonheur

- Discussing friends and friendship
- Making adjectives agree
- Translating a passage into French

Lire 1 Read about Nadia's friends. Copy and complete the sentences below by selecting the correct options.

Tu t'entends bien avec tes amis?

Myriam est ma meilleure amie.
Je m'entends très bien avec elle.
Elle est **patiente** et **sympa**.

Je ne m'entends pas bien avec mes **vieux** amis de l'école primaire.
Ils sont **ennuyeux**.
Ils ne sont pas **travailleurs**.

Je m'entends bien avec les filles de mon club de natation.
On s'amuse tout le temps bien ensemble.
Elles sont **sportives** et **actives**.

Je m'entends assez bien avec Sofiane.
Il est **travailleur** et **sérieux**.
J'adore son chien. Il est **beau**.

Nadia

vieux (vieille(s)) old

1 Nadia gets on **quite well** / **very well** with Myriam.
2 Nadia **gets on with** / **doesn't get on with** her old friends from primary school.
3 Nadia gets on well with **the girls** / **the boys** at her swimming club.
4 Nadia has fun with her swimming friends **all of the time** / **sometimes**.
5 Nadia gets on **quite well** / **very well** with Sofiane.
6 Nadia **loves** / **does not like** Sofiane's dog.

When a reflexive verb is negative, the negative goes around the **reflexive pronoun** and **verb**.
Je ne m'entends pas bien avec …
I do not get on well with …

Lire 2 Copy the grid and re-read the texts in exercise 1, paying attention to the adjectives in bold. Write each adjective in the correct column according to who it is describing. Then add the English translations.

masculine	feminine	masc plural	fem plural
	patiente (patient)		

Adjectives must agree with the person or noun they are describing. Most adjectives work like this:

masculine	feminine	masc plural	fem plural
– patient	add –e patiente	add –s patients	add –es patientes

Some adjectives follow different patterns:
sérieu**x** / sérieu**se**   acti**f** / acti**ve**

Others are irregular:
vi**eux** / vi**eille**   b**eau** / b**elle**

Some adjectives, such as **sympa**, never change.

Page 45

Écouter 3 Listen. Write down in English how well each speaker gets on with the person or people they mention. (1–4)

les amies de ma sœur my sister's friends (female)

Écouter 4 Listen again and write down in English how each person or group of people is described. (1–4)

Parler 5 In pairs, take turns to ask and answer the questions below.

- Tu t'entends toujours bien avec tes amis?
Pourquoi? / Pourquoi pas?

| Je m'entends (toujours) | (assez) bien | avec | mon ami(e). |
| Je ne m'entends pas (toujours) | très bien | | mes ami(e)s. |

Il est	amusant / travaill**eur** / sport**if** / sympa / ennu**yeux**.
Elle est	amusant**e** / travaill**euse** / sport**ive** / sympa / ennuy**euse**.
Ils sont	amusant**s** / travaill**eurs** / sport**ifs** / sympa / ennuy**eux**.
Elles sont	amusant**es** / travaill**euses** / sport**ives** / sympa / ennuy**euses**.

36 trente-six

Module 2

6 Read the quiz. Listen and note down the answers for Théo.

Qu'est-ce que c'est, un bon ami, pour toi?

1 Je préfère …
   a un ami proche.
   b un groupe d'amis sympa.
   c beaucoup d'amis amusants.

2 J'aime avoir …
   a des amis dans le monde réel.
   b des groupes d'amis différents.
   c beaucoup d'amis en ligne.

3 Mes amis sont …
   a sérieux.
   b intelligents.
   c fous.

4 Un bon ami …
   a écoute mes problèmes.
   b est patient.
   c est amusant.

proche	close
fou (folle)(s)	crazy, wild
l'affaire (f)	matter, business
la vie	life

Résultats

Maximum de a: Les amis sont très importants pour toi – c'est une affaire sérieuse!

Maximum de b: Tu t'entends toujours bien avec tes amis, c'est simple!

Maximum de c: Tu t'amuses bien avec tes amis; la vie, c'est amusant!

7 In pairs, do the quiz. Then read the results of the quiz and talk about whether or not you agree with them.

- Alors, première question. Je préfère un ami proche. Et toi?
- Je préfère beaucoup d'amis amusants.
- Ensuite, numéro deux. J'aime avoir …

- J'ai un maximum de a. Je suis d'accord. Et toi?
- J'ai un maximum de c. Je ne suis pas d'accord!

8 Listen to Pierre. How well does he get on with each person or group of people? Copy and complete the grid in English.

Who?	Gets on well? ✓ ✗	Why?	Extra details?
Ahmed			
basketball friends			
his father			
his friends from primary school			

9 Translate the sentences into French.

- I get on very well with my friend.
- She is hard-working and patient.
- I like to have lots of friends.
- A good friend listens to my problems.

Use a reflexive verb here.

Remember that you use *de* or *d'* after *beaucoup* (and never *des*).

Read the next sentence to see if this is masculine or feminine.

Make these adjectives agree.

Use *écoute*: there is no need for a word for 'to' here.

trente-sept **37**

3 Couleur famille

- Talking about what people look like
- Understanding the position of adjectives
- Describing a photo

Lire 1 Look at the photos. Write the correct letters to match **two** sentences to each photo. Then listen and check.

1. L'acteur français Omar Sy et sa fille Selly
2. Le footballeur français Kylian Mbappé et sa mère Fayza Lamari
3. Angèle, la chanteuse belge, et ses parents Laurence Bibot et Marka

a Elle est assez grande, comme sa mère.
b Elle a les cheveux longs et elle porte des lunettes.
c Il a les yeux marron de sa mère.
d Elle a les cheveux noirs de son père.
e Elle a les cheveux blonds et le visage long.
f Il a les cheveux très courts et il porte des lunettes de soleil.

sa fille	his/her daughter
comme sa mère	like his/her mother
de son père	of his/her father

Most adjectives come **after** the noun. **G**
Elle a le visage **long**.
Il a les cheveux **noirs**.
Page 46

Écouter 2 Listen and fill in the gaps with the correct word from the box. There are more words than gaps.

1 La femme a les cheveux ▩.
2 L'homme a les yeux ▩.
3 La personne a les cheveux ▩ et noirs.
4 La fille est assez ▩.
5 Le garçon a les yeux ▩.
6 L'enfant est très ▩.

grand   marron   gris   petite   longs
châtains   roux   bleus   court   blancs

Before you listen, read the sentences and predict which words could make sense in the gaps. When you listen, follow each sentence from the start.

ch is pronounced 'sh'.
Listen and repeat these words:
cheveux, **ch**âtains, **ch**ose.

Listen to these tongue-twisters. Then try saying them with a partner:

Sa**ch**a a**ch**ète une **ch**ose pour le **ch**ien de Ri**ch**ard.

Le **ch**anteur **ch**ante **ch**aque diman**ch**e.

Écrire 3 Write **four** short sentences to describe the photo.

Sur la photo,	il y a	cinq personnes.
Le garçon est / L'homme est / L'enfant est	assez très	grand. petit.
La fille est / La (jeune) femme est / La personne est		grande. petite.
Il a / Elle a	les cheveux	longs / courts. blonds / noirs / roux / châtains.
	les yeux	bleus / marron / verts.

trente-huit

Module 2

4 Look at the photo and read the description. Copy the texts, correcting the six mistakes.

Décris les personnes *(people)*

Sur la photo, il y a deux jeunes garçons, une femme et un chien.
Les filles ont les cheveux roux.

C'est où? *(location)*

Ils sont dans un restaurant. Il y a une route et une belle cuisine.

Que font-ils? *(activity)*

Ils font du vélo ensemble. L'homme regarde son portable.

| la route | road |

5 Listen and write down what is being described: people, location or activity. (1–4)

> Some adjectives go **in front of** the noun.
>
> une **belle** cuisine
> deux **jeunes** garçons
>
> Refer to page 46 for a list of other adjectives that come before the noun.
>
> Page 46

> When saying what people <u>are</u> doing, you don't need the verb 'to be' in French.
>
> she is cycling = elle **fait** du vélo
> they are eating = ils **mangent**

| à droite | on the right |

6 In pairs, describe the photo below. Remember to describe the people, location and activity.

Sur la photo, il y a	un (jeune) homme. une (jeune) femme. un garçon.
Il/Elle est	grand(e) / petit(e).
Ils sont	grands / petits.
Il/Elle a Ils ont	les cheveux (noirs). les yeux (marron).
Ils sont	dans un restaurant. en ville.
Il y a	une table. des personnes.
L'homme La femme	regarde … s'amuse.
Les personnes	mangent / parlent.

trente-neuf 39

4 La place des idoles

- Talking about positive role models
- Using direct object pronouns
- Using the present and perfect tenses

Écouter 1 Listen and read. Then find the French for the phrases below.

Qui est ton modèle dans la vie?

Mon modèle s'appelle Aïssa Maïga. Je la suis parce qu'elle est féministe. Elle est connue pour ses films. Elle lutte contre le racisme et le sexisme. Elle encourage l'égalité dans le cinéma et dans la société.

Mon modèle s'appelle Yannis Richardt. Je le suis parce qu'il est actif. Il est connu pour ses messages positifs. Il lutte pour l'environnement. Il partage des informations sur Instagram.

Mon modèle s'appelle Léna Mahfouf. Je la suis car elle est ordinaire. Elle est connue pour sa personnalité. Elle partage des vidéos sur la mode, le style de vie et ses expériences personnelles. Elle lutte contre le cyber-harcèlement.

1. I follow her
2. She is known for
3. She fights against
4. I follow him
5. He fights for
6. He shares news
7. she is ordinary
8. lifestyle
9. cyberbullying

suivre to follow (**je suis** I follow)

Lire 2 Re-read the texts from exercise 1. Copy and complete the grid in English.

Name	How are they described?	What are they known for?	What do they fight for/against?	What do they do?

Écouter 3 Listen. Then copy and complete the grid from exercise 2 in English for Gaëlle Prudencio.

Écouter 4 Listen and fill in the gaps.

Qu'est-ce que c'est, un bon modèle?

1. C'est une célébrité qui ___ les gens.
2. C'est une ___ qui inspire les autres.
3. C'est un ___ qui fait de bonnes ___.
4. C'est une ___ qui change les ___.
5. C'est un influenceur qui améliore ___ conditions de ___.

améliorer to improve

G A **direct object pronoun** replaces a noun that is the object in a sentence. It comes directly before the verb.

| masculine ('he'/'it') | le |
| feminine ('she'/'it') | la |

Je suis Yannis. → Je **le** suis.
I follow Yannis. → I follow **him**.

Je suis Aïssa. → Je **la** suis.
I follow Aïssa. → I follow **her**.

Page 46

qui means 'who' or 'that' and is useful for creating more complex sentences.

40 *quarante*

Module 2

5 Translate the sentences below about role models into English.

- Translate as 'role model'.
- Add 'a' here.
- Think about the English word order.
- Do you need a translation for this word here?
- Who does this refer to?

1 Un bon **modèle** aide les gens.
2 C'est une personne ordinaire qui change **les** choses.
3 Un exemple **de bon modèle**, c'est Arthur Baucheron.
4 **Je le suis** parce qu'il est intelligent et amusant.
5 Il m'inspire.

6 Read the text about Diane's role model, Arthur Baucheron. Is each statement below true or false?

Arthur Baucheron est né en France avec une maladie génétique. Il a partagé des photos sur les réseaux sociaux. Ensuite, il a reçu des questions sur son handicap.

Il est devenu une célébrité sur TikTok à cause de sa personnalité et sa créativité. Il a écrit un livre qui s'appelle *Les roues sur terre, la tête dans les étoiles*. Dans le livre, il parle de sa vie.

Maintenant, il est étudiant. Pour changer l'opinion publique, il crée des vidéos amusantes qui expliquent son handicap. Il montre que chaque personne peut faire une différence.

Diane

la maladie génétique	genetic condition
à cause de	because of
la roue	wheel
l'étoile (f)	star

Arthur Baucheron

1 Arthur was born in France.
2 He shared photos on social media.
3 He became a celebrity because of his music.
4 He wrote a blog about his life.
5 He is still studying at the moment.
6 He makes serious videos to change public opinion.

7 Re-read the text in exercise 6. Find the French for the verbs below.

1 he was born
2 he shared
3 he received
4 he became
5 he wrote
6 he speaks
7 he makes/creates
8 he shows

G

Use the **present tense** to describe what someone is doing now or usually does.

Il **lutte** pour l'environnement.   He **fights** for the environment.
Elle **encourage** l'égalité.   She **encourages** equality.

Use the **perfect tense** to talk about what someone did or has done in the past.

Il **a partagé** des photos.   He **shared** photos.

For verbs that take *être*, the past participle needs to agree with the subject.

Elle **est devenue** célèbre.   She **became** famous.

Page 47

8 Write a short paragraph about someone you follow. Include the following points:

- what makes a good role model
- who your role model is
- why you follow them
- what they do or have done.

Un bon modèle, c'est une personne qui	inspire les autres / aide les gens.
Mon modèle s'appelle	Arthur Baucheron / Aïssa Maïga.
Je le suis parce qu'il est	intelligent / féministe / acti**f** / amusant.
Je la suis parce qu'elle est	intelligent**e** / féministe / acti**ve** / amusant**e**.
Il/Elle m'inspire.	
Il/Elle partage Il/Elle a partagé	des photos positives sur les réseaux sociaux. des messages positifs sur les réseaux sociaux.
Il/Elle lutte Il/Elle a lutté	pour l'environnement. pour l'égalité. contre le racisme. contre le sexisme.

quarante-et-un 41

5 Famille, amour, gâteau

- Talking about celebrations
- Using the perfect, present and near future tenses
- Recognising adverbs

Lire 1 Read the captions (1–6). Write the letter of the correct photo for each caption.

1. Aujourd'hui, **c'est** l'anniversaire de Clara. **Je mange** au restaurant avec sa famille!

2. Samedi dernier, **je suis allé** à l'hôpital où **j'ai rencontré** ma nouvelle sœur!

3. **Mes mères vont se marier** cet après-midi! **Je vais danser** et **je vais faire** la fête.

4. Hier, **j'ai fait la fête** chez mon nouveau voisin. Bonjour et merci à Nathan!

5. **Je suis** au mariage d'Eva et Lucas. En ce moment, **je danse** et **je chante**!

6. Demain, **je vais avoir** un petit chat chez moi. **Ça va être** génial!

a #L'amourC'estL'amour
b #ChangementDeVie
c #PetiteFille
d #NouvelAnimal
e #BonAnniversaire
f #JeunesMariés

Chez means 'at' or 'to' someone's home.
chez mon nouveau voisin — at/to my new neighbour's house
chez moi — at/to my house

Lire 2 Re-read the photo captions and decide if each <u>event</u> (e.g. the birth, the wedding) is in the present, past or future.

Look or listen for different tenses and time phrases to spot if someone is referring to the present, past or future. **G**

	present	past	future
Tense	present e.g. *je mange*	perfect e.g. *j'ai rencontré*	near future e.g. *je vais danser*
Time phrase	e.g. *en ce moment*	e.g. *samedi dernier*	e.g. *demain*

Page 47

Lire 3 Re-read the photo captions and find <u>at least three</u> verbs in the present tense, the perfect tense and the near future tense. Then translate them into English.

Écouter 4 Listen. Which question do you hear in each conversation? Write the correct letter. (1–3)

a Normalement, qu'est-ce que tu fais pour ton anniversaire?
b L'année dernière, qu'est-ce que tu as fait pour ton anniversaire?
c L'année prochaine, qu'est-ce que tu vas faire pour ton anniversaire?

Écouter 5 Listen again. Copy and complete the grid in English. (1–3)

	When?	Activities
1		

present	perfect	near future	
Je vais	Je suis allé(e)	Je vais aller	chez (mon voisin) / en ville / au cinéma / au parc.
Je mange	J'ai mangé	Je vais manger	un grand repas / des pizzas / du gâteau.
Je reçois	J'ai reçu	Je vais recevoir	des cartes / des cadeaux.
Je danse / chante	J'ai dansé / chanté	Je vais danser / chanter	avec mes amis.

quarante-deux

Parler 6 In pairs, talk about how you celebrate your birthdays. Use the questions and key language from exercises 4 and 5.

Lire 7 Read the article. Answer the questions below in English.

Traditionnellement, au Québec, les élèves célèbrent la fin du lycée avec une grande fête. Alors, Toni organise une fête spéciale avec ses amis.

«J'ai déjà acheté ma robe et mes chaussures et on a invité nos profs. En ce moment, je choisis un restaurant et un groupe de musique. **Normalement**, c'est difficile! On va **certainement** beaucoup manger et danser. À minuit, je vais rentrer **directement** chez moi car la fête va être **extrêmement** fatigante!»

célébrer — to celebrate
alors — so, then, well
fatigant(e) — tiring

1 How do students in Quebec celebrate the end of school?
2 What has Toni already done?
3 What is Toni finding difficult?
4 What is going to happen at the event?
5 When is Toni going to go home and why?

Lire 8 Translate the adverbs in bold from the exercise 7 text into English.

G **Adverbs** are used to describe a verb, an adjective or a whole sentence. In English, they often end in '-ly'. In French, many adverbs are formed from adjectives.
Some are formed by adding **-ment** to the feminine form of an adjective, e.g.
traditionnelle → traditionnelle**ment**
normale → normale**ment**

The -ent at the end of a plural verb is silent. However, you do pronounce the **-ment** at the end of an adverb.
Listen to these sentences, then try saying them with a partner:
Traditionnelle**ment**, les élèves célèbr<u>ent</u> la fin du lycée.
Ils organis<u>ent</u> certaine**ment** une grande fête.

Écrire 9 Write a text about a celebration with family or friends. Include the following points:
- when and what you are going to be celebrating
- what you have already done to prepare
- what usually happens
- what is going to happen at the event.

L'année prochaine, Samedi prochain,	je vais célébrer on va célébrer	l'anniversaire de ma mère. la fin du lycée.
J'ai déjà	invité toute la famille. préparé un gâteau. acheté des vêtements.	
Normalement,	je vais chez (mon père). je mange (au restaurant / avec ma famille).	
Je vais On va	danser. beaucoup manger. faire la fête.	

Take care with your verbs.
- Is the action in the present, past or future?
- Which tense do you need?
- Have you formed the tense correctly?
- Check your work carefully when you've finished!

Module 2

quarante-trois 43

Grammaire 1

Reflexive verbs in the present tense (Unit 1, page 34)

Écouter 1 Listen and write the letter of the correct picture for each sentence. Listen again and write the reflexive verb in English. (1–4)

Example: 1 d, you …

a b c d

Reflexive verbs often refer to your body, clothing or relationships. They have a reflexive pronoun before the verb.

se lever (*to get up*)	s'entendre (*to get on*)
je **me** lève	je **m'**entends
tu **te** lèves	tu **t'**entends
il/elle/on **se** lève	il/elle/on **s'**entend

se lever is a stem-changing verb: the '*e*' changes to '**è**' in the *je*, *tu* and *il/elle/on* forms.

me, **te** and **se** are contracted to **m'**, **t'** and **s'** in front of a verb that begins with a vowel or *h*.

Écrire 2 Copy and complete the sentences with the correct reflexive pronouns.

Example: 1 Je m'entends bien avec mon frère.

1 Je ▢ entends bien avec mon frère.
2 Elle ▢ repose chez sa grand-mère.
3 On ▢ amuse au centre sportif.
4 Il ▢ habille à huit heures.
5 Le week-end, je ▢ lève à midi.
6 On ne ▢ entend pas bien.

Possessive adjectives (Culture, page 33)

Parler 3 In pairs, take turns to throw a dice twice: the first time, choose the possessive adjective; the second time, choose the noun. Say the phrase in French.

- my
- your (singular)
- his/her/one's
- our
- your (plural/polite)
- their

- step-mother
- sister
- half-brother
- father
- grandparents
- friends

Possessive adjectives are words such as 'our', 'your', 'his' and 'her'.

	masculine	feminine	plural
my	**mon**	**ma**	mes
your (singular)	**ton**	**ta**	tes
his/her/one's	**son**	**sa**	ses
our	notre	notre	nos
your (formal/plural)	votre	votre	vos
their	leur	leur	leurs

The possessive adjective must agree with the noun that follows it, rather than with the 'possessor':
*Claire et **son** frère*   Claire and her brother

💡 When saying 'step' parent, add **beau** or **belle** before the family member:
beau-père, belle-mère

When saying 'half-brother'/'step-brother' or 'half-sister'/'step-sister', add **demi**:
demi-frère, demi-sœur

💡 When used with a singular noun that starts with a vowel or *h*, you always use *mon*, *ton* or *son*, even for a feminine noun.
*un**e** ami**e*** ➝ **ton** ami**e**

quarante-quatre

Adjectival agreement (Unit 2, page 36)

Adjectives are used to describe nouns, including people. They agree with the gender of the noun they are describing and whether it is singular or plural.

Most adjectives follow this pattern.

masculine	feminine	masc plural	fem plural
amusant	amusant**e**	amusant**s**	amusant**es**

Some adjectives follow different patterns. Here are some examples.

ending	masculine	feminine	masc plural	fem plural
-e	calme	calme	calme**s**	calme**s**
-eux/-eur	sérieu**x**	sérieu**se**	sérieu**x**	sérieu**ses**
-f	acti**f**	acti**ve**	acti**fs**	acti**ves**
-il/-el	naturel	naturel**le**	naturel**s**	naturel**les**
-en/-on	bon	bon**ne**	bon**s**	bon**nes**
-al/-ial	génia**l**	génia**le**	génia**ux**	génia**les**
-er	prem**ier**	prem**ière**	prem**iers**	prem**ières**

Some adjectives never change, e.g. **sympa**, **marron**.

Some adjectives follow their own special pattern.

masculine	feminine	masc plural	fem plural
vieu**x***	vieille	vieux	vieille**s**
beau*	be**lle**	beau**x**	belle**s**
nouveau*	nouve**lle**	nouveau**x**	nouvelle**s**

💡 * Before a masculine singular noun beginning with a vowel or *h*, the masculine adjective becomes **vieil**, **bel** or **nouvel**:

un **vieil** homme (an old man); un **bel** animal (a beautiful animal); un **nouvel** ami (a new friend).

Lire 4
Copy and complete the grid, putting the adjectives under the correct headings. Then <u>underline</u> any plural adjectives.

masculine	feminine	either masculine or feminine
Example: amusant		

amusant, actifs, sympa, belle, nouveaux, travailleuse, sportives, calme, grand

Écouter 5
Listen to the adjectives. Copy out the one that you hear. (1–6)

Example: 1 patiente

1 patient / patiente
2 amusant / amusante
3 sportif / sportive
4 sérieux / sérieuse
5 grand / grande
6 actif / active

In the masculine forms of adjectives like *amusant* and *grand*, the final consonant is silent. However, in the feminine forms (*amusante* and *grande*), we pronounce the consonant before the final 'e'.

Lire 6
Copy out the text, choosing the correct form of each adjective in **bold**. Then translate the text into English.

Je m'appelle Norah. Je suis **patient** / **patiente**, mais je ne suis pas **sportif** / **sportive**. Mon frère est très **indépendant** / **indépendants**. Mes sœurs sont toujours **travailleuses** / **travailleurs**. Mes oncles ne sont pas **actifs** / **actives**.

quarante-cinq 45

Grammaire 2

The position of adjectives (Unit 3, pages 38 and 39)

Parler 1 In pairs. Partner A chooses one of the people. Partner B asks questions to find out who Partner A chose. Then swap over.

- *C'est un homme?*
- *Oui.*
- *Est-ce qu'il a les yeux verts?*
- *Oui.*
- *Est-ce qu'il porte des lunettes rouges?*
- *Oui.*
- *Est-ce qu'il s'appelle Thomas?*
- *Oui!*

C'est	un homme / une femme?			
Est-ce qu'il Est-ce qu'elle	a	les	cheveux	noirs / châtains / blonds?
			yeux	marron / verts?
	porte	des	lunettes	bleues / rouges?

Most adjectives come **after** the noun, e.g. *les yeux marron, les cheveux blancs*.

However, these common adjectives go **in front of** the noun: *beau, jeune, vieux, bon, mauvais, grand, petit, haut, nouveau*

Thomas   Raphaël
Lola   Yasmina

Écrire 2 Copy and complete the French translations with the missing adjectives. Think carefully about where each adjective should go.

1 I have two tiring little brothers. J'ai deux ▢ frères ▢.
2 Their sister is playing with a big white rabbit. Leur sœur joue avec un ▢ lapin ▢.
3 Our father loves his old green bike. Notre père adore son ▢ vélo ▢.
4 My friend is sharing a funny new message. Mon ami partage un ▢ message ▢.

Direct object pronouns (Unit 4, page 40)

Écrire 3 Put the words into the correct order to form sentences.

Example: 1 *Tu me regardes.*

1 me tu regardes
2 il aime t'
3 le suis je
4 elle fait la
5 l' ils encouragent
6 pas invite vous il ne

Écrire 4 Re-write these sentences, replacing the underlined words with direct object pronouns. Then translate your sentences into English.

Example: 1 *Elle les partage. She shares them.*

1 Elle partage <u>les vidéos</u>.
2 J'aime <u>l'actrice</u>.
3 Il ne regarde jamais <u>son portable</u>.
4 Ils admirent <u>le chanteur</u>.
5 Elles invitent <u>ton frère et toi</u>.

A direct object pronoun replaces a noun that is the object in a sentence. It usually goes in front of the verb.
Est-ce que tu partages le gâteau?
Are you sharing **the cake**?
Oui, je le partage.   Yes, I'm sharing **it**.

Here are the direct object pronouns:

me	me
te	you (singular)
le	him/it
la	her/it
vous	you (plural)

In front of a verb that begins with a vowel, **le** and **la** change to **l'**, e.g. *Je l'aime.*

In a negative structure, the direct object pronoun goes between the *ne* and the verb: *Non, je ne le partage pas.* No, I'm not sharing it.

Using the present and perfect tenses together (Unit 4, page 41)

Écouter 5 Listen to the sentences and note down whether you hear the present or perfect tense. (1–5)
1. Je partage des photos. / J'ai partagé des photos.
2. Il lutte contre le racisme. / Il a lutté contre le racisme.
3. Elle fait des vidéos. / Elle a fait des vidéos.
4. J'encourage l'égalité. / J'ai encouragé l'égalité.
5. On améliore les conditions de vie. / On a amélioré les conditions de vie.

Tense	To talk about …	Examples
Present tense	• what is happening now • what you usually do • what someone or something is like	*Il fait une vidéo.* *Je lutte tous les jours pour l'égalité.* *Elle est sympa.*
Perfect tense	completed events or actions in the past	*J'ai partagé des photos.* *Il a reçu des messages.* *On est allé(e)s au cinéma.*

The present, perfect and the near future (Unit 5, page 42)

Lire 6 Read each sentence and decide on the timeframe (past, present or future). Then write out each sentence, putting the verb in brackets into the correct tense.

Example: 1 present. Le soir, je **mange** en ville.

Look for different tenses and time phrases to spot if someone is referring to the past, present or future.

Timeframe:	present	past	future
Tense:	present je chante	perfect j'ai chanté	near future je vais chanter
Time phrase:	en ce moment	lundi dernier	demain

1. Le soir, on **(manger)** en ville.
2. L'année prochaine, elle **(danser)**.
3. Hier, il **(recevoir)** beaucoup de cartes.
4. Le mois dernier, je **(chanter)** avec mes amis.
5. Normalement, tu **(faire)** des gâteaux.
6. Dans huit jours, je **(préparer)** un grand repas.

C'est parti!

Lire 7 Read the text and answer the questions (1–4) in the coloured lozenges.

1. These are present tense verbs. Find <u>three</u> more in the text.

3. This is in the perfect tense. Find another verb in the perfect tense.

Aujourd'hui, c'est mon anniversaire. Je suis très content!
Normalement, le week-end, je m'amuse au centre sportif. Mes amis jouent au tennis.
J'ai invité toute ma famille chez moi.
Hier, j'ai préparé un gâteau délicieux. J'adore ça!
On va manger un grand repas. La fête va être extrêmement amusante!

2. What kind of verb is this and what does it mean?

4. What tense is this?

Parler 8 Listen to the text from exercise 7. In pairs, take turns to read out the text. Listen carefully to each other's pronunciation.

Remember to:
- pronounce the **-ment** at the end of adverbs
- keep **-ent** silent at the end of verbs
- watch out for final consonants such as **-s**, **-t**, **-x**, **-p** and **-d** that are usually silent.

Module 2 — Contrôle de lecture et d'écoute

Reading

Lire 1

My friends. Read Nathan's blog on friendship. Write down the word for the gap in each sentence, using a word from the box. There are more words than gaps.

> Salut!
>
> Je m'appelle Nathan. Au collège, j'ai beaucoup d'amis, mais mes amis proches sont mes amis de l'école primaire. Je ne m'entends pas bien avec les jeunes à l'école de musique.
>
> Pour moi, un bon ami doit être sympa. En plus, il doit avoir des passions intéressantes. Mes amis sont assez sportifs et ils passent beaucoup de temps avec moi. J'aime ça.
>
> Mon frère pense qu'il faut aimer les mêmes choses. Moi, je ne suis pas d'accord!
>
> Tu as beaucoup d'amis?
>
> Nathan

For each gap, there may be two or three possible answers. Make sure you read the text well to choose the correct one.

a Nathan met his closest friends at ___ school.
b For Nathan, a good friend must be ___.
c His friends are quite ___.

| hard-working | kind | sporty | interesting |
| secondary | primary | music | |

Lire 2

Equality. Read these comments from Clara and Yanis on an internet forum. Make notes **in English** under the headings below. You do not need to write in full sentences.

▼ #Clara#

J'organise un concert public. Le concert lutte pour l'égalité et le respect.

Les gens sont souvent trop cruels. Chaque personne a **le droit d'être*** libre et égale. Venez au concert si vous êtes d'accord!

*le droit d'être   the right to be

▼ #Yanis#

Dans notre société, il y a trop de problèmes à cause du racisme ou du sexisme.

Je lutte contre la violence aussi. La communication et les conversations sont très importantes pour trouver une solution. Tout le monde peut faire une différence.

In this type of task, you will have two possible answers in the text but each question only asks for one. So, make sure you only write one!

a Clara
  (i) One thing the concert is fighting for
  (ii) One thing everyone has the right to be

b Yanis
  (i) One thing that causes problems in society
  (ii) One thing that is important in order to find a solution

48 quarante-huit

3 Family celebrations. Translate the following sentences into English.

a J'aime les anniversaires et les fêtes.
b Normalement, mon père achète un gâteau au supermarché.
c Je déteste les cartes, j'adore les cadeaux.
d L'année dernière, j'ai organisé un repas spécial.
e Je pense que je préfère manger au restaurant.

These words will help you to work out which tenses to use.

Listening

4 My daily routine. Raphaël is talking about his and his sister's daily routines. What does he say? Listen to the recording and for each sentence write down the correct option (A–C).

1 Every morning, Raphaël gets up at …
  A 6.30 a.m.
  B 7.15 a.m.
  C 7.30 a.m.

2 Raphaël and his sister … together in the morning.
  A go to the park
  B eat breakfast
  C watch TV

3 Raphaël prefers …
  A getting dressed before eating.
  B eating before getting dressed.
  C eating dinner.

Focus on what Raphaël prefers.

5 Celebrating family. Listen to this advert promoting an annual family event in Canada. What activities take place? Write the letter (A–F) for each of the three correct options.

A	competitions
B	games
C	films
D	dancing
E	eating
F	concerts

Read options A–F carefully and think about what you hear. Do all the details match?

6 Dictation. You are going to hear someone talking about identity.

a Sentences 1–3: write down the missing words. For each gap, you will write one word in French.

1 J'ai ___ ans et je suis ___.
2 Ma ___ habite au ___.
3 Je ___ le ___.

Listen carefully to these words as you may not have heard them before.

b Sentences 4–6: write down the full sentences that you hear, in French.

Module 2 Contrôle oral

Read aloud

Parler 1 Look at this task card. With a partner, take turns to read out the five sentences, paying attention to the underlined letters.

> Jade, your Belgian friend, has emailed you to tell you about her family.
>
> Read out the text below to your teacher.
>
> > J'habite en France.
> >
> > Dans ma famille, il y a mes j<u>eu</u>nes s<u>œu</u>rs et mon p<u>è</u>re.
> >
> > Je v<u>ai</u>s f<u>ai</u>re la f<u>ê</u>te pour le Nouvel An.
> >
> > Je prépare un grand repas.
> >
> > Le diman<u>ch</u>e, je me l<u>è</u>ve tard et je me repo<u>s</u>e.

Take extra care with how you pronounce the underlined sounds.
- *ch* sounds like 'sh'
- *è, ê* and *ai* are pronounced the same
- *œu* and *eu* are pronounced the same in these words
- *s* in between vowels sounds like 'z'.

Remember that every final *s* in this text is silent!

Écouter 2 Listen and check your pronunciation.

Parler 3 Listen to the teacher asking the two follow-up questions. Translate each question **into English** and prepare your own answers **in French**. Then listen again and respond to the teacher.

Remember to answer in full sentences.

Role play

Parler 4 Look at the role-play card and prepare what you are going to say.

> **Setting:** At the concert ticket office
>
> **Scenario:**
> - You are at a concert ticket office in France with friends.
> - The teacher will play the part of the person at the ticket office and will speak first.
> - The teacher will ask questions **in French** and you must answer **in French**.
> - Say a few words or a short phrase/sentence for each prompt. One-word answers are not sufficient to gain full marks.
>
> **Task:**
> 1 Say how many tickets you would like.
> 2 Say how old you are.
> 3 Say what you want to do after the concert.
> 4 Say who you normally listen to music with.
> 5 Ask a question about timings.

Start with *Je voudrais*.

Use *Je veux*.

You could use *... à quelle heure?*

Parler 5 Practise what you have prepared. Then, using your notes, listen and respond to the teacher.

Écouter 6 Now listen to Mathis doing the role-play task. **In English**, note down (a) how he **answers** the questions for task prompts 1, 2, 3 and 4 and (b) what question he **asks** for task prompt 5.

cinquante

Picture task

Écouter 7 Look at the exam card below and read the **first part** of the task. Then listen to Emma describing the picture. Answer the questions **in English**.

a What does Emma say about the person in the centre?
b Who does she describe in the most detail and what does she mention?
c Where are they according to Emma? Do you agree?
d What does she say about what the people are doing?

Describe this picture.
Your description must cover:
- people
- location
- activity.

When you have finished your description, you will be asked **two questions** relating to the picture. Say a short phrase/sentence in response to each question. One-word answers will not be sufficient to gain full marks.

You will then move on to a **conversation** on the broader thematic context of **My personal world**.

During the conversation, you will be asked questions in the present, past and future tenses. Your responses should be as **full and detailed** as possible.

To describe someone's hair and eyes, use *il/elle a* or *ils/elles ont* + *les cheveux/les yeux* + colour.

Parler 8 Prepare your own description of the picture, mentioning **people**, **location** and **activity**. Then, with a partner, take turns to describe the picture.

> Sur la photo, il y a …

Parler 9 Read the **second part** of the task. Then listen to the two follow-up questions and respond to the teacher. Remember: you only need to give a short answer to each one.

Écouter 10 Read the **third part** of the task. The teacher asks Emma: *Est-ce que tu t'entends bien avec ta famille?* Listen and write down the words to complete the sentences.

1 Normalement, je m'entends bien avec ma ▭.
2 Mon frère est très ▭ et ▭ avec moi.
3 Ma ▭ aime les ▭, comme moi.
4 Hier, je suis allée au ▭ avec ma sœur. C'était ▭.

Écouter 11 Listen to Emma answering the question: *Qu'est-ce que tu vas faire avec tes ami(e)s ce week-end?* Write down (a) <u>one</u> thing she's going to do this weekend, and (b) <u>one</u> thing she has already done.

Parler 12 Prepare your own answers to the Module 2 questions on page 226. Your responses should be as **full and detailed** as possible. Then practise with a partner.

> Remember to use opinion phrases, time phrases and connectives, and a range of verbs in the present, past and near future tenses for yourself and other people.

cinquante-et-un 51

Module 2 — Contrôle écrit

40–50 word writing task

Écrire 1 Look at this writing exam task and then, for each bullet point:
1. think about what vocabulary you have learned which you could use in your answer. For example:
   - **nouns** and **verbs** to say what someone does
   - **verbs of opinion** and **adjectives** to explain reasons
   - how to explain what you are going to do in the future.
2. write down <u>two or three</u> ideas for what you could write about.
3. write down which tense(s) you will need to use in your answer.

> Write a text for a website about a person who has inspired you.
>
> You **must** include the following points:
> - what your role model does
> - your opinion about them
> - what you are going to do in the future to help a cause.
>
> Write your answer **in French**. You should aim to write between 40 and 50 words.

Lire 2 Read Ana's answer to the exam task. Answer questions 1–3 in the coloured shapes.

1. What do these **time expressions** mean? What tenses does Ana use in each sentence?

3. What does this **connective** mean? What other connective does she use?

> Mon modèle s'appelle Magaajyia Silberfeld. Tous les jours, elle lutte pour l'égalité. Elle encourage l'égalité dans le cinéma et la société.
>
> Je l'aime parce qu'elle inspire les autres. Je pense qu'elle est travailleuse.
>
> À l'avenir, je vais partager des messages pour lutter contre le racisme et le sexisme.

2. Using this **direct object pronoun** means Ana doesn't have to repeat 'Magaajyia Silberfeld'. Where else could she use a pronoun to avoid repetition?

Écrire 3 Prepare your own answer to the 40–50 word writing task in exercise 1.
- Think about how you can develop your answer for each bullet point.
- Look back at your notes from exercises 1 and 2.
- Write a **brief** plan and organise your answer into paragraphs.
- Write your answer and then carefully check the accuracy of what you have written.

80–90 word writing task

Écrire 4 Look at this writing exam task and then, <u>for each bullet point</u>:
1. think about what vocabulary you have learned which you could use in your answer. For example:
   - **nouns** and **verbs** to describe someone
   - **verbs of opinion** and **adjectives** to explain reasons
   - language to say what you did recently with that person
   - how to explain what your plans are for their next birthday.
2. write down <u>three or four</u> ideas for what you could write about.
3. write down which tense(s) you will need to use in your answer.

> Write about your friends.
>
> You **must** include the following points:
> - a description of a friend who is important to you
> - the reasons they are important to you
> - something you have done recently with them
> - what you are going to do to celebrate their birthday.
>
> Write your answer **in French**. You should aim to write between 80 and 90 words.

⭐ You don't have to tell the truth! Stick to what you've learned to say in French, and don't worry if it doesn't accurately describe your friend and your activities together in real life.

52 cinquante-deux

5 Read Mehdi's answer to the exam task. Answer questions 1–5 in the coloured shapes.

> Salut Lucie,
>
> J'ai beaucoup d'amis. Une amie importante s'appelle Diane et Diane est très originale et assez sportive. À mon avis, elle n'est jamais négative.
>
> Diane est spéciale pour moi car elle aime écouter mes problèmes. Elle s'entend très bien avec ma famille. Elle rit tout le temps!
>
> Récemment, avec Diane, je suis allé dans une association où on a discuté du respect et de l'égalité. Je pense que c'est vraiment intéressant.
>
> Cette année, pour son anniversaire, on va aller au concert d'Indila. Elle aime beaucoup Indila. Après, on va parler avec nos amis au club de jeunes.
>
> Mehdi

1 Which **tense** is this? What other examples of this tense can you find? Does he use any other tenses?

2 How could he **avoid repetition** by using pronouns here? Find one more example of using a pronoun in the text.

3 This is an example of **complex language**. What does it mean? Find three more examples from the text.

4 This word shows a **variety of vocabulary**. What does it mean? Find two more examples.

5 Which connective could he use here to form an **extended sentence**? What other connectives does he use?

6 Read Mehdi's answer again. Note **in English**:
a at least three details about Diane
b two details about why Diane is important to Mehdi
c two details about what Mehdi and Diane have done recently
d two reasons why Mehdi wants to go to see Indila in concert

7 Prepare your own answer to the 80–90 word writing task in exercise 4.
- Think about how you can develop your answer for each bullet point.
- Look back at your notes from exercises 4 and 5.
- Look at the 'Challenge checklist' and consider how you can show off your French!
- Write a **brief** plan and organise your answer into paragraphs.
- Write your answer and then carefully check the accuracy of what you have written.

Challenge checklist

🌶	✓ Past, present and future timeframes ✓ Connectives, time phrases, sequencers ✓ Some extended sentences ✓ Different opinion phrases
🌶🌶	✓ A wide range of tenses ✓ Different persons of the verb ✓ A variety of opinions ✓ Negatives (e.g. *ne … jamais*) ✓ A wide range of interesting vocabulary
🌶🌶🌶	✓ Phrases with more than one verb ✓ Infinitive phrases (e.g. *j'aime* + infinitive) ✓ Complex language (e.g. reflexive verbs, *je pense que* …) ✓ Positive/negative phrases ✓ A variety of connectives

Module 2 Vocabulaire

Key:
bold = this word will appear in higher exams only
* = this word is not on the vocabulary list but you may use it in your own sentences

Libre d'être moi (pages 32–33)

Mon identité	My identity
Qu'est-ce qui fait ton identité?	What defines your identity?
Il/Elle est né(e) …	He/She was born …
au *Québec.	in Quebec.
en France.	in France.
Il/Elle vient …	He/She comes …
du *Sénégal.	from Senegal.
de *Mauritanie.	from Mauritania.
Il/Elle est fan de …	He/She's a fan of …
Ce qui fait mon identité, c'est …	What defines my identity is …
*mon genre.	my gender.
mon groupe d'amis.	my group of friends.
ma famille.	my family.
ma langue.	my language.
ma personnalité.	my personality.
ma religion.	my religion.
Il/Elle parle (anglais et *wolof).	He/She speaks (English and Wolof).
Tu es d'accord?	Do you agree?
Oui, je suis d'accord.	Yes, I agree.
Non, je ne suis pas d'accord.	No, I do not agree.
À mon avis, …	In my opinion, …
*masculin(e)	masculine
*féminin(e)	feminine
non-binaire	non-binary
transgenre	transgender
gay	gay
hétéro(sexuel(le))	straight
lesbien(ne)	lesbian
bisexuel(le)	bisexual
avec moi	with me
pour toi	for you

Un week-end en famille (pages 34–35)

Il y a combien de personnes dans ta famille?	How many people are there in your family?
Dans ma famille, il y a (deux / trois / quatre) personnes.	In my family, there are (two / three / four) people.
Il y a …	There is/are …
J'habite avec …	I live with …
ma mère / belle-mère.	my mother / step-mother.
ma sœur / demi-sœur.	my sister / step (half)-sister.
mon père / beau-père.	my father / step-father.
mon frère / demi-frère.	my brother / step (half)-brother.
Qu'est-ce que tu fais le week-end, en famille?	What do you do at the weekend with your family?
Le samedi / Le dimanche …	On Saturday / Sunday …
matin,	morning,
après-midi,	afternoon,
soir,	evening,
à … heures,	at … o'clock,
Après, …	After, …
Ensuite, …	Next, …
Plus tard, …	Later, …
Je joue …	I play …
Je m'amuse …	I have fun …
Je m'habille.	I get dressed.
Je me lève.	I get up.
Je me repose.	I rest. (I relax.)
Je vais au lit.	I go to bed.
et	and
donc	therefore, so
car	because

L'amitié est la clé du bonheur (pages 36–37)

Tu t'entends (toujours) bien avec tes amis?	Do you (always) get on well with your friends?
Pourquoi? / Pourquoi pas?	Why? / Why not?
Je m'entends (toujours) (assez / très) bien avec …	I (always) get on (quite / very) well with …
Je ne m'entends pas (toujours) (très) bien avec …	I don't (always) get on (very) well with …
mon ami(e).	my friend.
mon/ma meilleur(e) ami(e).	my best friend.
mes amis.	my friends.
Il/Elle est (assez) …	He/She is (quite) …
Ils/Elles sont (très) …	They are (very) …
amusant(e)(s).	fun.
ennuyeux/ennuyeuse(s).	boring.
patient(e)(s).	patient.
sérieux/sérieuse(s).	serious.
sportif(s)/sportive(s).	sporty.
sympa.	nice.
travailleur(s)/travailleuse(s).	hard-working.
Qu'est-ce que c'est, un bon ami, pour toi?	What is a good friend, for you?
Je préfère …	I prefer …
un ami proche.	a close friend.
un groupe d'amis sympa.	a group of nice friends.
beaucoup d'amis amusants.	lots of fun friends.
J'aime avoir …	I like to have …
des amis dans le monde réel.	friends in the real world.
des groupes d'amis différents.	different groups of friends.
beaucoup d'amis (en ligne).	lots of friends (online).
Mes amis sont …	My friends are …
fous.	crazy.
intelligents.	intelligent.
Un bon ami écoute mes problèmes.	A good friend listens to my problems.

Module 2

Couleur famille (pages 38–39)

Décris les personnes	Describe the people
L'enfant / La personne est …	The child / The person is …
Le garçon / La fille est …	The boy / The girl is …
L'homme / La (jeune) femme est …	The man / The (young) woman is …
grand(e) / petit(e).	tall / short.
Il/Elle a le visage long.	He/She has a long face.
Ils/Elles ont les cheveux …	They have … hair.
blancs / blonds.	white / blond
châtains / roux.	chestnut brown / red
gris / noirs.	grey / black
courts / longs.	short / long
Il/Elle a les yeux …	He/She has … eyes.
bleus / marron / verts.	blue / brown / green
Il/Elle porte …	He/She is wearing …
Ils/Elles portent …	They are wearing …
des lunettes (de soleil).	(sun)glasses.
Sur la photo, il y a (cinq) personnes.	In the photo, there are (five) people.
C'est où?	Where is it?
Ils sont …	They are …
dans un restaurant.	in a restaurant.
en ville.	in town.
Il y a …	There is/are …
une route.	a road.
une table.	a table.
des personnes.	some people.
Que font-ils?	What are they doing?
L'homme / La femme …	The man / The woman …
regarde …	is looking at …
s'amuse.	is having fun.
Les personnes / Les amis …	The people / The friends …
font du vélo.	are cycling.
mangent.	are eating.
parlent.	are talking.

La place des idoles (pages 40–41)

Qui est ton modèle dans la vie?	Who is your role model in life?
Mon modèle s'appelle …	My role model is called …
Je le suis parce qu'il est …	I follow him because he is …
Je la suis parce qu'elle est …	I follow her because she is …
actif/active.	active.
*féministe.	a feminist.
ordinaire.	ordinary.
Il/Elle m'inspire.	He/She inspires me.
Il/Elle partage … sur les réseaux sociaux.	He/She shares … on social media.
Il/Elle a partagé … sur les réseaux sociaux.	He/She shared … on social media.
des messages positifs	positive messages
des photos positives	positive photos
Il/Elle lutte …	He/She fights …
Il/Elle a lutté …	He/She fought …
pour l'égalité.	for equality.
pour l'environnement.	for the environment.
contre le racisme.	against racism.
contre le sexisme.	against sexism.
Il/Elle est devenu(e) célèbre.	He/She became famous.
Qu'est-ce que c'est, un bon modèle?	What is a good role model?
Un bon modèle, c'est une personne qui …	A good role model is someone who …
aide les gens.	helps people.
inspire les autres.	inspires others.
encourage l'égalité.	encourages equality.

Famille, amour, gâteau (pages 42–43)

Normalement, qu'est-ce que tu fais pour ton anniversaire?	What do you normally do for your birthday?
L'année dernière, qu'est-ce que tu as fait pour ton anniversaire?	Last year, what did you do for your birthday?
L'année prochaine, qu'est-ce que tu vas faire pour ton anniversaire?	Next year, what are you going to do for your birthday?
Je vais / Je suis allé(e) / Je vais aller …	I go / I went / I am going to go …
chez mon voisin.	to my neighbour's house.
chez moi.	home.
au cinéma / au parc.	to the cinema / to the park.
en ville.	into town.
Je mange / J'ai mangé / Je vais manger …	I eat / I ate / I am going to eat …
un grand repas.	a big meal.
des *pizzas.	pizza.
du gâteau.	cake.
Je reçois / J'ai reçu / Je vais recevoir …	I receive / I received / I am going to receive …
des cadeaux / des cartes.	presents / cards.
Je danse / J'ai dansé / Je vais danser …	I dance / I danced / I am going to dance …
Je chante / J'ai chanté / Je vais chanter …	I sing / I sang / I am going to sing …
avec mes amis.	with my friends.
L'année prochaine, / Samedi prochain, on va *célébrer …	Next year, / Next Saturday, we are going to celebrate …
l'anniversaire de ma mère.	my mother's birthday.
la fin du lycée.	the end of sixth form.
J'ai déjà …	I have already …
acheté des vêtements.	bought some clothes.
invité toute la famille.	invited the whole family.
préparé un gâteau.	made a cake.
Normalement, …	Normally, …
je vais chez mon père.	I go to my father's house.
je mange (au restaurant / avec ma famille).	I eat (at a restaurant / with my family).
Je vais / On va …	I am going to / We are going to …
beaucoup manger.	eat a lot.
faire la fête.	party.

Modules 1–2 Révisions de grammaire

Plurals (Pages 20 and 22)

Écrire 1 Copy and complete the plural forms of the nouns.

Example: 1 une émission → dix émissions

1 une émission → dix
2 un gâteau → trois
3 le journal → les
4 l'animal → les
5 une table noire → cinq
6 un bateau bleu → trois
7 une grande pizza → des
8 un jeu intéressant → des

> To make a noun plural, you normally add -s.
> Some nouns have a plural form which ends in -x.
> - -al to -aux → animal to animaux
> - -eau to -eaux → château to châteaux
> - -eu to -eux → jeu to jeux
>
> Nouns which already end in -x, -z or -s don't change in the plural form.
> Remember that if you are changing a noun into the plural form, the adjective ending will also need to change.

Écrire 2 Re-write the singular verb forms, changing them into the plural form.

Example: 1 il déteste → ils détestent

1 il déteste – ils
2 tu vas – vous
3 elle est – elles
4 j'ai – nous
5 il a fêté – ils
6 elle sort – elles
7 tu viens – vous
8 on a fait – nous

> Watch out for any other words (articles, adjectives etc.) which you also need to change to the plural form, as well as the plural nouns and verb forms.

Écrire 3 Re-write these sentences, changing the <u>underlined</u> subject and verb into the plural form.

Example: 1 Les profs jouent au tennis de table.

1 <u>Le prof joue</u> au tennis de table.
2 <u>Ma tante va</u> au centre sportif.
3 <u>L'élève est</u> toujours travailleur.
4 <u>Ton frère se lève</u> à onze heures.
5 <u>Sa sœur a couru</u> un kilomètre.

Perfect tense verbs (Pages 16, 22 and 47)

Lire 4 Read the sentences. Write whether each sentence has a perfect tense verb that uses *avoir* or *être* as the auxiliary verb. Then translate the sentences into English.

Example: 1 être – I went to the Taylor Swift concert with my dad and my sister.

1 Je suis allée au concert de Taylor Swift avec mon père et ma sœur.
2 C'est la première fois que Taylor Swift est venue à Londres.
3 Le concert a commencé à huit heures et demie.
4 Nous avons dansé et chanté.
5 Nous sommes sortis du stade à onze heures.

> The vast majority of verbs use *avoir* as the auxiliary verb in the perfect tense. However, there are a group of very useful verbs that use *être* as the auxiliary verb.
>
> | Verb | Perfect tense | |
> |---|---|---|
> | aller (to go) | je suis allé(e) | I went |
> | arriver (to arrive) | je suis arrivé(e) | I arrived |
> | rester (to stay) | je suis resté(e) | I stayed |
> | sortir (to go out) | je suis sorti(e) | I went out |
> | venir (to come) | je suis venu(e) | I came |
>
> Some other verbs that also use *être* as the auxiliary verb are: *descendre* (to go down), *entrer* (to enter), *monter* (to go up), *partir* (to leave), *retourner* (to return), *revenir* (to come back) and *tomber* (to fall).
>
> Remember that the past participle needs to agree with the subject of verbs that take *être*, e.g. *elle est restée, ils sont sortis*.

Révisions de grammaire — Modules 1–2

Écrire 5 Copy and complete the sentences with the correct form of the auxiliary verb.
1 Elle ___ allée chez son grand-père. (être)
2 Il ___ lutté contre les règles scolaires. (avoir)
3 On ___ fêté l'anniversaire de mon frère. (avoir)
4 Nous ___ arrivés très tôt. (être)
5 Pourquoi ___-vous invité toute la famille? (avoir)
6 J' ___ lu un magazine et j' ___ surfé sur Internet. (avoir)
7 Ils ___ restés à la maison hier soir. (être)
8 Est-ce que tu ___ sorti à neuf heures et demie? (être)

Negatives (Pages 11, 17 and 21)

Lire 6 Read the sentences. Make each one negative by adding the phrase given in brackets to the underlined verb. Then translate the negative sentences into English.
Example: 1 Mon père n'aime pas regarder la télé. → My dad doesn't like watching TV.
1 Mon père <u>aime</u> regarder la télé. (ne … pas)
2 Nous <u>allons</u> au théâtre avec mes parents. (ne … jamais)
3 Je <u>discute</u> souvent avec mes amis. (ne … pas)
4 Elle <u>est</u> allée chez sa grand-mère. (ne … pas)
5 J'<u>ai</u> mangé au restaurant samedi dernier. (ne … rien)

Asking questions (Pages 12, 18 and 21)

You have seen lots of ways of forming questions in Modules 1 and 2.
- Intonation (making your voice go up at the end) — Tu es sportif?
- Using *est-ce que* for a yes/no question — **Est-ce que** tu partages des photos sur Instagram?
- Using *est-ce que* after a question word — Quand **est-ce que** tu regardes des vidéos?
- Using *quel, quelle, quels, quelles* (what/which) — **Quel** est ton film préféré?
- Inverting the subject and the verb, after a question word — Que **fais-tu** le week-end, en famille?
- Using *qu'est-ce que* — **Qu'est-ce que** tu as fait le week-end dernier?

Écrire 7 Copy the questions. Then re-write them using the question starters given in brackets.
Example: 1 Tu as une vie active? Est-ce que tu as une vie active?
1 Tu as une vie active? (*Est-ce que tu …*)
2 Que fais-tu en ligne? (*Qu'est-ce que …*)
3 Tu suis qui? (*Qui est-ce …*)
4 Tu es allé(e) où le week-end dernier? (*Où …*)
5 Tu fais quoi cet après-midi? (*Que …*)
6 Tu as un film préféré? (*Quel est …*)

Using a range of tenses (Pages 23 and 47)

Écrire 8 Translate the conversation into French.

I often watch TV with my parents at the weekend, but last Saturday, they went to the cinema. Do you like going to the cinema?

No, I never go to the cinema because it's very expensive. Next weekend, I'm going to watch a film online.

- This will go after the verb.
- Use *aimer* + infinitive.
- This is an adjective and needs to go after the noun.
- Use the perfect tense and remember the verb *aller* uses the auxiliary *être*.
- Remember the negative parts go around the verb or the auxiliary.
- Use the near future tense.

cinquante-sept 57

Module 3 — Ma vie scolaire

Au collège chez nous
- Learning about school life in francophone countries
- Describing photos

La vie au collège dans le monde francophone

C'est comment, la vie au collège? Voici les réponses de deux jeunes de pays différents.

Emma, en France

Salut! <u>Je suis en quatrième</u> au collège Jacques Brel à Toulouse en France.

<u>J'adore le collège</u> et j'aime bien voir mes amis tous les jours.

Le bâtiment principal est très grand et il y a une cantine moderne.

En France, <u>on n'a pas d'uniforme</u> au collège: c'est excellent! En plus, on n'a pas de cours de religion.

Matthieu, au Sénégal

Salut! <u>J'ai treize ans</u> et je suis en cinquième au collège Saint François à Dakar au Sénégal.

Le collège est bilingue et on étudie toutes les matières en français et en anglais. <u>Ma matière préférée, c'est la musique</u>.

Au collège, on a une académie de foot, et le week-end, on joue avec des footballeurs professionnels. <u>Voici une photo de mon équipe</u> sur le terrain de foot.

le bâtiment	building
en plus	in addition
bilingue	bilingual

1 Listen and read. Then answer the questions in English.
1. Who has practice at the weekends?
2. Who says they like seeing their friends every day?
3. Who is musical?
4. Who is in the equivalent of Year 8?
5. Whose school building is big?

Year groups in *collège*:
sixième — Year 7
cinquième — Year 8
quatrième — Year 9
troisième — Year 10

Whereas in the UK school year groups count upwards, in most of the Francophone world, they count downwards.

After *collège*, students go to *lycée* for three years to prepare for their final exams, the *baccalauréat* (*bac*).

2 Re-read the texts in exercise 1. Match the <u>underlined</u> phrases with the English translations below.
1. I love school
2. I am in Year 9
3. My favourite subject is music.
4. Here is a photo of my team
5. I am 13 years old
6. we don't have a uniform

G The definite article 'the' changes according to the noun:

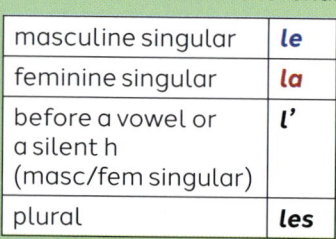

masculine singular	le
feminine singular	la
before a vowel or a silent h (masc/fem singular)	l'
plural	les

You often need the definite article in French even where we wouldn't use it in English, e.g.
Ma matière préférée, c'est le théâtre.
My favourite subject is drama.

Look for examples of this in exercise 2.

Page 70

58 cinquante-huit

Zone de culture — Module 3

Écouter 3 Look at the photo and listen. Put the words in the statements in the correct order. Is each statement true or false? (1–4)

1. jeunes / sur / il y a / trois / la photo
2. un uniforme / portent / scolaire / ils
3. une salle de classe / sont / dans / ils
4. un court de tennis / il y a / des arbres / et

Écrire 4 Write four sentences to describe this photo, including the people, location and activity.

Les personnes (people)

Sur la photo, il y a	un prof / deux personnes / trois jeunes.
Il y a	un garçon / deux garçons et une fille / deux filles.
Le prof porte	une cravate noire.
Un garçon porte	un pantalon gris / marron une chemise bleue / blanche et des baskets noires / blanches.
Une fille porte	un tee-shirt rose / jaune et un short bleu / noir.
Ils portent	un uniforme scolaire.

C'est où? (location)

Ils/Elles sont	à la cantine / au collège / sur le terrain de foot.
← À gauche, il y a	un professeur / des arbres.
→ À droite, il y a	des élèves / des tables / de la nourriture.

Que font-ils? (activity)

Les élèves / Les enfants	discutent / mangent / jouent ...
Le/La prof Un garçon / Une fille	discute / mange / joue ...

Parler 5 In pairs, describe one of the photos below, including the people, location and activities.

- Use or adapt phrases from the boxes above.
- Check that your adjectives agree with the noun (e.g. *une chemise blanche*).

cinquante-neuf 59

1 Quelle est ta matière préférée?

- Talking about school subjects and school life
- Using comparative adjectives
- Giving opinions with reasons

Parler 1 In pairs, take turns to read out the subjects for each day in the timetable. Then listen and check.

> Take care with the words that look very similar to the English – the pronunciation may be very different!

Lire 2 Read what these students say about their subjects. Translate the phrases in **bold** into English.

Quelle est ta matière préférée et pourquoi?

	lundi	mardi
8h00	les maths	l'informatique
9h00	l'anglais	la biologie
10h00	récréation	
10h15	la chimie	les maths
11h15	le français	l'EPS
12h15	déjeuner	
13h30	la musique	
14h30		le français
15h30	le théâtre	l'histoire-géo

Ma matière préférée est le théâtre, car je suis très créative.
J'aime aussi les maths parce que la prof est sympa.
— Alice

Ma matière préférée est la biologie parce que je suis forte en sciences.
Je déteste l'anglais parce que **le prof est très sévère.**
— Zélie

Ma matière préférée est la musique parce que c'est passionnant.
J'adore chanter et jouer du piano.
— Mehdi

Ma matière préférée, c'est l'EPS parce que je suis sportif.
Je n'aime pas l'informatique car **on a trop de devoirs.**
— Arthur

l'informatique (f)   ICT
l'EPS (f)   PE

Lire 3 Re-read the texts. Copy and complete the sentences below in English.
1 Drama is Alice's ▢.
2 She likes maths because ▢.
3 Mehdi's favourite subject is ▢.
4 He loves ▢ and ▢ the piano.
5 Zélie is ▢ at science.
6 She does not like ▢.
7 Arthur is ▢.
8 He ▢ ICT.

Écouter 4 Listen to the teenagers talking about their favourite subjects. Then copy and complete the grid in English. (1–4)

	Favourite subject	Reason
1		

Parler 5 In pairs, take turns to ask and answer the following questions.
- *Quelle est ta matière préférée? Pourquoi?*
- *Ma matière préférée est (l'anglais) parce que (la prof est sympa).*
- *Tu n'aimes pas quelle matière? Pourquoi?*
- *Je déteste (les sciences) parce que (je suis faible en biologie).*

Ma matière préférée est J'aime J'adore Je n'aime pas Je déteste	le français la biologie l'anglais les maths	parce que	c'est facile / utile / amusant / intéressant / passionnant. c'est difficile / inutile / ennuyeux. je suis créati**f**/créati**ve**. je suis sporti**f**/sporti**ve**. le/la prof est sympa / sévère.
		parce qu'	on a trop de devoirs.
Je suis fort(**e**) en Je suis faible en	anglais / informatique / maths.			

6 Écouter

Listen and read sentences 1–4. Then translate them into English. Finally, listen and note down details for sentences 5–8.

1 La musique est moins utile que l'anglais.
2 Le théâtre est plus amusant que les maths.
3 Les sciences sont plus difficiles que l'histoire-géo.
4 L'informatique est moins intéressante que le français.

G

You use comparative adjectives to compare things.

plus + adjective + **que**   more + adjective + than
moins + adjective + **que**   less + adjective + than

The adjective must agree (in gender and number) with the first noun:

Le français est **plus** intéressant **que** l'histoire-géo.
French is more interesting than history and geography.

La chimie est **moins** important**e** **que** les maths.
Chemistry is less important than maths.

Page 70

7 Parler

Choose a pair of subjects. In pairs, take turns to give your opinions and make a comparison.

- Quelle est ta matière préférée?
- Ma matière préférée est …
  parce que …
  À mon avis, c'est plus … que …

À mon avis,	c'est plus amusant que …
Je pense que	**le** français est plus (facile) que (la chimie).
	la biologie est moins (intéressant**e**) que (les maths).
	les maths sont plus (difficile**s**) que (l'anglais).

a   b   c   d

8 Lire

Listen and read the text. Answer the questions in English.

Luis

Moi, je suis élève au collège du Vieux Port à la Martinique. En ce moment, je suis en quatrième.

Le premier cours commence à 7h45, mais le collège finit à 14h, car l'après-midi, il fait très chaud. La pause-déjeuner dure cinquante minutes.

Je n'ai pas de matière préférée, mais je déteste la technologie car c'est ennuyeux. Je pense que la musique est plus intéressante que la technologie. Je n'aime pas les sciences parce que les sciences sont difficiles.

durer   to last

1 Which year is Luis in?
2 Why do lessons at Luis's school finish at 14:00?
3 How long is Luis's lunch break?
4 Why does Luis hate technology?
5 Which subject does Luis think is more interesting than technology?
6 Does Luis like science? Why / Why not?

9 Écrire

Write a text about your school subjects and life at school. Include the following points:

- your favourite subject and why
- which subjects you don't like, with reasons
- comparisons of some of your subjects
- information about your school day.

Use some connectives to extend your sentences: *et, mais, car, parce que*.

Ma matière préférée, c'est les sciences car c'est intéressant …

Je n'aime pas la musique parce que le prof est sévère …

L'EPS est plus amusante que la technologie …

Les cours commencent à … et finissent à …

soixante-et-un 61

Module 3

2 C'est injuste!

- Discussing school rules
- Using *il faut* + infinitive
- Expressing opinions, agreeing and disagreeing

Lire 1 Read the school rules. Write the letter of the correct picture for each school rule.

Règlement intérieur

✓
1. Il faut porter l'uniforme scolaire.
2. Il faut faire ses devoirs.
3. Il faut respecter les profs.

✗
4. Il ne faut pas arriver en retard.
5. Il ne faut pas manger en classe.
6. Il ne faut pas utiliser son portable en classe.

le règlement intérieur — set of rules

a b c d e f

Merci, madame!

G
To talk about rules, use:
il faut + **infinitive**
Il faut **porter** l'uniforme scolaire.   You have to wear school uniform.
il ne faut pas + **infinitive**
Il ne faut pas **arriver** en retard.   You must not arrive late.

Page 71

Écouter 2 Listen to Enzo and Nadia talking about the school rules. Note down the number of the rule they mention from exercise 1, and if they agree (✓) or disagree (✗) with the rule. (1–6)

Example: 1 6, ✗

Qu'est-ce que tu penses des règles?					
À mon avis, Je pense que	c'est	un peu assez très trop	important juste	parce que parce qu' car	c'est essentiel pour les examens. c'est utile pour le travail scolaire.
					il faut respecter les autres.
			injuste nul stupide strict		l'uniforme scolaire est pratique. l'uniforme scolaire n'est pas confortable.
					j'ai des problèmes avec le bus.

la règle — rule

Parler 3 In pairs, talk about the school rules from exercise 1 and give your opinions.

- Il faut / Il ne faut pas …
  À mon avis, c'est …
  Tu es d'accord?
- Oui, je suis d'accord parce que …
  Non, je ne suis pas d'accord parce que ….
  Je pense que …

Try to extend your answers by giving reasons for your opinions. You can use these connectives to do this (both meaning 'because'):
car / parce que

Écrire 4 Write at least <u>three</u> ridiculous school rules in French.

Il faut manger de la pizza en classe.
Il ne faut pas faire ses devoirs.

62 soixante-deux

Écouter 5 Listen and read. Then find the French for the phrases below.

Les règles scolaires et TikTok

Au collège Saint Paul à la Martinique, on a organisé des manifestations. Les élèves ont lutté pour avoir le droit de porter un short ou une jupe en été. Ils pensent qu'il fait trop chaud pour un pantalon. Les élèves ont aussi demandé à avoir le droit de quitter le collège pendant l'heure du déjeuner.

Les élèves ont filmé les manifestations et utilisé TikTok pour partager des vidéos. La directrice du collège a refusé de changer toutes les règles. Madame Quirin dit, «Il faut écouter les élèves et respecter leurs opinions, mais il faut aussi préparer les jeunes pour la vie et le travail.» Mais les élèves peuvent maintenant porter un short ou une jupe en été.

la manifestation — protest
la directrice du collège — headteacher

1 the students can now wear
2 in summer
3 to have the right to
4 to share videos
5 you have to listen to the students

> Start with any words that you already know. For example, you might not know the French for 'share', but you should be able to spot 'videos'.

Lire 6 Read the article again, and copy and complete the sentences below in English.

1 They protested because they wanted to wear ▬ in summer.
2 They also wanted the right to ▬ during the lunch hour.
3 They used TikTok to ▬.
4 The headteacher refused to ▬.
5 She thinks that you have to prepare young people for ▬.

Parler 7 In pairs, take turns to read out the first paragraph of the article, paying careful attention to your pronunciation.

Écrire 8 Translate these sentences into French.

Use *Il faut* + infinitive.

1 You have to respect the rules.
2 It's fair because it's essential for exams.
3 I think that school uniform isn't practical.
4 I can wear trousers.
5 I shared videos of my school online.

Which words could you use to say 'because'?

Use *Je peux* + infinitive.

Negatives go around the verb.

Remember that the perfect tense is made of the part of *avoir* or *être*, and the past participle.

soixante-trois 63

3 As-tu fait des progrès?

- Talking about what has happened at school
- Using irregular verbs in the perfect tense
- Pronouncing *oi* and *oy*

Écouter 1 Listen to the teachers giving feedback to Lucas and Manon at parents' evening. For each student, write the letters of the four statements the teacher makes, in the order in which you hear them. (1–2)

Une soirée parents-profs

a Tu as <u>appris</u> beaucoup de choses.

b Tu as <u>écrit</u> une histoire extraordinaire.

c Tu as <u>fait</u> beaucoup de progrès.

d Tu as <u>lu</u> beaucoup de livres.

e Tu as <u>bu</u> du coca en classe.

f Tu as <u>mis</u> des lunettes de soleil.

g Tu as <u>reçu</u> de mauvaises notes.

h Tu as <u>ri</u> pendant un examen.

Lucas — Manon

mauvais(e)(s) bad

Lire 2 Look at the infinitives of these these irregular verbs. What is the past participle for each one (underlined in exercise 1)? Copy out the correct sentence from exercise 1 next to each infinitive.

Example: 1 *mettre*: Tu as <u>mis</u> des lunettes de soleil.

1 mettre (*to put (on)*)
2 lire (*to read*)
3 faire (*to do/make*)
4 apprendre (*to learn*)
5 rire (*to laugh*)
6 boire (*to drink*)
7 recevoir (*to receive*)
8 écrire (*to write*)

> **G** Lots of verbs are irregular and have **irregular past participles**, e.g.
> *lire* (to read) → *j'ai* **lu** (I read)
> *faire* (to do/make) → *tu as* **fait** (you did/made)
> Page 71

Lire 3 Translate the sentences from exercise 1 into English.

Écouter 4 Listen to the teenagers talking about positive and negative things that happened in their lessons. Then copy and complete the grid in English. (1–3)

	School subject	Positive	Negative
1			

Parler 5 Listen to the tongue-twister. Then read it aloud, paying attention to your pronunciation of the sound *oi*.

C'est incr**oy**able, mais j'ai oublié mes dev**oi**rs d'hist**oi**re tr**oi**s f**oi**s.

incroyable incredible, unbelievable

> If you know how to say *trois*, this can help you pronounce the *oi* sound in other words.

64 *soixante-quatre*

Module 3

6 Écouter
Listen to and read Gabriel's school report. Is each statement below true or false?

En maths et en sciences, Gabriel a reçu de bonnes notes et il n'a jamais oublié ses devoirs. En histoire-géo, il a fait beaucoup de progrès. Il est très créatif, et en musique, il a écrit une chanson géniale.

Par contre, Gabriel n'a pas fait beaucoup d'efforts en anglais et en français. Malheureusement, son professeur de français dit qu'il n'a pas lu son livre. Donc, il n'a rien appris et il a reçu de mauvaises notes.

oublier to forget

> **G**
> In the perfect tense, **negatives** go around the part of *avoir* or *être*.
> *Je **n'ai pas** lu le livre.*
> I haven't read the book.
>
> *Tu **n'as jamais** fait tes devoirs.*
> You have never done your homework.
>
> *Il **n'a rien** appris.*
> He didn't learn anything. / He learned nothing.
>
> Page 73

1. Gabriel received good grades in maths and science.
2. He forgot his homework.
3. He hasn't made progress in history and geography.
4. In music, he wrote a great song.
5. He hasn't made an effort in English and French.
6. He didn't read his English book.

7 Parler
In pairs, choose to be either Diane or Thomas and tell your partner what you have done or not done at school.

Diane
- learned a lot in French
- never forgot her homework
- put on sunglasses

Thomas
- made lots of progress in music
- made no effort in English
- received bad grades

> En ..., j'ai ...
> En plus, j'ai ...
> Par contre, je n'ai pas ...

> To say 'in' a subject (e.g. 'in music'), use **en** + the subject.
> You don't need *le/la/l'/les* as well.
>
> **en** musique

8 Écrire
Write a paragraph about your own progress at school this year, using the key language from the grid. Include:
- details about your progress in different subjects
- things that you have and haven't done
- opinions.

En anglais, En français, En histoire-géo, En musique,	j'ai reçu de bonnes notes / de mauvaises notes. j'ai appris beaucoup de choses. j'ai bu du coca en classe. j'ai fait	des efforts / beaucoup de progrès / mes devoirs.
Je n'ai jamais oublié mes devoirs.		
Je n'ai pas fait d'efforts.		
Je n'ai rien appris.		

J'aime J'adore	l'anglais les sciences	parce que car	c'est génial. c'est intéressant.
Je n'aime pas Je déteste	les maths le théâtre		c'est nul. c'est ennuyeux.

soixante-cinq

4 Souvenirs d'école

- Talking about what school used to be like when you were younger
- Using verbs in the imperfect tense
- Translating into French

1 Listen and read. Put the headings in the order in which the information appears in the text.

Salut, je m'appelle Théo et j'habite à Antsiranana dans le nord de Madagascar.

Quand j'étais petit, j'allais à l'école à pied. Mon école primaire s'appelait ECAR Sainte Thérèse et il y avait un énorme terrain de foot. Le foot, c'était mon sport préféré. Tous les jours pendant la pause-déjeuner, je jouais au foot avec mes amis.

À l'école, j'aimais beaucoup l'anglais et aussi la musique. De temps en temps, je lisais des magazines en anglais!

Après l'école, j'aidais mon frère sur son bateau. Il était pêcheur. C'était assez difficile pour un enfant! Puis le soir, je retournais à la maison et je mangeais avec toute la famille. Après, je faisais mes devoirs ou je regardais un peu la télévision.

l'école (f) primaire — primary school
le pêcheur — fisherman

Madagascar

a what he used to do straight after school
b information about his school subjects
c what he used to do at lunchtime
d how he used to get to school
e what he used to do when he got home

2 Find the French for the verbs below, choosing from the underlined words in the text.

1 I used to be / I was
2 I used to like
3 I used to go
4 I used to read
5 I used to do
6 it used to be / it was
7 there used to be / there was

G

The **imperfect tense** is used to talk about what things were like in the past / what used to happen.
To form the imperfect tense, remove the *-ons* from the *nous* form of the verb in the present tense:
regarder (to watch) → *nous regardons* (we watch) → **regard-**
Then add these endings:

je regard**ais**	I used to watch
tu regard**ais**	you (singular) used to watch
il/elle/on regard**ait**	he/she/we used to watch

The verb *être* has the stem **ét-**, e.g. *c'**ét**ait* (it used to be / it was).

Page 72

3 Listen to Nadia talking about what life was like at primary school. Choose the correct answer for each question. Write 'a' or 'b'.

1 What did you use to be like?
  a very hard-working
  b not very hard-working
2 How did you use to get to school?
  a by bus
  b by bike
3 What subjects did you use to like?
  a maths and music
  b maths and drama
4 What did you use to do at lunchtime?
  a eat in the canteen
  b play football outside
5 What did you use to do after school?
  a watch TV with brother
  b read music magazines

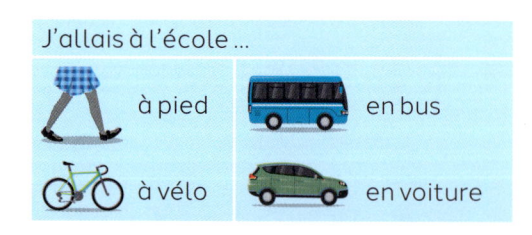

J'allais à l'école ...
à pied — en bus
à vélo — en voiture

66 *soixante-six*

4 Parler
In pairs, take turns to ask and answer the questions.
- *Quand tu étais petit(e), tu étais comment?*
  - *J'étais… / Je n'étais pas…*
- *Tu allais à l'école comment?*
  - *J'allais à l'école…*
- *Qu'est-ce que tu aimais, comme matières?*
  - *J'aimais le/la/l'/les…*
- *Qu'est-ce que tu faisais pendant la pause-déjeuner?*
  - *Je faisais / Je jouais / Je mangeais…*
- *Qu'est-ce que tu faisais après l'école?*
  - *Je regardais / Je lisais / J'allais…*

> When there is an **-s-** in the middle of a word, **between two vowels**, it is pronounced as a 'z' sound.
> Listen and repeat these phrases:
> *je fai**s**ais*
> *une mai**s**on*
> *la télévi**s**ion*
> Take care to pronounce them correctly if you use them in exercise 4.

5 Lire
Read the sentences. Write the letters of the three correct sentences for each picture. Then listen and check.

- a Elle m'envoyait des cartes d'anniversaire.
- b Elle me disait que je n'étais pas travailleur.
- c Elle n'était jamais contente.
- d Elle me parlait avec respect.
- e Elle me donnait de bonnes notes.
- f Elle me donnait trop de devoirs.

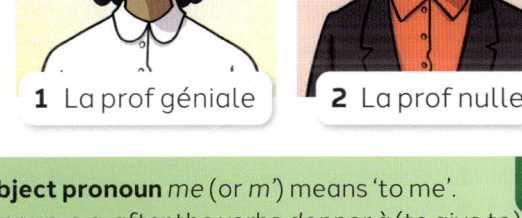

1 La prof géniale   2 La prof nulle

6 Lire
Which one of the six phrases in exercise 5 does not include an indirect object pronoun? From the five that do, choose any three to translate into English.

Example: Elle me donnait de bonnes notes. She used to give me good grades.

> **G**
> The **indirect object pronoun** *me* (or *m'*) means 'to me'.
> It replaces *à* + noun, e.g. after the verbs *donner à* (to give to) and *parler à* (to speak to).
> The word 'to' is not always used in English.
> Indirect object pronouns go before the verb.
>
> *Il **me** parlait.*   He used to talk **to me**.
> *Tu **m'**envoyais des cadeaux.*   You used to send **me** presents.
>   You used to send presents **to me**.
>
> Page 72

7 Écrire
Write out the jumbled words/phrases to make sentences.

1 parlais | avec patience | Tu | me
2 envoyait | m' | des lettres | Il
3 me | des cartes d'anniversaire | donnait | Elle
4 Tu | disais | travailleur | que j'étais | me

8 Écrire
Copy out the parallel translations, completing the missing words.

1	When I was ___, I used to like ___.	___ j'étais petit(e), j'___ l'école.
2	I used to play tennis ___ the lunch break.	Je ___ au tennis pendant la pause-déjeuner.
3	___ favourite teacher was called Mr Gasson.	Mon ___ préféré ___ Monsieur Gasson.
4	He used to give me birthday ___.	Il ___ donnait des cartes ___.

soixante-sept 67

5 Les langues et l'avenir

- Talking about learning languages
- Using the imperfect, present and near future tenses
- Using negatives in different timeframes

Lire 1
Read the text. Find the French for the phrases below.

Laurent
Quand j'étais plus jeune, j'habitais à Paris. Au collège, j'apprenais l'anglais.

Maintenant, j'habite à Nice et je suis élève au lycée hôtelier. Je travaille dans de grands hôtels et j'ai l'occasion de parler anglais et italien avec mes collègues.

L'année prochaine, je vais travailler dans un hôtel traditionnel à Turin, en Italie. Je vais utiliser une appli de langues sur mon portable pour améliorer mon italien.

Zahra
Avant, j'habitais à Arolla, un petit village à la montagne en Suisse. Au collège et au lycée, j'apprenais l'allemand.

En ce moment, je suis étudiante à l'université de Genève. J'étudie le commerce. J'ai dix heures de cours par semaine, donc je continue à apprendre l'allemand.

L'année prochaine, je vais continuer à améliorer mon allemand. Je vais regarder des films allemands et je vais écouter des podcasts en allemand.

le lycée hôtelier	hospitality school
l'allemand (m)	German
le commerce	business

1 when I was younger
2 now
3 next year
4 before
5 at the moment

Lire 2
Re-read the texts in exercise 1. Find three different verbs in the imperfect tense, six verbs in the present tense and five verbs in the near future tense.

Tense:	imperfect	present	near future
To talk about …	what **used to** happen	what **is** happening **now**	what is **going to** happen
être (to be)	j'étais	je suis	je vais être
aller (to go)	j'allais	je vais	je vais aller
faire (to do/make)	je faisais	je fais	je vais faire
apprendre (to learn)	j'apprenais	j'apprends	je vais apprendre

Lire 3
Re-read the texts in exercise 1. Answer the questions in English.
1 Where did Laurent use to live?
2 Where is he doing work placements now?
3 Where is he going to work next year?
4 What language did Zahra use to learn at school?
5 What is she studying at university at the moment?
6 How is she going to improve her German skills?

> Pay attention to the tense used in each question. This will help you to locate the answer in the text more confidently.

Écouter 4
Listen to Kader and Agathe talking about languages. Then copy and complete the grid in English.

	Before	Now	In the future
Kader			
Agathe			

soixante-huit

Écouter 5 Listen. Write the correct verb phrase from the box to fill each gap. Then write what tense each verb is in (imperfect, present or near future).

Example: 1 j'écoutais, imperfect

Avant, **1** des podcasts en anglais, mais maintenant **2** des films américains ou canadiens.

En ce moment, **3** l'espagnol et je le trouve passionnant. Bientôt, **4** des cours d'allemand aussi parce que c'est une langue très utile.

L'année prochaine, **5** dans une entreprise de marketing à Paris. En ce moment, **6** des cours de français.

À l'école primaire, **7** les langues assez difficiles. À l'avenir, je **8** une appli pour améliorer mon italien.

- je prends
- j'apprends
- je vais utiliser
- je regarde
- je vais prendre
- j'écoutais
- je vais travailler
- je trouvais

l'espagnol (m) Spanish

Parler 6 Listen and repeat the words on the right. Then, in pairs, take turns to read out sentences 1 and 2, paying attention to your pronunciation of the sound *ien*.

1 J'aime b**ien** l'ital**ien**, mais je ne comprends r**ien**.
2 Comb**ien** de langues parle-t-il, Jul**ien**, ton ami canad**ien**?

b**ien**   ital**ien**
r**ien**   canad**ien**
comb**ien**   Jul**ien**

Écouter 7 Listen and write down the negative you hear in each sentence (1–5). Listen again and note in English what the people don't do.

G

ne … pas	not
ne … jamais	never
ne … personne	not anyone/no one
ne … rien	nothing

Most **negatives** are in two parts and go around the verb:
*Je **ne** regarde **jamais** de films français.*
I never watch French films.
*Je **ne** connais **personne** qui travaille à l'étranger.*
I don't know anyone who works abroad.
*Je **ne** faisais **rien** en classe.*
I didn't use to do anything in class.

Remember that in the near future, the negative goes around the part of the verb *aller*:
*Je **ne** vais **pas** écouter de podcasts en italien.*

Page 73

Lire 8 Translate the sentences below into English. Each pair of sentences is in a different tense.

1 Je n'écoute rien en classe.
2 Je ne déteste personne.
3 Je ne trouvais pas les langues intéressantes.
4 Je n'allais jamais à l'étranger.
5 Je ne vais pas regarder de films allemands.
6 Je ne vais jamais faire mes devoirs.

Parler 9 In pairs, take turns to ask and answer the following questions.

1 Est-ce que tu apprenais une langue à l'école primaire? *(imperfect tense)*
Oui, j'apprenais (le français) et (l'espagnol).
Non, je n'apprenais pas de langue.

2 Tu apprends quelles langues au collège? *(present tense)*
Au collège, j'apprends (l'allemand) et (l'italien).
En ce moment, j'apprends (le français), mais je n'apprends pas (l'espagnol).

3 Comment est-ce que tu vas améliorer ton français à l'avenir? *(near future tense)*
À l'avenir, je vais
- regarder des films (allemands).
- écouter des podcasts en (français).
- utiliser une appli sur mon portable.
- lire des magazines en (français).

soixante-neuf 69

Grammaire 1

The definite article (Culture, page 58)

1 Copy and complete the sentences with the correct definite article (*le, la, l'* or *les*). Then translate the sentences into English.

1 Je n'aime pas ___ histoire car c'est ennuyeux.
2 ___ musique est ma matière préférée.
3 Je pense que ___ professeur est assez amusant.
4 ___ cours commencent à neuf heures du matin.
5 Au collège, ___ uniforme est très strict.
6 Ma sœur aime ___ anglais, mais moi, je préfère ___ maths.

Comparative adjectives (Unit 1, page 61)

> Use comparative adjectives to compare things:
> **plus** + adjective + **que**   more + adjective + than
> **moins** + adjective + **que**   less + adjective + than
> **aussi** + adjective + **que**   as + adjective + as
>
> 💡 The adjective must agree (in gender and number) with the first noun:
> **La** musique est aussi amusant**e** que l'anglais.
> Music is as fun as English.

2 Listen and complete the dictation task.

1 La géographie est ___ amusante que l'histoire.
2 La ___ est moins ennuyeuse que la ___.
3 Thomas est ___ que Maxime.
4 Le théâtre est ___ intéressant que les ___.
5 La cantine est ___ grande que la ___ de classe.
6 Le court de tennis est ___ ___ le terrain de foot.

3 Write out the words in the correct order to form sentences using the comparative. Then listen and check.

Example: 1 L'informatique est plus intéressante que le français.

1 plus | le français | intéressante | que | est | L'informatique
2 important | est | plus | la technologie | que | Le sport
3 amusante | La musique | l'anglais | est | moins | que
4 les maths | est | La biologie | aussi | ennuyeuse | que

> The first school subject in each sentence has a capital letter.

4 In pairs, play 'comparatives tennis'. Partner A 'serves' by saying a sentence according to the prompts. Partner B 'returns' by disagreeing and swapping the order of the two school subjects. Make sure that you make the adjective agree with the first noun! Swap who 'serves' each time.

• *Le français est plus amusant que la géographie.*
▪ *Non, la géographie est plus amusante que le français.*

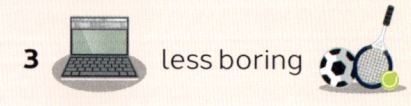

1  more fun 
2  more interesting 
3 less boring
4 more important

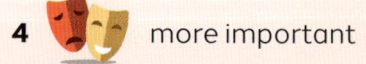

Module 3

Using *il faut* + infinitive (Unit 2, page 62)

Écrire 5 Copy and complete the French translations with the missing words.

1 *You have to wear school uniform.* ▬▬▬ porter l'uniforme scolaire.
2 *You have to respect the teachers.* ▬▬▬ les profs.
3 *You must not arrive late.* ▬▬▬ arriver en retard.
4 *You must do your homework.* ▬▬▬ ses devoirs.
5 *You must not eat in class.* ▬▬▬ en classe.

The perfect tense (Unit 3, page 64)

Lire 6 Copy and complete the sentences, choosing the correct irregular past participle from the box for each gap.

1 Qu'est-ce que tu as ▬ au collège hier?
2 Elle a ▬ des baskets.
3 Olivier a ▬ beaucoup de progrès.
4 J'ai ▬ un magazine de musique.
5 Nous avons ▬ du café ce matin.
6 Ils ont ▬ des cadeaux.

lu   mis   appris   reçu   fait   bu

> Remember, the perfect tense includes an **auxiliary verb** (part of *avoir* or *être*) and a **past participle**, e.g.
> *j'ai mangé* (I ate)
>
> Verbs that take **être** must agree with the subject (the person who is doing the action): *elle est allée* (she went)
>
> You form the past participle of regular -*er* verbs like this:
> étud**ier** (to study) ⟶ étudi**é**
>
> However, many verbs are irregular and have irregular past participles, e.g.
> *faire* (to do/make) ⟶ fait
> *mettre* (to put) ⟶ mis
> *apprendre* (to learn) ⟶ appris

Écrire 7 Copy out the sentences, putting the verbs in brackets into the perfect tense.

Example: 1 *J'ai travaillé dur pour l'examen.*

1 J' (**travailler**) dur pour l'examen.
2 À midi, nous (**manger**) à la cantine.
3 Elle (**faire**) ses devoirs de maths.
4 En classe d'histoire-géo, elles (**regarder**) un film.
5 Tu (**prendre**) combien de temps pour déjeuner?
6 Nous (**lire**) un magazine de sport.

> Think carefully about whether the verb is a regular -*er* verb or if you need to use an irregular past participle.

Lire 8 Translate the sentences from exercise 7 into English.

Lire 9 Find the <u>two</u> mistakes in each sentence and write out the corrected sentence in French.

1 En anglais, je reçu de mauvaises notes et je n'ai rien apprendu.
2 Il n'as jamais fait ses devoirs et il as ri pendant un examen.
3 Elle a allé au café avec ses amies.
4 Nous avoir écouté un podcast mais nous n'avons pas lire de magazines en français.

soixante-et-onze 71

Grammaire 2

The imperfect tense (Unit 4, page 66)

The imperfect tense is used to talk about what things were like in the past / what used to happen.
To form the imperfect tense, remove the *-ons* from the *nous* form of the verb in the present tense, e.g.
jouer (to play) → *nous jouons* → *jou-*

Then add these endings:

je jou**ais**	I used to play
tu jou**ais**	you (singular) used to play
il/elle/on jou**ait**	he/she/we used to play

The verb être has the stem **ét-**:
*j'**ét**ais* (I used to be / I was)

> Take care with verbs ending in **-ger**: the *nous* form in the present tense has an extra *e*, so 'I used to eat' is *je mangeais*.

Lire 1
Translate the sentences into English.

1 Quand j'étais à l'école primaire, j'aimais bien mon professeur.
2 Mon frère allait au collège à vélo.
3 J'allais à l'école à pied avec mon père.
4 Pendant la pause-déjeuner, je lisais beaucoup de livres.
5 Après l'école, je jouais souvent au tennis.

Parler 2
In pairs, take turns to read out the sentences from exercise 1. Pay particular attention to the pronunciation of the imperfect tense verbs. Then listen and check.

Écrire 3
Copy out the sentences, putting the verbs in brackets into the imperfect tense.

1 J'___ plus sportif. (*être*)
2 J'___ à la cantine. (*aller*)
3 Tu n'___ pas ton collège. (*aimer*)
4 Elle ___ un énorme sandwich. (*manger*)
5 Je ___ au rugby pour l'école. (*jouer*)
6 Il ___ assez intelligent. (*être*)

Indirect object pronouns (Unit 4, page 67)

Indirect object pronouns mean 'to me', 'to him' etc. They are used to replace *à* + noun, e.g. after the verbs *donner à* (to give to), *parler à* (to speak to) and *envoyer à* (to send to). The word 'to' is not always used in English.

(to) me — **me** or **m'**
(to) you (singular) — **te** or **t'**
(to) him/her — **lui**
(to) you (plural or polite) — **vous**

Indirect object pronouns go before the verb.
*Il **me** parle en français.* He speaks **to me** in French.

Lire 4
Copy out the parallel translations, completing the missing words.

Example: 1 I used to talk to him every day. Je lui parlais tous les jours.

1	I ___ to him every day.	Je ___ parlais tous les jours.
2	___ used to send me birthday cards.	Le prof ___ envoyait des cartes d'anniversaire.
3	Did ___ use to give you too much homework?	Est-ce qu'il ___ donnait trop de devoirs?
4	He used to ___ to me a lot.	Il ___ parlait beaucoup.
5	I used to give her ___ every year.	Je ___ donnais un cadeau chaque année.

72 soixante-douze

Module 3

The near future tense (Unit 5, page 68)

> Remember that the near future tense is formed by using the present tense of the verb *aller* + an **infinitive**, e.g.
> *Je vais **faire** des progrès.* I am going to make progress.
> *Elle va **utiliser** une appli.* She is going to use an app.

Écouter 5 Listen. Write the words from the boxes in the correct order to complete these questions.

Example: 1 *Est-ce que tu vas …?*

1 Est-ce que … ?
2 Comment est-ce que … ?
3 À quelle heure est-ce que … ?
4 Pourquoi est-ce que … ?

vas	à la cantine	manger	tu	demain
nous	le français	allons	apprendre
commencer	la pause-déjeuner	va
tu	aller	ne vas pas	au collège

Using negatives in different timeframes (Unit 5, page 69)

Écrire 6 Read the grammar box on page 69. Make these sentences negative by putting the negative expression in brackets in the correct place. Then translate the sentences into English.

Example: 1 *Les règles ne sont pas justes.* The rules …

1 Les règles sont justes. (*ne … pas*)
2 Elle jouait au foot pendant la récréation. (*ne … jamais*)
3 Je vais apprendre en classe. (*ne … rien*)
4 La prof était amusante. (*ne … jamais*)

Lire 7 Complete the English translation of these negative sentences and questions.

1 Je ne comprends rien en classe de maths.   I don't …
2 Tu n'as rien fait pendant la pause-déjeuner?   Didn't you do …
3 Ce matin, au collège, je n'ai vu personne.   This morning, I didn't …
4 Est-ce que tu ne vas jamais faire tes devoirs?   Are you never …

C'est parti!

Écrire 8 Translate the sentences into French.

1 I used to love music.
2 My teacher was very happy.
3 I did not use to learn a language.

Use the imperfect tense in each sentence.

4 I like school.
5 Lessons are hard because the teachers are strict.
6 I don't learn anything in German but the teacher is nice.

Think about where you need to include the definite article (the word for 'the').

7 I am going to go abroad.
8 She is going to listen to podcasts.
9 We are going to read a lot of books in French.

You need to use the near future tense in these sentences.

soixante-treize **73**

Module 3 — Contrôle de lecture et d'écoute

Reading

Lire 1

My school. Read Maria's blog on her school. Write the letter (A–F) for each of the **three** correct statements.

Bonjour!

Je n'aime pas mon collège car les règles ne sont jamais justes et la cour est trop petite. Les enfants dans ma classe sont sympa. J'adore mon uniforme car c'est simple mais ce n'est pas pratique. Les études sont importantes pour mon avenir.

Maria …

A	likes her school.	D	likes her classmates.
B	thinks the rules are fair.	E	wears a practical uniform.
C	thinks the playground is small.	F	thinks her studies are important.

Watch out for negatives.

Lire 2

A new school. Read Charlie's blog. Write down the correct option (A–C) for each question.

Je suis en troisième et je vais bientôt être en seconde au lycée. La rentrée est en septembre et j'ai déjà acheté mon sac et mes stylos, mais je cherche encore un ordinateur portable.

Le bâtiment principal du lycée est très beau et il y a un terrain de foot, mais je pense que le **règlement*** est trop strict. Si tu arrives en retard, tu as une **colle** de 30 minutes après le lycée!

Je vais aller au lycée en car parce que je n'ai pas de vélo et j'habite loin du lycée.

*le règlement   set of rules

1 Charlie will soon be in Year …
  A 9.
  B 10.
  C 11.

2 He has not yet bought …
  A a bag.
  B a laptop.
  C some pens.

3 At the sixth form college, he doesn't like the …
  A rules.
  B canteen.
  C building.

4 He is going to go to sixth form college …
  A by bike.
  B by coach.
  C by car.

5 Which of these is the best translation for the word **colle**?
  A club
  B detention
  C homework

74 *soixante-quatorze*

Lire 3

School studies. Translate the following sentences **into English**.

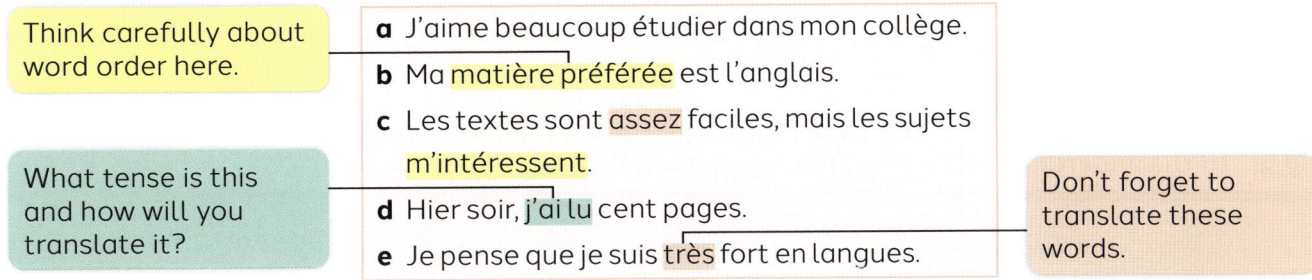

Think carefully about word order here.

a J'aime beaucoup étudier dans mon collège.
b Ma matière préférée est l'anglais.
c Les textes sont assez faciles, mais les sujets m'intéressent.
d Hier soir, j'ai lu cent pages.
e Je pense que je suis très fort en langues.

What tense is this and how will you translate it?

Don't forget to translate these words.

Listening

Écouter 4

My subjects. Ahmed is talking about his subjects in a podcast. What does he say? Write down the word or phrase for the gap in each sentence, using the words from the box. There are more words/phrases than gaps.

a Before, Ahmed used to prefer ▭.
b Ahmed doesn't find his subjects ▭.
c This year he has made ▭ progress in English.
d Ahmed is currently in ▭.
e Ahmed is going to ▭ studying music.

| maths | easy | French | a lot of | no | English |
| continue | sixth form | stop | Year 10 | difficult |

Before you listen, start by predicting which words could work in each gap.

Écouter 5

a **School rules.** Lucas is discussing school rules. What does he say? Listen to the recording and answer the following questions **in English**. You do not need to write in full sentences.

1 Why does Lucas think rules are important?
2 Which rule does he not agree with?

b Lola and Mohamed are talking about school rules. Which rules do they like and dislike? Listen to the recording, then copy and complete the following table **in English**. You do not need to write in full sentences.

	Lola ...	Mohamed ...
likes ...		
dislikes ...		

Écouter 6

Dictation. You are going to hear someone talking about school.

a Sentences 1–3: write down the missing words. For each gap, you will write one word **in French**.

1 Mon ▭ est ▭.
2 Je ▭ un uniforme ▭.
3 J'▭ l'anglais et l'▭.

Listen carefully to these words as you may not have heard them before.

b Sentences 4–6: write down the full sentences that you hear, **in French**.

Make sure you read your answers carefully to check they make sense. Your knowledge of grammar and vocabulary will help you in the dictation task.

soixante-quinze 75

Module 3 Contrôle oral

Read aloud

Parler 1 Look at this task card. With a partner, take turns to read out the five sentences, paying attention to the underlined letters and the highlighted liaisons.

> Alex, your Swiss friend, has emailed you to tell you about his school.
>
> Read out the text below to your teacher.
>
> J'aime mon collège.
> Mon collège est assez grand et moderne.
> Je préfère la musique car c'est utile.
> Je pense que l'anglais est très difficile pour moi.
> J'apprends beaucoup de choses mais on a trop de devoirs.

Take extra care with how you pronounce the underlined sounds:
- *s* between two vowels
- *oi* sounding the same as 'wha'
- *ais*
- silent *s* at the end of these words.

Remember your liaisons between the highlighted sounds.

Écouter 2 Listen and check your pronunciation.

Parler 3 Listen to the teacher asking the two follow-up questions. Translate each question **into English** and prepare your own answers **in French**. Then listen again and respond to the teacher.

A short sentence is fine but one-word answers are not sufficient to gain full marks.

Role play

Parler 4 Look at the role-play card and prepare what you are going to say.

> **Setting:** At the train station
>
> **Scenario:**
> - You are at a train station in France, applying for a student card.
> - The teacher will play the part of the person at the ticket office and will speak first.
> - The teacher will ask questions **in French** and you must answer **in French**.
> - Say a few words or a short phrase/sentence for each prompt. One-word answers are not sufficient to gain full marks.
>
> **Task:**
> 1. Say the name of your school.
> 2. Say how old you are.
> 3. Say what you think of travelling by train.
> 4. Ask a question about the price of the card.
> 5. Say where you are going to with your card.

Start with *J'ai*.

You could start with *Combien coûte ...?*

Parler 5 Practise what you have prepared. Then, using your notes, listen and respond to the teacher.

Écouter 6 Now listen to Thomas doing the role-play task. **In English**, note down (a) how he **answers** the questions for task prompts 1, 2, 3 and 5 and (b) what question he **asks** for task prompt 4.

Picture task

Écouter 7 Look at the exam card below and read the **first part** of the task. Then listen to Maxime describing the picture. Answer the questions **in English**.

a What does Maxime say about the pupils?
b Where are they, according to Maxime? Do you agree?
c What else does he mention?

Describe this picture.

Your description must cover:

- people
- location
- activity.

To talk about what someone is wearing, remember to use *porte/portent*.

When you have finished your description, you will be asked **two questions** relating to the picture. Say a short phrase/sentence in response to each question. One-word answers will not be sufficient to gain full marks.

You will then move on to a **conversation** on the broader thematic context of **Studying and my future**.

During the conversation, you will be asked questions in the present, past and future tenses. Your responses should be as **full and detailed** as possible.

Parler 8 Prepare your own description of the picture, mentioning **people**, **location** and **activity**. Improve your original description, using some of the details and vocabulary that Maxime used in his description. Then, with a partner, take turns to describe the picture.

Sur la photo, il y a ...

Parler 9 Read the **second part** of the task. Then listen to the two follow-up questions and respond to the teacher. Remember: you only need to give a short answer to each one.

Écouter 10 Read the **third part** of the task. The teacher asks Maxime: *Quel est ton avis sur les règles du collège?* Listen and write down **in English** (a) <u>two</u> rules he mentions, (b) what he thinks of school rules, and (c) what happened this morning.

Écouter 11 The teacher asks Maxime: *Qu'est-ce que tu vas faire demain au collège?* Listen and write down <u>three</u> things he says he is going to do tomorrow.

Parler 12 Prepare your own answers to the Module 3 questions on page 226. Your responses should be as **full and detailed** as possible. Then practise with a partner.

soixante-dix-sept 77

Module 3 — Contrôle écrit

80-90 word writing task

Écrire 1 Look at this writing exam task and then, <u>for each bullet point</u>:

1 think about what vocabulary you have learned which you could use in your answer. For example:
- **nouns** and **verbs** to talk about your favourite subject
- **verbs of opinion** and **adjectives**
- language for **narrating a story** about what you did recently in a lesson
- how to explain your plans for the next school year or beyond.

2 write down <u>three or four</u> ideas for what you could write about.

3 write down which tense(s) you will need to use in your answer.

Write to your friend about your favourite subject.

You **must** include the following points:
- your favourite subject and why you like it
- subjects you don't like and why
- something you have done in a lesson recently
- what subjects you're going to study in future.

Write your answer **in French**. You should aim to write between 80 and 90 words.

Make sure you cover all four bullet points of the task to maximise your marks.

Lire 2 Read Diane's answer to the exam task. Answer questions 1–5 in the coloured shapes.

1 This is an example of **complex language**. What does it mean? Find <u>three</u> more examples from the text.

3 How could she **avoid repetition** by using a different verb here?

5 Which connective could she use here to form an **extended sentence**? What other connectives does she use?

Salut,

Ma matière préférée est l'anglais parce que c'est plus intéressant que les maths. Je pense que c'est passionnant et je trouve ça facile. Plus tard, je veux devenir professeure et je vais travailler à l'étranger.

Je n'aime pas la musique. En troisième, la prof me donne trop de devoirs et je ne joue pas d'un instrument. Je n'aime pas l'histoire car c'est nul.

Récemment, en théâtre, on a regardé un film et après on a discuté. C'était génial!

L'année prochaine, je vais continuer le français. J'adore parler une autre langue.

Diane

2 This word shows a **variety of vocabulary**. What does it mean? Find <u>two</u> more examples.

4 Which **tense** is this? What other examples of this tense can you find? Does she use any other tenses?

soixante-dix-huit

Lire 3
Read Diane's answer again. Answer the questions in English.

a What does Diane say about English exactly? Give two details.
b What does she say about music? Give two details.
c What did she recently do in her drama lesson?
d Why is she going to continue studying French?

Écrire 4
Prepare your own answer to the 80–90 word writing task in exercise 1.

- Think about how you can develop your answer for each bullet point.
- Look back at your notes from exercises 1 and 2.
- Look at the 'Challenge checklist' and think about how you can show off your French!
- Write a **brief** plan and organise your answer into paragraphs.
- Write your answer and then carefully check the accuracy of what you have written.

Challenge checklist

🌶
- ✓ Past, present and future timeframes
- ✓ Connectives, time phrases, sequencers
- ✓ Some extended sentences
- ✓ Different opinion phrases

🌶🌶
- ✓ A wide range of tenses (e.g. imperfect, near future)
- ✓ Different persons of the verb (e.g. *on, la prof*)
- ✓ A variety of opinions
- ✓ Negatives (e.g. *ne … pas*)
- ✓ A wide range of interesting vocabulary

🌶🌶🌶
- ✓ Phrases with more than one tense
- ✓ Complex language (e.g. *je pense que*, comparatives, direct object pronouns)
- ✓ Positive/negative phrases
- ✓ A variety of connectives

Translation

Écrire 5
Rearrange the French words to translate the English sentences.

1 *I wear a green uniform.*
   porte / Je / un / vert / uniforme
2 *I think that my maths teacher is patient.*
   prof / pense / patient / maths / de / Je / mon / que / est
3 *There are lots of clubs after the lessons.*
   clubs / de / beaucoup / Il / après / y / les / a / cours
4 *Yesterday I forgot my exercise book.*
   oublié / j' / cahier / mon / ai / Hier

Écrire 6
Translate the sentences into French.

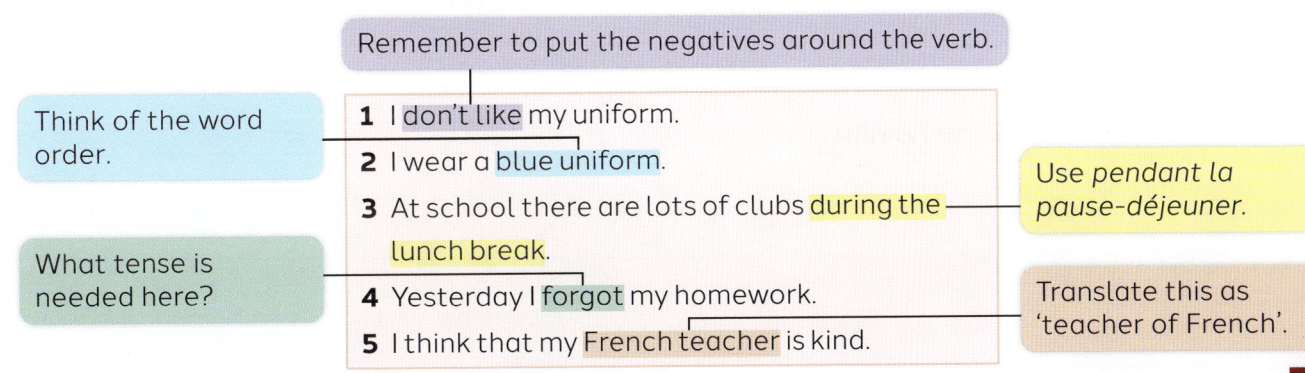

Remember to put the negatives around the verb.

Think of the word order.

1 I don't like my uniform.
2 I wear a blue uniform.
3 At school there are lots of clubs during the lunch break.

Use pendant la pause-déjeuner.

What tense is needed here?

4 Yesterday I forgot my homework.
5 I think that my French teacher is kind.

Translate this as 'teacher of French'.

Module 3 Vocabulaire

Key:
bold = this word will appear in higher exams only
* = this word is not on the vocabulary list but you may use it in your own sentences

Au collège chez nous (pages 58–59)

C'est comment, la vie au collège? — What is life at school like?
Je suis en ... — I am in ...
  quatrième / troisième. — Year 9 / 10.

Les personnes — *People*
Sur la photo, il y a ... — In the photo, there is/are ...
  un prof. — a teacher.
  deux personnes. — two people.
  trois jeunes. — three young people.
Il y a ... — There is/are ...
  un garçon. — a boy.
  deux garçons et une fille. — two boys and a girl.
Le prof porte ... — The teacher is wearing ...
  une cravate noire. — a black tie.
Un garçon porte ... — A boy is wearing ...
  un pantalon gris / marron. — grey / brown trousers.
  une chemise bleue. — a blue shirt.
  des baskets noires. — black trainers.
Une fille porte ... — A girl is wearing ...
  un *tee-shirt rose / jaune. — a pink / yellow t-shirt.
  un *short bleu / noir. — blue / black shorts.

Ils portent un uniforme scolaire. — They are wearing a school uniform.

C'est où? — *Where is it?*
Ils/Elles sont ... — They are ...
  à la *cantine. — in the canteen.
  au collège. — at school.
  dans une salle de classe. — in a classroom.
  sur le terrain de foot. — on the football pitch.
À gauche / droite, il y a ... — On the left / right, there is/are ...
  un professeur. — a teacher.
  des élèves. — some pupils.
  des tables. — some tables.

Que font-ils? — *What are they doing?*
Les élèves / enfants ... — The pupils / children ...
  discutent / mangent. — are talking / eating.
  jouent. — are playing.
Le/La prof / Un garçon / Une fille ... — The teacher / A boy / A girl ...
  discute / mange / joue. — is talking / eating / playing.

Quelle est ta matière préférée? (pages 60–61)

Quelle est ta matière préférée et pourquoi? — *What is your favourite subject and why?*
Ma matière préférée est ... — My favourite subject is ...
  l'anglais. — English.
  le français. — French.
  le théâtre. — drama.
  la *biologie. — biology.
  la *chimie. — chemistry.
  *l'EPS. — PE.
  *l'histoire-géo. — history and geography.
  *l'informatique. — ICT.
  la musique. — music.
  les maths. — maths.
  les sciences. — science.
J'aime (l'anglais) parce que c'est ... — I like (English) because it's ...
  amusant / facile. — fun / easy.
  génial / utile. — great / useful.
J'adore (*l'EPS) parce que ... — I love (PE) because ...
  je suis *créatif/créative. — I'm creative.
  je suis sportif/sportive. — I'm sporty.
  le/la prof est sympa. — the teacher is nice.

Je n'aime pas (les sciences) parce que c'est ... — I don't like (science) because it's ...
  difficile. — difficult.
  ennuyeux. — boring.
  inutile. — useless.
Je déteste (*l'histoire-géo) parce que/qu' ... — I hate (history and geography) because ...
  le/la prof est **sévère**. — the teacher is strict.
  on a trop de devoirs. — we have too much homework.
Je suis fort(e) / faible en ... — I'm good / bad at ...
  anglais / *informatique. — English / ICT.
À mon avis, c'est plus amusant que ... — In my opinion, it's more fun than ...
Je pense que ... — I think that ...
  le français est plus/moins passionnant que ... — French is more/less exciting than ...
  la musique est plus/moins intéressante que ... — music is more/less interesting than ...
  les maths sont plus/moins utiles que ... — maths is more/less useful than ...

C'est injuste! (pages 62–63)

Il faut ... — You have to ...
  porter l'uniforme scolaire. — wear the school uniform.
  faire ses devoirs. — do your homework.
  respecter les profs. — respect the teachers.

Il ne faut pas ... — You must not ...
  arriver en retard. — arrive late.
  manger en classe. — eat in class.
  utiliser son portable en classe. — use your phone in class.

Qu'est-ce que tu penses des règles? — *What do you think of the rules?*
À mon avis, c'est ... — In my opinion, it's ...
Je pense que c'est ... — I think that it's ...
  un peu / assez ... — a bit / quite ...
  très / trop ... — very / too ...
  important. — important.
  juste / injuste. — fair / unfair.
  nul / strict. — rubbish / strict.
  *stupide. — stupid.
parce que/qu' / car ... — because / as ...
  c'est essentiel pour les examens. — it's essential for exams.

quatre-vingts

c'est utile pour le travail scolaire.	it's useful for schoolwork.	Tu es d'accord?	Do you agree?
il faut respecter les autres.	you must respect others.	Oui, je suis d'accord.	Yes, I agree.
l'uniforme scolaire (n') est (pas) confortable / pratique.	the school uniform is (not) comfortable / practical.	Non, je ne suis pas d'accord.	No, I do not agree.
		Je peux porter …	I can wear …
j'ai des problèmes avec le bus.	I have problems with the bus.	J'ai partagé des vidéos de mon collège en ligne.	I shared videos of my school online.

As-tu fait des progrès? (pages 64–65)

J'ai …	I have …	ri pendant un examen.	laughed during an exam.
Tu as / Il/Elle a …	You have / He/She has …	Je n'ai pas / Tu n'as pas / Il/Elle n'a pas …	I have not / You haven't / He/She hasn't …
appris beaucoup de choses (en anglais).	learned lots of things (in English).	fait d'efforts en …	made an effort in …
fait beaucoup de progrès (en français).	made a lot of progress (in French).	bu de *coca en classe.	drunk cola in class.
fait mes/tes/ses devoirs.	done my/your/his/her homework.	Je n'ai jamais oublié mes devoirs.	I have never forgotten my homework.
bu du *coca en classe.	drunk cola in class.	Je n'ai rien appris.	I have learned nothing.
écrit une histoire extraordinaire.	written an extraordinary story.	Il/Elle n'a rien appris.	He/She has learned nothing.
fait des efforts.	made an effort.	En (théâtre), j'ai …	In (drama), I have …
lu beaucoup de livres.	read lots of books.	Par contre, je n'ai pas …	On the other hand, I haven't …
mis des lunettes de soleil.	put on sunglasses.	*En plus, j'ai …	In addition, I have …
reçu de bonnes / mauvaises notes (en musique).	got good/bad grades (in music).		

Souvenirs d'école (pages 66–67)

Quand tu étais petit(e), tu étais comment?	When you were little, what were you like?	Je lisais / J'allais …	I read / I went …
J'étais / Je n'étais pas … (très) travailleur/ travailleuse.	I was / I wasn't … (very) hard-working.	Il y avait un(e) prof génial(e) / nul(le). Il/Elle …	There was a great / rubbish teacher. He/She …
		m'envoyait des cartes d'anniversaire.	sent me birthday cards.
Tu allais à l'école comment?	How did you go to school?	n'était jamais content(e).	was never happy.
J'allais à l'école …	I went to school …	me parlait avec respect / *patience.	spoke to me with respect / patience.
à pied / à vélo.	on foot / by bike.		
en bus / en voiture.	by bus / by car.	me donnait de bonnes notes / trop de devoirs.	gave me good grades / too much homework.
Qu'est-ce que tu aimais, comme matières?	Which subjects did you like?	Quand j'étais petit(e), …	When I was little, …
J'aimais le/la/l'/les …	I liked …	j'aimais l'école.	I liked school.
Qu'est-ce que tu faisais pendant la pause-déjeuner?	What did you do during the lunch break?	je jouais au tennis pendant la pause-déjeuner.	I played tennis during the lunch break.
Qu'est-ce que tu faisais après l'école?	What did you do after school?	mon/ma prof préféré(e) s'appelait …	my favourite teacher was called …
Je faisais / Je jouais …	I did / I played …	C'était …	It was …
Je mangeais / Je regardais …	I ate / I watched …		

Les langues et l'avenir (pages 68–69)

Est-ce que tu apprenais une langue à l'école *primaire?	Did you learn a language at primary school?	À l'avenir, je vais …	In the future, I am going to …
Oui, j'apprenais …	Yes, I learned …	regarder des films.	watch films.
*l'allemand.	German.	écouter des *podcasts.	listen to podcasts.
*l'espagnol.	Spanish.	utiliser une appli sur mon portable.	use an app on my phone.
*l'italien.	Italian.	lire des *magazines.	read magazines.
Non, je n'apprenais pas de langue.	No, I didn't learn a language.	Je ne vais pas écouter de *podcasts en *italien.	I am not going to listen to podcasts in Italian.
Tu apprends quelles langues au collège?	Which languages are you learning at school?	Je ne regarde jamais de films français.	I never watch French films.
Au collège, j'apprends …	At school, I am learning …		
En ce moment, j'apprends …, mais je n'apprends pas …	At the moment, I am learning …, but I am not learning …	Je ne connais personne qui travaille à l'étranger.	I do not know anyone who works abroad.
		Je ne faisais rien en classe.	I did not use to do anything in class.
Comment est-ce que tu vas améliorer ton (français) à l'avenir?	How are you going to improve your (French) in the future?		

Module 4 — En pleine forme

Sain ou malsain?

- Describing and giving opinions about dishes
- Understanding advice in the *vous*-form imperative

Des plats du monde francophone

A la France: les religieuses 🇫🇷 #PâtisseriesFrançaises

B le Québec: la poutine #PlatQuébécois

C la Tunisie: le couscous 🇹🇳 #CouscousTraditionnel

D la Belgique: les gaufres 🇧🇪 #GoûtDeBelgique

E le Sénégal: le thiéboudienne 🇸🇳 #PlatTraditionnelSénégalais

le plat — dish

Il y a	du	chocolat. fromage / poisson. riz / sucre.
	de la	glace / sauce. viande.
	des	frites / fruits. légumes.

Écouter 1 Look at the photos and captions, then listen. Write the letter of the correct dish. (1–5)

Parler 2 How do you pronounce these words? Read them out, then listen and check.

1 le goût (*the taste*)
2 délicieux (*delicious*)
3 sain (*healthy*)
4 malsain (*unhealthy*)
5 les légumes (*vegetables*)
6 les végans (*vegans*)
7 les végétariens (*vegetarians*)

Écouter 3 Listen and note down in English (a) if they think each dish is healthy or unhealthy, and (b) which foods are mentioned. (1–2)

Parler 4 In pairs, discuss the dishes in the photos above.

- À ton avis, le plat A, c'est sain?
- À mon avis, il a bon goût, mais c'est malsain.
- Pourquoi?
- Parce que dans ce plat, il y a …

👍	👎
C'est sain.	C'est malsain.
C'est bon pour la santé.	C'est mauvais pour la santé.
Le plat a bon goût.	Je n'aime pas le goût.
C'est parfait pour les végétariens.	Ce n'est pas bon pour les végans.

quatre-vingt-deux

Zone de culture

Module 4

MANGERBOUGER.FR

RÉPUBLIQUE FRANÇAISE — Liberté Égalité Fraternité

Santé publique France

Mangez mieux!
- Mangez au moins cinq fruits et légumes tous les jours.
- Buvez moins de boissons sucrées.

au moins — at least

Bougez plus!
- Faites au moins une heure d'activité physique tous les jours.
- Pour les distances de moins de cinq kilomètres, choisissez le vélo ou la marche à pied.
- Essayez un nouveau sport.

Dormez bien!
- Allez au lit tôt.
- Arrêtez d'utiliser votre portable au moins une heure avant de dormir.

50 petites astuces pour manger mieux et bouger plus

l'astuce (f) — tip

Manger Bouger is a campaign by the French government to help people of all ages with their health and fitness. The website *mangerbouger.fr* has lots of hints and tips about healthy eating and exercise.

Note these two meanings of the word *moins*:
moins de (+ noun) — less, fewer
au moins — at least

Écouter 5
Listen to and read the text above. Then copy and complete the translation of each piece of advice.

1 Eat at least ▭ fruits and vegetables every day.
2 Drink fewer ▭.
3 Do at least ▭ every day.
4 For distances of less than five kilometres, choose ▭ or ▭.
5 Try a ▭.
6 Go to bed ▭.
7 Stop using your mobile phone at least ▭ before sleeping.

G
The *vous*-form imperative is often used to give instructions or advice.
It is the present tense of the verb without the word '*vous*':
vous allez (you go) → *Allez!* (Go!)
vous buvez (you drink) → *Buvez!* (Drink!)
vous dormez (you sleep) → *Dormez!* (Sleep!)
vous faites (you make/do) → *Faites …!* (Do …!)
vous choisissez (you choose) → *Choisissez!* (Choose!)
vous mangez (you eat) → *Mangez!* (Eat!)

Page 94

Écrire 6
Choose options from the box to write as many pieces of good and bad advice as possible. Write your sentences in both French and English.

Example: Allez moins souvent au centre sportif. – Go to the sports centre less often.

Buvez	moins de	coca.
Mangez	plus de	frites / chocolat.
Faites	moins d' plus d'	exercice.
	de la natation plus souvent.	
Allez		moins souvent au centre sportif. au collège à pied ou à vélo. au lit plus tard.
Dormez	au moins huit heures toutes les nuits.	
Essayez	un nouveau sport.	

quatre-vingt-trois 83

1 Bon appétit!

- Talking about meals and mealtimes
- Using the partitive article (*du, de la, de l', des*)
- Using present and perfect tenses in translations

Écouter 1 Listen and read. Then copy and complete the grid in English.

	Breakfast	Lunchtime	Snack	Dinner
Drinks …	coffee			
Eats …				

Qu'est-ce que tu manges (normalement)?

Mes repas

Qu'est-ce que tu manges pour le petit-déjeuner?
Pour le petit-déjeuner, je bois du café et si j'ai le temps, je mange du pain.

Qu'est-ce que tu manges et bois à midi?
À midi, je mange au collège. Normalement, je choisis de la viande avec des légumes. Ensuite, je mange des fruits parce que c'est sain! Je bois du lait.

Est-ce que tu manges quelque chose après les cours?
Après les cours, si j'ai faim, je mange un sandwich. Quand j'ai soif, je bois seulement de l'eau. C'est bon pour la santé.

Normalement, qu'est-ce que tu manges le soir?
Le soir, on mange en famille. Normalement, on mange quelque chose de léger, comme du poisson ou des œufs. On boit du lait.

le repas — meal
j'ai faim — I'm hungry
j'ai soif — I'm thirsty

Lire 2 Re-read the text in exercise 1. Then find the French for the phrases below.
1 I eat at school
2 if I have time
3 because it's healthy
4 I only drink
5 we eat something light
6 normally, I choose

G
In French, the partitive article ('some') agrees with the noun it refers to:

masculine singular	feminine singular	before a vowel sound	plural
du poisson	**de la** viande	**de l'** eau	**des** légumes

After a negative or a quantity, just use **de** (**d'** before a vowel):
Je ne mange pas de viande.   Je bois beaucoup d'eau.

Page 94

Écouter 3 Listen to Sam talking about what they eat and drink during the day. Note down in English what they have for breakfast, lunch, after school and in the evening.

Parler 4 Listen and repeat the following words, paying attention to your pronunciation.

en, souv**en**t, comm**en**t   p**ain**, s**ain**, mat**in**
d**an**s, m**an**ge, qu**an**d   **im**portant, f**aim**
t**em**ps, ch**am**bre

Take care with the pronunciation of the letter combinations **in bold** in exercise 4. They are nasal sounds. Say them at the back of your throat, as if you have a cold!

There are four different ways of spelling each sound:
- *en, an, em, am*
- *ain, in, im, aim*

Listen and repeat the tongue-twister:
*Qu**an**d j'ai f**aim**, je m**an**ge souv**en**t du p**ain**.*
*C'est **im**port**an**t de m**an**ger s**ain**.*

Parler 5 Prepare your answers to the questions in exercise 1. Then, in pairs, take turns to interview your partner.

- *Qu'est-ce que tu prends pour le petit-déjeuner?*
- *Pour le petit-déjeuner, je mange des céréales et je bois …*

84 *quatre-vingt-quatre*

Module 4

Écouter 6 Look at the sentences and predict the missing words. Then listen and fill in the gaps.

1 Le ___ est bon pour la santé.
2 Pour le ___, je bois du ___.
3 À midi, je mange de la ___ avec des ___.
4 C'est un ___ délicieux et ___.
5 Quand j'ai ___, je mange des ___.

- Look at the words <u>before</u> and <u>after</u> each gap.
- Spot grammar clues (e.g. *du* is followed by a <u>masculine</u> noun).
- Check your spelling and accents!

Lire 7 Read the text. Is each statement below true or false?

Bienvenue à Chef de Cuisine Junior!

Yasmina, qu'est-ce que tu as fait?

J'ai préparé un tagine car ma famille vient d'Algérie.

Ce matin, je suis allée au marché et j'ai acheté beaucoup de légumes.

Traditionnellement, dans ce plat, il y a de la viande. Mais moi, j'ai mis des olives.

Le résultat de la compétition
Yasmina a gagné quatre étoiles. ★★★★☆

Jules, qu'est-ce que tu as fait?

J'ai préparé une recette malgache car ma famille vient de Madagascar.

J'ai fait ça avec du poisson, des légumes et du lait de coco.

J'ai essayé la recette chez moi et toute ma famille a adoré ça!

Le résultat de la compétition
Jules a gagné cinq étoiles. ★★★★★

1 Yasmina's family is from Algeria.
2 She went to the market yesterday.
3 Her dish contained meat.
4 Jules's meal included fish and vegetables.
5 He tried making the meal at home.
6 His family didn't like it.

l'étoile (f)	star
la recette malgache	Madagascan recipe
le lait de coco	coconut milk

G Use the perfect tense to say what you did. There are three parts:

subject	auxiliary verb	past participle	
Je	suis	allé(e)	I went
J'	ai	fait	I did/made
Elle	a	adoré	she loved

How many perfect tense verbs can you find in the text in exercise 7?

Page 96

Écrire 8 Translate these sentences into French.

1 For breakfast, I often eat bread.
2 When I am thirsty, I drink water.

- These are both in the present tense.
- Both need a partitive article (*du/ de la/ de l'/ des*).
- Take care with where you place the word for 'often'.

3 This morning, I made a French dish.
4 I bought lots of fish at the market.

- These are both in the perfect tense.
- Take care with where you place the word for 'French'.
- Use *de* after *beaucoup*.

quatre-vingt-cinq 85

2 Bien dans ma peau

- Talking about good mental health
- Using modal verbs (*devoir, vouloir, pouvoir*)
- Giving advice

Écouter 1 Listen to the teenagers talking about how they feel and why. Note down (a) the letter of the correct emoji, and (b) the reason in English. (1–4)

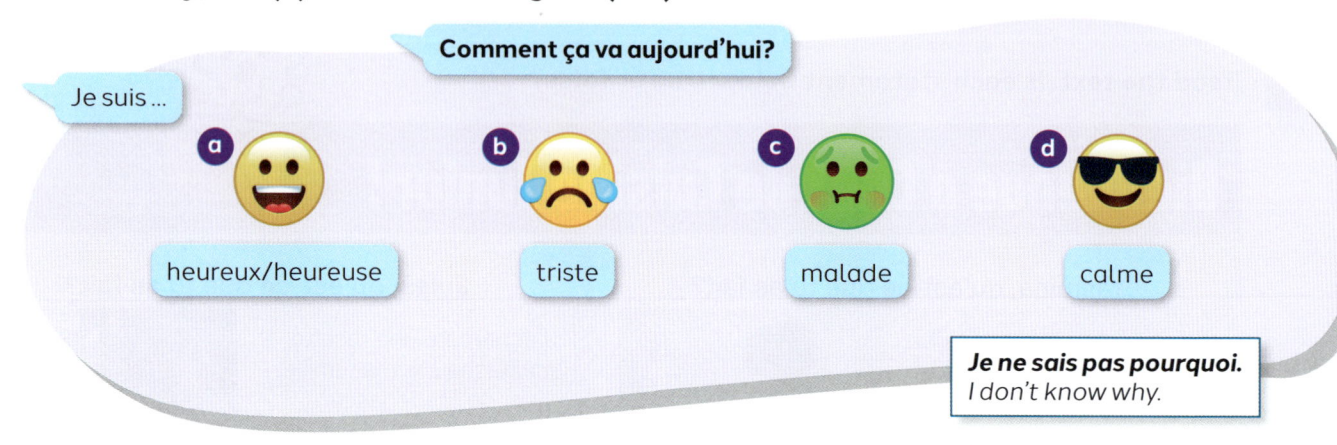

Comment ça va aujourd'hui?

Je suis …

- a heureux/heureuse
- b triste
- c malade
- d calme

Je ne sais pas pourquoi.
I don't know why.

Écouter 2 Listen again. Match the advice given below to the speakers. (1–4) Some of the advice may be used more than once.

- a Fais de la cuisine. (*Do some cooking.*)
- b Parle avec moi. (*Speak to me.*)
- c Va au lit. (*Go to bed.*)
- d Reste calme. (*Stay calm.*)
- e Écoute de la musique. (*Listen to music.*)

> **G**
> You use the *tu*-form imperative to give advice or instructions to someone you know well.
>
> The *tu*-form of the imperative works like this:
> *tu écoutes* (you listen) → *Écoute!* (Listen!)
> *tu vas* (you go) → *Va!* (Go!)
> *tu restes* (you stay) → *Reste!* (Stay!)
> Note that you drop the final 's' from the verb.
>
> In the negative, *ne/n'… pas* goes around the verb:
> *Ne parle pas.* (Don't speak.)
>
> Page 95

Parler 3 In pairs, put yourselves in the place of the teenagers in these two photos. Ask and answer questions about how you are doing.

- ● *Comment ça va aujourd'hui?*
- ■ *Je suis triste.*
- ● *Pourquoi es-tu triste?*
- ■ *Je suis triste parce que j'ai perdu mon chien.*
- ● *Reste calme et parle avec moi!*

Comment ça va aujourd'hui? Ça ne va pas?	Ça va très bien. Ça ne va pas bien.
Pourquoi es-tu …?	Je suis (un peu / assez / très / vraiment) triste car … Je suis heureux/heureuse parce que …

86 *quatre-vingt-six*

Module 4

4 Read the forum posts. Write the letter of the correct piece of advice below for each problem. Then listen and check. (1–4)

D'ados à ados

Ne continue pas en silence – partage ton problème ici! D'autres ados donnent des conseils.

1 Le soir, j'adore jouer à des jeux vidéo contre mes amis. Mais je dors mal.
@megajeuxfan

2 J'ai beaucoup de travail scolaire en ce moment. Je suis tout le temps très stressée avec les examens.
@mimilou5

3 En ce moment, je suis triste car je ne m'entends pas bien avec mon père. À mon avis, il est trop strict.
@anon2012

4 Mon meilleur ami a changé de collège et maintenant je suis tout seul – je dois trouver de nouveaux amis, mais comment?
@basketsrouges

a Tu dois parler avec tes profs. Ils peuvent t'aider. Bouge un peu aussi – fais une activité physique.

b Je suis sûr qu'il t'aime. Parle avec lui. Tu peux être heureuse.

c Tu dois arrêter de passer du temps devant l'ordinateur avant d'aller au lit. C'est difficile de dormir après les jeux vidéo, les écrans sont mauvais.

d Si tu veux trouver de nouveaux amis, tu peux devenir membre d'un club sportif. Cherche en ligne ou sur les réseaux sociaux.

l'ado (m/f)	adolescent, teenager
donner des conseils	to give advice
avec lui	with him

G

These are key modal verbs in the present tense:

devoir (to have to/must)	**pouvoir** (to be able to/can)	**vouloir** (to want (to))
je dois	je peux	je veux
tu dois	tu peux	tu veux
il/elle/on doit	il/elle peut	il/elle veut
nous devons	nous pouvons	nous voulons
vous devez	vous pouvez	vous voulez
ils/elles doivent	ils/elles peuvent	ils/elles veulent

Modal verbs are usually followed by another verb in its <u>infinitive</u> form:

Tu **dois** <u>rester</u> calme.
You must stay calm.

Je **veux** <u>trouver</u> le bonheur.
I want to find happiness.

Negatives go around the modal verb:
Il <u>ne</u> **peut** <u>pas</u> parler avec son prof.
He can't talk to his teacher.

Page 95

5 Copy out the parallel translations, completing them with the missing words.

1	I want to change ▢▢.	Je ▢▢ changer de collège.
2	She must ▢▢▢▢.	▢▢ doit trouver son chien.
3	He wants to go to a ▢▢▢.	Il ▢▢ ▢▢ à un cours de yoga.
4	▢▢ stay calm!	On ne peut pas rester ▢▢!
5	You must work this weekend.	▢▢ ▢▢ ce week-end.
6	You can be ▢▢!	▢▢ ▢▢ être heureux!

The closed sound **-eu** rhymes with 'd**eu**x'.

Listen and repeat the sentences:
Je p**eu**x être h**eu**r**eu**x.
Il v**eu**t montrer qu'il p**eu**t être sér**ieu**x.
Je ne v**eu**x pas faire mes devoirs.

6 Write a reply to this post on the *D'ados à ados* forum.

Je suis souvent très stressée et, au collège, je n'ai pas d'énergie. Pendant les cours, je ne peux pas écouter et je ne veux pas parler avec mes profs. Donnez-moi des conseils, s'il vous plaît!

Tu peux …   Parle …
Tu dois …   Bouge …
Si tu veux …

quatre-vingt-sept 87

3 Ça ne va pas?

- Describing illness and accidents
- Using the perfect tense (with both *avoir* and *être*)
- Booking a doctor's appointment

Parler 1 In pairs, look at the pictures and use your knowledge of French pronunciation to predict how to say each part of the body. Then listen and check.

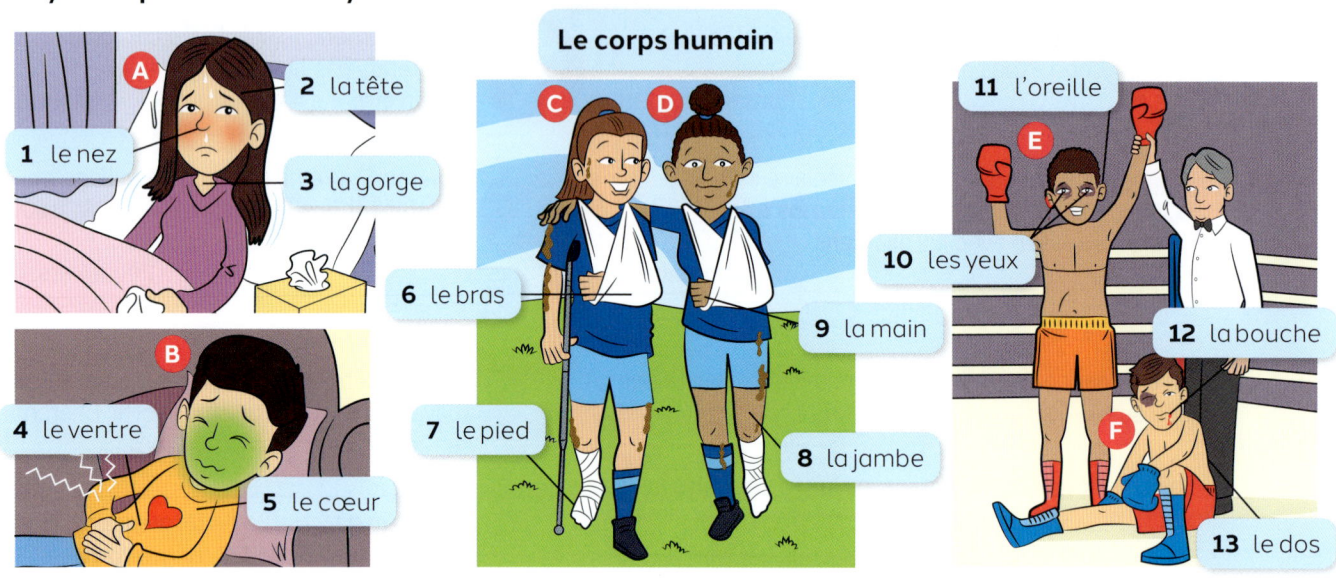

Le corps humain

1. le nez
2. la tête
3. la gorge
4. le ventre
5. le cœur
6. le bras
7. le pied
8. la jambe
9. la main
10. les yeux
11. l'oreille
12. la bouche
13. le dos

Écouter 2 Listen to the conversations. Note down (a) the letter of the person from exercise 1, and (b) the outcome/advice (a–d) that you hear. (1–4)

le médecin — doctor

a Reste à la maison. Essaye de boire quelque chose. (*Stay at home. Try to drink something.*)
b Ce n'est pas sérieux, mais allez chez le médecin. (*It's not serious, but go to the doctor.*)
c Reste au lit. Essaye de dormir. (*Stay in bed. Try to sleep.*)
d Ne bougez pas. Je vais appeler une ambulance. (*Don't move. I'm going to call an ambulance.*)

G To say that something hurts or is sore, use *avoir mal à* + noun:
à + **le** = **au**   à + **les** = **aux**

masculine noun	feminine noun	plural noun
J'ai mal **au** dos.	J'ai mal **à la** tête.	J'ai mal **aux** yeux.
I have a sore back.	I have a headache.	I have sore eyes.

G Remind yourself how to form the **imperative**, using the grammar boxes on pages 83 and 86. Read the examples in exercise 2. The first and third pieces of advice are in the *tu* form; the second and fourth pieces of advice are in the *vous* form.

Parler 3 In pairs, take turns to read the message out, paying attention to your pronunciation. Listen and check. Then translate the text into English.

> Ma fille Emma ne peut pas aller au collège parce qu'elle est malade. Elle a mal à la gorge et elle a chaud.
> Demain, je vais prendre rendez-vous chez le médecin.

These expressions in French use *avoir* (to have), not *être* (to be):
avoir chaud — to be hot
avoir froid — to be cold
avoir faim — to be hungry
avoir soif — to be thirsty

prendre rendez-vous — to make an appointment

Écouter 4 Listen to the two voicemails left on a school answerphone. Note down in English why the students are absent. (1–2)

88 *quatre-vingt-huit*

5 Read the dialogue of a call to a doctor's surgery. Listen and note down in French <u>five</u> differences between what you read and what you hear.

- **Allô? Je peux vous aider?**
- Bonjour. Je voudrais prendre rendez-vous, s'il vous plaît.
- **Bien sûr. Quel est le problème?**
- J'ai mal au <u>bras</u> et mal à la <u>main</u>.
- **Vous voulez un rendez-vous pour quand?**
- Demain <u>après-midi</u>, s'il vous plaît.
- **Pas de problème.**
- Le rendez-vous est à quelle heure, s'il vous plaît?
- **À <u>deux</u> heures.**
- Quelle est l'adresse, s'il vous plaît?
- **C'est dans la rue du Marché, au numéro <u>quinze</u>.**
- Merci. Au revoir.

6 Find the French for these expressions in the conversation in exercise 5. Write the French out in full.

1 What is the address?
2 No problem.
3 I would like to make an appointment.
4 Can I help you?
5 What is the problem?
6 What time is the appointment?

7 In pairs, create <u>two</u> dialogues, using the one in exercise 5 as a model.

ailments: headache and fever
appointment wanted for: today
time: 3:00
address: number 10

ailment: earache
appointment wanted for: Wednesday
time: 10:30
address: number 25

8 Listen and read. Copy and complete the grid in English. (1–2)

	Injury	When	How / Where
1	arm		

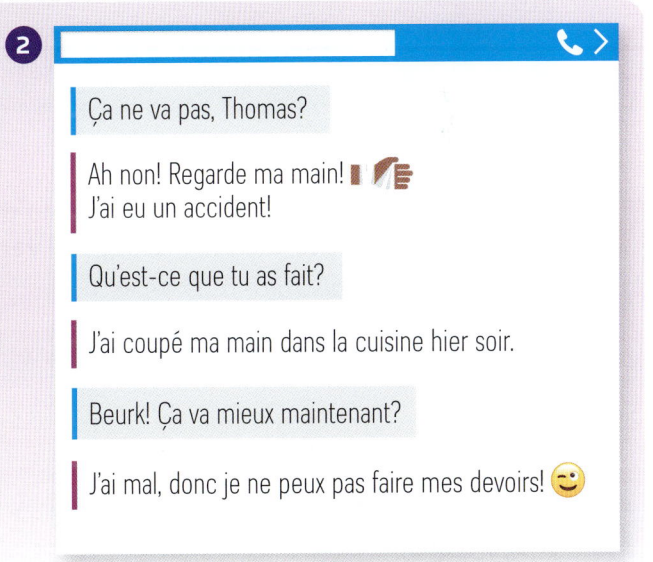

1
- Coucou, Lucie. Ça va?
- Non. J'ai eu un accident! J'ai mal au bras!
- Oh là là! Qu'est-ce que tu as fait?
- Ce matin, je suis tombée de vélo. Je suis allée à l'hôpital.
- Quelle horreur! Tu as mal?
- Non, parce que j'ai pris des médicaments. Ça va mieux maintenant.

tomber to fall

2
- Ça ne va pas, Thomas?
- Ah non! Regarde ma main! J'ai eu un accident!
- Qu'est-ce que tu as fait?
- J'ai coupé ma main dans la cuisine hier soir.
- Beurk! Ça va mieux maintenant?
- J'ai mal, donc je ne peux pas faire mes devoirs!

9 Write a message about another accident. Use your own ideas.

Example: J'ai eu un accident. Je suis tombé(e) ... J'ai mal ... Je suis allé(e) ...

G Use the perfect tense to say what happened in the past. Most verbs use *avoir* as the auxiliary verb:
J'**ai** eu un accident.   I had an accident.
J'**ai** pris des médicaments.   I took some medicine.

But some important verbs use *être* as the auxiliary verb:
Je **suis** allé(e) à l'hôpital.   I went to hospital.
Je **suis** tombé(e) de vélo.   I fell off my bike.

Page 96

quatre-vingt-neuf 89

4 Je change ma vie

- Saying what you are going to do to improve your life
- Using the near future tense
- Using *plus* and *moins*

1 Listen and read. Then write the letter of the correct photo for each speaker. (1–6)

Qu'est-ce que tu vas faire pour améliorer ta vie?

1. Je vais manger plus de légumes.
2. Je vais prendre des cours de danse.
3. Je vais moins penser à moi et je vais aider les autres.
4. Je vais être plus patient(e) avec ma petite sœur.
5. Je vais aller à la piscine chaque week-end.
6. Je ne vais pas faire mes devoirs à la dernière minute.

les autres other people

2 Translate the sentences in exercise 1 into English.

> **G**
> Use the near future tense to say 'going to' (or will) do something.
> Put the infinitive of the verb you want to use after the present tense of the verb **aller**.
> je **vais** manger — I am going to eat
> tu **vas** aider — you are going to help
> il/elle/on **va** travailler — he/she is / we are going to work
>
> Negatives in the near future tense go around the part of *aller*:
> Je <u>ne</u> vais <u>pas</u> manger de chocolat. I am not going to eat chocolate.
>
> Page 96

3 In pairs, look at the verbs in the box and decide if they are an infinitive or a part of *aller*. Copy and complete the text, using the verbs. Then listen and check.

Example: 1 Je vais <u>faire</u> plus de vélo.

> va   travailler   être   faire   vais   parler   va   boire   avoir

Les bonnes résolutions

Moi – Alessandro

Santé
1. Je vais ____ plus de vélo.
2. Mon ami Louis ____ jouer au tennis tous les jours.
3. Ma mère Sylvie va ____ plus d'eau.

Famille
4. Je ____ aider ma mère et mes grands-parents.
5. Mon ami Louis ne va pas ____ impatient avec son frère.
6. Ma mère Sylvie va ____ une meilleure attitude avec ses sœurs.

Collège
7. Je ne vais pas ____ en même temps que la prof.
8. Mon ami Louis va ____ plus dur en cours de maths.
9. Ma mère Sylvie ____ arriver avant ses élèves.

90 *quatre-vingt-dix*

Module 4

4 Parler In pairs, take turns to answer each of the criticisms by saying what you are going to do differently in the future.

- Tu ne manges pas assez de légumes.
- À l'avenir, je vais manger plus de légumes.

1 Tu ne manges pas assez de légumes.
2 Tu ne fais pas assez de sport.
3 Tu ne travailles pas sérieusement au collège.
4 Tu n'aides pas à la maison.
5 Tu n'es pas très patient(e).
6 Tu ne vas pas souvent au centre sportif.

- Use *plus* to say 'more' (or 'more' + adjective/adverb):
  Je vais aider plus. I am going to help more.
  Je vais être plus calme. I am going to be calmer.
- Use *plus* **de/d'** to say 'more' + noun:
  Tu vas manger plus **de** fruits. You are going to eat more fruit.
  Je vais faire plus **d'**exercice. I am going to do more exercise.

5 Lire Look at the *Mission Bien-Être* calendar and read the two blogs. For each blogger, write down in French the three days on the calendar that have inspired them to change their lifestyle.

Mission Bien-Être Plus heureux – Plus sympa – Tous les jours

le rêve   dream

lundi	mardi	mercredi	jeudi	vendredi	samedi	dimanche
Aujourd'hui, mange bien. Choisis des repas sains.	Bouge. Fais quelque chose d'actif.	Ne va pas au lit tard. Reste calme.	Apprends quelque chose de nouveau.	Écris tes rêves et tes projets pour l'avenir.	Dis bonjour à tes voisins /voisines.	N'utilise pas ta tablette une heure avant de dormir.

The calendar suggestions use the *tu*-form imperative of the verb:
mange bien (**eat** well)
ne **va** pas au lit tard (don't **go** to bed late)

1 Je veux être plus actif. Je vais faire du vélo tous les jours. Je vais aussi commencer une nouvelle activité – demain, je vais prendre un cours de guitare! Je veux manger moins de choses sucrées. Je vais aller au marché pour acheter des légumes. Je vais préparer des repas végétariens sains.
                                                              Clément

2 Je veux mieux dormir, alors je vais aller au lit plus tôt. Je veux avoir plus d'amis, donc je vais parler avec la nouvelle famille qui habite dans l'appartement numéro dix. Je veux beaucoup voyager à l'avenir. Je vais écrire mes projets de vacances dans un cahier.
                                                              Nadia

6 Écouter Listen to each person and note down (a) what they want to do, and (b) what they are going to do in the future. (1–3)

Both *je vais* and *je veux* are followed by an infinitive:
je vais + infinitive   I am going to …
je veux + infinitive   I want to …

7 Écrire Write a list of five resolutions for yourself.

Je veux Je vais	faire	plus de vélo. une nouvelle activité. quelque chose d'actif.
	être	plus actif/active. en forme.
	manger plus de / moins de	fruits / légumes. chocolat / fromage.
	jouer	au tennis. au rugby.
	aller	au lit plus tôt.

quatre-vingt-onze 91

5 Mieux vivre

- Talking about lifestyle changes
- Using the imperfect, present and near future tenses
- Distinguishing between tenses when listening

Écouter 1 Listen to the podcast and read the texts. Copy and complete the sentences in English.

Quand tu étais plus jeune, ta vie était comment?

En ce moment, comment est ta vie?

À l'avenir, qu'est-ce que tu vas faire?

Sarah
- Quand j'étais ado, j'habitais dans un quartier difficile à Paris. J'étais membre d'un gang et je n'étais pas heureuse.
- Maintenant, j'étudie la musique et j'écris des chansons. Je vais dans des collèges et je parle de ma vie aux élèves.
- À l'avenir, je vais aider d'autres jeunes comme moi. Je vais changer des vies, avec la musique et la danse.

Malik
- Quand j'étais plus jeune, je ne faisais rien le soir, car je n'avais pas beaucoup d'amis. J'étais timide et j'étais victime de racisme. C'était très difficile.
- Maintenant, j'ai une chaîne sur YouTube et je lutte contre le racisme. Je suis plus fort et plus heureux.
- À l'avenir, je vais être politicien et je vais travailler pour l'égalité. Je ne vais jamais accepter l'inégalité.

1 Sarah used to live ▁▁. She was a member of ▁▁.
2 Now she studies ▁▁ and she ▁▁. She talks to students about ▁▁.
3 In the future, she is going to help ▁▁. She is going to change ▁▁ with ▁▁.
4 Malik didn't use to have ▁▁. He was ▁▁ and he was a victim of ▁▁.
5 Now, he has a YouTube channel and he ▁▁ against racism. He is ▁▁ and ▁▁.
6 In the future, he is going to be a ▁▁. He is going to work for ▁▁.

| lutter pour/contre | to fight for/against |
| l'inégalité (f) | inequality |

G There are two parts to most **negatives** in French:
ne ... pas   not
ne ... rien nothing
ne ... jamais never

Remember that the two parts of the negative go around the verb:
Je n'étais pas fort(e).   I wasn't strong.
Je ne vais jamais être politicien.
I am never going to be a politician.

Lire 2 Re-read the texts in exercise 1. Then find four phrases in the negative and translate them into English.

Lire 3 In exercise 1, find at least four verbs in the imperfect tense, four in the present tense and four in the near future tense. Translate them into English.

Écouter 4 Listen and read. Then fill in the gaps with the verb(s) that you hear. Then note what tense the sentence is in (imperfect, present or near future). (1–4)

Example: 1 *je vais être, …*

1 À l'avenir, ▁▁ professeur de danse. ▁▁ avec des jeunes handicapés.
2 Quand ▁▁ jeune, ▁▁ beaucoup d'amis. ▁▁ heureux.
3 Maintenant, ▁▁ triste. ▁▁ beaucoup d'espoir pour l'avenir.
4 ▁▁ les victimes de racisme en ligne. ▁▁ contre l'inégalité.

G You use:
- the **imperfect tense** to say what you used to do
  je travaillais   (I used to work)
- the **present tense** to say what you do now
  je travaille   (I work)
- the **near future tense** to say what you are going to do
  je vais travailler   (I am going to work)

Watch out for these irregular verbs:

	imperfect	present	near future
avoir (to have)	j'avais (I used to have)	j'ai (I have)	je vais avoir (I am going to have)
être (to be)	j'étais (I used to be)	je suis (I am)	je vais être (I am going to be)
faire (to do/make)	je faisais (I used to do/make)	je fais (I do/make)	je vais faire (I am going to do/make)

Page 97

92 *quatre-vingt-douze*

5 Read the text and choose the correct word to complete each sentence.

Sadio Mané est joueur de foot. Il est né au Sénégal et quand il était petit, il habitait dans un petit village. «La vie était dure», dit Sadio.

À dix-neuf ans, il a commencé sa carrière professionnelle avec l'équipe française de Metz. Il a ensuite joué pour les équipes de Southampton, Liverpool et Bayern Munich.

Maintenant, Sadio gagne des milliers d'euros! Pourtant, il reste modeste et il est très généreux: il a déjà payé pour la construction d'un lycée et d'un hôpital dans son village au Sénégal.

À l'avenir, Sadio va continuer à aider les Sénégalais. Il va travailler pour l'association *Right to Play*, qui lutte pour les droits des enfants. «Je crois que la base du succès, c'est le travail, de croire en ses rêves et le respect de soi-même», dit-il.

il est né	he was born
des milliers	thousands
l'association (f)	charity
croire en ses rêves	to believe in one's (your) dreams
soi-même	oneself (yourself)

1 Sadio Mané grew up in **France** / **Senegal** / **Canada**.
2 His early life was **happy** / **easy** / **hard**.
3 He started his professional career when he was **seventeen** / **eighteen** / **nineteen**.
4 Sadio earns thousands of **pounds** / **euros** / **dollars**.
5 In the future, he is going to **work for** / **help** / **give money to** *Right to Play*.

6 Listen to Sacha. Copy and complete the table in English.

When he was young	At the moment	In the future

7 Read the notes on the two celebrities with your partner, then create a podcast interview with one of them. Use the questions from exercise 1.

Rachel Keke
- Grew up in Ivory Coast (*en Côte d'Ivoire*)
- Used to work in a hotel
- Now a politician (*politicienne*) in France
- Fights for the rights of workers (*les travailleurs*)
- Is going to continue to fight for equality

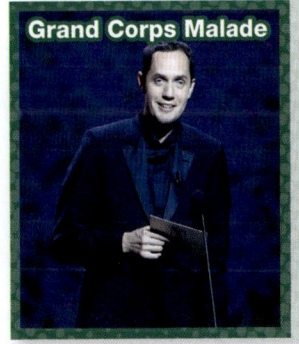

Grand Corps Malade
- Grew up in France
- Used to play tennis and basketball
- Now writes songs and poems (*des poèmes*)
- Is also an actor (*acteur*)
- Is going to sing and act (*jouer*) in films

8 Imagine you are the other famous person from exercise 7. Write a short article about your life.

Example: Je m'appelle … J'habitais …

Quand j'étais jeune, j'habitais …
Je travaillais dans …
Je jouais …

Maintenant, je lutte pour …
Je suis …
J'écris …

À l'avenir, je vais continuer à …
Je vais chanter …
Je vais jouer …

Rachel Keke used to clean hotel rooms. In 2019, she organised a successful strike for better pay and working conditions for hotel cleaners. She became an MP in 2022.

Grand Corps Malade (real name Fabien Marsaud) is a slam poet, actor and musician. He changed his name after a diving accident which damaged his spine and affected his legs. Can you work out what his new name means?

quatre-vingt-treize

Grammaire 1

The partitive article (Unit 1, page 84)

Écrire 1 Axel's parents want him to eat properly while they are out for the day. Look at their message. Imagine you are Axel and write out your meal plan in full.

Example: Pour le petit-déjeuner, je mange du pain et je bois …

> Axel, voici ton plan repas:
> Le petit-déjeuner – le pain, le café
> Le déjeuner – le riz, l'eau
> Après l'école – les fruits, le thé
> Le dîner – la viande, les légumes, le lait
> Pas de chocolat, pas de frites

You use the partitive article to say 'some'. It must agree with the noun it refers to.

masculine singular	feminine singular	before a vowel sound	plural
du poisson	**de la** viande	**de l'** eau	**des** légumes

After a **negative** or a **quantity**, these shorten to *de* (*d'* before a vowel):
Je ne mange pas *de* poisson. I don't eat fish.
Je bois beaucoup *d'*eau.   I drink a lot of water.

💡 In French, you use the partitive article even when we would not use 'some' in English:
Je mange **du** poisson avec **des** légumes.
I eat fish with vegetables.
Je ne mange pas *de* viande ou *de* fromage.
I don't eat meat or cheese.

Parler 2 Your French exchange partner has never been to the UK before. They ask you about some typical dishes. In pairs, take turns to be the exchange partner. Create **three** conversations, using the ideas below.

- *Qu'est-ce que c'est, le Lancashire hotpot?*
- *Dans ce plat, il y a du/de la/des …*

Lancashire hotpot – meat, vegetables

Yorkshire pudding – eggs, milk

Welsh rarebit – bread, cheese

The imperative (Culture, page 83 and Unit 2, page 86)

Écrire 3 Read the grammar boxes about the imperative on pages 83 and 86. Then put the French words into the correct order to translate these sentences into French.

1. Eat lots of fruit and vegetables.   de fruits | Mangez | et | de légumes | beaucoup
2. Talk to your family or your friends.   Parle | tes amis | ou | ta famille | avec | avec
3. Do some sport – play football.   au football | Faites | du sport – | jouez
4. Don't watch TV – go to bed.   au lit | Ne | pas | regarde | la télé – | va

Lire 4 Note down if each sentence in exercise 3 is in the *tu-* or *vous-*form of the imperative.

94 *quatre-vingt-quatorze*

Module 4

5 **Listen. Which form of the imperative do you hear? Write *tu* or *vous* and choose the correct English translation from the box. (1–5)**

Example: 1 *tu* – Listen to some music.

Go to school on foot.
Listen to some music.
Stay in bed.
Do some exercise.
Go to the sports centre.

With -**er** verbs in the imperative:
- the *tu*-form ending is silent: Écout**e**!
- the *vous*-form ending is pronounced: Écout**ez**!

Irregular verbs are different in spelling and sound:

	tu-*form*	***vous-*form**
aller *(to go)*	Va	Allez
faire *(to do/make)*	Fais	Faites

The present tense of modal verbs (Unit 2, page 87)

The modal verbs *pouvoir*, *vouloir* and *devoir* are usually followed by an infinitive.

pouvoir *(to be able to, can)*
je p<u>eux</u>
tu p<u>eux</u>
il/elle/on p<u>eut</u>
nous pouvons
vous pouvez
ils/elles peuvent

vouloir *(to want (to))*
je v<u>eux</u>
tu v<u>eux</u>
il/elle/on v<u>eut</u>
nous voulons
vous voulez
ils/elles veulent

devoir *(to have to, must)*
je d<u>ois</u>
tu d<u>ois</u>
il/elle/on d<u>oit</u>
nous devons
vous devez
ils/elles doivent

💡 The underlined parts of each modal verb are pronounced the same. Think carefully about which spelling of the verb you need in exercise 6.

6 **Look at the sentences and predict what modal verb goes in each gap. There is often more than one possibility. Then listen and fill in the gaps.**

1 Je ___ trouver de nouveaux amis. Qu'est-ce que je ___ faire?
2 Il ___ essayer de parler avec lui s'il ___ être plus heureux.
3 Si tu ___ mieux dormir, tu ___ arrêter de regarder ton portable au lit.
4 Mon meilleur ami ne ___ pas parler avec ses parents. Vous ___ l'aider?
5 Mon frère et moi ___ être en forme, donc nous ___ faire plus de sport.

7 **In pairs, take turns to read out the advice poster. Give feedback on each other's pronunciation. Then listen and check.**

Pay special attention to the pronunciation of these sounds:

eu – count to two in French. These words rhyme with '*d**eu**x*' or '*délici**eu**x*'.
ou – make a small 'o' with your lips to form this sound (*n**ou**s*, *t**ou**jou**rs*).
oi – count to three in French. This sound is also in '*tr**oi**s*' or '*m**oi**'.

Si tu veux être heureux ou heureuse ...

▶ Tu dois avoir une vie active. Tu peux faire du sport ou essayer une nouvelle activité.

▶ Tu dois bien dormir. Tu peux lire un bon livre avant de dormir.

▶ Tu dois parler avec quelqu'un quand tu as des problèmes. Tu peux toujours en parler avec nous.

| si | if |

8 **Find the French for the following modal verb expressions in the poster in exercise 7. Write them out in English and French.**

1 You must have
2 You can read
3 You must speak
4 If you want to be
5 You can do
6 You must sleep well

quatre-vingt-quinze 95

Grammaire 2

The perfect tense (Unit 1, page 85 and Unit 3, page 89)

1 Copy out the sentences, filling in the gaps with the correct **auxiliary verb** and **past participle** from the box. Then listen and check.

> ai fait   ai pris   ai fini   ai commencé
> avons mangé   ai trouvé   ai servi   suis allé

1 Le week-end dernier, j'___ un gâteau d'anniversaire pour ma mère.
2 D'abord, je ___ au supermarché pour acheter tous les ingrédients.
3 J'ai cherché des recettes en ligne et j'___ une recette pour un gâteau au chocolat.
4 J'___ à préparer le gâteau le matin, et j'___ le gâteau à 14h30.
5 Le soir, ma famille et moi ___ ensemble et en dessert, j'___ mon gâteau.
6 Le gâteau était vraiment délicieux! J'___ une photo pour Instagram.

Zachary

You use the perfect tense to say what you <u>did</u> or <u>have done</u>.
Remember, there are two parts to the perfect tense:
1 the auxiliary verb (part of *avoir* or *être*)
2 the past participle.

Different groups of verbs work in different ways:
- Regular **-er** verbs, e.g. *regarder* (to watch)
  j'**ai** regard**é** (I watched)
- Regular **-ir** verbs, e.g. *choisir* (to choose)
  elle **a** chois**i** (she chose)
- Regular **-re** verbs, e.g. *attendre* (to wait)
  nous **avons** attend**u** (we waited)
- Some verbs are irregular, e.g. *prendre* (to take)
  j'**ai** pris (I took)
- Some verbs use *être*, e.g. *aller* (to go)
  elle **est** all**ée** (she went)

You may not know every word in the sentences, or every verb in the box, but can you guess what any new words might be according to the context and the other words in the sentence?

The near future tense (Unit 4, page 90)

2 Separate out these words to make accurate near future tense sentences.

Example: 1 *Je vais manger du couscous.*

1 jevaismangerducouscous
2 ellevaboireducoca
3 onvaprendredescoursdetennis
4 nousallonsfairedelanatation
5 ilsvontaiderlesautres

For the near future tense, use the correct part of **aller** followed by the infinitive:

je **vais** manger	I am going to eat
tu **vas** parler	you are going to speak
il/elle/on **va** être	he/she is / we are going to be
nous **allons** avoir	we are going to have
vous **allez** faire	you are going to do
ils/elles **vont** aller	they are going to go

<u>Negatives</u> go around the part of **aller**.

Je ne vais pas faire mes devoirs.
I am not going to do my homework.

---

3 Translate the sentences in exercise 2 into English.

Example: 1 *I am going to eat couscous.*

quatre-vingt-seize

4 Copy and complete each sentence in the near future tense with the correct part of *aller* and the correct infinitive from the box. Then make up <u>three</u> sentences in the near future tense using the remaining three infinitives.

Example: 1 *Elle **va aller** à la piscine tous les week-ends.*

1 Elle ▭ à la piscine tous les week-ends.
2 Il ▭ plus gentil avec sa petite sœur.
3 Tu ▭ plus d'efforts au collège, surtout en maths.
4 Nous ▭ au handball chaque semaine.
5 Ils ▭ cinq fruits ou légumes tous les jours.

acheter	être
aller	faire
avoir	jouer
écouter	manger

Using three tenses (imperfect, present and near future) (Unit 5, page 92)

5 Read the grammar box on page 92. Then, in pairs, play 'tenses tennis'. Take turns to change each present tense sentence into both the imperfect and the near future tenses.

- *J'habite à Toulouse.*
- *J'habitais à Toulouse.*
- *Je vais habiter à Toulouse.*

1 *J'habite à Toulouse.* → (imperfect) → (near future)
2 *J'ai une chaîne sur YouTube.* → (imperfect) → (near future)
3 *Je travaille dans un magasin.* → (imperfect) → (near future)
4 *Je suis timide.* → (imperfect) → (near future)
5 *J'ai beaucoup d'amis.* → (imperfect) → (near future)
6 *J'aide mes grands-parents.* → (imperfect) → (near future)

6 Translate the passage fully into French by changing the English words/phrases in bold.

When j'étais **young**, je **used to go swimming** tous les week-ends.
Maintenant, **I don't do** de sport. **I go to school** en bus.
À **the future**, je vais **take dance lessons**.

C'est parti!

7 Listen and complete the sentences with the missing word or words. Remember, some verb forms sound the same (e.g. *je <u>veux</u>, il/elle <u>veut</u>*), so think carefully about which spelling you need.

1 D'habitude, le midi au collège, je ▭ du poisson avec des frites.
2 Ma sœur ▭ être végane.
3 Pour être en forme, on ▭ avoir une vie active.
4 En ce moment, je ne ▭ pas beaucoup de sport.
5 J'ai mal à la jambe parce que je ▭ tombé de vélo.
6 À l'avenir, je ▭ aller au collège en bus.
7 Quand j'étais plus jeune, j' ▭ souvent triste.
8 Un jour, je ▭ être professeur de sport dans un collège.

> Write something down for every gap, even if you're not 100% sure.

Module 4 — Contrôle de lecture et d'écoute

Reading

Lire 1

Staying healthy. Read these comments from an internet forum. Make notes **in English** for each person under the following headings. You do not need to write in full sentences.

a Change they have made
b Reason why

Nadia:
Avant, je ne faisais pas beaucoup de sport mais maintenant, je fais une activité physique régulière pour être bien physiquement et dans ma tête.

Zoé:
Quand j'avais douze ans, je n'étais pas active et je mangeais beaucoup de fastfood. Maintenant j'ai changé! Je suis végétarienne parce que je pense que c'est un choix plus sain.

Sacha:
J'ai changé ce que je mange. Je mange moins de choses comme les gâteaux et je choisis des fruits parce que mon docteur a dit que c'est une bonne idée pour moi.

> These texts contain verbs that refer to the present and the past. Use the time expressions *avant*, *maintenant* and *quand j'avais … ans* to help you work out the meaning of the texts.

Lire 2

Eat well. Read this guide about healthy eating.

Une vie saine est importante pour tout le monde, pas seulement pour les enfants ou les adolescents.
- Pour être en bonne santé, il ne faut pas avoir beaucoup d'argent, ce n'est pas difficile et ça ne prend pas énormément de temps.
- Avant de faire de grands changements, il faut parler avec ses amis et ses parents. Mais il est plus important de parler avec une équipe médicale.
- On ne mange pas assez de légumes ou de poisson. Mais ce qui est malsain, c'est le **grignotage** toute la journée, comme les **chips***, les fruits, les gâteaux …

*les chips crisps

a Complete the sentences below. For each sentence, write the correct letter (A–C).

(i) The guide is for …
   A teenagers only.   B children only.   C everyone.

(ii) According to the guide, being healthy …
   A is easy.   B is expensive.   C takes a lot of time.

(iii) Advice should mainly come from …
   A friends.   B doctors.   C parents.

(iv) According to the guide, we don't eat enough …
   A crisps.   B fruit.   C fish.

b Which of these is the best translation for the word **grignotage**? Write down the correct letter.

   A dieting   B snacking   C buying

> This question is testing your ability to work out the meaning of a word that you haven't seen before (e.g. by looking at the **context** in which it is used). Which of the three options is the most likely translation?

quatre-vingt-dix-huit

Module 4

Lire 3
Being a vegetarian. Translate the following sentences **into English**.

a Je n'aime pas manger de la viande.
b Beaucoup de mes amis sont végétariens.
c Je pense que c'est un choix plus sain.
d J'ai parlé à mes amis et j'ai lu un livre sur le sujet.
e Mais mes parents pensent qu'il faut manger de la viande pour être en bonne santé.

> Take care to get your tenses right.

> This word suggests that there is a different opinion.

Listening

Écouter 4
Fast food. Fathia is talking about fast food. What does she say? Write down the word for the gap in each sentence, using a word from the box. There are more words than gaps.

a According to Fathia's parents, fast food is ___.
b They also think that the ___ is not good.
c ___ have not changed.
d Fathia prefers the ___ she gets.
e Fathia doesn't really like ordering from a ___.

> Which French words/phrases might you hear?
>
> tasty   unhealthy   service   price
> clients   recipes   person   cheap
> machine   offers   food

> Listen out for 'distractors' (i.e. words/phrases that are mentioned but not needed for any of your answers). These test your ability to listen for **detail**, not simply gist.

Écouter 5
A bad day! You hear Jules talking about a bad day he had recently. Listen to the recording and, for each question, write the correct letter (A–C).

1 Jules was …
   A in the park.
   B in the countryside.
   C at the beach.

2 Jules fell over after …
   A he tripped up.
   B he saw his friend.
   C his friend pushed him.

3 Now, Jules has a sore …
   A leg.
   B arm.
   C head.

4 Jules is sad because he can't …
   A go out.
   B run.
   C play sport.

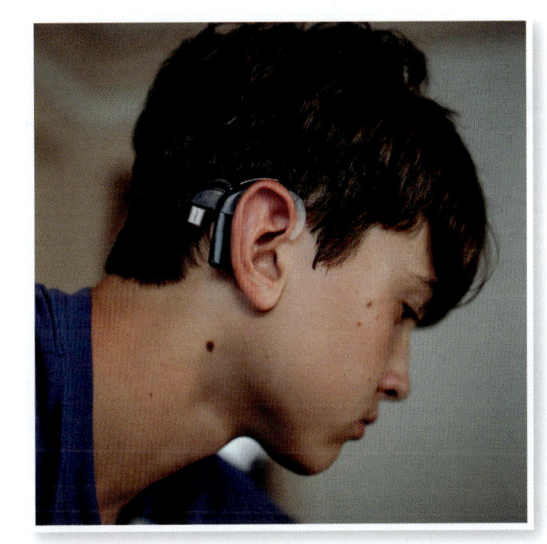

Écouter 6
Dictation. You are going to hear someone talking about food.

a Sentences 1–3: write down the missing words. For each gap, you will write one word **in French**.

   1 Le ___ est ___.
   2 Je ___ un ___ chaque matin.
   3 Le ___ est trop ___.

> Take care with adjectives in this activity. Each adjective will need to agree with the noun in the sentence. Is it masculine or feminine?

b Sentences 4–6: write down the full sentences that you hear, **in French**.

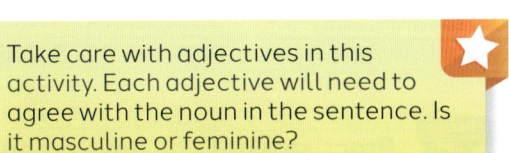

quatre-vingt-dix-neuf 99

Module 4 Contrôle oral

Read aloud

Parler 1 Look at this task card. With a partner, take turns to read out the five sentences, paying attention to the underlined letters and the highlighted liaison.

> Maxime, your Swiss friend, has emailed you to tell you about his daily life.
>
> Read out the text below to your teacher.
>
> J'aime prendre du pain.
> Quand j'ai faim, je choisis un fruit.
> C'est très important pour la santé.
> Normalement, je mange beaucoup de légumes le matin.
> Malheureusement, je pense que les repas malsains sont délicieux!

Take extra care with how you pronounce the underlined sounds:
- an, en
- ain, in, aim, im
- u.

Remember that in this text, a final t is silent.

Remember to make the liaison here.

Écouter 2 Listen and check your pronunciation.

Parler 3 Listen to the teacher asking the two follow-up questions. Translate each question **into English** and prepare your own answers **in French**. Then listen again and respond to the teacher.

Role play

Parler 4 Look at the role-play card and prepare what you are going to say.

> **Setting:** At the doctor's surgery
>
> **Scenario:**
> - You are at a doctor's surgery in France.
> - The teacher will play the part of the doctor and will speak first.
> - The teacher will ask questions **in French** and you must answer **in French**.
> - Say a few words or a short phrase/sentence for each prompt. One-word answers are not sufficient to gain full marks.
>
> **Task:**
> 1 Say what the problem is.
> 2 Say how much it hurts.
> 3 Say who you are with.
> 4 Say how long you are staying in France for.
> 5 Ask what you need to do.

E.g. 'I have a backache.'

Use *pour* followed by a length of time.

You can use *Ça fait … mal* and add *un peu / très / assez*.

You could use *je dois* in your question.

Parler 5 Practise what you have prepared. Then, using your notes, listen and respond to the teacher.

Écouter 6 Now listen to Rachid doing the role-play task. **In English**, note down (a) how he **answers** the questions for task prompts 1, 2, 3 and 4, and (b) what question he **asks** for task prompt 5.

100 *cent*

Picture task

Écouter 7 Look at the exam card below and read the **first part** of the task. Then listen to Ana describing the picture. Answer the questions **in English**.

a In Ana's opinion, where are the five people in the picture? Do you agree?
b What does she say about the person at the front?
c What does she think the other people are doing? Do you agree?
d What do you think the verb *attendre* means?

Describe this picture.

Your description must cover:

- people
- location
- activity.

When you have finished your description, you will be asked **two questions** relating to the picture. Say a short phrase/sentence in response to each question. One-word answers will not be sufficient to gain full marks.

You will then move on to a **conversation** on the broader thematic context of **Lifestyle and wellbeing**.

During the conversation, you will be asked questions in the present, past and future tenses. Your responses should be as **full and detailed** as possible.

> To talk about where people are, you can use a preposition followed by a pronoun – e.g. *derrière lui* (behind him), *devant elle* (in front of her).

Parler 8 Prepare your own description of the picture, mentioning **people, location** and **activity**. Then, with a partner, take turns to describe the picture.

> Sur la photo, il y a …

Parler 9 Read the **second part** of the task. Then listen to the first two follow-up questions and respond to the teacher. Remember: you only need to give a short answer to each one.

Écouter 10 Read the **third part** of the task. The teacher asks Ana: *Qu'est-ce que tu as mangé au dîner hier soir?* Listen and write down the missing word or words for each gap.

> Hier soir, j'ai acheté beaucoup de ⬛1 et du poisson. J'ai fait un ⬛2 pour mes amis. C'était délicieux. J'ai bu de ⬛3 . Je n'ai pas pris de dessert mais ⬛4 a mangé du fromage. Je ⬛5 végétarienne mais je n'aime pas trop manger ⬛6 .

Écouter 11 Listen to Ana answering the question: *Qu'est-ce que tu voudrais manger demain et pourquoi?*

Write down **in English** the food Ana would like to eat for each meal.

a breakfast   b lunch   c dinner

Parler 12 Prepare your own answers to the Module 4 questions on page 226. Your responses should be as **full and detailed** as possible. Then practise with a partner.

cent-un 101

Module 4 Contrôle écrit

40–50 word writing task

Écrire 1 Look at this writing exam task and then, for each bullet point:
1. think about what vocabulary you have learned which you could use in your answer. For example:
   - **nouns** and **verbs** to talk about what you often eat
   - **verbs of opinion** and **adjectives** to explain your opinion
   - how to say what you are going to eat this weekend.
2. write down <u>two or three</u> ideas for what you could write about.
3. write down which tense(s) you will need to use in your answer.

> Write about food that you often eat.
>
> You **must** include the following points:
> - details about what you often eat
> - your opinion on what you often eat
> - what you are going to eat this weekend.
>
> Write your answer **in French**. You should aim to write between 40 and 50 words.

Make sure you vary your vocabulary and avoid repetition.

Lire 2 Read Emma's answer to the exam task. Answer questions 1–5 in the coloured shapes. Write down **in English** five details that she gives.

1. This word shows a **variety of vocabulary**. What does it mean? Find <u>two more</u> examples.

2. Which **connective** could she use here to form an **extended sentence**? What other connective does she use?

> Je mange souvent de la cuisine internationale car c'est vraiment pratique.
>
> J'aime manger des pâtes avec des légumes de saison. Je suis végétarienne. Je ne mange jamais de viande.
>
> Ce week-end, je vais voir ma belle-mère. Ma belle-mère va préparer un énorme gâteau. Je pense que ça va être délicieux!

3. This is an example of **complex language**. What does it mean? Find <u>three</u> more examples from the text.

4. How could Emma **avoid repetition** by using a pronoun here?

5. Which **tense** is this?

80–90 word writing task

Écrire 3 Look at this writing exam task and then, for each bullet point:
1. think about what vocabulary you have learned which you could use in your answer. For example:
   - **nouns** and **verbs** to talk about keeping healthy
   - **verbs of opinion** and **adjectives** to explain your point of view
   - language for **narrating a story** about what you have recently done
   - how to explain what you are going to change and why.
2. write down <u>three or four</u> ideas for what you could write about.
3. write down which tense(s) you will need to use in your answer.

> Write to your friend about keeping healthy.
>
> You **must** include the following points:
> - what you can do to keep healthy in your area
> - your opinion of doing sports
> - what you have done recently to keep fit
> - things you are going to change in your daily life.
>
> Write your answer **in French**. You should aim to write between 80 and 90 words.

You don't have to tell the truth! Stick to what you've learned to say in French, and don't worry if it doesn't accurately describe your real life.

102 cent-deux

Lire 4 Read Dorian's answer to the exam task in exercise 3. Answer questions 1–5 in the coloured shapes.

1 This is an example of **complex language**. What does it mean? Find <u>three</u> more examples from the text.

2 Which **connective** has he used here? What other connectives does he use?

3 This word shows a **variety of vocabulary**. What does it mean? Find <u>two</u> more examples.

4 Which **tense** is this? What other examples can you find? Does he use any other tenses?

5 He **avoids repetition** by using a direct object pronoun here, but what does the sentence mean?

Dans ma ville il y a un centre sportif. On peut faire de la natation ou faire du sport pour être en bonne santé.

J'aime le sport parce que c'est génial. J'adore jouer en équipe avec mes amis. On s'amuse! Mais le sport est assez fatigant.

Récemment, je suis allé à la campagne pour faire du vélo avec ma famille. Après, j'ai mangé des pizzas car j'avais faim! Je les adore!

En général je suis en forme mais je voudrais aller au lit plus tôt et manger moins de pizza!

Lire 5 Read Dorian's answer again. Answer the following questions **in English**.
a What can you do where Dorian lives to keep fit?
b What positive things does he say about sport?
c What negative things does he say about sport?
d What did he recently do with his family?
e What <u>two</u> things would he like to change?

Écrire 6 Prepare your own answer to the 80–90 word writing task in exercise 3.
- Think about how you can develop your answer for each bullet point.
- Look back at your notes from exercises 3 and 4.
- Look at the 'Challenge checklist' and consider how you can show off your French!
- Write a **brief** plan and organise your answer into paragraphs.
- Write your answer and then carefully check the accuracy of what you have written.

Challenge checklist

🌶️
- ✓ A range of opinions (e.g. *j'aime, je n'aime pas*)
- ✓ Negatives (*ne ... pas*)
- ✓ *C'est* + adjective

🌶️🌶️
- ✓ A variety of opinion structures (e.g. *je pense que c'est ...*)
- ✓ Opinion verbs with infinitives (*j'aime jouer*)
- ✓ A range of connectives (*et, mais, ou*)
- ✓ A wide range of interesting vocabulary

🌶️🌶️🌶️
- ✓ Past, present and future timeframes
- ✓ Connectives / time phrases / sequencers
- ✓ Some extended sentences (*parce que ...*)
- ✓ Different opinion phrases
- ✓ Complex language (e.g. *pour* + infinitive, reflexive verbs)
- ✓ Direct object pronouns

Module 4

cent-trois

Module 4 Vocabulaire

Key:
bold = this word will appear in higher exams only
* = this word is not on the vocabulary list but you may use it in your own sentences

Sain ou malsain? (pages 82–83)

Dans ce **plat**, il y a …	In this dish, there is/are …
du chocolat / fromage	chocolate / cheese
du poisson / riz / sucre	fish / rice / sugar
de la glace / *sauce	ice cream / sauce
de la viande	meat
des frites / fruits / légumes	chips / fruit / vegetables
À ton avis, le **plat**, c'est sain?	In your opinion, is the dish healthy?
C'est sain / malsain.	It is healthy / unhealthy.
C'est bon / mauvais pour la santé.	It is good / bad for your health.
Le **plat** a bon goût.	The dish tastes good.
Je n'aime pas le goût.	I don't like the taste.
C'est parfait pour les végétariens.	It's perfect for vegetarians.
Ce n'est pas bon pour les végans.	It's not good for vegans.
À mon avis, il a bon goût, mais c'est malsain.	In my opinion, it tastes good, but it's unhealthy.
le goût	the taste
délicieux	delicious
Buvez plus de/moins de *coca!	Drink more/less cola!
Mangez plus de/moins de frites et de chocolat!	Eat more/less chips and chocolate!
Faites plus/moins d'exercice!	Do more/less exercise!
Faites de la natation plus/ moins souvent!	Go swimming more/less often!
Allez plus/moins souvent au centre sportif!	Go to the sports centre more/less often!
Allez au collège à pied ou à vélo!	Go to school on foot or by bike!
Allez au lit plus tôt / tard!	Go to bed earlier / later!
Dormez au moins huit heures toutes les nuits!	Sleep at least eight hours every night!
Essayez un nouveau sport!	Try a new sport!

Bon appétit! (pages 84–85)

Qu'est-ce que tu manges (normalement)?	What do you (usually) eat?
Qu'est-ce que tu manges pour le petit-déjeuner?	What do you eat for breakfast?
Qu'est-ce que tu manges et bois à midi?	What do you eat and drink at lunchtime?
Est-ce que tu manges quelque chose après les cours?	Do you eat something after school?
Normalement, qu'est-ce que tu manges le soir?	What do you usually eat in the evening?
Pour le petit-déjeuner, …	For breakfast, …
À midi, …	At lunchtime, …
Après les cours, …	After school, …
Normalement, le soir, …	Usually, in the evening, …
je bois / on boit …	I / we drink …
je mange / on mange …	I / we eat …
je choisis …	I choose …
du café / lait	coffee / milk
du pain / poisson / *poulet	bread / fish / chicken
des *céréales / fruits	cereal / fruit
des légumes	vegetables
des œufs / *olives / pâtes	eggs / olives / pasta
de l'eau	water
un **plat** français	a French dish
un *sandwich	a sandwich
Je mange souvent des œufs.	I often eat eggs.
Quand j'ai soif, …	When I'm thirsty, …
Si j'ai faim, …	If I'm hungry, …
beaucoup de (légumes)	lots of (vegetables)

Bien dans ma peau (pages 86–87)

Comment ça va aujourd'hui?	How are you today?
Ça ne va pas?	Are you OK?
Ça va très bien.	I am very well.
Ça ne va pas bien.	I am not well/good.
Je suis …	I am …
un peu / assez …	a bit / quite …
très / vraiment …	very / really …
heureux/heureuse.	happy.
triste.	sad.
malade.	ill.
calme.	calm.
Pourquoi es-tu …?	Why are you …?
Je suis … parce que / car …	I am … because / as …
j'adore jouer à des jeux vidéo contre mes amis.	I love playing video games against my friends.
je ne travaille pas ce week-end.	I am not working this weekend.
je ne m'entends pas bien avec (mon père).	I don't get on with (my father).
j'ai beaucoup de travail scolaire.	I have lots of school work.
je suis tout le temps / souvent **stressé(e)** avec les examens.	I am always / often stressed with exams.
je dors mal.	I am sleeping badly.
j'ai perdu mon chat / chien.	I have lost my cat / dog.
je dois trouver de nouveaux amis.	I must find new friends.
je n'ai pas d'énergie.	I don't have any energy.
mon meilleur ami a changé de collège.	my best friend has changed school.
mon équipe a gagné.	my team won.
Je ne sais pas pourquoi.	I don't know why.
Écoute de la musique.	Listen to music.
Fais de la cuisine.	Do some cooking.
Parle avec moi.	Speak to me.
Reste calme.	Stay calm.
Va au lit.	Go to bed.
Bouge un peu.	Move a bit.
je veux changer …	I want to change …

je peux parler …	I can speak …	tu dois travailler …	you must work …
elle doit trouver …	she must find …	tu peux être …	you can be …
il veut aller …	he wants to go …		

Ça ne va pas? (pages 88–89)

Le corps **humain**	The human body
le bras	the arm
le cœur	the heart
le dos	the back
le nez	the nose
le pied	the foot
le ventre	the stomach
la bouche	the mouth
la gorge	the throat
la jambe	the leg
la main	the hand
l'oreille	the ear
la tête	the head
les yeux	the eyes
*Allô? Je peux vous aider?	Hello? Can I help you?
Bonjour. Je voudrais prendre rendez-vous, s'il vous plaît.	Hello. I would like to make an appointment, please.
Bien sûr. Quel est le problème?	Of course. What is the problem?
J'ai (très) mal (au bras) et mal (à la tête / à l'oreille).	I have a (very) sore (arm) and a (headache / earache).
Vous voulez un rendez-vous pour quand?	When would you like an appointment?
Demain après-midi.	Tomorrow afternoon.
Aujourd'hui / Mercredi, s'il vous plaît.	Today / Wednesday, please.
Pas de problème.	No problem.
Le rendez-vous est à quelle heure, s'il vous plaît?	What time is the appointment, please?
À deux / trois / dix heures (et demie).	At (half past) two / three / ten.
Quelle est l'adresse, s'il vous plaît?	What is the address, please?
C'est dans la rue (du Marché), au numéro (dix / quinze / vingt-cinq).	It is in (Market) Street, at number (ten / fifteen / twenty-five).
Merci. Au revoir.	Thank you. Goodbye.
J'ai eu un accident.	I had an accident.
Je suis tombé(e) (de vélo).	I fell (off my bike).
Je suis allé(e) à l'hôpital.	I went to hospital.
J'ai chaud / froid.	I am hot / cold.
J'ai faim / soif.	I am hungry / thirsty.
le médecin	the doctor

Je change ma vie (pages 90–91)

Qu'est-ce que tu vas faire pour améliorer ta vie?	What are you going to do to improve your life?
Les bonnes *résolutions	Good resolutions
Je vais manger plus de légumes / fruits.	I am going to eat more vegetables / fruit.
Je vais prendre des cours de danse.	I am going to take dance classes.
Je vais moins penser à moi et je vais aider les autres.	I am going to think less about myself and I am going to help others.
Je vais être plus patient(e) avec ma petite sœur.	I am going to be more patient with my little sister.
Je vais aller à la piscine chaque week-end.	I am going to go to the swimming pool every weekend.
Je ne vais pas faire mes devoirs à la dernière minute.	I am not going to do my homework at the last minute.
À l'avenir, je vais / je veux …	In the future, I am going to / I want to …
aider ma mère et mes grands-parents.	help my mother and my grandparents.
aider plus à la maison.	help around the house more.
aller plus souvent au centre sportif.	go to the sports centre more often.
aller au lit plus tôt.	go to bed earlier.
être plus actif/active / en forme.	be more active / in better shape.
faire une nouvelle activité.	do a new activity.
faire plus de sport / de vélo.	do more sport / cycling.
jouer au tennis / *rugby.	play tennis / rugby.
manger moins de chocolat / fromage.	eat less chocolate / cheese.
travailler plus **sérieusement** au collège.	work harder at school.
Je ne vais pas …	I am not going to …
Il/Elle va arriver / jouer …	He/She is going to arrive / play …
Il/Elle ne va pas être …	He/She is not going to be …

Mieux vivre (pages 92–93)

Quand tu étais plus jeune, ta vie était comment?	When you were younger, how was your life?
Quand j'étais petit(e) …	When I was little …
Quand j'étais jeune / *ado, …	When I was young / a teenager …
j'habitais en *Côte d'Ivoire / France.	I lived in Ivory Coast / France.
je jouais au tennis / basket.	I played tennis / basketball.
je travaillais dans un hôtel.	I worked in a hotel.
En ce moment, comment est ta vie?	At the moment, how is your life?
Maintenant, …	Now, …
je suis acteur/actrice.	I am an actor.
je suis *politicien(ne).	I am a politician.
j'écris des chansons.	I write songs.
je lutte pour les droits des **travailleurs**.	I fight for the rights of workers.
À l'avenir, qu'est-ce que tu vas faire?	In the future, what are you going to do?
À l'avenir, …	In the future, …
je vais *continuer à …	I am going to continue to …
je vais chanter / écrire …	I am going to sing / write …

Module 5 — Numéro vacances

Voudrais-tu voyager?
- Talking about holidays and accommodation
- Using *pour* + infinitive

Pourquoi voudrais-tu voyager?

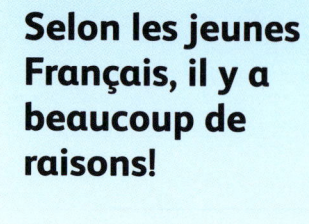

Selon les jeunes Français, il y a beaucoup de raisons!

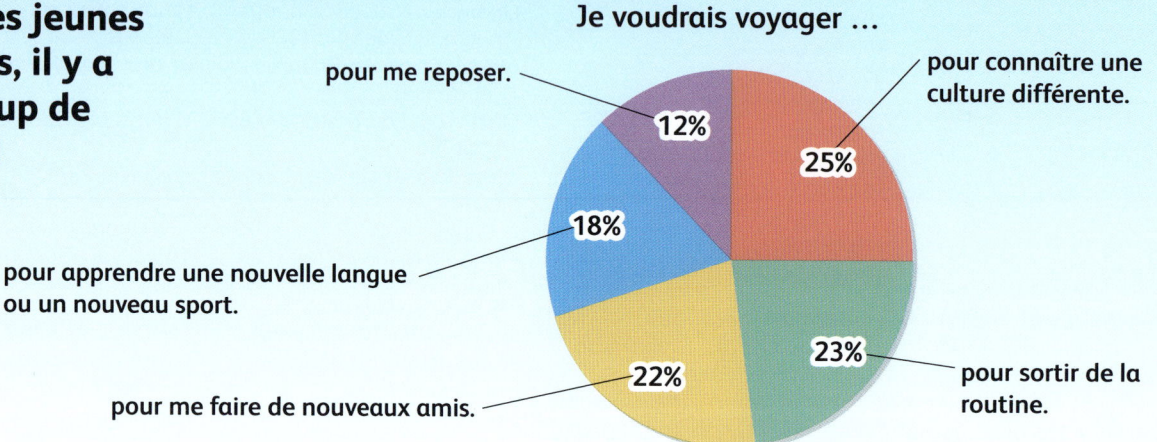

Je voudrais voyager …
- pour me reposer. — 12%
- pour connaître une culture différente. — 25%
- pour sortir de la routine. — 23%
- pour me faire de nouveaux amis. — 22%
- pour apprendre une nouvelle langue ou un nouveau sport. — 18%

Logements étonnants

Le Village Flottant de Pressac
Où: dans la Vienne
Description: un village calme sur l'eau
Équipement: une piscine, un grand choix de restaurants
Parfait pour: être près de la nature

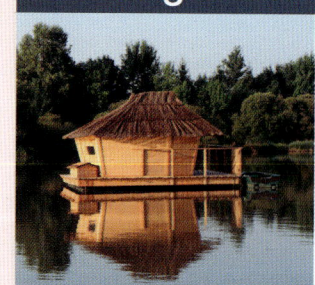

La Troglo à Plumes
Où: dans le Maine-et-Loire
Description: une maison historique et confortable
Équipement: trois chambres, une belle vue sur la campagne
Parfait pour: se couper du monde

Le camping Le Haut-Village
Où: en Loire-Atlantique
Description: un camping avec des logements étonnants – avion, voitures de train et de métro
Équipement: des aires de jeux pour enfants, des terrains de sport
Parfait pour: s'amuser en famille sur la côte

L'Hôtel de la Cité à Carcassonne
Où: dans l'Aude
Description: un hôtel-château au cœur d'une vieille ville
Équipement: des chambres confortables, un grand jardin
Parfait pour: se reposer

étonnant(e)	surprising, amazing, incredible
flottant(e)	floating
se couper du monde	to switch off from the world
l'aire (f) de jeux	playground

L'Aude, la Loire-Atlantique, le Maine-et-Loire and la Vienne are all French *départements*. These are similar to counties in the UK.

106 cent-six

Zone de culture — Module 5

1 Lire — Read the results of the survey at the top of page 106 and answer the questions.

What percentage of young people would like to travel so they can …
1 rest?
2 learn a new language or sport?
3 change their routine?
4 get to know a different culture?
5 make new friends?

2 Écouter — Listen to the interviews and note in English **two** reasons why each person would like to travel. (1–3)

> **G** *Je voudrais* means 'I would like' and is in the conditional. Follow it with an <u>infinitive</u> such as *voyager* to say what you would like to do:
> *Je voudrais <u>voyager</u>.*   I would like to travel.
> Pages 108 and 118

> **G** Use *pour* + infinitive to say 'in order to':
> *pour sortir de la routine*
> in order to change (my) routine

3 Parler — In pairs, talk about why you would like to travel.

- *Pourquoi voudrais-tu voyager?*
- *Je voudrais voyager pour … et pour …*
  Et toi, pourquoi voudrais-tu voyager?
- *Je voudrais voyager pour … et …*

Je voudrais voyager pour	me reposer.
	me faire de nouveaux amis.
	connaître une culture différente.
	sortir de la routine.
	apprendre une nouvelle langue.
	apprendre un nouveau sport.

4 Écouter — Read the article called *Logements étonnants* on page 106. Then listen. For each conversation, write 'Le Village', 'La Troglo', 'Le camping' or 'L'Hôtel'. (1–8)

5 Parler — In pairs, choose one of the places to stay, then make up your own version of the dialogue below, changing the <u>underlined</u> phrases.

- *Où voudrais-tu passer tes vacances?*
- *Je voudrais passer mes vacances dans <u>le Village Flottant</u>.*
- *C'est où?*
- *C'est <u>dans la Vienne</u>.*
- *Qu'est-ce que c'est?*
- *C'est <u>un village calme sur l'eau</u>.*
- *Qu'est-ce qu'il y a là-bas?*
- *Il y a <u>une piscine</u> et <u>un grand choix de restaurants</u>.*
- *Qu'est-ce qu'on peut faire?*
- *On peut <u>être près de la nature</u>.*

là-bas over there

> Ch**â**teau, h**au**t, se rep**o**ser and c**ô**te all contain the same sound. Say this sound with rounded lips and your tongue back.
>
> In French, *h* is always silent.
>
> Listen and repeat these sentences:
> **H**uit **h**ommes **h**eureux **h**abitent dans l'**h**ôtel **h**istorique.
> Vos ch**â**t**eaux** sur l'**eau** sont près de la c**ô**te.

6 Écrire — Write a description of one of the places in the *Logements étonnants* texts on page 106. Include:

- where it is
  La Troglo à Plumes est dans le Maine-et-Loire.
- what it is
  C'est une maison …
- what there is
  Il y a …
- what you can do there.
  On peut …

cent-sept 107

1 Des vacances de rêve

- Talking about your ideal holiday
- Using the conditional of *vouloir*
- Giving reasons for your preferences

Écouter 1
Listen and write the <u>four</u> correct letters for each speaker. (1–4)

Quel type de vacances voudrais-tu?

Je voudrais …

- **a** des vacances calmes.
- **b** des vacances éco-responsables.
- **c** des vacances culturelles.
- **d** des vacances actives.

Où voudrais-tu passer tes vacances idéales?

Je voudrais passer mes vacances …

- **e** à la campagne.
- **f** à la montagne.
- **g** sur une île ou sur la côte.
- **h** en ville.

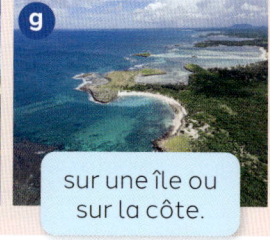

Comment voudrais-tu voyager?

Je voudrais voyager …

- **i** en avion privé.
- **j** en bateau.
- **k** en train.
- **l** à dos de chameau.

Où voudrais-tu loger?

Je voudrais loger …

- **m** sous une tente.
- **n** dans un hôtel de luxe.
- **o** dans une ferme.
- **p** dans un château.

loger to stay

G
The conditional of *vouloir* is used to say what you would like:
je voud**rais** — I would like
tu voud**rais** — you would like
il/elle/on voud**rait** — he/she/we would like

You can use it with an <u>infinitive</u> to say what you would like to do:
Je voudrais <u>voyager</u>. — I would like to travel.

You can also use it with **a noun**:
Je voudrais **des vacances calmes**. — I would like a quiet holiday.

Page 118

Parler 2
In pairs, take turns to ask and answer the <u>four</u> questions from exercise 1.

- Quel type de vacances voudrais-tu?
- Je voudrais <u>des vacances calmes</u>. Et toi, quel type de vacances voudrais-tu?
- Je voudrais <u>des vacances éco-responsables</u>. Où voudrais-tu passer tes vacances idéales?
- Je voudrais passer mes vacances <u>à la campagne</u>. Et toi, …

The **gn** in *monta**gn**e* and *campa**gn**e* is pronounced a bit like the middle of 'onion' in English. It is made up of two sounds: 'n' and 'yuh'.

Listen to the sound and the words. In pairs, try saying '*monta**gn**e, campa**gn**e*' repeatedly, getting faster each time. How many sets can you say correctly?

108 cent-huit

3 Read the texts. Match each picture (a–f) to one of the phrases in bold.

Example: a – *visiter de beaux sites,* b …

Spécial vacances: des vacances idéales!

Je voudrais aller au Maroc avec ma famille parce que je préfère les **vacances culturelles**.

Je voudrais aller en ville parce que je voudrais **acheter des vêtements**.

Et pour me reposer, je voudrais **passer du temps à la piscine**.

Mehdi

Je voudrais aller à l'île de Vanuatu pour passer des **vacances éco-responsables** avec mon ami Alex.

Il voudrait **faire de la natation avec des poissons** dans l'eau claire parce qu'il aime les poissons. Moi aussi! Après, on voudrait **faire la fête sur la plage**!

Chloé

Je voudrais aller à la campagne avec mon amie Zoé car j'aime les **vacances actives**.

Zoé voudrait **faire des activités passionnantes** car elle adore le danger!

On aime aussi le tourisme, donc on voudrait **visiter de beaux sites**.

Jade

4 Re-read the texts in exercise 3. Choose the correct option to complete each sentence.

1 Mehdi would like to go into town because he would like to **buy clothes / visit tourist sites**.
2 He would like to go to the swimming pool in order to **get some exercise / rest**.
3 Chloé would like to go to Vanuatu in order to have **an environmentally responsible holiday / a calm holiday**.
4 Her friend Alex would like to go swimming because he likes **fish / the sea**.
5 Jade would like to go to the countryside because she likes **walking / active holidays**.
6 Jade's friend Zoé would like to do exciting activities because she loves **a challenge / danger**.

5 Listen to the podcast about ideal holidays. Look at pictures a–f in exercise 3. For each speaker, write down (a) the letter of the activity they would like to do, and (b) their reason, in English. (1–4)

6 Write a presentation about your dream holiday. Include:
- what type of holiday you would like to have
- where you would like to go
- what you would like to do.

Give reasons for your preferences.

7 In groups, take turns to read out your presentations.

> There are different ways to explain why you would like to do something.
> - because you like, love or prefer something:
>   … *parce que je préfère* les vacances culturelles.
>   … *car elle adore* le danger.
> - because you would like to do something:
>   … *parce que je voudrais* acheter des vêtements.
> - in order to do something:
>   … *pour* me reposer.

> Je voudrais des vacances … car …
> Je voudrais passer mes vacances … parce que …
> Je voudrais aller … / faire … / visiter … parce que … / pour …

cent-neuf 109

2 On part pour la Corse

- Discussing what you can see and do on holiday
- Forming different types of questions
- Giving advice with *il faut*, *on doit* and *on peut*

Écouter 1 Listen and write down the letter of each holiday top tip. (1–5)

Qu'est-ce qu'il faut faire en Corse?

Il faut …

a essayer les desserts locaux.
b connaître la culture corse. 
c faire une visite en bateau. 
d pratiquer un sport extrême. 
e aller à la plage. 

Écouter 2 Listen again and note down in English the extra advice given. (1–5)

Il faut … On doit … On peut …

aller au marché.
faire du vélo. 
monter une montagne. 
réserver toutes les activités. 
visiter le musée de Bastia. 

tout/toute/tous/toutes all

G To give advice you can use *il faut* (you must), *on doit* (you must) or *on peut* (you can) followed by an infinitive.
il faut faire you must do   *on doit réserver* you must book
on peut aller you can go

Page 118

Lire 3 Translate these sentences into English.

Corte
1 Il faut visiter cette ville pour comprendre l'histoire de la Corse.
2 On peut monter des montagnes.
3 On doit aller au marché pour acheter des souvenirs.
4 Et après, on peut réserver une table à un restaurant pour essayer les desserts traditionnels.

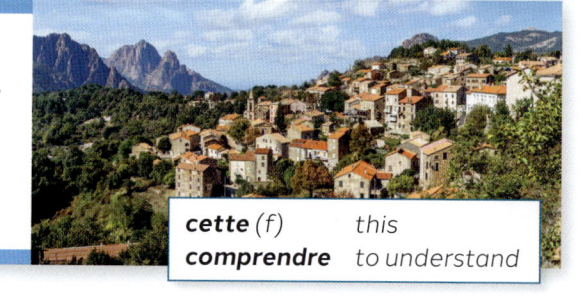

cette (f) this
comprendre to understand

Parler 4 In pairs, take turns to read out the sentences from exercise 3, paying particular attention to your pronunciation of the sound *on/om*. Then listen and check.

Listen and repeat this nasal sound and the words. To make this sound, put your mouth into a round shape and push your lips forward.
on, om
b**on**   m**on**ter   c**om**prendre

110 cent-dix

Module 5

Lire 5 Read the conversation. Copy and complete each question with the correct phrase from the box. Then listen and check.

> à quelle heure   où est   combien coûte l'entrée   est-ce que   quels jours

1. ● ▨ **le château?**
   ■ *Il est près du marché.*
2. ● **Le château est ouvert** ▨ **de la semaine?**
   ■ *Il est ouvert du mardi au dimanche. Il est fermé le lundi.*
3. ● **Le château ouvre et ferme** ▨ **?**
   ■ *Il ouvre à huit heures et ferme à midi.*
4. ● ▨ **pour le château?**
   ■ *L'entrée pour le château coûte trois euros pour les adultes. C'est gratuit pour les enfants.*
5. ● ▨ **les animaux sont acceptés?**
   ■ *Non, les animaux ne sont pas acceptés.*

> **G**
> To ask if something is the case, you can put 'est-ce que' in front of a sentence:
> *C'est ouvert.* (It's open.) →
> **Est-ce que** *c'est ouvert?* (Is it open?)
>
> To ask for other types of information, use question words like:
> *où* (where)
> *combien* (how much or how many)
> *à quelle heure* (at what time)
> *quel/quelle/quels/quelles* (which)
>
> Page 118

Lire 6 Copy out the grid. Re-read the conversation in exercise 5 and complete the first row.

	Location	Days open	Opening time	Closing time	Price	Animals allowed?
1 Castle						
2 Museum						
3 Park						

Écouter 7 Listen and complete the grid from exercise 6 for the conversations about the museum and the park. (2–3)

Parler 8 You are in a tourist information office in Ajaccio, in Corsica. In pairs, choose an attraction and take part in the conversation. Then swap roles and talk about the other attraction.

1. ● [Ask where the attraction is.]
   ■ *C'est …*
2. ● [Ask which days it is open.]
   ■ *C'est ouvert du … au …*
3. ● [Ask about opening times.]
   ■ *… ouvre à … et ferme à …*
4. ● [Ask the entrance price.]
   ■ *L'entrée coûte …*
5. ● [Ask if animals are allowed.]
   ■ *Oui, les animaux sont acceptés. / Non, les animaux ne sont pas acceptés.*

Visitez Ajaccio

La Grande Maison de la Corse
De 10h à 17h30
Ouvert tous les jours
Adultes: 7€
Gratuit pour les enfants et les personnes handicapées
Près de l'office de tourisme

Le Parc Aventure
De 9h à 18h
Ouvert du jeudi au mardi
Enfants: 12€
Adultes: 22€
Près du château

l'office (m) *de tourisme*   tourist information office

cent-onze

3 Le monde en fête

- Talking about festivals
- Using the perfect and imperfect tenses together
- Understanding more complex sentences using *qui*

Les fêtes du monde francophone

Écouter 1 Listen and read. Then answer the questions by writing the letter of the correct festival.

a) Le carnaval à la Martinique
C'est un festival qui se passe en février. Le carnaval dure plusieurs jours et nuits!
Il y a des parades avec des danseurs et il y a beaucoup de touristes dans les rues.
C'est une fête amusante.

b) La fête des goyaviers à la Réunion
C'est un événement qui se passe en juin.
Les chefs préparent des desserts avec des goyaves, qui sont de petits fruits rouges.
Il y a des marchés, des jeux pour les enfants et des concerts. C'est une fête populaire.

c) Le festival international des Masques et des Arts au Burkina Faso
C'est un événement qui se passe en février et en mars.
On écoute de la musique traditionnelle. Il y a des masques qui viennent de divers pays d'Afrique et des spectacles étonnants.
C'est un festival culturel.

le goyavier	*guava tree*
la goyave	*guava (fruit)*
divers(e)	*various*

Which festival …
1 has chefs preparing fruit desserts?
2 has traditional music?
3 lasts several days and nights?
4 features masks from various African countries?
5 has lots of tourists in the streets?
6 is described as a fun festival?
7 has amazing shows?
8 takes place in June?

Écouter 2 Listen to the description of the festival. Choose the correct option to complete each sentence.
1 *La Fête du Citron®* takes place in **February / April**.
2 Chefs prepare **desserts / cakes**.
3 There are sculptures made with yellow and orange **objects / fruits**.
4 Tourists love the **markets / parades**.
5 It's a **popular / fun** festival.

> **G** *Qui* is a relative pronoun that helps you extend your sentences.
> It can be translated as 'who', 'which' or 'that':
> *C'est un festival **qui** se passe en février.*
> It's a festival that takes place in February.
> Page 119

Écrire 3 Write about *Le Festival d'Avignon* using the notes below.

Le Festival d'Avignon
July
- shows
- concerts
- parade
- games for children
Popular and cultural

C'est un festival / une fête qui se passe en	janvier / février / mars …	
Il y a	des	danseurs / concerts. groupes de musique. marchés / masques. jeux pour les enfants. parades / spectacles.
		beaucoup de touristes.
C'est	un festival	amusant / culturel / populaire.
	une fête	amusante / culturelle / populaire.

112 *cent-douze*

Module 5

4 Read the text. Correct the mistake in each of the sentences below. (1–6)

En février dernier, je suis allée chez mon oncle qui habite à la Martinique.

J'étais très contente car c'était le carnaval!

Pendant plusieurs jours, il y avait beaucoup de gens dans les rues.

J'ai vu des danseurs et j'ai écouté de la musique. J'ai aussi dansé, c'était amusant!

Un autre jour, je suis allée au marché. Il y avait beaucoup d'activités.

J'ai mangé du sorbet coco qui est comme une glace. C'était délicieux!

J'ai adoré ma première expérience du carnaval. C'était extraordinaire!
Lola

1 Last February, Lola went to her friend's house in Martinique.
2 For several days, there were lots of people on the beaches.
3 Lola listened to music and played as well.
4 Another day, she went to the park.
5 She didn't enjoy the coconut sorbet.
6 She loved her second visit to the carnival.

Use words like **plusieurs** (several) and **beaucoup de** (lots of) for variety.
Beaucoup is usually followed by **de** unless the noun begins with a vowel or h.

beaucoup **de g**ens   beaucoup **d'a**ctivités

G The **perfect tense** is used to talk about single actions that happened in the past:
Je suis allé(e) chez mon oncle. I went to my uncle's house.

One of the uses of the imperfect tense is to describe what something was like:
J'étais contente. I was happy.
C'était extraordinaire. It was extraordinary.
Il y avait beaucoup de gens. There were lots of people.

Can you find more examples of each tense in the exercise 4 text?

Page 119

---

5 Listen. Then copy and complete the grid in English. (1–2)

	What was there?	What did they do?	What was it like?
1 Dunkirk Carnival			
2 Winter Festival			

6 In pairs, take turns to talk about the two festivals below.

- Est-ce que tu es allé(e) à une fête?
- Oui, je suis allé(e) au … / à la …
- Qu'est-ce qu'il y avait?
- Il y avait …
- Qu'est-ce que tu as fait?
- J'ai mangé … / dansé / vu … / écouté …
- C'était comment?
- C'était …

Le carnaval de Binche
Shows and concerts
Ate local desserts
Fun

Le carnaval de Nice
Dancers and music
Danced
Extraordinary

7 Translate these sentences into French.

Use the imperfect tense.

1 Last April, I went to my aunt's house.
2 It was the Festival of Rice.
3 There was a market and I listened to music in the street.
4 Another evening, I ate a lot of rice. It was delicious!

Use *la fête du riz*.

Use the perfect tense. Think about whether you need to use *avoir* or *être* for each verb.

cent-treize 113

4 Guide de voyage

- Reviewing and booking holiday accommodation
- Using negatives in the imperfect and perfect tenses
- Identifying positive and negative opinions

Lire 1 Read the reviews of the hotel. Write the letter of the correct picture for each of the phrases in bold in the texts.

Comment était l'hôtel?

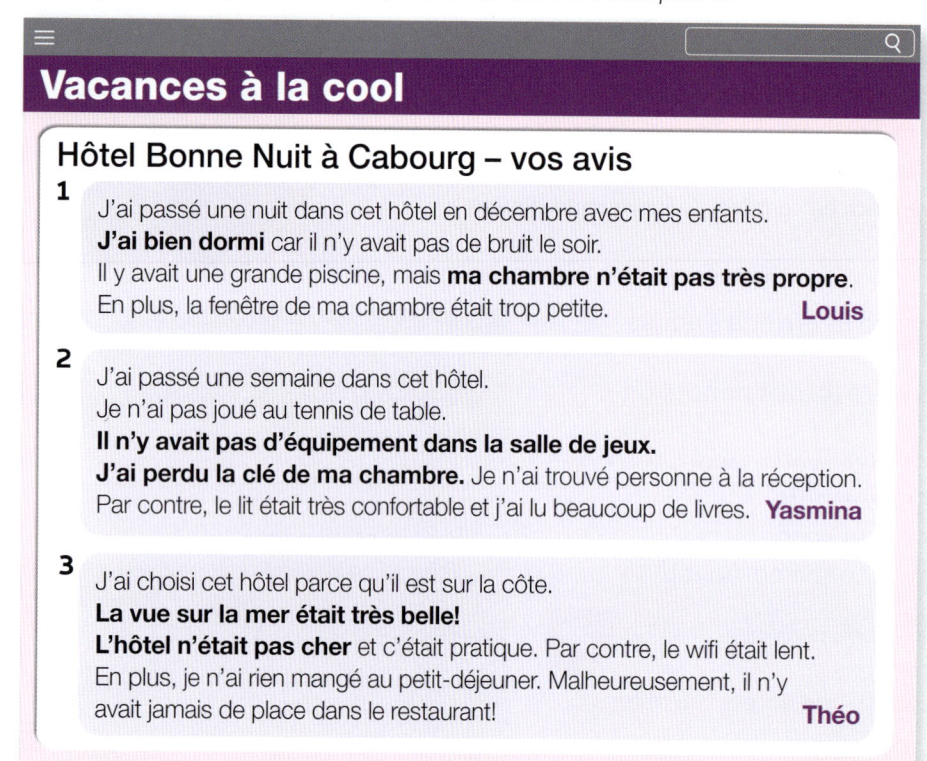

Example: J'ai bien dormi – b; ma chambre n'était pas …

Vacances à la cool

Hôtel Bonne Nuit à Cabourg – vos avis

1 J'ai passé une nuit dans cet hôtel en décembre avec mes enfants. **J'ai bien dormi** car il n'y avait pas de bruit le soir. Il y avait une grande piscine, mais **ma chambre n'était pas très propre**. En plus, la fenêtre de ma chambre était trop petite. — **Louis**

2 J'ai passé une semaine dans cet hôtel. Je n'ai pas joué au tennis de table. **Il n'y avait pas d'équipement dans la salle de jeux.** **J'ai perdu la clé de ma chambre.** Je n'ai trouvé personne à la réception. Par contre, le lit était très confortable et j'ai lu beaucoup de livres. — **Yasmina**

3 J'ai choisi cet hôtel parce qu'il est sur la côte. **La vue sur la mer était très belle!** **L'hôtel n'était pas cher** et c'était pratique. Par contre, le wifi était lent. En plus, je n'ai rien mangé au petit-déjeuner. Malheureusement, il n'y avait jamais de place dans le restaurant! — **Théo**

Lire 2 Re-read the reviews in exercise 1. Then answer the questions below.

Who …
1 spent one week at the hotel?
2 had a window that was too small?
3 found no-one at reception?
4 ate nothing for breakfast?
5 thought there was no noise at night?
6 says there was never space in the restaurant?

> **G**
> In the imperfect tense, negatives go around the verb:
> L'hôtel **n'**était **pas** cher.
> The hotel was **not** expensive.
> Il **n'**y avait **jamais** de place dans le restaurant.
> There was **never** space in the restaurant.
>
> In the perfect tense, most negatives go around the part of *avoir* or *être*:
> je **n'ai pas** joué   I did **not** play
> je **n'ai rien** mangé   I ate **nothing**
> je **ne** suis **jamais** allé   I have **never** been
>
> *Personne* goes after the past participle:
> Je **n'**ai trouvé **personne**. I found **no-one**.
>
> Page 119

Écouter 3 Listen to people talking about their stay in a hotel. Are they positive (**P**) or negative (**N**) about the following things? (1–3)

1 a the breakfast   b the pool
2 a the room   b the restaurant
3 a the bed   b the price

> When you hear a negative, don't assume it means a negative opinion. For example, *il n'y avait pas de bruit* means 'there wasn't any noise', which is a positive opinion in this context.

114 cent-quatorze

Module 5

Parler 4
Listen to these sentences. Then practise saying them with a partner.

> **En** déc**em**bre, j'ai trouvé **un** excell**en**t c**am**ping.
> Les **en**fa**n**ts m**an**gent d**an**s **un** restaur**an**t.

Listen and repeat these two nasal sounds. Try to say them from the back of your throat.

un
en   an   em   am

Écrire 5
Imagine that you have stayed at this hotel. Write a review.
- Say how long you spent in this hotel.
- Say what the hotel and room were like.
- Describe a problem in the hotel.

Hôtel Pause Parfaite

J'ai passé une nuit / deux nuits / une semaine dans cet hôtel.		
L'hôtel	(n') était (pas)	pratique / cher.
Le lit		confortable.
Le wifi		lent.
La vue		belle.
La chambre		propre.
La fenêtre		(trop) petit(e).
Il n'y avait pas	de	place dans le restaurant.
		bruit.
	d'équipement.	
J'ai perdu la clé.		
Je n'ai trouvé personne à la réception.		
Je n'ai rien mangé.		
Je n'ai pas joué.		

Écouter 6
Listen and read. Copy and complete the grid in English. Then listen and complete the grid for the next two conversations. (1–3)

	Number of rooms	Number of people	Number of nights	Question asked – Is there …?
1				

- Bonjour. Je peux vous aider?
- Bonjour. J'ai réservé <u>deux chambres</u> pour <u>deux personnes</u>.
- Pas de problème. C'est pour combien de nuits?
- C'est pour <u>trois nuits</u>. Ça coûte combien?
- Ça coûte cinquante euros par nuit. Je peux voir vos passeports?
- Oui, les voilà. Est-ce qu'il y a <u>une salle de jeux</u> dans l'hôtel?
- Oui, bien sûr.

G The French word for 'in' depends on the context.
- inside something: **dans** ma chambre, **dans** l'hôtel
- in a named town: **à** Cabourg
- in the town centre: **au** centre-ville
- in town: **en** ville

Page 120

Parler 7
In pairs, create two new versions of the dialogue in exercise 6, using the pictures in the boxes.

a) 🛏️ 👤 🌙×4 🍽️

b) 🛏️🛏️ 👤👤 🌙×1 🏖️

Écrire 8
Write an email to book holiday accommodation using the prompts from the box.

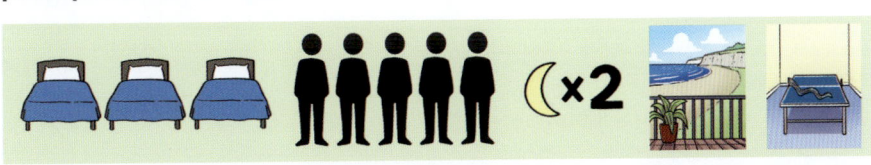

You could use *Bonjour* to start your email and end with *Merci* and *Au revoir*. You could use expressions like *Je voudrais* + an infinitive verb like *réserver*.

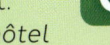

cent-quinze **115**

5 Vive les vacances!

- Talking about staycation activities
- Using a range of tenses
- Using *si* + the present tense + the near future tense

Écouter 1 Listen to the conversations about today's weather. Write the letters of the two correct pictures for each one. (1–4)

Quel temps fait-il aujourd'hui?

a Il fait chaud.
b Il fait froid.
c Il fait beau.
d Il fait mauvais.
e Il y a du soleil.
f Il y a du vent.
g Il pleut.

Lire 2 Read and listen. Then copy and complete the sentences in English.

Ça va bientôt être les vacances! Qu'est-ce qu'on va faire?

J'ai beaucoup d'idées pour les vacances!

- S'il fait beau, je vais faire du vélo à la campagne.
- S'il y a du soleil, je vais organiser un concert au parc avec mes amis. Ça va être super amusant!
- S'il fait chaud, je vais faire du camping car j'adore dormir dans une tente.
- S'il fait mauvais, je vais faire un repas. J'adore les pâtes!
- S'il y a du vent, je vais prendre le train et m'amuser à la plage avec ma famille.
- S'il fait froid, je vais aller au musée avec mon frère parce qu'on aime l'histoire.
- S'il pleut, je vais rester à la maison et je vais faire une appli! Ça va être cool!

1 If the weather is nice, Clément is going to ▇ in the ▇.
2 If it's sunny, he's going to ▇ with his friends.
3 If it's hot, he's going to ▇.
4 If it's bad weather, he's going to ▇.
5 If it's windy, he's going to ▇ and enjoy himself ▇.
6 If it's cold, he's going to ▇ with ▇.
7 If it rains, he's going to ▇ and he's going to ▇.

G To say **what you are going to do** <u>if something happens or is a particular way</u> (for example, the weather), use:
<u>Si</u> + **present tense** + **near future tense**

<u>S'il fait</u> froid, je **vais rester** chez moi.
If it's cold, I am going to stay at home.

Remember that the near future is formed by using the correct part of *aller* + an infinitive.

Page 120

Parler 3 In pairs, adapt the dialogue below to talk about your weekend plans.

- *Qu'est-ce que tu vas faire ce week-end?*
- *S'il fait beau, je vais m'amuser à la plage.*
- *Bonne idée! Et s'il pleut?*
- *Je vais aller au musée.*
- *S'il fait chaud? Qu'est-ce que tu vas faire?*
- …

S'il fait beau / chaud / mauvais / froid,	je vais	aller … faire … prendre … organiser … rester … m'amuser …
S'il y a du vent / du soleil,		
S'il pleut,		

116 cent-seize

Module 5

4 Read the texts. Find the French for the phrases below.

Dorian: Normalement, pendant les grandes vacances, je suis avec ma grand-mère.
L'année dernière, j'ai passé trop de temps sur les réseaux sociaux car il faisait froid. Ce n'était pas bon pour ma santé.
Cette année, je vais apprendre une nouvelle langue. Ça va être génial!

Eva: L'été dernier, j'ai passé des vacances extraordinaires! Il faisait mauvais et je ne suis pas partie en vacances. J'ai passé beaucoup de temps en ville avec mes amis et j'ai adoré ça.
Mais cet été, je vais aller à Paris en train avec ma mère et on va monter à la tour Eiffel. Ça va être intéressant!

Inès: Normalement, je joue au tennis avec mes amies pendant les grandes vacances. C'est amusant.
Un jour, l'été dernier, je suis allée au parc à vélo. Il faisait gris et il y avait du vent et je suis tombée de vélo. Aïe!
Cette année, je vais faire quelque chose de moins actif!

1 I spent too much time
2 it was cold
3 I didn't go on holiday
4 it was grey
5 it was windy
6 I'm going to do something less active

> Use the imperfect tense to describe what the weather was like in the past:
> *Il faisait chaud.* It was hot.
> *Il y avait du soleil.* It was sunny.

> **G** When referring to the present, past and future, you need to use several tenses. For the past, use the imperfect tense for descriptions and the perfect tense for single, completed actions.
> Page 120

5 Re-read the texts in exercise 4. Write down the letters for the two correct pictures for each text. Then decide if each picture refers to an event in the present, in the past or in the future.

Example: Dorian: a – present, ...

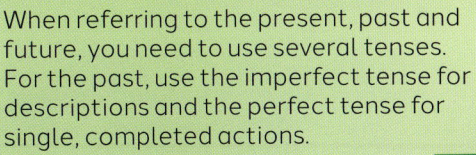

a, b,  c,  d,  e,  f

6 Listen to Lola and Rachid talking about their holidays. Which timeframe do they use to talk about each of the categories below? Write 'past', 'present' or 'future' for each one. (1–6)

Lola 1 accommodation 2 activities 3 transport
Rachid 4 food 5 a problem 6 weather

7 Write a text about your holidays in the past, present and future.

> As in the texts in exercise 4, try to extend your answer by recycling structures and vocabulary that you have met in different contexts.

Normalement,	pendant les grandes vacances,	je reste ... / je vais ... je joue ... / je loge ...	C'est amusant. C'est génial.
L'été dernier, L'année dernière,	j'ai passé	du temps ... mes vacances ...	C'était super. C'était nul.
	j'ai fait ... je suis allé(e) ... je (ne) suis (pas) parti(e) en vacances.		
	il faisait froid / il y avait du vent.		
Cet été, Cette année,	je vais aller ... / je vais faire ... je vais apprendre ...		Ça va être cool / extraordinaire.

cent-dix-sept 117

Grammaire 1

The conditional of *vouloir* (Unit 1, pages 108 and 109)

Lire 1 Read the grammar box on the conditional of *vouloir* on page 108. Then copy out the sentences below, choosing the correct form of the conditional each time.

1 Je **voudrait** / **voudrais** passer des vacances avec mes amis Luc et Lucie.
2 On **voudrais** / **voudrait** passer nos vacances à la campagne.
3 Moi, je **voudrait** / **voudrais** aller en vacances à vélo.
4 Lucie, elle **voudrait** / **voudrais** voyager en train.
5 Luc, il **voudrais** / **voudrait** aller en vacances en bateau.
6 Et toi, où **voudrait** / **voudrais**-tu passer tes vacances idéales?

Giving advice using *il faut*, *on doit* and *on peut* followed by an infinitive (Unit 2, page 110)

Parler 2 Read the grammar box about giving advice with *il faut* (you must), *on doit* (you must) and *on peut* (you can) followed by an infinitive on page 110. Then, in pairs, take turns to be the holidaymaker and the person who works in a tourist information office in Corsica. The holidaymaker says one thing that they like. Their partner then suggests something they *must* or *can* do.

- J'aime l'histoire.
- On peut visiter des musées.
  J'aime la natation …
- …

J'aime J'adore	l'histoire. la natation. le danger. le shopping. les desserts.

Il faut visiter la Corse!
- aller à la plage
- pratiquer un sport extrême
- visiter des musées
- aller au marché
- réserver une table dans un restaurant

Forming questions (Unit 2, page 111)

Lire 3 Read the grammar box on the different ways of forming questions on page 111. Match the question beginnings and endings below, and write the questions out in full. Then translate the questions into English.

1 Le musée ouvre et ferme — ouvert quels jours de la semaine?
2 Combien coûte — est le marché?
3 Où — à quelle heure?
4 Est-ce que les animaux — l'entrée pour le château?
5 Le restaurant est — sont acceptés?

Écouter 4 Listen to the six questions. The answers below are in the wrong order. Write the letter of the correct answer for each question you hear. (1–6)

a Il ouvre à onze heures.
b Le parc est près du château.
c Il ferme à minuit.
d Il est ouvert du jeudi au dimanche.
e Non, les animaux ne sont pas acceptés.
f L'entrée pour le parc est gratuite.

cent-dix-huit

The relative pronoun *qui* (Unit 3, page 112)

5 Re-write each pair of sentences as one sentence. For 1–3, replace the underlined words with *qui*. For 4–6, work out which word or words you should replace.

Example: 1 *J'ai un oncle qui habite en Asie.*

1. J'ai un oncle. <u>Mon oncle</u> habite en Asie.
2. Il y a des chefs. <u>Les chefs</u> préparent des desserts.
3. C'est une fête. <u>La fête</u> dure trois jours.
4. J'ai un ami. Mon ami aime les parades.
5. Il y a des danseurs. Les danseurs viennent d'Afrique.
6. C'est un festival. Le festival se passe en novembre.

> Relative pronouns such as *qui* refer to a noun that has just been mentioned.
>
> *Qui* can be translated as 'who', 'which' or 'that'. You can use it to join two sentences together:
>
> *Il y a un restaurant. Le restaurant s'appelle Bon Appétit.*
>
> *Il y a un restaurant **qui** s'appelle Bon Appétit.*

Using the perfect and imperfect tenses together (Unit 3, page 113)

6 Read the grammar box on using the perfect and imperfect tenses together on page 113. Then copy out the sentences. Circle each imperfect tense verb and underline each perfect tense verb.

1. Je suis allé chez mon oncle, il y avait beaucoup de gens.
2. J'ai écouté de la musique, c'était extraordinaire.
3. J'étais content car il a vu ma famille.
4. Mon amie est allée au marché mais elle était fatiguée.

> To form the imperfect tense, remove the *-ons* from the *nous* form of the verb in the present tense, e.g.
> *regarder* (to watch) → *nous regardons* → *regard-*
> Then add these endings:
> *je regardais*   *tu regardais*   *il/elle/on regardait*
>
> The verb *être* has the stem *ét-*
> *c'était* (it used to be/it was).

> 💡 The imperfect tense is used to talk about what <u>you were doing</u> during a certain period of time:
> *Hier matin, entre 7 heures et 9 heures, <u>je travaillais</u>.*
> Yesterday morning, between 7 and 9 a.m., <u>I was working</u>.

7 Sabrina the detective wants to know what these people were doing last night between 8 and 10 p.m. Read their alibis and translate them into English.

> Qu'est-ce que tu faisais hier soir entre 20 heures et 22 heures?

1. Je jouais au football au parc avec Sadio Mané.
2. Je chantais en concert avec Angèle.
3. Je regardais un film au cinéma avec Aïssa Maïga.
4. J'organisais un concert avec le groupe Teriya.
5. J'écrivais des chansons avec Grand Corps Malade.
6. Je luttais pour l'égalité avec Rachel Keke.

Negatives in the imperfect and perfect tenses (Unit 4, page 114)

8 Read the grammar box about negatives in the imperfect and perfect tenses on page 114. Listen, then copy and complete the sentences with the missing negatives. Translate the sentences into English. (1–8)

1. Ce ▢ était ▢ amusant.
2. Il ▢ y avait ▢ à l'hôtel.
3. Je ▢ étais ▢ patient.
4. Il ▢ y avait ▢ dans la chambre.
5. Elle ▢ a trouvé ▢.
6. Il ▢ a ▢ fait.
7. Je ▢ ai ▢ bien dormi.
8. Il ▢ est ▢ allé au marché.

> Remember that *ne* shortens to *n'* in front of a vowel.

Grammaire 2

Saying 'in' (Unit 4, page 115)

Lire 1 Copy out each sentence and complete it with the correct word for 'in'.
1 Il y a des parades ___ la rue.
2 Il a fait du vélo ___ campagne.
3 Ma mère habite ___ montagne.
4 Il y a un musée ___ centre-ville.
5 J'achète des souvenirs ___ ville.
6 Il passe une semaine ___ Paris.

> The word for 'in' depends on where you are talking about:
> - inside something: **dans** une chambre
> - in the countryside or mountains: **à la** campagne, **à la** montagne
> - in the town centre: **au** centre-ville
> - in town: **en** ville
> - in a named town: **à** Paris

Using *si* + the present tense + the near future tense (Unit 5, page 116)

Écrire 2 Put the words in the correct order to make sentences. Then write the letter of the correct weather condition for each sentence.

Example: 1 S'il fait beau, je vais jouer au basket. b

1 beau fait s'il jouer je au vais basket
2 fait s'il froid visiter vas le tu musée
3 s'il chaud fait faire elle du va vélo
4 s'il du y a soleil s'amuser au va on parc
5 fait acheter vais des mauvais souvenirs s'il je
6 on faire du pleut va camping ne s'il pas
7 du aller s'il au va vent y concert on a

a b  c  d  e  f  g

> *Si* + weather phrase in the present tense, + near future tense
>
> When using a reflexive verb, remember to make the reflexive pronoun agree with the person doing the action:
> *je* vais **m'**amuser   **on** va **s'**amuser

Talking about the present, past and future (Unit 5, page 117)

Écouter 3 Listen and write down which of the verbs in bold you hear each time. Then identify the name of the tense. (1–8)

Example: 1 Il faisait – imperfect

1 **Il faisait** / **Il fait** tout le temps froid.
2 **Je vais jouer** / **Je joue** en ligne chez moi.
3 **Je voyage** / **J'ai voyagé** à vélo ou en bus.
4 **Je vais manger** / **J'ai mangé** des pâtes.
5 **On chante** / **On va chanter** ensemble.
6 **Je suis tombé** / **Je vais tomber** de cheval.
7 **C'était** / **C'est** très amusant.
8 **On s'amuse** / **On va s'amuser** en famille.

> *le cheval* — horse
>
> When referring to the present, you usually use the **present tense**.
> When referring to the future, you usually use the **near future tense** (*aller* + an infinitive).
> When referring to the past, you need to choose between the **perfect tense** and the **imperfect tense**.
> - Use the **perfect tense** for completed actions.
> - Use the **imperfect tense** for descriptions and to say what was happening or what used to happen.

120 cent-vingt

Module 5

Écrire 4 Copy out the sentences, filling in the gaps by translating the verbs in brackets into French.
1 Normalement, pendant les grandes vacances, ▭ chez moi. (*I stay*)
2 ▭ au parc avec mes amis. (*I go*)
3 ▭ au football. (*We play*)
4 L'année dernière, ▭ du temps avec ma famille à la campagne. (*I spent*)
5 ▭ à la plage. (*I went*)
6 Mais ▭ très froid. (*it was*)
7 Cet été, ▭ deux semaines chez mon ami. (*I'm going to spend*)
8 ▭ ! (*We are going to have fun*)

C'est parti!

Parler 5 In pairs, play 'trapdoor'.
- Partner A: in secret, select one of the three options for each of numbers 1 to 7 in the sentences below.
- Partner B: your goal is to read out the sentences from start to finish, filling in gaps 1 to 7 with the options that your partner chose. Start to read out the story. Each time you get to a number, make a choice. If you read out what your partner selected, you can continue reading. If you don't, Partner A shouts 'trapdoor!' and you have to go back to the beginning.
- Then swap roles!

Je voudrais passer mes vacances idéales **1** en ville / à la campagne / à la montagne avec mes amis et on voudrait **2** aller à la plage. / faire du sport. / visiter de beaux sites.

En vacances, **3** on peut / on doit / il faut connaître une culture différente.

L'année dernière, je suis allé(e) à une fête. C'est une fête qui **4** se passe en mars. / dure une semaine. / est célèbre.

Je n'ai **5** rien mangé / pas dansé / trouvé personne **6** parce qu'il y avait du vent. / parce qu'il faisait froid. / parce que c'était ennuyeux.

Cet été, s'il fait chaud, je vais **7** retourner / m'amuser / danser à la fête.

Lire 6 Translate the sentences from exercise 5, with your own options for each of gaps 1 to 7, into English.

cent-vingt-et-un 121

Module 5 — Contrôle de lecture et d'écoute

Reading

Lire 1 *A French hotel.* Read the extract from a hotel brochure.

> L'hôtel est dans une ancienne école. Il y a un beau jardin de cent mètres et tout le monde adore la large porte d'entrée.
>
> Il n'y a pas de **brasserie**, mais on peut commander quelque chose à manger car il y a un service de chambre.

a Complete the sentences below. For each sentence, write the correct letter (A–C).

   (i) The hotel is in an old …
      A school.   B hospital.   C station.

   (ii) All the visitors love the …
      A clock.   B balcony.   C door.

b Which of these is the best translation for the word *brasserie*? Write down the correct letter.

   A swimming pool   B tennis court   C restaurant

Lire 2 *Travelling.* Read these comments from Ahmed and Léa on an internet forum. Make notes **in English** under the headings below. You do not need to write in full sentences.

> **#Ahmed#**
> Quand je suis en vacances, j'aime apprendre un nouveau sport ou une nouvelle langue. Je ne voudrais pas passer trop de temps à la piscine. Je voudrais voyager pour visiter les sites pour les touristes et pour me faire de nouveaux amis.

> **#Léa#**
> À l'étranger, moi et mon ami, nous aimons manger des fromages locaux et des desserts traditionnels. En vacances, on peut se reposer, mais pas moi – je préfère être active. Voyager, c'est un moyen de comparer les cultures et de sortir de la routine.

a Ahmed
   (i) One thing Ahmed likes to learn
   (ii) One reason he would like to travel

b Léa
   (i) One thing Léa likes to eat on holiday
   (ii) One reason she would like to travel

> There is more than one correct answer for each question. But watch out for negatives, like *je ne voudrais pas* or *pas moi*, which completely change the meaning of the sentence.

3 A food festival. Translate the following sentences **into English**.

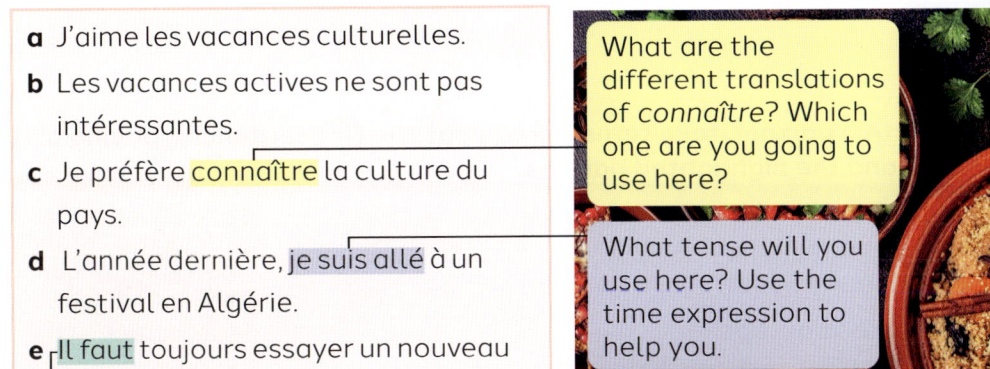

a J'aime les vacances culturelles.
b Les vacances actives ne sont pas intéressantes.
c Je préfère connaître la culture du pays.
d L'année dernière, je suis allé à un festival en Algérie.
e Il faut toujours essayer un nouveau type de cuisine.

What are the different translations of connaître? Which one are you going to use here?

What tense will you use here? Use the time expression to help you.

Think carefully about how to translate this impersonal verb.

Listening

4 Transport. Yanis, Myriam and Thomas are talking about transport to go on holiday. What do they say? Listen to the recording and, for each sentence, write down the correct option (A–C).

a Yanis's favourite way to go on holiday is …
   A by car.   B by plane.   C by train.
b When he's older, Yanis thinks he will go on holiday …
   A by plane.   B by car.   C by train.
c According to Myriam, her journey last year was …
   A very expensive.   B too long.   C good for the environment.
d On holiday, Thomas travelled by …
   A horse.   B bike.   C boat.

Which timeframes do you hear when Yanis talks about his favourite means of transport? Is he just talking about now?

You are going to hear each of these options, but which one is linked to Myriam's journey last year?

5 A weather forecast. You hear this weather report for the region where you are staying on holiday. What does it say? Write down the word for the gap in each sentence, using a word from the box. There are more words than gaps.

a In the morning, it's going to be ___.
b The weather is going to be nice in the ___.
c The weather is going to be ___ in the south.

cold   sunny   hot   west
north   east   south

6 Dictation. You are going to hear someone talking about a campsite.

a Sentences 1–3: write down the missing words. For each gap, you will write one word **in French**.

  1 C'est ___ les ___.
  2 Au camping, il y a une ___ et des ___.
  3 J'adore le ___ de ___.

b Sentences 4–6: write down the full sentences that you hear, **in French**.

You can't usually hear if a noun is singular or plural. Look at the article (un/une/des/le/la/l'/les) to help you decide.

In sentences 4 and 5, beware of liaisons.

cent-vingt-trois

Module 5 Contrôle oral

Read aloud

Parler 1 Look at this task card. With a partner, take turns to read out the five sentences, paying attention to the underlined letters and the highlighted liaisons.

> Eva, your Swiss friend, has emailed you to tell you about the type of accommodation she prefers.
>
> Read out the text below to your teacher.
>
> On est en vacances.
> J'aime dormir dans un hôtel confortable.
> Il y a beaucoup de monde.
> À mon avis, il faut réserver une chambre.
> Quand il fait trop chaud, le camping est une mauvaise décision.

Take extra care with how you pronounce the underlined sounds:
- o, au, ô
- on.

Remember that in this text the *h* is silent.

Don't forget to make the liaisons by sounding the last consonant and linking it to the next word.

Écouter 2 Listen and check your pronunciation.

Parler 3 Listen to the teacher asking the two follow-up questions. Translate each question **into English** and prepare your own answers **in French**. Then listen again and respond to the teacher.

Role play

Parler 4 Look at the role-play card and prepare what you are going to say.

> **Setting:** At the campsite
>
> **Scenario:**
> - You are at a campsite in France.
> - The teacher will play the part of the employee and will speak first.
> - The teacher will ask questions **in French** and you must answer **in French**.
> - Say a few words or a short phrase/sentence for each prompt. One-word answers are not sufficient to gain full marks.
>
> **Task:**
> 1 Say how long you would like to stay.
> 2 Say how many people it is for.
> 3 Say why you are in France.
> 4 Say what you want to do in the area.
> 5 Ask about facilities at the campsite.

E.g. start with *Je voudrais*.

You could use *Je veux* ... followed by an infinitive.

Use *C'est pour* ...

You could use *Est-ce qu'il y a* ...

Parler 5 Practise what you have prepared. Then, using your notes, listen and respond to the teacher.

Écouter 6 Now listen to Fathia doing the role-play task. **In English**, note down (a) how she **answers** the questions for task prompts 1, 2, 3 and 4, and (b) what question she **asks** for task prompt 5.

124 *cent-vingt-quatre*

Picture task

Écouter 7 Look at the exam card below and read the **first part** of the task. Then listen to Camille describing the picture. Answer the questions **in English**.

a In Camille's opinion, where are the four people in the picture? Do you agree?
b What does she say about the person in the foreground?
c What does she think the other people are doing? Do you agree?

Describe this picture.

Your description must cover:
- people
- location
- activity.

When you have finished your description, you will be asked **two questions** relating to the picture. Say a short phrase/sentence in response to each question. One-word answers will not be sufficient to gain full marks.

You will then move on to a **conversation** on the broader thematic context of **Travel and tourism**.

During the conversation, you will be asked questions in the present, past and future tenses. Your responses should be as **full and detailed** as possible.

> To talk about a group of similar people, you can use prompts to set them apart – e.g. *la première fille* (the first girl), *la deuxième fille* (the second girl), *l'autre fille* (the other girl), *la dernière fille* (the last girl).

Parler 8 Prepare your own description of the picture, mentioning **people, location** and **activity**. Then, with a partner, take turns to describe the picture.

> Sur la photo, il y a ...

Parler 9 Read the **second part** of the task. Then listen to the two follow-up questions and respond to the teacher. Remember: you only need to give a short answer to each one.

Écouter 10 Read the **third part** of the task. The teacher asks Camille: *Qu'est-ce que tu as fait pendant les grandes vacances l'année dernière?* Listen and write down **in English** what she did, and her opinion about it.

Écouter 11 Listen to Camille answering the question: *Quel type de vacances voudrais-tu?*

Write down in English the following details of Camille's ideal holiday:

a Where?   b Why?   c Who with?   d For how long?

Listen again and write down <u>three</u> examples where Camille uses the conditional of *vouloir* + an infinitive.

Parler 12 Prepare your own answers to the Module 5 questions on page 227. Your responses should be as **full and detailed** as possible. Then practise with a partner.

Module 5 Contrôle écrit

80–90 word writing task

1 Look at this writing exam task and then, <u>for each</u> bullet point:

1 think about what vocabulary you have learned which you could use in your answer. For example:
   - **nouns** and **verbs** to talk about holiday activities and problems
   - **verbs of opinion** and **adjectives** to explain your point of view
   - language for **narrating a story** about what went wrong
   - *je voudrais* + **infinitive** to express how you **would like** to spend your summer holidays.
2 write down <u>three or four</u> ideas for what you could write about.
3 write down which tense(s) you will need to use in your answer.

> Write about the summer holidays for a forum.
>
> You **must** include the following points:
> - how you usually spend your summer holiday
> - your opinion on (the length of) the summer holiday
> - a disaster that happened during your last holiday
> - your ideal way to spend your summer holiday.
>
> Write your answer **in French**. You should aim to write between 80 and 90 words.

Make sure your ideas are linked and that you write a coherent piece of writing (a piece that makes sense as a whole).

2 Read Sarah's answer to the exam task. Answer questions 1–5 in the coloured shapes.

2 This phrase shows a **variety of vocabulary**. What does it mean? Find <u>two</u> more examples.

1 Which connective could she use here to form an **extended sentence**? What other connectives does she use?

3 How could she **avoid repetition** by using an alternative phrase here?

4 This is an example of **complex language**. What does it mean? Find <u>three</u> more examples from the text.

5 Which **tense** is this? What other examples can you find? Does she use any other tenses?

> Salut!
>
> Normalement, je reste en Angleterre en été. Les vacances d'été à l'étranger sont chères.
>
> Je pense que les vacances d'été sont trop longues, mais en réalité, six semaines sans collège, c'est génial!
>
> L'été dernier, on a eu un problème. Nous sommes arrivés à notre maison de vacances, mais il y avait une autre famille! Ma mère a téléphoné à l'entreprise de vacances. C'était la mauvaise adresse!
>
> Mes vacances idéales? Je voudrais visiter un pays francophone car je voudrais parler une autre langue.

3 Read Sarah's answer again. Answer the following questions.
   a Why does Sarah's family normally stay in England in the summer?
   b What does she enjoy about the long summer break?
   c What disaster happened to her family on their last holiday?
   d Where would she like to spend her ideal holiday and why?

126 *cent-vingt-six*

Module 5

Écrire 4 **Prepare your own answer to the 80–90 word writing task in exercise 1.**
- Think about how you can develop your answer for each bullet point.
- Look back at your notes from exercises 1 and 2.
- Look at the 'Challenge checklist' and consider how you can show off your French!
- Write a **brief** plan and organise your answer into paragraphs.
- Write your answer and then carefully check the accuracy of what you have written.

Challenge checklist

🌶️	✓ Past, present and future timeframes ✓ Connectives / time phrases / sequencers ✓ Some extended sentences ✓ Different opinion phrases
🌶️🌶️	✓ A wider range of tenses (e.g. conditional of *vouloir*) ✓ Different persons of the verb (e.g. he/she/it) ✓ Weather phrases (e.g. *il fait …*) ✓ A wide range of interesting vocabulary (e.g. *francophone, à l'étranger*)
🌶️🌶️🌶️	✓ The perfect tense and imperfect tense together ✓ Complex language (e.g. *sans*, reflexive verbs) ✓ Using *nous* and *on* ✓ More varied connectives (*mais en réalité …*)

Translation

Écrire 5 **Complete the gaps with a word from the box and translate the whole sentence into English. There are more words than gaps.**

> veux   faut   peut   dansé   fait   y   peux

a Il ___ a beaucoup de choses à faire dans ma région.
b En hiver, il ___ froid.
c En vacances, on ___ connaître la culture du pays.
d L'année dernière, j'ai ___ à une fête.
e En vacances, il ___ essayer les desserts locaux.

Écrire 6 **Translate the following five sentences into French.**

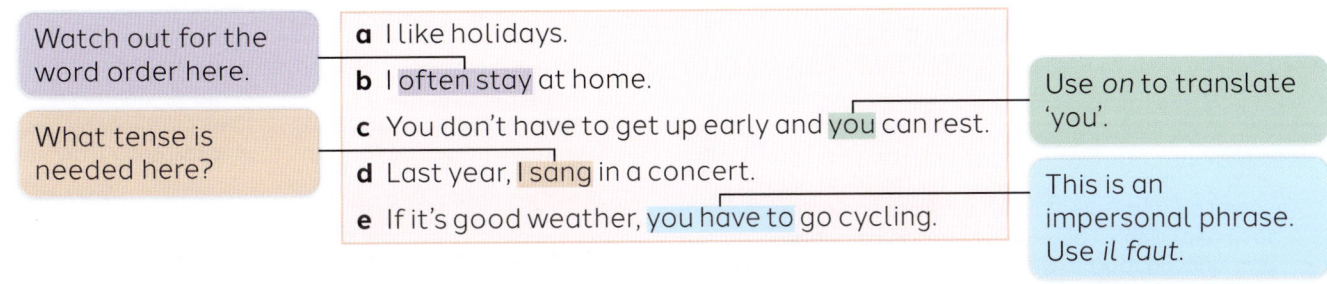

Watch out for the word order here.
What tense is needed here?

a I like holidays.
b I often stay at home.
c You don't have to get up early and you can rest.
d Last year, I sang in a concert.
e If it's good weather, you have to go cycling.

Use on to translate 'you'.
This is an impersonal phrase. Use il faut.

Module 5 Vocabulaire

Key:
bold = this word will appear in higher exams only
* = this word is not on the vocabulary list but you may use it in your own sentences

Voudrais-tu voyager? (pages 106–107)

Pourquoi voudrais-tu voyager?	Why would you like to travel?
Je voudrais voyager pour …	I would like to travel to …
apprendre une nouvelle langue / un nouveau sport.	learn a new language / sport.
connaître une culture différente.	get to know a different culture.
me faire de nouveaux amis.	make new friends.
me reposer.	rest. (relax.)
sortir de la *routine.	escape the routine.
Où voudrais-tu passer tes vacances?	Where would you like to spend your holiday?
Je voudrais passer mes vacances …	I would like to spend my holiday …
au camping.	at a campsite.
à l'hôtel.	at a hotel.
à la maison.	at home.
dans le village.	in the village.
C'est où?	Where is it?
Qu'est-ce que c'est?	What is it?
C'est …	It is …
un camping avec des logements étonnants.	a campsite with amazing accommodation.
un hôtel-château au cœur d'une vieille ville.	a castle hotel in the heart of an old town.
une maison historique et confortable.	a historic and comfortable house.
un village calme sur l'eau.	a quiet village on the water.
Qu'est-ce qu'il y a là-bas?	What is there?
Il y a …	There is/are …
un grand choix de restaurants.	a large choice of restaurants.
un grand jardin.	a big garden.
une belle vue sur la campagne.	a beautiful view of the countryside.
une piscine.	a swimming pool.
des *aires de jeux pour enfants.	play areas for children.
des chambres confortables.	comfortable bedrooms.
des terrains de sport.	sports grounds.
Qu'est-ce qu'on peut faire?	What can you do?
On peut …	You can …
être près de la nature.	be close to nature.
s'amuser en famille sur la côte.	have fun as a family on the coast.
se couper du monde.	switch off from the world.
se reposer.	rest. (relax.)

Des vacances de rêve (pages 108–109)

Quel type de vacances voudrais-tu?	What type of holiday would you like?
Je voudrais …	I would like …
des vacances calmes.	a quiet holiday.
des vacances *éco-responsables.	an eco-friendly holiday.
des vacances culturelles.	a cultural holiday.
des vacances actives.	an active holiday.
Où voudrais-tu passer tes vacances idéales?	Where would you like to spend your ideal holiday?
Je voudrais passer mes vacances …	I would like to spend my holiday …
à la campagne.	in the countryside.
à la montagne.	in the mountains.
sur une île ou sur la côte.	on an island or on the coast.
en ville.	in a town.
Comment voudrais-tu voyager?	How would you like to travel?
Je voudrais voyager …	I would like to travel …
en avion privé.	in a private plane.
en bateau / en train.	by boat / by train.
Où voudrais-tu *loger?	Where would you like to stay?
Je voudrais *loger …	I would like to stay …
sous une tente.	in a tent.
dans un hôtel de *luxe / un château / une ferme.	in a luxury hotel / a castle / a farm.
Il/Elle voudrait …, parce qu'il/elle préfère … car il/elle adore …	He/She would like to …, because he/she prefers … as he/she loves …
acheter des vêtements.	to buy clothes.
faire des activités passionnantes.	to do exciting activities.
faire de la natation avec des poissons.	to swim with fish.
passer du temps à la piscine.	to spend time at the swimming pool.
visiter de beaux sites.	to visit beautiful sites.
Je voudrais … pour me reposer.	I would like to … (in order) to rest (relax).

On part pour la Corse (pages 110–111)

Qu'est-ce qu'il faut faire en *Corse?	What must you do in Corsica?
Il faut … / On doit …	You must …
On peut …	You can …
essayer les desserts locaux.	try the local desserts.
connaître la culture *corse.	get to know Corsican culture.
faire une visite en bateau.	go on a boat trip.
pratiquer un sport extrême.	practise an extreme sport.
aller à la plage.	go to the beach.
aller au marché.	go to the market.
faire du vélo.	go cycling.
monter une montagne.	climb a mountain.
réserver toutes les activités.	book all the activities.
visiter le musée de *Bastia.	visit the Bastia museum.
Où est le château / la piscine?	Where is the castle / swimming pool?
Il/Elle est ouvert(e) quels jours de la semaine?	Which days of the week is it open?
Il/Elle ouvre et ferme à quelle heure?	What time does it open and close?

Combien coûte l'entrée pour le château?	How much does entry for the castle cost?	Est-ce que les animaux sont acceptés?	Are animals allowed?

Le monde en fête (pages 112–113)

C'est un festival / une fête qui se passe en (janvier).	It is a festival that happens in (January).	il y avait …	there was/were …
Il y a des …	There are …	beaucoup d'activités.	lots of activities.
danseurs / concerts.	dancers / concerts.	beaucoup de gens.	lots of people.
groupes de musique.	music groups.	de la musique dans la rue.	music in the street.
jeux pour les enfants.	games for children.	Qu'est-ce que tu as fait?	What did you do?
marchés / *masques.	markets / masks.	J'ai mangé … / dansé / écouté …	I ate … / danced / listened to …
*parades / spectacles.	parades / shows.	Un autre jour / soir, j'ai entendu … / vu …	Another day / evening, I heard … / saw …
Il y a beaucoup de touristes.	There are lots of tourists.	C'était comment?	How was it?
C'est un événement / une fête …	It is a(n) … event / festival.	C'était …	It was …
amusant(e) / culturel(le).	fun / cultural	amusant.	fun.
En (avril) dernier, je suis allé(e) chez ma tante / mon oncle.	Last (April), I went to my aunt / uncle's house.	délicieux.	delicious.
C'était (la fête du riz / le *carnaval).	It was (the Festival of Rice / the carnival).	extraordinaire.	extraordinary.
Qu'est-ce qu'il y avait?	What was there?	J'ai adoré ma première expérience (du festival / de la fête).	I loved my first experience (of the festival).
Pendant plusieurs jours, …	For several days …		

Guide de voyage (pages 114–115)

Comment était l'hôtel?	What was the hotel like?	Il n'y avait pas de bruit le soir.	There was no noise in the evening.
J'ai passé une nuit / deux nuits / une semaine dans cet hôtel.	I spent a night / two nights / a week in this hotel.	Il n'y avait pas d'équipement (dans la salle de jeux).	There was no equipment (in the games room).
L'hôtel …	The hotel …	Il n'y avait jamais de place dans le restaurant.	There was never space in the restaurant.
Le lit / Le *wifi …	The bed / wifi …	J'ai bien dormi.	I slept well.
La vue (sur la mer) / La chambre / La fenêtre … était / n'était pas …	The (sea) view / bedroom / window … was / was not …	J'ai perdu la clé de ma chambre.	I lost my room key.
beau/belle.	beautiful.	Je n'ai trouvé personne à la *réception.	I found no-one at reception.
cher/chère.	expensive.	Je n'ai rien mangé (au petit-déjeuner).	I ate nothing (at breakfast).
confortable.	comfortable.	Je n'ai pas joué (au tennis de table).	I did not play (table tennis).
lent(e).	slow.		
(trop) petit(e).	(too) small.		
pratique.	practical.		
propre.	clean.		

Vive les vacances! (pages 116–117)

Quel temps fait-il aujourd'hui?	What is the weather like today?	je vais à la campagne.	I go to the countryside.
Il fait / faisait …	It is / was …	je joue au tennis.	I play tennis.
chaud / froid.	hot / cold.	je *loge dans un hôtel.	I stay in a hotel.
beau / mauvais.	nice / bad weather.	L'été dernier, / L'année dernière, …	Last summer, / Last year, …
Il y a / avait …	It is / was …	j'ai passé du temps / mes vacances …	I spent time / my holidays …
du soleil / du vent.	sunny / windy.	j'ai fait …	I did …
Il pleut.	It is raining.	je suis allé(e) …	I went …
Qu'est-ce qu'on va faire?	What are we going to do?	je suis parti(e) / je ne suis pas parti(e) en vacances.	I went / I didn't go on holiday.
Qu'est-ce que tu vas faire ce week-end?	What are you going to do this weekend?	Cet été, / Cette année, …	This summer, / This year, …
S'il fait beau / froid …	If it's nice / cold weather …	je vais …	I am going to …
je vais …	I am going to …	aller à Paris.	go to Paris.
aller au musée.	go to the museum.	faire quelque chose de plus / moins actif.	do something more / less active.
faire du vélo.	go cycling.	apprendre une nouvelle langue.	learn a new language.
prendre un train …	take a train …		
organiser un concert.	organise a concert.	Ça va bientôt être les vacances!	It is going to be the holidays soon!
rester chez moi.	stay at home.		
m'amuser à la plage.	have fun at the beach.		
Normalement, pendant les grandes vacances, …	Normally, during the summer holidays, …		

Modules 1–5 Révisions de grammaire 1

Using different articles (Pages 58, 84 and 94)

1 Copy and complete these sentences with the correct definite article (*le/la/l'/les*) or indefinite article (*un/une/des*).

Example: 1 Ma matière préférée, c'est l'histoire.

1 Ma matière préférée, c'est ___ histoire.
2 Sur la photo, il y a ___ maison.
3 Quand j'étais jeune, ma matière préférée était ___ musique.
4 ___ parc est ouvert tous les jours.
5 Il n'y avait pas beaucoup d'activités pour ___ jeunes.
6 ___ rendez-vous est à dix heures.

2 Copy and complete the sentences, choosing the correct partitive article to complete each one.

1 À l'avenir, je vais faire **du / de la / des** sport chaque jour.
2 Le vendredi, je mange **du / de l' / des** poisson.
3 Tu as acheté **du / de la / de** viande au marché?
4 Il y a beaucoup **du / de / des** plages au Portugal.
5 Je ne bois jamais **du / de l' / d'** eau.

> After a <u>negative</u> or a <u>quantity</u>, just use *de* (*d'* before a vowel).

Choosing the correct word for 'in' (Pages 115 and 120)

3 Copy out the parallel translations, completing the missing words.

1	Je voudrais dormir ___ une ferme.	I ___ ___ to sleep in a ___.
2	Elle a trouvé un portable ___ la salle de classe?	Did she ___ a ___ ___ in the classroom?
3	Tu achetais des fruits au marché ___ ville?	Did you used to ___ fruit at the ___ in ___?
4	Est-ce qu'il a passé ses vacances ___ Espagne?	Did he ___ his ___ in ___?
5	As-tu visité un musée ___ Maroc?	___ you ___ a ___ in Morocco?

> There are several words for 'in'.
> - *au* + masculine country, or <u>in</u> the town centre
> - *en* + feminine country, or <u>in</u> town
> - *à* + village/town/city
> - *dans* – inside something

Comparative adjectives (Pages 61 and 70)

4 Copy and complete the comparative sentences with the correct adjective from the box.

1 La musique est plus ___ que l'anglais.
2 À mon avis, TikTok est moins ___ que Facebook.
3 Mon père trouve les émissions de sport plus ___ que les informations.
4 Je pense que les voyages en bateau sont aussi ___ que les voyages en train.

> agréables
> passionnantes
> amusante
> ennuyeux

> The comparative adjective needs to agree with the <u>first</u> noun mentioned.

5 Translate the sentences into English.

1 Ma sœur est plus intelligente que mes frères.
2 Le lit à l'hôtel était moins confortable que mon lit.
3 Le déjeuner est aussi important que le petit-déjeuner.
4 Tu trouves Netflix moins cher qu'un film au cinéma?

130 cent-trente

Révisions de grammaire 1 — Modules 1–5

Indefinite adjectives

6 Copy and complete the sentences with the French translation of the indefinite adjectives in brackets.

1 J'ai une heure de devoirs pour ▨ matière. *(each, every)*
2 Le couscous est bon, mais j'aime ▨ les plats. *(all)*
3 ▨ les fêtes sont très amusantes pour ma famille. *(all)*
4 Est-ce que tu regardes des vidéos sur TikTok ▨ soir? *(each, every)*
5 Elle va ▨ le temps à la plage avec son chien. *(all)*
6 Pendant les vacances, tu vas à la piscine ▨ jour? *(each, every)*

> Indefinite adjectives talk about people or things in a general way, without being specific.
> chaque — each, every
> tout/toute/tous/toutes — all, the whole
>
> A definite article isn't needed with *chaque* but is needed with *tout*.
> chaque jour
> tous **les** jours

Direct object pronouns and indirect object pronouns (Pages 40, 46, 67 and 72)

7 Copy out the sentences. Circle the object pronoun and write if it is a direct (D) or indirect (I) object pronoun.

Example: 1 Je (la) regarde tous les soirs. → D

1 Je la regarde tous les soirs.
2 Nous l'avons chanté quatre fois.
3 Il ne lui envoie pas de carte d'anniversaire.
4 Il va la voir en concert demain soir.
5 Je vous ai vu au centre commercial.

> Object pronouns go before the verb.
> In the perfect tense, they go **before** the auxiliary verb (*avoir* or *être*).
> In the near future tense, they go **before** the infinitive.

8 Re-write the sentences, replacing the underlined noun with the direct object pronoun in brackets. Make sure you put the pronoun in the correct place in the sentence.

1 Vous cherchez <u>la salle de classe</u>? (la)
2 Je vais acheter <u>la voiture</u>. (l')
3 Elle a attendu <u>moi</u>. (m')
4 Je lis <u>le journal</u> tous les jours. (le)

9 Replace the underlined noun with the indirect object pronoun in brackets. Make sure you put the pronoun in the correct place in the sentence.

1 Il donne un gâteau <u>à moi</u>. (me)
2 Tu envoyais des cartes d'anniversaire <u>à ta sœur</u>? (lui)
3 Elle parlait <u>à toi</u> avec respect. (te)
4 Le prof donne trop de devoirs <u>à vous</u>. (vous)

Expressions with *avoir* (Page 88)

10 Read the sentences and match up the correct halves. Then translate them into English.

1 J'ai froid et je …
2 Elle avait faim …
3 Tu n'as pas chaud …
4 Ils vont avoir …

a … donc elle a mangé un sandwich.
b … très soif après le match.
c … ne veux pas aller dehors.
d … à la plage?

> There are lots of useful expressions using *avoir* in French, some of which are the equivalent of 'to be' expressions in English.
> avoir chaud — to be hot
> avoir froid — to be cold
> avoir faim — to be hungry
> avoir soif — to be thirsty

cent-trente-et-un 131

Modules 1–5 Révisions de grammaire 2

Modal verbs (Pages 87 and 95)

Modal verbs include *pouvoir*, *vouloir* and *devoir*. They are all followed by an infinitive.

Je veux acheter un gâteau. — I want to buy a cake.
Je peux sortir ce samedi. — I can go out this Saturday.
Je dois faire mes devoirs. — I have to do my homework.

Savoir is also a modal verb.

savoir – to know (how to)	
je sais	nous savons
tu sais	vous savez
il/elle/on sait	ils/elles savent

Lire 1 Separate out the words to make accurate sentences. Then match them up with the English translations.

1 tupeuxfairetesdevoirsplustard
2 ellenesaitpasdanser
3 jeneveuxpassallerauconcert
4 nousdevonssortircesoir
5 ildoitparleràsongrandpère

a She doesn't know how to dance.
b He has to speak to his grandfather.
c You can do your homework later.
d I don't want to go to the concert.
e We have to go out tonight.

Écrire 2 Copy and complete the sentences with the correct form of the verb in brackets.

1 Tu ___ écrire un article. (*devoir*)
2 Il ___ voyager en avion. (*vouloir*)
3 Vous ___ faire vos devoirs de maths? (*pouvoir*)
4 Un bon ami ___ être sympa. (*devoir*)
5 Est-ce que tu ___ faire du judo? (*savoir*)
6 Nous ne ___ pas acheter la maison. (*pouvoir*)

Infinitive expressions (Pages 62, 71, 91 and 107)

Écrire 3 Choose one option from each column to make at least four logical sentences. Write out your sentences in French. Then translate them into English.

Example: Il faut aller au collège – You have to go to school.

Il faut	aller	les profs.
Il ne faut pas	arriver	ses devoirs.
Il est interdit de/d'	boire	au collège.
Il est essentiel de/d'	écouter	de l'eau.
	faire	du piano.
	jouer	en classe.
	manger	en retard.
	voyager	en train.

il faut (+ infinitive)	you have to
il ne faut pas (+ infinitive)	you must not
il est interdit de (+ infinitive)	it is forbidden to
Il est essentiel de (+ infinitive)	it is essential to
pour (+ infinitive)	in order to

Écrire 4 Copy out the parallel translations, completing the missing words.

1	Le ___, je me lève tôt ___ aller chez ma grand-mère.	On weekends, I ___ early to go to my ___ house.
2	Pour ___ en forme, il faut faire du ___.	___ to be healthy, you must ___ sport.
3	Tu ___ les réseaux sociaux pour ___ des photos?	Do you use ___ media to share ___?
4	On va à l'___ pour se ___.	We ___ to the hotel ___ rest.
5	Pour avoir de bonnes ___, il ne faut ___ manger en classe.	In order to ___ good grades, you ___ not eat in class.

132 cent-trente-deux

Révisions de grammaire 2 — Modules 1–5

Talking about the past (Pages 71, 72 and 96)

5 Copy and complete the perfect tense sentences with the correct auxiliary verb from the box.
1. J'___ fait beaucoup de progrès cette année.
2. Nous ___ passé une nuit dans cet hôtel en décembre.
3. Elle ___ allée au marché pour acheter des pommes.
4. Je ne ___ pas resté chez moi le week-end dernier.
5. Tu n'___ pas très bien dormi?

as   ai   avons   est   suis

6 Write the French words in the correct order to translate the English sentences.
1. I used to watch music clips. — des clips / regardais / Je / de musique
2. There were lots of people. — beaucoup de / avait / Il / monde / y
3. She used to find English boring. — trouvait / Elle / ennuyeux / l'anglais
4. It was hard for me. — pour / C'était / moi / dur
5. It was sunny. — soleil / y / Il / du / avait

7 For each of these past tense sentences, write whether the underlined verb is in the perfect tense or imperfect tense. Then translate the sentences into English.
Example: 1 Perfect tense – I read a very good book.
1. J'<u>ai lu</u> un très bon livre.
2. Elle <u>a acheté</u> une robe pour la fête.
3. Tu <u>allais</u> à l'école primaire à pied?
4. J'<u>étais</u> très triste à cause des examens.
5. Elles <u>ont dormi</u> sous une tente dans la forêt.
6. Je <u>gagnais</u> souvent les matchs de tennis.

Using verbs in a range of tenses (Pages 97 and 120)

8 In each set of verbs, one is in a different tense from the other three. Write down which is the odd one out, and the tense of the other three: perfect, imperfect, present or near future tense.
Example: 1 j'ai acheté is the odd one out. The other three are in the present tense.
1. nous mangeons / il y a / j'ai acheté / ils travaillent
2. je jouais / tu as étudié / c'était / on regardait
3. nous allons rester / je vais voyager / il va aller / vous avez
4. je n'ai pas vu / il est allé / vous chantez / ils sont restés
5. elle va danser / elle aimait / je partais / tu faisais
6. c'est / on boit / vous allez / tu vas ouvrir

9 Translate the sentences into French.
1. I like seeing my friends every day.
2. She doesn't want to eat lots of vegetables.
3. Last weekend, we went to my aunt's house.
4. The hotel wasn't expensive.
5. If it's hot, I am going to go to the beach.

For 'seeing', use the infinitive voir.
Take care with where you place the negative.
Just use de for the partitive article after a quantity.
Use chez ma tante for 'to my aunt's house'.
The first part of the sentence needs a present tense verb and the second part a near future tense verb.

cent-trente-trois 133

Module 6 — Notre planète

Madagascar: miroir du monde?
- Understanding infographics about the environment
- Practising numbers and percentages

Madagascar is a large island located to the southeast of Africa.

The main languages spoken there are Malagasy and French.

There are more unique species of plants and animals living in Madagascar than on the entire African continent. More than 80 per cent of its species can be found nowhere else on Earth.
Source: https://www.usaid.gov/madagascar/environment-and-climate-change

a silky sifaka lemur, one of the many endangered species of Madagascar

Lire 1
Read the infographic. Then answer each question (1–6) with the correct number from the box. Write your answer in French.

L'écologie à Madagascar

concerné(e) — concerned
rarement — rarely

À ton avis, est-ce que l'écologie est importante?
- Oui, très importante **87%**
- Oui, assez importante **11%**
- Pas très importante **1%**
- Pas du tout importante **1%**

Es-tu concerné(e) par la planète?
- Très concerné(e) **61%**
- Assez concerné(e) **34%**
- Un peu concerné(e) **3%**
- Pas du tout concerné(e) **2%**

Est-ce que tu aides à protéger l'environnement?
- Oui, chaque jour **40%**
- Oui, souvent **26%**
- De temps en temps **26%**
- Non, rarement **7%**
- Non **1%**

onze   soixante-et-un   trente-quatre   vingt-six   quatre-vingt-sept   quarante

What percentage of respondents …
1. think that ecology is very important?
2. think that ecology is quite important?
3. are very concerned about the planet?
4. are quite concerned about the planet?
5. help to protect the environment every day?
6. help to protect the environment from time to time?

Écouter 2
Listen and write down the number that you hear. Check your answers and then write each number as a word in French. (1–8)

1 26 / 28   4 52 / 56   7 81 / 83
2 31 / 41   5 65 / 75   8 93 / 97
3 45 / 49   6 66 / 76

20	vingt	61	soixante-et-un
30	trente	64	soixante-quatre
40	quarante	71	soixante-et-onze
50	cinquante	86	quatre-vingt-six
60	soixante	98	quatre-vingt-dix-huit
70	soixante-dix		
80	quatre-vingts		
90	quatre-vingt-dix		
100	cent		
200	deux-cents		
1000	mille		

pour cent — *per cent*
vingt-deux pour cent — *twenty-two per cent*

cent-trente-quatre

Zone de culture
Module 6

Écouter 3 Listen and write down the correct percentage for each environmental problem. There are two options too many. (1–5)

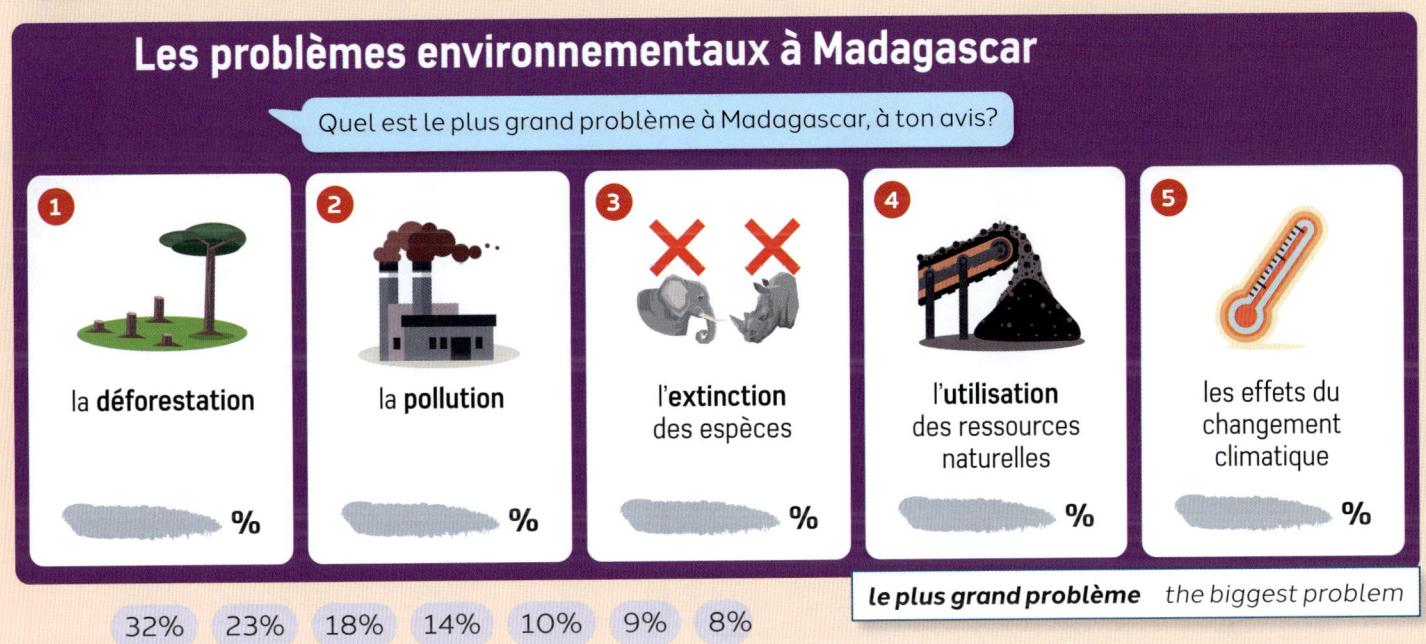

Les problèmes environnementaux à Madagascar

Quel est le plus grand problème à Madagascar, à ton avis?

1. la **déforestation** — %
2. la **pollution** — %
3. l'**extinction** des espèces — %
4. l'**utilisation** des ressources naturelles — %
5. les effets du changement climatique — %

32% 23% 18% 14% 10% 9% 8%

le plus grand problème — the biggest problem

The sound **-tion** is pronounced a bit like 'ss-ee-on'.

As you do exercise 3, listen carefully to how the words in bold are pronounced.

Note that all nouns ending in **-tion** are feminine!

Parler 4 In pairs, take turns to read out the following words, paying attention to the *-tion* sound. Then listen and check.

- la pollution
- l'extinction
- la protection
- l'organisation
- la solution
- la population

All of the words in exercise 4 are cognates. This means that they look the same as, or are similar to, English words, and mean the same things. Other examples of cognates in this unit include *l'environnement* and *la planète*. Which other cognates can you spot in the unit?

Parler 5 Conduct a survey. Copy out the grid, then ask the question below to at least eight people in your class. Keep a tally of your results.

Quel est le plus grand problème dans ta région, à ton avis?

À mon avis, c'est …

la déforestation	
la pollution	
l'extinction des espèces	
l'utilisation des ressources naturelles	
les effets du changement climatique	

Écrire 6 Write some sentences in French to summarise the findings from your survey.

Une personne pense que
Deux / Trois / Quatre personnes pensent que
(le plus grand problème) c'est …

cent-trente-cinq 135

1 Notre monde est beau

- Talking about geography and the climate
- Using comparative adjectives
- Learning about francophone countries

Lire 1 Read the cards. Is each statement below true (write *vrai*) or false (write *faux*)? Then listen and check. (1–5)

La France

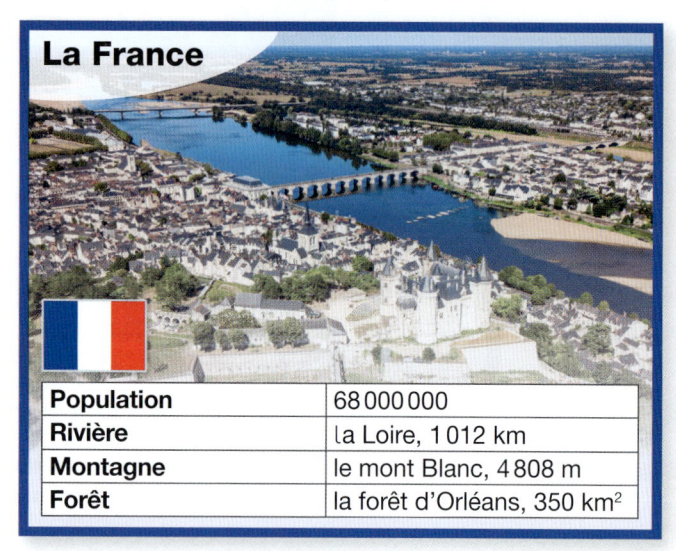

Population	68 000 000
Rivière	la Loire, 1 012 km
Montagne	le mont Blanc, 4 808 m
Forêt	la forêt d'Orléans, 350 km²

La République démocratique du Congo (RDC)

Population	103 000 000
Rivière	le Congo, 4 700 km
Montagne	le pic Marguerite, 5 109 m
Forêt	la forêt tropicale congolaise, 154 135 km²

1 Le mont Blanc est plus haut que le pic Marguerite.
2 Le Congo est plus long que la Loire.
3 La forêt d'Orléans est plus grande que la forêt tropicale congolaise.
4 La population de la France est moins grande que la population de la République démocratique du Congo.
5 La Loire est moins longue que le Congo.

G Remember, you use comparative adjectives to compare things:
plus + adjective + **que**   more + adjective + than
moins + adjective + **que**   less + adjective + than

The adjective must agree (in gender and number) with the first noun:
Le Congo est plus long que la Loire. The Congo is longer than the Loire.
La forêt d'Orléans est moins grande que la forêt tropicale congolaise. The forest of Orléans is less big/smaller than the Congo rainforest.

masculine	feminine	
grand	grande	big
haut	haute	high
long	longue	long

Page 146

Écrire 2 Using the information in the card about Canada and the cards in exercise 1, copy and complete the sentences.

1 La population du Canada est moins grande que ▭.
2 Le Mackenzie est plus long que ▭.
3 Le mont Logan est ▭.
4 La forêt boréale canadienne est ▭.

⭐ Compare some of the geographical features to those in France and some to those in Democratic Republic of the Congo.

Le Canada

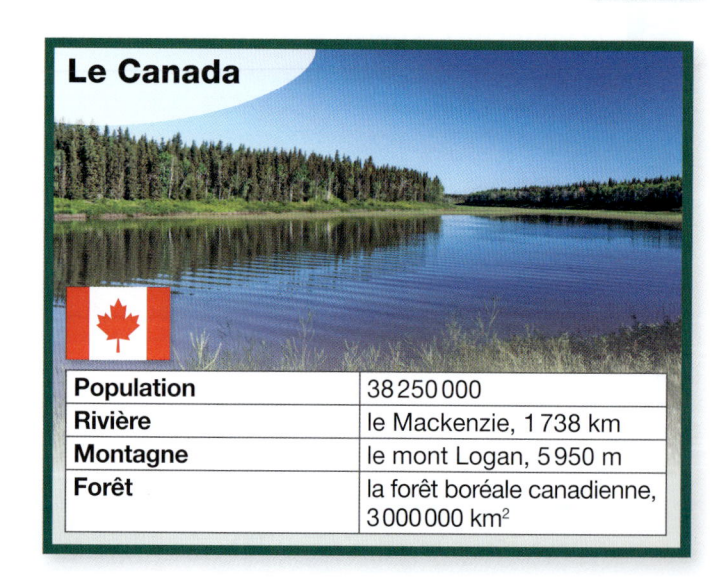

Population	38 250 000
Rivière	le Mackenzie, 1 738 km
Montagne	le mont Logan, 5 950 m
Forêt	la forêt boréale canadienne, 3 000 000 km²

136 cent-trente-six

Module 6

Lire 3 Read the texts. Find the French for the phrases below.

Notre monde est *beau*

l'ours (m)	bear
la baleine	whale
le paysage	landscape

Le Canada est bien connu pour ses hautes montagnes et ses grandes forêts.

La forêt boréale canadienne est plus grande que les forêts de France.

Au Canada, il y a beaucoup d'animaux, comme par exemple des ours noirs et des baleines.

En hiver et au printemps, il fait très froid et il neige beaucoup. Il fait plus froid qu'en France, par exemple!

La République démocratique du Congo (RDC) est en Afrique.

Le paysage est divers. Il y a de grandes villes et de petits villages.

La RDC est bien connue pour ses montagnes et son volcan, le Nyiragongo.

Dans le nord, il pleut beaucoup en automne. Le soir, il y a du brouillard.

En été et au printemps, il fait très chaud. Il fait plus chaud qu'en Europe!

1 is well known for
2 like for instance
3 it snows a lot
4 in the north, it rains a lot in autumn
5 in the evening, there is fog

au printemps	in spring
en été	in summer
en automne	in autumn
en hiver	in winter

Lire 4 Re-read the texts in exercise 3. Are the statements below true of Canada (write 'C') or Democratic Republic of the Congo (write 'DRC')?

1 This country is well known for its forests.
2 This country's mountains are described as high.
3 This country has a varied landscape.
4 This country is very hot in summer.
5 The text about this country mentions lots of animals.
6 This country has large cities and small towns.

Écouter 5 Listen and write down the missing words in French. Then translate the sentences into English. (1–5)

1 ▢ en Suisse.
2 La Suisse est connue pour ses ▢ et ses lacs.
3 En ▢, dans les Alpes, il ▢ beaucoup.
4 Dans ma région, en ▢, il fait ▢.
5 Il ne fait ▢ très ▢.

le lac lake

Parler 6 In pairs, play 'trapdoor'.
- Partner A: in secret, select one of the options for each of numbers 1 to 5 in the sentences below.
- Partner B: start to read out the sentences. When you get to a number, if you read out what your partner selected, you can continue. If you don't, Partner A shouts 'trapdoor' and you have to go back to the beginning!
- Then swap roles.

Ma région est connue pour ses ❶ forêts / montagnes / lacs.

❷ En été / Au printemps, ici, ❸ il fait beau / il fait chaud / il pleut

et ❹ en hiver / en automne, ❺ il fait mauvais / il fait froid / il neige.

cent-trente-sept 137

2 Planète en danger

- Talking about environmental problems
- Talking about future weather
- Pronouncing the 'open o'

Lire 1 Look at the photos and read the captions. Copy and complete the grid in French. Listen and check.

Problèmes	Solutions possibles

Quel est le problème le plus important pour la planète?

a) la destruction des forêts
b) le recyclage
c) la pollution de l'air
d) la faim
e) le changement climatique
f) la pollution de la mer
g) les transports électriques
h) planter plus d'arbres et de fleurs

Écouter 2 Listen. What are these students talking about? Write the letter of the correct photo from exercise 1. (1–8)

l'arbre (m) tree
la fleur flower

Lire 3 Read the texts. Then answer the questions below by writing the correct name.

Adaline
Je pense que la destruction des forêts est une catastrophe! Ça cause le changement climatique.

Lucas
La pollution de la mer tue les poissons. Je trouve que la protection de la mer sauve les animaux et améliore l'environnement.

Zachary
La pollution de l'air est un problème énorme. Les transports électriques améliorent la situation. Le recyclage aussi!

Khalida
À mon avis, le changement climatique cause la faim dans le monde. C'est un grand problème pour la population humaine.

tuer to kill

Who …
1 wants to protect the sea?
2 is concerned by hunger?
3 thinks that deforestation is a problem?
4 is concerned by air pollution?

Parler 4 Listen and repeat the following words.

protéger   notre   pollution   forêt
améliorer   catastrophe

The French **o** is an open sound in these words.

138 *cent-trente-huit*

Module 6

Écouter 5 Look at the map. Listen and read. Then write down the letter of the correct city for each weather forecast. (1–4)

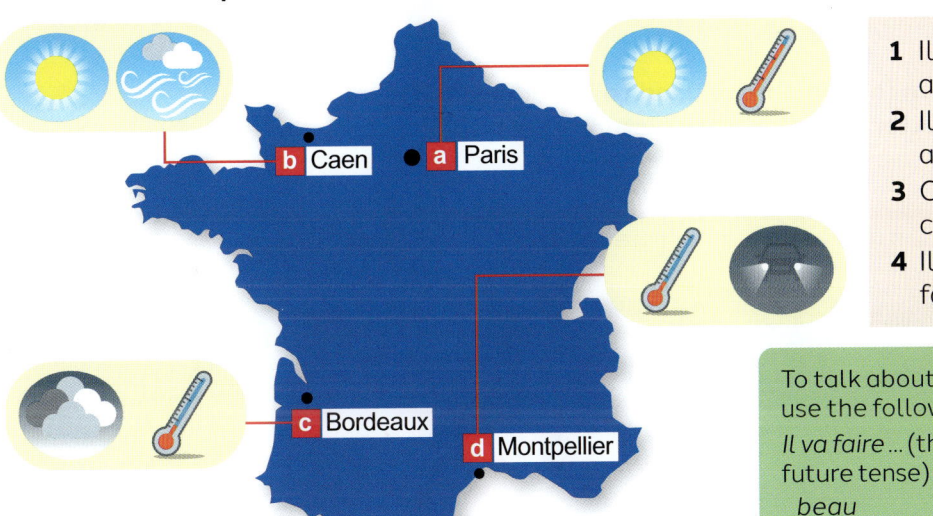

b Caen
a Paris
c Bordeaux
d Montpellier

1 Il y aura du soleil, mais il y aura aussi du vent.
2 Il va faire très froid et il y aura aussi du brouillard.
3 Ce week-end, il va faire chaud et il y aura du soleil.
4 Il va faire mauvais et il va faire froid.

G To talk about the weather in the future, use the following structures:

Il va faire … (the near future tense)	Il y aura … (this is 'il y a' in the future)
beau	du soleil
chaud	du vent
froid	du brouillard
mauvais	

Page 147

Parler 6 In pairs, talk about what the weather will be like, using the prompts below.

- Quel temps va-t-il faire?
- Il va faire … Il y aura …

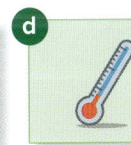

a   b   c   d

Lire 7 Read the text. Match each underlined phrase to one of the pictures (a–d) below.

Le climat en 2050? Le choix est à nous!

On lutte pour limiter le réchauffement de la planète à 1,5°C. Voici deux scénarios possibles …

Scénario A ✓

1 <u>Les nouvelles technologies, comme les voitures électriques par exemple, vont limiter le danger.</u>
2 <u>On va sauver les habitats des animaux et limiter la pollution de la mer.</u>
3 <u>On va limiter le réchauffement de la planète.</u> Les pays vont être plus froids ou plus chauds, mais les effets vont être moins extrêmes.

Scénario B ✗

4 <u>Il va faire beaucoup plus chaud.</u> Le changement climatique va continuer à cause de la pollution.
Le climat va être plus extrême.
Les effets du changement climatique vont avoir un impact terrible sur les animaux.

| le réchauffement (de la planète) | (global) warming |
| le pays | country |

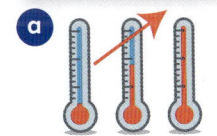

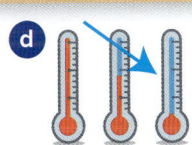

a   b   c   d

Écrire 8 Write four sentences using the grid. Then swap sentences with a partner and translate your partner's sentences into English.

À mon avis, Je pense que Je trouve que	la pollution le changement climatique la destruction des forêts	est	un problème énorme. une catastrophe.
	le recyclage la protection de la mer planter plus de fleurs et d'arbres	est	une solution possible.
		améliore	la situation.
	les transports électriques	sont	une solution possible.
		améliorent	la situation.

cent-trente-neuf 139

3 Des grands gestes

- Discussing what we can do together to protect the environment
- Using the present and perfect tenses
- Describing a photo taken outside in nature

Écouter 1 Listen, then write down (a) the phrase used to introduce the opinion, and (b) the letter of the correct picture. (1–6)

Qu'est-ce qu'il faut faire pour protéger l'environnement?

pour moi,   à mon avis,   je pense que   je trouve que   je crois que

a  Il faut travailler ensemble pour arrêter le changement climatique.

d Il faut être bénévole pour des projets verts.

b  Il faut respecter la nature.

e Il faut arrêter d'utiliser des produits en plastique.

c  Il faut lutter contre la pollution et la destruction des forêts.

f  Il faut organiser des manifestations pour la protection des animaux.

| le/la bénévole | volunteer |
| la manifestation | protest, demonstration |

Parler 2 Conduct a survey. Ask the question below to six people in the class.

- Qu'est-ce qu'il faut faire pour protéger l'environnement?
- À mon avis, / Pour moi, il faut …

Make your own speaking and writing more interesting by varying how you introduce your opinions. Remember that *que* changes to *qu'* in front of a vowel: *Je pense qu'il faut …*

Lire 3 Look at the picture. Copy and complete the sentences, choosing from the correct option each time. Then listen and check.

1 Sur la photo, il y a **cinq personnes** / **des amis** / **une famille**.
2 La femme a les cheveux **courts** / **longs et noirs** / **blonds**.
3 Ils sont dehors, **sur la côte** / **dans une forêt** / **à la montagne**.
4 Il fait **beau** / **mauvais** / **froid**.
5 Les gens **marchent** / **font du vélo** / **jouent**.
6 **Ils s'amusent.** / **Ils ne s'amusent pas.**

| dehors | outside |

Écrire 4 Write four sentences about this photo. Adapt some of the sentences from exercise 3.

140 cent-quarante

Module 6

5 Read the texts. Then answer the questions by writing 'Michel' or 'Charlotte'.

J'adore la nature et je crois qu'il faut travailler avec les autres pour arrêter le changement climatique. J'admire beaucoup Youna Marette. Elle est connue pour ses actions pour protéger l'environnement. Moi aussi, <u>je lutte contre la pollution</u>. J'écris un blog sur les projets verts et l'importance de donner de son temps.
Le mois dernier, <u>je suis allé à une manifestation à Paris</u> contre la destruction des forêts. J'ai pris le bus.
<u>J'ai rencontré des personnes sympa</u> et j'ai appris beaucoup de choses.

Michel

Je pense qu'il faut lutter contre la pollution.
<u>Je vais souvent à des manifestations</u> pour la protection de la planète. Je rencontre toujours des personnes intéressantes.
Au mois d'août, <u>j'ai participé à une manifestation</u> contre la pollution de l'air. Il y avait beaucoup de gens dans les rues et j'ai écouté Victor Noël, un jeune activiste. <u>J'ai passé du temps avec de nouveaux amis</u>.
Après la manifestation, j'ai écrit un article sur mon expérience pour le collège.

Charlotte

1. Who writes about giving time for green projects?
2. Who took public transport to a protest?
3. Who went to a protest about air pollution?
4. Who listened to a speaker?
5. Who learned lots of things?
6. Who has written about a recent protest for school?

Youna Marette   Victor Noël

6 Copy out each of the underlined phrases from the texts in exercise 5. Note down if each one is in the present tense or the perfect tense. Then translate the phrases into English.

G Remember that the perfect tense is formed of two parts: the auxiliary verb (part of *avoir* or *être*) and a past participle. Some past participles are irregular. The past participle of verbs that take *être* must agree with the subject.

	present	perfect
regular -er verbs, e.g. rencontrer (to meet)	je rencontre	j'**ai** rencontr**é**
écrire (to write)	j'écris	j'**ai écrit**
aller (to go)	je vais	je **suis allé**(**e**)

Page 147

7 Listen, then write down (a) the letter of the correct activity, and (b) the tense (present or perfect) used. (1–4)

a participating in protests
b giving time for green projects
c listening to activists
d writing blog posts

8 Translate these sentences into French.

1. In my opinion, we have to work together to stop pollution.
2. I fight for the protection of animals.
3. I admire Greta Thunberg because she fights against climate change.
4. Last week, I went to a demonstration against deforestation.
5. Afterwards, I wrote an article on my blog about my experience.

Which structure do you need to use here?
Beware of the plural of animal in French!
Do not forget to include an article.

cent-quarante-et-un 141

4 Des petits gestes

- Talking about day-to-day actions to protect the environment
- Using the imperfect tense to describe what you used to do
- Extending spoken and written answers

Écouter 1
Listen and write down the two correct letters for each speaker. (1–3)

les déchets (m) rubbish

a Je prends les transports en commun.

b Je ne mange pas de viande.

c Je recycle les déchets.

d Je n'utilise pas de produits en plastique.

e Je vais en ville à vélo et non pas en voiture.

f J'achète du papier recyclé.

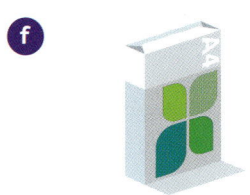

Parler 2
Play a memory game. Work in groups of four. Each person has to repeat what the previous person said, and add something new!

Qu'est-ce que tu fais pour protéger l'environnement?

- J'achète du papier recyclé.
- J'achète du papier recyclé et je prends les transports en commun.
- ▲ J'achète du papier recyclé, je prends les transports en commun et je ne mange pas de viande.
- ♦ J'achète du papier recyclé, je prends les transports en commun, je ne mange pas de viande et …

Lire 3
Read Tom's text. Copy and complete the sentences in English.

Sept jours pour sauver la planète!

Le lundi, je vais en ville à vélo. Je ne prends jamais la voiture.
Le mardi, je fais les courses. J'utilise toujours les mêmes sacs en plastique.
Le mercredi, je recycle les déchets: le papier et le plastique.
Le jeudi, j'achète des fruits et des légumes au marché.
Le vendredi, je travaille comme bénévole pour un projet qui protège les hérissons.
Le samedi, je prends toujours le bus pour aller chez ma grand-mère.
Le dimanche, je ne mange pas de viande. C'est mieux pour l'environnement.

les courses (f) (food) shopping
le hérisson hedgehog
mieux better

You sometimes need the definite article in French even where we wouldn't use it in English.
le lundi on Mondays
Je recycle **les** déchets.
I recycle rubbish.

1 On Mondays, he goes into town ▭. He never ▭.
2 On Tuesdays, he goes ▭. He always uses the same ▭.
3 On Wednesdays, he ▭.
4 On Thursdays, he buys ▭.
5 On Fridays, he works as a volunteer for ▭.
6 On Saturdays, he always ▭ in order to go ▭.
7 On Sundays, he doesn't ▭. It's better ▭.

Écrire 4
Write your own diary of a week to save the planet.

Expand on your answers by adding extra details where possible (e.g. where, when, who, what, how).

142 cent-quarante-deux

5 Read the text. Copy and complete the grid with the letters of the correct pictures.

What she used to do (imperfect)	What she does now (present)

Rosalie: Ma visite au Québec

L'année dernière, je suis allée au Québec. Ma visite a changé ma vie parce que là-bas, j'ai vu les effets du changement climatique!

Avant, je ne m'intéressais pas beaucoup à l'environnement, mais maintenant, après ma visite au Québec, je fais beaucoup d'efforts pour protéger l'environnement.

Par exemple, avant, je mangeais de la viande tous les jours. Maintenant, je ne mange pas de viande. Je suis végétarienne. En plus, dans ma famille, on achète nos légumes au marché.

Ensuite, je recycle les déchets et j'utilise du papier recyclé. Avant, je ne recyclais rien!

J'allais au collège en voiture, mais maintenant, je vais tous les jours au collège à pied – quand il fait beau mais aussi quand il pleut!

6 Re-read the text in exercise 5. Find the French for the phrases below.
1. my visit changed my life
2. I saw the effects of climate change
3. I wasn't very interested in the environment
4. I make a lot of effort to protect the environment
5. I didn't use to recycle anything

> **G**
> Use the **perfect tense** to talk about **single, completed events or actions in the past,** e.g. *ma visite a changé ma vie* (my visit changed my life – one action, completed). Look at page 141 to see how the perfect tense is formed.
>
> Use the **imperfect tense** to talk about **what happened in the past over a period of time** (what used to happen), e.g. *j'allais au collège en voiture* (I used to go to school by car – repeatedly). Look at page 148 to see how the imperfect tense is formed.
>
> **Page 148**

7 Listen. Then copy and complete the grid in English. (1–3)

	What did they use to do?	What do they do now?
1		

imperfect	present
j'utilisais	j'utilise / je n'utilise pas
je (ne) mangeais (pas)	je ne mange pas
je recyclais	je recycle
j'allais	je vais

8 In pairs, take turns to ask and answer the two questions.
- Quand tu étais plus jeune, qu'est-ce que tu faisais pour protéger l'environnement?
- Quand j'étais plus jeune, je m'intéressais beaucoup à l'environnement / je ne m'intéressais pas beaucoup à l'environnement. Je …
- Qu'est-ce que tu fais pour protéger l'environnement maintenant?
- Maintenant, je fais beaucoup d'efforts. Je …

> Can you extend your answer by also saying what you **didn't** use to do in the past? For example:
> *Je **ne** recyclais **pas** …*
> I did not use to recycle …
> *Je **ne** recyclais **jamais** …*
> I never used to recycle …

cent-quarante-trois 143

5 Innovation verte

- Discussing school environmental projects
- Using the present, perfect, imperfect and near future tenses
- Practising answering questions featuring a variety of tenses

Lire 1 Read the questions below. Which tense is each one in? Write 'present', 'perfect', 'imperfect', or 'near future'.

Innovation verte au collège

1. Quelle est votre innovation?
2. Quel était le problème, avant?
3. Et qu'est-ce que vous avez fait?
4. Et c'est comment, maintenant?
5. Et à l'avenir, qu'est-ce que vous allez faire?

Lire 2 Match each question (1–5) from exercise 1 to an answer (a–e) below. Then listen and check.

a On a parlé avec le directeur et **on a décidé d'organiser un jardin** et le recyclage de la nourriture en compost. On a arrêté le gaspillage.

b Il y avait beaucoup de gaspillage et **on jetait la nourriture à la poubelle avec les autres déchets. On ne faisait pas beaucoup pour protéger l'environnement**.

c **On va parler à une conférence** et participer à un concours interscolaire. On va aussi interdire les sacs en plastique au collège.

d Dans notre collège, on évite le gaspillage de nourriture. On fait pousser nos propres légumes dans le jardin de l'école. **On fait aussi du compost**.

e C'est beaucoup mieux! On lutte contre le changement climatique – **il n'y a pas de gaspillage de nourriture**. Ça fait une énorme différence.

la nourriture	food
le gaspillage	waste
la poubelle	bin
éviter	to avoid
faire pousser	to grow

Lire 3 Re-read the answers in exercise 2 and find the French for the phrases below, choosing from the phrases in **bold**.

1 there is no food waste
2 we also make compost
3 we decided to organise a garden
4 we did not (use to) do much to protect the environment
5 we are going to speak at a conference
6 we threw / used to throw food in the bin with the other rubbish

Tense	Used to talk about	Examples
present	what is happening now what you usually do what someone or something is like	Il travaille dans le jardin. On lutte pour l'environnement. C'est mieux!
perfect	single, completed actions in the past	J'ai écrit un blog. Elle est allée à une manifestation.
imperfect	what something or someone was like what used to happen in the past, over a period of time	C'était bien. On allait toujours au collège à pied.
near future	what is going to happen in the future	On va parler avec les profs.

Page 148

cent-quarante-quatre

Écouter 4

Listen to the conversation. Choose the correct option to complete each sentence. (1–5)

1 At our school **cars have been banned** / **new buses are in operation**.
2 Before, there **were too many cars on site** / **was too much air pollution**.
3 We encouraged pupils to come to school by **bike** / **bus**.
4 Now, although the journey is **slower** / **less practical**, it is better for the environment.
5 In the future, we will **encourage more people to walk** / **have free bikes that students can use**.

> **G**
> Comparative adverbs work in a similar way to adjectives, but they are invariable (i.e. there are not different masculine, feminine or plural forms). They are placed after the verb:
> *On arrive **plus vite** en avion.*
> You arrive more quickly by plane.
> *On voyage **moins vite** à vélo.*
> You travel less quickly by bike.
>
> Note these irregular forms:
> *bien* (well)   *mieux* (better)

Parler 5

In pairs, take turns to read out the matched answers and questions from exercises 1 and 2 to recreate the interview. Focus on good pronunciation.

> Before reading aloud, look at the interview and talk with your partner about how to pronounce:
> - the question words
> - the verbs in different tenses
> - the French words that look similar to English words. How many of these can you find?

Lire 6

Read the article. Answer the questions below in English.

Sac à dos électrique: le transport vert du futur?

Amir habite en France. Il est ingénieur.

Quand il était plus jeune, il voyageait toujours en voiture et il prenait l'avion pour partir en vacances.

Maintenant, Amir pense qu'il faut lutter contre le changement climatique et réduire la pollution. On voyage plus vite en avion, mais c'est pire pour la planète.

Amir a fait des recherches dans les transports verts. Récemment, il a fini un projet très important, un nouveau moyen de transport: le sac à dos électrique. C'est mieux pour l'environnement que les moyens de transport traditionnels.

À l'avenir, Amir va rechercher d'autres possibilités. Un sac à dos solaire, peut-être?

le sac à dos	backpack
l'ingénieur(e)	engineer
solaire	solar

1 What two things did Amir do when he was younger?
2 What does he think we should fight against now?
3 What has Amir researched?
4 What project has he recently finished?
5 What may he research in the future?

Écrire 7

Translate these sentences into French.

1 At school, we did not use to recycle rubbish.
2 Now we go to school by bike.
3 In the future, I am going to work in the garden.
4 Last month, I finished an important project.
5 Recently, I took the train in order to go on holiday.

> - Remember that you can use **on** to mean 'we'.
> - Take care with the tenses. You need the imperfect tense for one sentence, and the perfect for two of the sentences. Which ones?

cent-quarante-cinq

Grammaire 1

Numbers (Culture, page 134)

Lire 1 Read the language box on numbers on page 134. Then rewrite these calculations as figures. Put a tick next to the ones that have correct answers, and a cross next to the incorrect ones.

Example: 1 34 + 18 = 54 ✗

1 trente-quatre + dix-huit = cinquante-quatre
2 vingt-sept + quarante-et-un = soixante-huit
3 quatre-vingt-trois − vingt-deux = soixante-et-onze
4 soixante-cinq − onze = cinquante-deux
5 soixante-quinze − quatorze = soixante-et-un
6 treize × quatre = quarante-deux
7 seize × trois = quarante-huit
8 quatre-vingt-dix-neuf ÷ trois = trente-trois

Parler 2 In pairs, take turns to read out a number from one of the four cards. Your partner says the letter of the card that features the number.

- *soixante-sept*
- C

A

16	35
42	63

B

18	26
57	71

C

14	37
41	67

D

12	28
59	74

Comparative adjectives (Unit 1, page 136)

Lire 3 Copy and complete the sentences, choosing the correct form of the adjective each time.

1 Le pic Marguerite est plus **haut** / **haute** que le mont Blanc.
2 Le mois de juillet est aussi **chaud** / **chaude** que le mois de septembre.
3 La forêt d'Orléans est moins **grand** / **grande** que la forêt tropicale congolaise.
4 Le mois de janvier est plus **froid** / **froide** que le mois de juin.
5 La Loire est moins **long** / **longue** que le Congo.
6 Le mois de novembre est aussi **long** / **longue** que le mois d'avril.

> You use **comparative** adjectives to compare things:
> - *plus* + adjective + *que*
>   more + adjective + than
> - *moins* + adjective + *que*
>   less + adjective + than
> - *aussi* + adjective + *que*
>   as + adjective + as
>
> The adjective must agree (in gender and number) with the first noun:
> *La Loire est moins longue que le Congo.*
> The Loire is less long than the Congo. / The Loire is shorter than the Congo.
>
> 💡 Just like in English, 'good' and 'bad' are irregular in French:
> *bon(ne)(s)* (good)   *meilleur(e)(s)* (better)
> *mauvais(e)(s)* (bad)   *pire(s)* (worse)

146 cent-quarante-six

Module 6

Écouter 4 Listen to these people comparing modes of transport. For each person, write the letters of the two modes of transport and the comparison made in English. (1–6)

Example: 1 e, a – e less fast than a

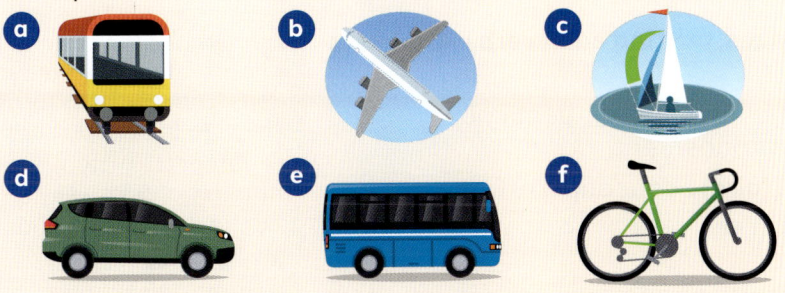

a b c
d e f

rapide	fast
facile	easy
propre	clean
pratique	practical
bon(ne)(s) pour l'environnement	good for the environment
mauvais(e)(s) pour l'environnement	bad for the environment

Talking about future weather (Unit 2, page 139)

Écrire 5 What is the weather going to be like in Belgium? Write a weather forecast for each of the cities on the map. Then listen and check.

Example: À Bruxelles, il y aura du soleil.

present	future
Il fait …	Il va faire …
Il y a …	Il y aura …

1 Bruxelles 
2 Liège 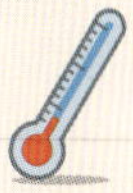
3 Namur 
4 Bruges 
5 Charleroi 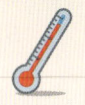
6 Anvers

Using the present and perfect tenses (Unit 3, page 141)

Écrire 6 Read the grammar box on page 141. Change the tense of the sentences below.
- Change 1–4 from the present to the perfect.
- Change 5–8 from the perfect to the present.

Example: 1 <u>J'ai participé</u> à des manifestations.

1 Je participe à des manifestations.
2 J'écris des articles pour le magazine du collège.
3 J'écoute des activistes.
4 Je prends le bus.
5 J'ai lutté contre la pollution.
6 Je ne suis pas allée à la manifestation.
7 J'ai rencontré des personnes intéressantes.
8 J'ai passé du temps avec de nouveaux amis.

Remember that some verbs are irregular. This could be either present tense forms, the past participle or both. If you are unsure, check the verb tables on pages 235–239.

cent-quarante-sept **147**

Grammaire 2

Using the imperfect tense (Unit 4, page 143)

Écrire 1 Copy and complete the sentences, putting each verb in brackets into the imperfect tense.

Example: 1 Quand j'<u>étais</u> plus jeune, je <u>faisais</u> beaucoup d'efforts pour l'environnement.

1 Quand j'**(être)** plus jeune, je **(faire)** beaucoup d'efforts pour l'environnement.
2 J'**(aller)** au collège à vélo.
3 J'**(utiliser)** souvent les transports en commun.
4 Je **(recycler)** le papier et le plastique.
5 Ma sœur ne **(manger)** pas beaucoup de viande.
6 Avant, qu'est-ce que tu **(faire)** pour protéger l'environnement?
7 Quand Zoé **(être)** au collège, elle ne **(recycler)** rien!
8 Marc **(acheter)** du papier recyclé.

> Remember, to form the imperfect tense, remove the *-ons* from the *nous* form of the verb in the present tense:
> *regarder* (to watch) →
> *nous regardons* → *regard-*
> Then add these endings:
> *je regardais*
> *tu regardais*
> *il/elle/on regardait*
>
> The verb *être* has the stem *ét-*:
> *c'était* (it used to be/it was)

Understanding when to use the perfect tense and when to use the imperfect tense (Unit 4, page 143)

Lire 2 Read the grammar box on page 143. Copy and complete the sentences, choosing the correct form of the verb from the options in bold. Then translate the sentences into English.

1 Quand j'étais petit, **je suis allée** / **j'allais** tous les jours à l'école à pied.
2 Le week-end dernier, **j'ai pris** / **je prenais** le bus.
3 Hier, **j'ai recyclé** / **je recyclais** des déchets et du papier.
4 Quand j'étais au collège, **j'ai participé** / **je participais** souvent aux manifestations.
5 Samedi dernier, au restaurant, **j'ai mangé** / **je mangeais** un plat végétarien.

Using the present, perfect, imperfect and near future tenses (Unit 5, page 144)

- Use the **present tense** for things that usually happen or are happening now.
- Use the **perfect tense** for single, completed actions in the past.
- Use the **imperfect tense** to say what used to happen in the past, over a period of time.
- Use the **near future tense** to refer to the future.

Écrire 3 Copy and complete the table. Choose from the verb forms in the box for the first three rows. Then complete the final three rows on your own.

present	perfect	imperfect	near future
je vais			je vais aller
je mange		je mangeais	
	j'ai acheté		je vais acheter
je participe			je vais participer
	j'ai recyclé		
		j'utilisais	

> je vais manger
> je suis allé(e)
> j'achète
> j'ai mangé
> j'allais
> j'achetais

148 cent-quarante-huit

Module 6

4 Listen. Which tense is each sentence in? Choose from the options. (1–6)

1 present / near future
2 present / perfect
3 present / imperfect
4 perfect / near future
5 imperfect / perfect
6 present / near future

5 Tense challenge! Ask your partner one of the four questions and say the letter of one of the pictures. Your partner must answer in the correct tense.
- Quand tu étais jeune, qu'est-ce que tu faisais pour protéger l'environnement? b
- Je recyclais les déchets. Qu'est-ce que tu as fait récemment pour protéger l'environnement? a
- J'ai acheté du papier recyclé. À l'avenir, …

Qu'est-ce que tu fais d'habitude pour protéger l'environnement?

Quand tu étais jeune, qu'est-ce que tu faisais pour protéger l'environnement?

Qu'est-ce que tu as fait récemment pour protéger l'environnement?

À l'avenir, qu'est-ce que tu vas faire pour protéger l'environnement?

a acheter du papier recyclé
b recycler les déchets
c aller au collège à vélo
d participer à une manifestation
e utiliser les transports en commun
f manger des plats végétariens

C'est parti!

6 Translate these sentences into English.
1 À mon avis, il faut lutter contre le changement climatique.
2 Quand j'étais jeune, je ne recyclais rien.
3 Maintenant, je vais en ville à pied et je prends souvent les transports en commun.
4 Samedi dernier, j'ai participé à une manifestation pour la protection des animaux.
5 Ce week-end, je vais acheter des fruits au marché.
6 À l'avenir, il va faire beaucoup plus chaud en été.
7 En hiver, il fait plus froid au Canada qu'en France.
8 Ma mère, qui a trente-neuf ans, ne mange pas de viande.

7 In pairs, take turns to read out the sentences from exercise 6.

Module 6 Contrôle de lecture et d'écoute

Reading

1 *Where I live.* Read this blog that Clément has written about his town.

> Salut tout le monde!
> Dans ma ville il y a quelques problèmes. Maintenant, le bruit causé par les voitures et le trafic n'est pas agréable. Avant, c'était plus calme ici! Et on trouve souvent des sacs en plastique dans notre parc! Nous avons assez de **poubelles*** mais l'eau de la rivière est moins saine qu'avant. C'est triste!

*la poubelle — bin

a Write down the word for the gap in each sentence, using the words from the box. There are more words than gaps.

(i) There was ___ noise in his town before.
(ii) Clément thinks there ___ enough bins in his local park.
(iii) The river is ___ .

> less   aren't   more   are   polluted   healthy   were

For each gap, there are two or three possible answers. Identify which words make sense in each gap and then choose the one that is correct.

The blog continues.

> Il y a quelques semaines, un groupe d'élèves de mon lycée a commencé un projet pour améliorer les conditions de vie dans notre ville. Ils vont au parc tous les jours pour mettre les **déchets*** dans les poubelles et ils demandent aux gens de ne pas jeter les déchets **par terre***. Habiter dans une ville saine et propre est important pour notre avenir, sans oublier notre santé mentale.

*les déchets — rubbish
*par terre — on the ground

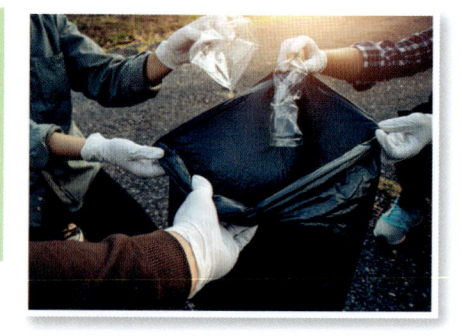

b Complete the sentences below. For each sentence, write the correct letter (A–C).

(i) To improve living conditions in Clément's town, a group of students …
   A started to act last year.
   B has already started to act.
   C will launch a project in a few weeks.

(ii) Every day they …
   A clean the park.
   B watch people in the park.
   C empty the bins.

c Answer the following questions **in English**. You do not need to write in full sentences.

(i) What do the students ask people to do?
(ii) According to the students, why is living in a clean environment important? Give <u>one</u> detail.

2 *Eco-friendly.* Translate the following sentences **into English**.

What tense is this? Use the time expression to help you.

a Je fais beaucoup pour protéger la planète.
b Ma famille utilise les transports en commun.
c J'utilise du papier recyclé chez moi.
d Hier, j'ai acheté des légumes au marché.
e Si j'ai le temps, j'aide un projet qui protège les animaux.

Think about how you are going to translate these prepositions.

Think about how you are going to translate this structure.

150 *cent-cinquante*

Listening

Écouter 3

A weather forecast. You are listening to tomorrow's weather forecast in France. What does it say? Write down the word for the gap in each sentence, using a word from the box. There are more words than gaps.

a In the south, it will be quite ___.
b In the north, the weather will be ___ and the temperatures will be ___ than today.
c In Paris, it will be ___ during the day.
d Motorists will be driving in ___ later on at night.

> Focus on what the weather is going to be like tomorrow.
>
> Beware of negatives and pay attention to other details in the sentence that might help you.

| good | hotter | foggy | wind | hot | bad |
| colder | freezing | windy | rain | cold |

Écouter 4

Town life.

a Jules is talking about living in a town. What does he say? Listen to the podcast and answer the following questions **in English**. You do not need to write in full sentences.

   (i) What does Jules like to do in town?
   (ii) What does he like most in town?

b Inès and Luis are talking about living in a town. What do they like and dislike? Listen to the podcast, then copy and complete the following table in English. You do not need to write in full sentences.

	Inès …	Luis …
likes …		
dislikes …		

> You won't always hear the French for 'I like' and 'I don't like'. You need to concentrate on positive and negative aspects, and focus on key words such as 'unfortunately' and 'but'.

Écouter 5

Dictation. You are going to hear someone talking about where they live.

a Sentences 1–3: write down the missing words. For each gap, you will write one word **in French**.

   1 Ma famille ___ à la ___.
   2 Il y a une ___ et des ___.
   3 À la ___, c'est propre et ___.

> Listen carefully to these words as you may never have seen them before.

b Sentences 4–6: write down the full sentences that you hear, **in French**.

cent-cinquante-et-un 151

Module 6 Contrôle oral

Read aloud

Parler 1 Look at this task card. With a partner, take turns to read out the five sentences, paying attention to the underlined letters and the highlighted liaisons and cognates.

> Medhi, your Belgian friend, has emailed you to tell you about the environment.
> Read out the text below to your teacher.
>
> La planète est en danger.
> La pollution est un problème énorme.
> Je recycle tous les jours pour protéger l'environnement.
> On doit utiliser souvent les transports en commun.
> Je vais à beaucoup de manifestations pour la protection des animaux.

Take extra care with how you pronounce the underlined sounds:
- *-tion* sounds like 'ss-ee-on'
- *u* and *ou* will sound differently.

Take extra care with how you pronounce cognates. The underlined letters will be pronounced very differently than in English.

Remember your liaisons!

Écouter 2 Listen and check your pronunciation.

Parler 3 Listen to the teacher asking the two follow-up questions. Translate each question **into English** and prepare your own answers **in French**. Then listen again and respond to the teacher.

A few words or a short phrase or sentence are enough. Try to avoid one-word answers.

Role play

Parler 4 Look at the role-play card and prepare what you are going to say.

Here you could say that you would like to go to the lake, the countryside, the forest, to the south …

You could ask if there are mountains or a river. Use *Est-ce qu'il y a …*

You could give your opinion using *J'aime* or *Je n'aime pas*.

Setting: At the tourist information office

Scenario:
- You are with your family at a tourist information office in France.
- The teacher will play the part of the employee and will speak first.
- The teacher will ask questions **in French**, and you must answer **in French**.
- Say a few words or a short phrase/sentence for each prompt. One-word answers are not sufficient to gain full marks.

Task:
1. Say what part/feature of the region you would like to visit.
2. Say when you want to go there.
3. Say why you want to go on the visit.
4. Ask a question about other features/parts you can visit.
5. Give your opinion of the region.

Parler 5 Practise what you have prepared. Then, using your notes, listen and respond to the teacher.

Écouter 6 Now listen to Gabriel doing the role-play task. **In English**, note down (a) how he **answers** the questions for task prompts 1, 2, 3 and 5, and (b) what question he **asks** for task prompt 4.

152 *cent-cinquante-deux*

Picture task

Écouter 7 Look at the exam card below and read the **first part** of the task. Then listen to Morgane describing the picture. Answer the questions **in English**.

a What does Morgane say about the people in the picture?
b Who does she describe in the most detail and what does she mention?
c Where does she say the four people are in the picture? Do you agree?
d What does she say about the man at the back?

> To talk about the people, you can use *assis* (sitting), *debout* (standing) and prepositions like *devant* (in front(of)) and *derrière* (behind).

Describe this picture.
Your description must cover:
- people
- location
- activity.

When you have finished your description, you will be asked **two questions** relating to the picture. Say a short phrase/sentence in response to each question. One-word answers will not be sufficient to gain full marks.

You will then move on to a **conversation** on the broader thematic context of **My neighbourhood**.

During the conversation, you will be asked questions in the present, past and future tenses. Your responses should be as **full and detailed** as possible.

Parler 8 Prepare your own description of the picture, mentioning **people**, **location** and **activity**. Then, with a partner, take turns to describe the picture.

> Sur la photo, il y a ...

Parler 9 Read the **second part** of the task. Then listen to the two follow-up questions and respond to the teacher. Remember: you only need to give a short answer to each one.

Écouter 10 Read the **third part** of the task. The teacher asks Morgane: *Qu'est-ce que tu as fait récemment pour protéger la planète?* Listen and read the list of verbs. Write down all the verbs that you can hear.

> j'ai pris   j'ai fait
> j'ai recyclé   j'ai utilisé
> je suis allée   je suis arrivée

Écouter 11 Listen to Morgane answering the question: *Est-ce que tu voudrais conduire à l'avenir?* Give (a) <u>one</u> reason why she would like to, and (b) <u>one</u> disadvantage she mentions.

Parler 12 Prepare your own answers to the Module 6 questions on page 227. Your responses should be as **full and detailed** as possible. Then practise with a partner.

> Remember to use opinion phrases, time phrases, connectives, and a range of verbs in the present, past and future tenses for yourself and other people.

cent-cinquante-trois 153

Module 6 Contrôle écrit

Photo description

Écrire 1 Describe the photo. Write four short sentences **in French**.

Write things that you know how to say. You could say who is in the photo, where they are and what they are doing. Use the *il/elle* and *ils/elles* parts of present tense verbs.

80–90 word writing task

Écrire 2 Look at this writing exam task and then, <u>for each bullet point</u>:

1 think about what vocabulary you have learned which you could use in your answer. For example:
 - **nouns** and **verbs** to talk about the environment and problems
 - **verbs of opinion** and **adjectives** to explain your point of view
 - language for **narrating a story** about what you did recently to help the environment
 - how to explain what your plans are to help the environment in the future.

2 write down <u>three or four</u> ideas for what you could write about.
3 write down which tense(s) you will need to use in your answer.

> Write about helping to protect the environment.
>
> You **must** include the following points:
> - how you help protect the environment at school
> - your opinion on helping to protect the environment
> - something you have done recently to help protect the environment
> - what you would like to do more of to help protect the environment.
>
> Write your answer **in French**. You should aim to write between 80 and 90 words.

Look at the vocabulary you have noted to help you think of ideas of what to write.

Lire 3 Read Chloé's answer to the exam task. Answer questions 1–5 in the coloured shapes.

1 This is an example of **complex language**. What does it mean? Find <u>three</u> more examples from the text.

2 This word shows a **variety of vocabulary**. What does it mean? Find <u>two</u> more examples.

4 Which **tense** is this? Does she use any other tenses?

5 How could she form an **extended sentence**? What other extended sentences does she include?

3 How could she **avoid repetition** by using another phrase?

> Salut!
>
> Au collège, je recycle le papier. Avant, j'achetais du fastfood dans du plastique mais maintenant je prépare mon déjeuner chez moi dans une boîte.
>
> Je pense qu'il faut protéger la planète. Je trouve que ma ville est moins propre car il y a trop de pollution. Je crois qu'on doit travailler ensemble pour protéger la planète.
>
> Récemment, j'ai écrit un blog pour la protection des animaux. Le changement climatique a un effet négatif sur la nature.
>
> À l'avenir, je vais arrêter de manger de la viande car je voudrais devenir végétarienne.
>
> Chloé

154 cent-cinquante-quatre

Module 6

4 **Read Chloé's answer again. Make notes in English about the following points:**
a what Chloé says she does to help protect the environment
b two details about her opinion about helping to protect the environment
c one detail about what Chloé has done recently
d what she is going to do in the future.

5 **Prepare your own answer to the 80–90 word writing task in exercise 2.**
- Think about how you can develop your answer for each bullet point.
- Look back at your notes from exercises 2 and 3.
- Look at the 'Challenge checklist' and consider how you can show off your French!
- Write a **brief** plan and organise your answer into paragraphs.
- Write your answer and then carefully check the accuracy of what you have written.

Challenge checklist

🌶	✓ Past, present and future timeframes ✓ Connectives / time phrases / sequencers ✓ Some extended sentences ✓ Different opinion phrases
🌶🌶	✓ A wide range of tenses ✓ Different persons of the verb ✓ A variety of ways to give your opinion ✓ A wide range of interesting vocabulary
🌶🌶🌶	✓ Phrases with more than one tense ✓ Infinitive phrases (e.g. *on doit, il faut*) ✓ Complex language (e.g. *avant,* + imperfect tense) ✓ Comparatives ✓ A variety of connectives

Translation

6 **Translate the following five sentences into French.**

Does each adjective go before or after the noun? Remember to make them agree.

Remember to use arrêter in the perfect tense. This is then followed by de + the infinitive.

a I fight for the environment.
b Climate change is a catastrophe.
c In my opinion, it's a big problem.
d Last year I stopped travelling by plane.
e I think that electric means of transport are a possible solution.

Remember to use en + type of transport.

Use les transports.

Remember to spot complex grammatical structures such as 'I stopped travelling ...'.

cent-cinquante-cinq 155

Module 6 Vocabulaire

Key:
bold = this word will appear in higher exams only
* = this word is not on the vocabulary list but you may use it in your own sentences

Madagascar: miroir du monde? (pages 134–135)

Les nombres	Numbers
vingt, vingt-six	twenty, twenty-six
trente, trente-quatre	thirty, thirty-four
quarante	forty
cinquante	fifty
soixante	sixty
soixante-dix	seventy
quatre-vingts, quatre-vingt-six	eighty, eighty-six
quatre-vingt-dix	ninety
cent	one hundred
deux-cents	two hundred
mille	one thousand
pour cent	per cent
vingt-deux pour cent	twenty-two per cent

À ton avis, est-ce que *l'écologie est importante? — In your opinion, is ecology important?
Oui, *l'écologie est très / assez importante. — Yes, ecology is very / quite important.
Non, l'*écologie n'est pas très / n'est pas du tout importante. — No, ecology is not very / not at all important.

Es-tu **concerné(e) par** la planète? — Are you concerned about the planet?
Oui, je suis très / assez / un peu **concerné(e) par** la planète. — Yes, I am very / quite / a bit concerned about the planet.
Non, je ne suis pas du tout **concerné(e) par** la planète. — No, I am not at all concerned about the planet.
Est-ce que tu aides à protéger l'environnement? — Do you help to protect the environment?
Oui, chaque jour / souvent. — Yes, every day / often.
De temps en temps. — From time to time.
Non, **rarement**. — No, rarely.

la *déforestation — deforestation
les effets du changement **climatique** — the effects of climate change
*l'extinction des **espèces** — the extinction of species
l'utilisation des ressources naturelles — the use of natural resources
l'organisation — the organisation
la population — the population
la protection — the protection
la solution — the solution

Notre monde est beau (pages 136–137)

plus / moins grand(e) que … — bigger / less big than …
plus / moins long(ue) que … — longer / less long than …
plus / moins haut(e) que … — higher / less high than …

La *Suisse est bien connue pour ses forêts / montagnes. — Switzerland is well known for its forests / mountains.
Au Canada, il y a beaucoup d'animaux, comme **par** exemple … — In Canada, there are lots of animals, like for example …
En *République démocratique du Congo, il y a de grandes villes et de petits villages. — In the Democratic Republic of the Congo, there are large towns and small villages.
Le **paysage** est divers. — The landscape is varied.

Dans ma région, … — In my region, …
Dans le nord, … — In the north, …
Au printemps, … — In spring, …
En été, … — In summer, …
En automne, … — In autumn, …
En hiver, … — In winter, …
  il fait plus chaud / froid … qu'en France / Europe. — it is hotter / colder … than in France / Europe.
  il neige / pleut beaucoup. — it snows / rains a lot.
  il y a du brouillard. — it is foggy.

Planète en danger (pages 138–139)

Quel est le problème le plus important pour la planète? — Which is the most important problem for the planet?
À mon avis, … — In my opinion, …
  le changement **climatique** … — climate change …
  la destruction des forêts … — destruction of the forests …
  la faim … — hunger …
  la pollution de l'air … — air pollution …
  la pollution de la mer … — sea pollution …
    est un problème énorme. — is an enormous problem.
    est une catastrophe. — is a catastrophe.
Je pense que … — I think that …
  *planter plus d'**arbres** et de **fleurs** … — planting more trees and flowers …
  la protection de la mer … — the protection of the sea …
  le recyclage … — recycling …
    améliore la situation. — is improving the situation.
    est une solution possible. — is a possible solution.

va sauver les *habitats des animaux. — is going to save animal habitats.
Je trouve que … — I find that …
  les transports électriques … — electric transport …
  les nouvelles technologies … — new technologies …
    améliorent la situation. — are improving the situation.
    sont une solution possible. — are a possible solution.
    vont **limiter** le danger. — are going to limit the danger.

Quel temps va-t-il faire? — What is the weather going to be like?
Il va faire beau / chaud. — It is going to be nice / hot weather.
Il va faire froid / mauvais. — It is going to be cold / bad weather.
Il y aura du soleil / du vent / du brouillard. — It will be sunny / windy / foggy.

Module 6

Des grands gestes (pages 140–141)

Qu'est-ce qu'il faut faire pour protéger l'environnement?	What must we do to protect the environment?
À mon avis, / Pour moi, il faut …	In my opinion, / For me, we must …
Je pense / crois qu'il faut …	I think / find that we must …
arrêter d'utiliser des **produits** en plastique.	stop using plastic products.
être *bénévole pour des projets verts.	volunteer for green projects.
lutter contre la pollution et la destruction des forêts.	fight against pollution and the destruction of forests.
organiser des **manifestations** pour la protection des animaux.	organise demonstrations for the protection of animals.
respecter la nature.	respect nature.
travailler ensemble pour arrêter le changement **climatique**.	work together to stop climate change.
Sur la photo, il y a quatre personnes / des amis.	In the photo, there are four people / some friends.
La femme a les cheveux longs et noirs.	The woman has long, black hair.
Ils sont dehors, à la montagne.	They are outside, in the mountains.
Il fait beau.	It is nice weather.
Les gens marchent.	The people are walking.
Ils s'amusent. / Ils ne s'amusent pas.	They are having fun. / They are not having fun.
*J'admire beaucoup …	I admire … a lot.
La semaine dernière, j'ai participé à une **manifestation** pour / contre …	Last week, I took part in a demonstration for / against …
J'ai rencontré des personnes intéressantes / sympa.	I met some interesting / nice people.
Après, j'ai écrit un **article** / *blog sur mon expérience.	Afterwards, I wrote an article / blog about my experience.

Des petits gestes (pages 142–143)

Qu'est-ce que tu fais pour protéger l'environnement?	What do you do to protect the environment?
J'achète du papier recyclé.	I buy recycled paper.
Je ne mange pas de viande.	I do not eat meat.
Je prends (toujours) les transports en commun.	I (always) take public transport.
Je recycle les **déchets**.	I recycle rubbish.
Je n'utilise pas de **produits** en plastique.	I do not use plastic products.
Je vais en ville à vélo et non pas en voiture.	I go to town by bike and not by car.
Quand tu étais plus jeune, qu'est-ce que tu faisais pour protéger l'environnement?	When you were younger, what did you do to protect the environment?
Quand j'étais plus jeune, je (ne) m'intéressais (pas) beaucoup à l'environnement.	When I was younger, I was (not) very interested in the environment.
Avant, …	Before, …
j'utilisais / je (ne) mangeais (pas) / je recyclais / j'allais	I used / I ate (did not eat) / I recycled / I went
Qu'est-ce que tu fais pour protéger l'environnement maintenant?	What do you do to protect the environment now?
Maintenant, …	Now, …
je fais beaucoup d'efforts.	I make a big effort.
j'utilise / je ne mange pas …	I use / I do not eat …
je recycle / je vais …	I recycle / I go …
je suis végétarien(ne).	I am vegetarian.
C'est mieux pour l'environnement.	It is better for the environment.

Innovation verte (pages 144–145)

Quelle est votre *innovation?	What is your innovation?
Dans notre collège, …	At our school, …
on **évite** le *gaspillage de **nourriture**.	we avoid food waste.
on fait *pousser nos propres légumes dans le jardin de l'école.	we grow our own vegetables in the school garden.
on fait (aussi) du *compost.	we (also) make compost.
on lutte contre le changement **climatique**.	we fight against climate change.
Quel était le problème, avant?	What was the problem before?
On ne faisait pas beaucoup pour protéger l'environnement.	We did not do a lot to protect the environment.
Il y avait beaucoup de *gaspillage.	There was a lot of waste.
On jetait la **nourriture** à la *poubelle avec les autres **déchets**.	We threw food in the bin with the other rubbish.
On ne recyclait pas.	We did not recycle.
Et qu'est-ce que vous avez fait?	And what did you do?
On a parlé avec le **directeur**.	We spoke to the head teacher.
On a décidé d'organiser …	We decided to organise …
un jardin.	a garden.
le recyclage de la **nourriture** en *compost.	recycling of food into compost.
On a arrêté le *gaspillage.	We stopped waste.
Et c'est comment, maintenant?	And how are things now?
Il n'y a pas de *gaspillage de **nourriture**.	There is no food waste.
C'est beaucoup mieux!	It is a lot better!
Ça fait une énorme différence.	It makes an enormous difference.
Et à l'avenir, qu'est-ce que vous allez faire?	And in the future, what are you going to do?
On va parler à une *conférence.	We are going to speak at a conference.
On va participer à un **concours** *interscolaire.	We are going to participate in an inter-school competition.
On va interdire les sacs en plastique au collège.	We are going to ban plastic bags at school.
On arrive plus/moins vite en avion / à vélo.	You arrive more/less quickly by plane / by bike.
C'est mieux / pire pour la planète que les moyens de transport traditionnels.	It is better / worse for the planet than traditional means of transport.

cent-cinquante-sept

Module 7 — Mon petit monde à moi

À louer, à vendre
- Understanding adverts
- Using demonstrative adjectives (*ce, cet, cette, ces*)

Appartements à louer

A — Appartement 650€ / mois
ROUEN — 1 chambre

B — Appartement 1 030€ / mois
DIEPPE — 2 chambres

C — Appartement 800€ / mois
DEAUVILLE — 3 chambres

Clé des symboles
- chambre(s)
- cuisine
- avec accès pour les personnes handicapées
- salle de bains
- entrée
- jardin

le centre-ville	city centre
l'accès pour les personnes handicapées	access for disabled people
le fauteuil roulant	wheelchair

1 Près du centre-ville
Grand appartement avec trois chambres
Cuisine moderne, jardin
Accès pour les personnes handicapées avec un fauteuil roulant

2 Dans le centre-ville
Agréable appartement pour une personne
Une salle de bains
Jardin

3 À vingt minutes du centre-ville
Deux chambres
Une cuisine
Très moderne

Lire 1 Match each text (1–3) with an advert (A–C).

Écouter 2 Look at the adverts and listen. Write the letter of the flat these people are talking about. (1–2)

Parler 3 How do you pronounce these words? Read them out, then listen and check.

accès pour les personnes h**a**ndic**a**pées   **a**dresse
app**a**rtem**e**nt   s**a**lle de b**a**ins   **e**ntrée   ch**a**mbre   cuisine

Notice the difference between the bold **a** sound and the underlined nasal sounds.

Parler 4 In pairs, talk about the third advert above. Describe the flat and give your opinion.
- Cet appartement est grand?
- Il y a …
- Est-ce qu'il y a un/une …?
- Oui, il y a un/une … / Non, il n'y a pas de/d' …
- Qu'est-ce que tu penses de cet appartement?
- À mon avis, c'est assez / très / trop / un peu …

Not sure whether to use *un* or *une* in exercise 4?
Many (but not all) nouns that end in a consonant are masculine (e.g. **un** appartement).
Many (but not all) nouns that end in -e are feminine (e.g. **une** cuisine).

Remember, *un* and *une* change to **de/d'** after a negative:
Il n'y a pas **de** jardin. Il n'y a pas **d'**accès pour les personnes handicapées.

158 cent-cinquante-huit

Zone de culture

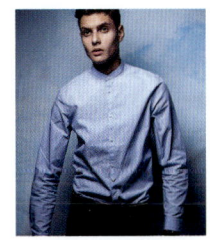

Module 7

Tendance mode

A Chemise bleue — Maintenant 13,00€

B Tee-shirt gris — 22,99€

C Robe — Maintenant 14,50€

D Pantalon noir — 39,99€

E Chaussures noires — 34,99€

assez	enough
trop	too (much)
seulement	only

Écouter 5 Look at the adverts and listen. Write down (a) the letter of the item of clothing they are talking about, and (b) if they are going to buy it. (1–3)

Parler 6 In pairs, make up a dialogue using one of the other adverts above.

- Qu'est-ce que tu vas porter pour aller … ?
- Je vais acheter ce (pantalon) / cette (robe) / ces (chaussures) …

G The demonstrative adjective 'this' varies in French according to gender.

masculine singular	feminine singular	plural
ce tee-shirt (this tee-shirt)	**cette** robe (this dress)	**ces** chaussures (these shoes)

Note: Before a masculine noun that starts with a vowel, you use **cet**. This creates a liaison to make the pronunciation easier: *cet appartement* (this flat).

Page 170

Qu'est-ce que tu vas	porter acheter	pour aller à la fête	de fin d'année? de ton ami(e)?
Je vais Je voudrais		ce tee-shirt / ce pantalon, … cette chemise / cette robe, … ces baskets / ces chaussures, …	
… mais		c'est trop cher pour moi. je n'ai pas assez d'argent.	

Écrire 7 Write a message to a French friend about what you are thinking of wearing or buying for a birthday party this weekend. Ask their opinion.

Pour aller à la fête d'anniversaire ce week-end, je pense que je vais acheter / porter (ce pantalon bleu) avec (ces chaussures noires). Qu'est-ce que tu penses de (ce pantalon)?

Remember, adjectives of colour go after the noun in French and must agree with the noun:

ce pantalon vert   *cette chemise verte*
ces baskets vertes

Blanc (white) is irregular in the feminine forms: *blanche(s)*.

Marron (brown) is invariable (it does not agree).

cent-cinquante-neuf 159

1 Là où j'habite

- Describing your town or village
- Using indefinite adjectives *chaque, tous, tout(e)(s)*
- Using the correct preposition for 'in'

Écouter 1 In pairs, take turns to read out the compass points. Then listen and check.

le nord
le nord-ouest • le nord-est
l'ouest • l'est
le sud-ouest • le sud-est
le sud

Écouter 2 Listen and read. Then copy and complete the sentences in English.

Fathia: J'habite en Algérie dans un petit village près de la capitale, Alger. Alger se trouve sur la côte, dans le nord du pays. La partie ancienne de la ville s'appelle la médina. Chaque jour, beaucoup de touristes viennent visiter ce quartier. Dans la médina, il y a des petites rues avec beaucoup de beaux bâtiments blancs et la Grande Mosquée. Habiter à la campagne est ennuyeux, car il n'y a rien à faire. Je voudrais habiter en ville.

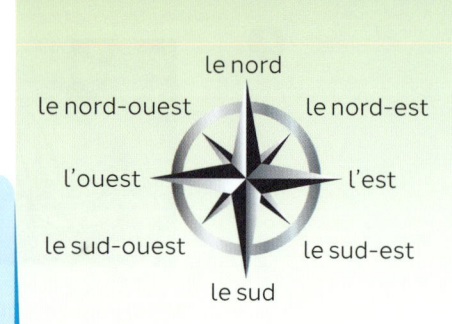

Sofiane: Ma famille et moi habitons à Rouen. C'est une grande ville dans le nord-ouest de la France. Il y a une partie historique, avec beaucoup de vieux bâtiments et de musées. Il y a aussi une partie moderne, avec beaucoup d'entreprises. Habiter ici est parfait pour moi, parce que je peux faire les magasins ou sortir avec tous mes amis.

la médina	medina (usually the historical district/old town in North African cities; the word comes from Arabic and means 'city')
se trouver	to be located/situated
la mosquée	mosque

1 Fathia lives in a ▨, near ▨.
2 Algiers is in the ▨ of Algeria. The streets in the medina have lots of ▨ buildings, and the Great Mosque.
3 Fathia thinks living in the ▨ is ▨. She would like to live ▨.
4 Sofiane lives in Rouen, which is a ▨ in the ▨ of France.
5 There is a ▨ part with ▨ businesses.
6 He thinks it's the perfect place to live, because he can ▨ or ▨ with all his friends.

The verb *habiter* means 'to live (in a place)'.

habiter
j'habite
tu habites
il/elle/on habite
nous habitons
vous habitez
ils/elles habitent

Lire 3 Translate the sentences into English.
1 Tous mes amis habitent à la campagne.
2 Toutes les rues sont petites.
3 Je fais tout le temps les magasins.
4 Chaque année, je pars en vacances dans le nord de la France.
5 Toute ma famille aime habiter en ville.

G Indefinite adjectives talk about people or things in a general way, without being specific:
chaque — each, every
tout/toute/tous/toutes — all, the whole, every

They need to agree with the noun in number and gender, just like all adjectives.

masculine singular	*tout le temps* (all the time)	*chaque jour* (every day)
feminine singular	*toute ma famille* (my whole family)	*chaque année* (each year)
masculine plural	*tous mes amis* (all my friends)	
feminine plural	*toutes les filles* (all the girls)	

Page 170

160 *cent-soixante*

Module 7

4 Listen to the interviews. Then copy and complete the grid in English. (1–2)

> Est-ce que tu habites dans une ville ou un village?

> Où se trouve ta ville / ton village?

> Comment est ta ville / ton village?

> Est-ce que tu aimes habiter dans cette ville / ce village? Pourquoi?

	Town / Village	Country	Location details	Size and description	Opinion and reason
1	Town (Dakar)				

5 In pairs, take turns to ask and answer the questions from exercise 4.
- *Est-ce que tu habites dans une ville ou un village?*
- *J'habite dans une petite ville.*
- *Où se trouve ta ville?*
- *Elle se trouve dans le nord-est de l'Angleterre.*

6 Read the text. Then answer the questions in English.

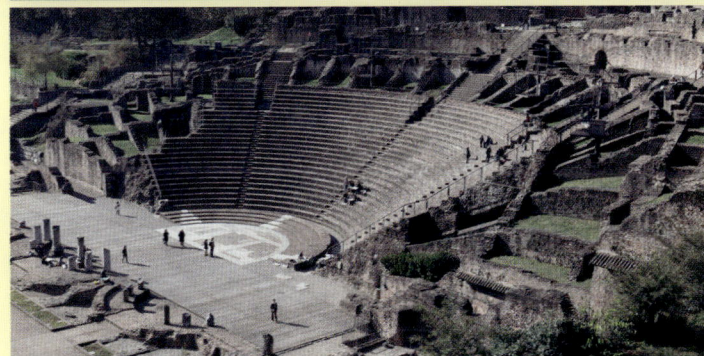

J'habite à Montréal, qui est une des plus grandes villes du Québec, au Canada. J'adore habiter dans cette ville, parce qu'il y a toujours quelque chose à faire.

L'année dernière, je suis allé en vacances à Lyon. Lyon se trouve dans le sud-est de la France. J'ai trouvé que certaines parties de Lyon étaient comme des quartiers de Montréal, avec beaucoup de bâtiments modernes. Mais la ville de Lyon est plus ancienne que Montréal.

Je suis très content d'habiter à Montréal mais un jour, je voudrais passer plus de temps à Lyon.

Hugo

1 Why does Hugo love living in Montreal?
2 Where is Lyon?
3 According to Hugo, in what way is Lyon similar to Montreal?
4 In what way does he say Lyon is different from Montreal?
5 What would he like to do one day?

7 Translate the sentences into French.

1 I live in Dinan, in the west of France.
2 I love living in Dinan.
3 Every year, I visit England with my parents.
4 Last year, I visited York.
5 There are lots of beautiful buildings in York.

> There are different words for 'in' depending on the context. Make sure you use the correct one.
> **dans** + point of compass — **dans** le sud-est
> **à** + name of town/village — **à** Londres
> **en** + feminine country — **en** France
> **au** + masculine country — **au** Canada

cent-soixante-et-un 161

2 Sur la bonne route

- Asking for and understanding directions
- Using *à* and *de* with the definite article
- Using negatives to talk about your town

Écouter 1 Listen to the people talking about where they want to go, and the directions. Write the letters of the correct place and the correct map. (1–3)

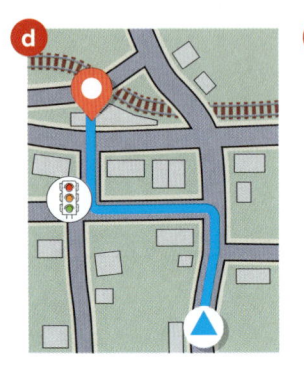

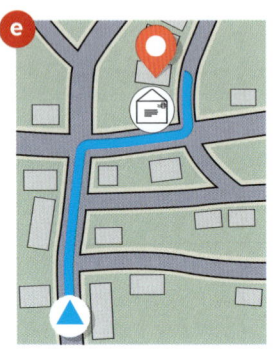

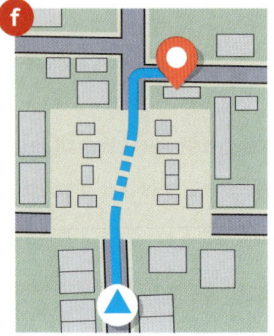

a b c

d e f

la gare	station
les feux (m)	traffic lights
la place	square

Allez / Continuez	tout droit.
Tournez	à gauche / à droite.
Traversez	le pont.
Prenez	la première / la troisième rue à gauche / à droite.
C'est loin / près d'ici?	

Pronounce the letter **r** as a raspy sound in the back of your throat.
The letters **th** are always pronounced 't' in French.
Listen and repeat the sentence.
*Tou**r**nez à d**r**oite à côté du **th**éât**r**e.*

Lire 2 Copy and complete the text with the correct word or phrase from the boxes below. There are three words/phrases you don't need. Then listen and check.

The prepositions *à* and *de* merge with **le** and **les** to form new words. **G**

		le	la	l'	les
à	pour aller ...	**au** parc?	**à la** gare?	à l'hôpital?	**aux** magasins?
de	à côté ...	**du** musée	**de la** poste	de l'hôtel	**des** toilettes

Page 171

Pour aller ⬜1 musée, allez tout droit et tournez à gauche ⬜2 feux. Traversez le pont, puis tournez à droite au coin ⬜3 rue. Le musée est sur la place, près ⬜4 jardin public, à côté ⬜5 Hôtel Bellevue et du théâtre.

de la   aux   à la   du
des   à l'   au   de l'

| le pont | bridge |
| le coin | corner |

Parler 3 In pairs, make up two dialogues using the maps below.

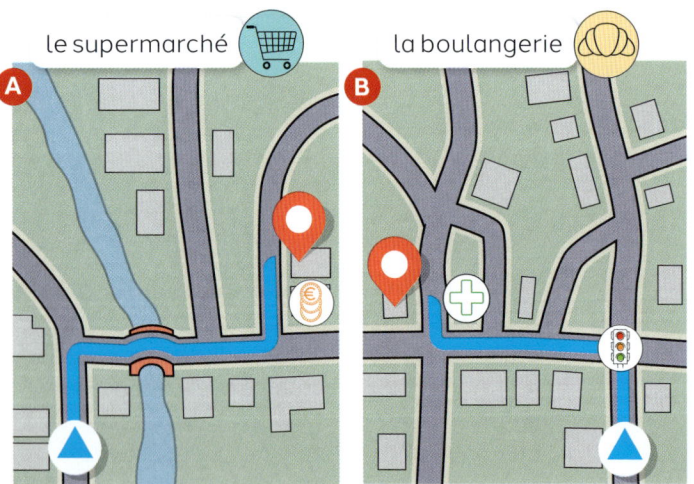

le supermarché   la boulangerie

A   B

Pour aller	au supermarché, à la boulangerie,	s'il vous plaît?
Prenez	la première / la troisième rue à gauche / à droite.	
Traversez	la place. le pont.	
Tournez	à gauche / à droite aux feux.	
C'est à côté	de la banque. de la pharmacie. du jardin public.	
C'est loin? C'est près d'ici?	Oui, ... Non, ...	
Et voilà, vous êtes arrivé(e)(s)!		

162 *cent-soixante-deux*

4 Read the sentences. Then listen and fill in the gaps.
1 On peut acheter du pain au ▨.
2 À Paris, il faut visiter les ▨.
3 Il n'y a pas de ▨ dans ma ville.
4 Au centre-ville, il y a une ▨.

> Look at the words before each gap for clues, e.g. is the word going to be masculine or feminine? Singular or plural?

5 Listen and read. Then note down if each statement is true or false.

Où habites-tu? Qu'est-ce que tu aimes? Qu'est-ce que tu n'aimes pas?

La parole aux jeunes Belges!

Enzo
Dans mon village, il n'y a rien et il n'y a personne de mon âge. Mais je suis content d'habiter ici car c'est un endroit calme.

Nadia
J'habite au centre-ville et il y a une pâtisserie et beaucoup de cafés dans ma rue. Il y a même un hôpital en face de notre maison. Malheureusement, il n'y a pas de cinéma.

Zoé
Il y a beaucoup de trafic devant notre appartement et ce n'est jamais calme. Il y a du bruit et la pollution est terrible.

Maxime
Dans mon quartier, il y a quelques petits magasins. C'est pratique pour faire les courses. Il y a aussi une pharmacie derrière la maison.

> **G** The following prepositions are followed by *de*:
> *près de* — near to
> *loin de* — far from
> *à côté de* — next to
> *en face de* — opposite
>
> The following are used on their own:
> *devant* — in front of
> *derrière* — behind
> *entre* — between
>
> Page 171

malheureusement	unfortunately
le quartier	neighbourhood
quelques	some
faire les courses	to go food shopping

1 Enzo enjoys living in his village.
2 Nadia lives next to a hospital.
3 It's very quiet where Zoé lives.
4 Maxime can go shopping where he lives.

> **G** Like most negatives, the following go around the verb:
> *ne ... pas* — not
> *ne ... jamais* — never, not ever
> *ne ... rien* — not anything, nothing
> *ne ... personne* — nobody, no one
>
> For a reminder about other negative expressions, see page 68.
>
> Page 171

6 Translate the negative phrases that are underlined from exercise 5 into English.

7 Write a paragraph about the place where you live. Include:
- where exactly your town or village is
- what it is like (e.g. big, small, old, modern, pretty ...)
- what there is and is not in your town/village
- whether you like living there and why / why not.

Include at least two negative expressions in your writing.

J'habite	dans	un village près de Manchester. une ville dans le nord-est de l'Angleterre.
Ma ville est		grande / petite / vieille / belle.
Mon village est		grand / petit / vieux / beau.
Il y a	un	supermarché / musée. hôtel / hôpital.
	une	banque / poste / gare.
	beaucoup de quelques	cafés / magasins.
Malheureusement, Mais		il n'y a personne de mon âge. il n'y a rien à faire. il n'y a pas de cinéma. ce n'est jamais calme.

cent-soixante-trois 163

3 Tendances et shopping

- Talking about shopping for clothes
- Using *de* to indicate possession
- Practising shopping role plays

Écouter 1 Listen and read. Then translate the sentences in bold into English.

@Mohammed

J'ai acheté **ce beau tee-shirt blanc** et je l'ai mis pour aller à la fête de mon meilleur ami. Je l'ai porté avec **mon pantalon noir et mes chaussures noires**. Il n'a pas coûté cher et les couleurs sont cool! 😎

#teeshirtcool

@Jade

J'ai vu **cette belle jupe verte et grise** dans un magasin de mode mais elle n'était pas à ma taille! J'ai cherché dans les autres magasins du centre commercial sans succès. Puis j'ai trouvé la jupe en ligne! C'est une bonne marque et elle va super bien avec **ma chemise blanche et rose** et le sac à main vert de ma sœur.

#manouvellejupe

@Gabriel

Ouais! J'ai vendu mes vieilles baskets sur Vinted pour un très bon prix! Avec l'argent, j'ai acheté **cette cravate jaune et bleue** et **ces chaussettes noires, orange et violettes** comme cadeau pour l'anniversaire de mon père. Papa a dit qu'il allait les mettre pour aller au bureau la semaine prochaine! 😆

#cadeaudanniversaire

mettre	to put on (*j'ai mis* / put on (past))
la taille	size
sans succès	without success
le sac à main	handbag

Lire 2 Re-read the posts in exercise 1. Who …
1 bought something online?
2 sold something online to buy a birthday present?
3 wore what they bought to their best friend's party?
4 sold something online (for a very good price)?

G

In English, an apostrophe is used to indicate possession:
my best friend's birthday; my brother's shoes

In French, you use *de* (of):
l'anniversaire de ma meilleure amie ('the birthday of my best friend')
les chaussures de mon frère ('the shoes of my brother')

Page 172

Lire 3 Find, copy out and translate **three** phrases in exercise 1 which use *de* to indicate possession.

Écouter 4 Listen to the teenagers talking about their clothes shopping. Copy and complete the grid in English. (1–2)

	What did they buy? (item(s) and colour)?	Where did they buy it/them?	How much did it/they cost?	When will they wear it/them?
1				

neuf/neuve	brand new

164 *cent-soixante-quatre*

Module 7

Parler 5 In pairs, take turns to read out Jade's text from exercise 1. Give feedback on each other's pronunciation.

> If you add **-e** or **-es** to *vert* or *gris*, you pronounce the final consonant.
> Listen and repeat the words.
> vert   ver**t**e
> gris   gri**s**es

Écouter 6 Listen and read. Then note down the French for the English phrases.

A

- Qu'est-ce que vous cherchez?
- Je cherche une chemise bleue ou blanche.
- C'est pour vous?
- Oui, c'est pour moi. C'est pour la fête de mon amie.
- Vous aimez cette chemise? Elle coûte combien, s'il vous plaît?
- Vingt euros soixante-dix.
- Je peux payer par carte?
- Bien sûr. La caisse est là-bas.
- Caisses

B

- Bonjour. Je peux vous aider?
- Je voudrais échanger ce tee-shirt, s'il vous plaît.
- Quel est le problème?
- Malheureusement, il est trop petit.
- Désolée. Je n'ai pas d'autres tee-shirts dans cette couleur.
- Avez-vous la même chose en noir?
- Oui, voilà. Ça va comme ça?
- Je peux l'essayer, s'il vous plaît?
- Pas de problème.

1 It's for me.
2 How much does it cost?
3 Can I pay by card?
4 The checkout is over there.
5 I'd like to exchange …
6 Unfortunately, it's too small.
7 Do you have the same thing in …?
8 Can I try it on, please?

Parler 7 In pairs, create <u>two</u> new shopping dialogues using the ones above as a model. Change as many details as possible, e.g. clothing, colours, prices, sizes.

- Qu'est-ce que vous cherchez?
- Je cherche <u>un pantalon noir ou gris</u>.

Écrire 8 Write a social media post about an item of clothing you bought online which wasn't quite right.

- Describe what item you bought …
- … and for what special occasion you bought it.
- Mention where you found/saw it/them …
- … and how much it/they cost.
- Mention a problem (too small, too big).

J'ai acheté	ce pantalon noir cette jupe bleue ces chaussures blanches	pour l'anniversaire de ma sœur.
J'ai trouvé ça	dans un magasin de mode.	
Il/Elle a coûté Ils/Elles ont coûté	quarante euros. peu / beaucoup d'argent. cher.	
Il/Elle n'a pas coûté Ils/Elles n'ont pas coûté	cher.	
Malheureusement, Mais	il/elle est trop petit(e). ils/elles sont trop grand(e)s.	

cent-soixante-cinq   **165**

4 La maison de mes rêves

- Describing your ideal home
- Working out if adjectives go before or after the noun
- Using *si* clauses

Écouter 1 Listen and read. Then note down the quiz answers for Thomas. (1–4)

Ta maison idéale

1 Plus tard, je voudrais habiter dans …
- a un château ancien à la campagne.
- b une petite maison en bois à la montagne.
- c un bel appartement neuf.
- d une vieille maison comme dans les films d'horreur!

2 Je voudrais avoir …
- a une cuisine propre et moderne.
- b un bon accès pour les personnes handicapées avec un fauteuil roulant.
- c ma propre chambre calme et confortable.
- d de grandes fenêtres.

3 C'est moins important pour moi d'avoir …
- a beaucoup d'espace.
- b une salle de sport.
- c un joli jardin.
- d des voisins sympa.

4 Si j'étais riche, je voudrais avoir …
- a une télévision à grand écran dans ma chambre.
- b un cinéma privé pour regarder les derniers films.
- c une piscine pour moi tout(e) seul(e).
- d un sauna ou un jacuzzi.

le bois — wood

Parler 2 In pairs, do the quiz.
- *Question numéro un. Plus tard, je voudrais habiter dans un bel appartement neuf. Et toi?*
- *Moi, je voudrais habiter …*

Lire 3 Re-read the quiz. Find and note down in French:
- <u>two</u> phrases with an adjective/adjectives <u>after</u> the noun only
- <u>two</u> phrases with an adjective/adjectives <u>before</u> the noun only
- <u>two</u> phrases with adjectives before <u>and</u> after the noun.

Lire 4 In pairs, take turns to choose a number (1–4) and a letter (a–d) from the quiz, and to translate the full sentence.
- *2d*
- *I would like to have big windows.*

Most adjectives (including colours) go <u>after</u> the noun.
However, the following usually go <u>in front</u> of the noun: grand, petit, joli, beau, vieux.
A noun can have adjectives before and after it, e.g. *une <u>grande</u> et <u>belle</u> maison <u>moderne</u>*.

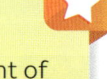

G Some adjectives have a different meaning before and after the noun.
une maison <u>ancienne</u>	an ancient/old house
une <u>ancienne</u> amie	a former friend
une chambre <u>propre</u>	a clean bedroom
ma <u>propre</u> chambre	my own bedroom
un appartement <u>cher</u>	an expensive flat
un <u>cher</u> oncle	a dear uncle

Page 172

166 cent-soixante-six

5 Listen and write down in English what each person's dream or wish is. (1–4)

Example: 1 To buy a new flat in the city centre.

6 Read the text. What do the five words/phrases in blue mean in English?

J'habite avec ma mère et ma sœur dans un appartement. C'est moderne et confortable, mais il y a **peu d'espace** et je dois partager ma chambre avec ma sœur. Si j'avais le choix, je voudrais habiter dans une grande maison, avec ma propre chambre.

En face de notre appart, il y a un vieux bâtiment. Il n'y a personne dans le bâtiment – il est **vide**. Si j'étais riche, je voudrais acheter ce grand bâtiment.

Je rêve d'avoir une chambre avec une belle vue sur la ville. Pour moi, c'est essentiel d'avoir **des chambres d'amis**. Je voudrais aussi avoir une grande cuisine et **une salle à manger**. Enfin, je voudrais avoir **une salle de jeux** pour jouer au tennis de table et aux jeux vidéo.

Voilà la maison de mes rêves!

Eva

Sometimes, you can work out the meaning of unfamiliar words from the context.
What do you think the missing word is in the English translation?
Il n'y a personne dans le bâtiment – il est vide.
No one lives in the building – it is …

Compound words can also give you clues:
la salle = room
manger = to eat
la salle à manger = …

G

You can use *si* ('if') with a verb in the imperfect tense, followed by *je voudrais* (the conditional of *vouloir*) to express your dreams and wishes:
Si j'étais riche, je voudrais avoir une grande maison.
If I were rich, I would like to have a big house.

Page 173

7 Re-read the text. Then answer the questions in English.
1. What does Eva say about her flat? Give two details.
2. What is the main thing she dislikes about living there?
3. Where would Eva live if she had the choice? Give two details.
4. Where is the old building she would like to buy?
5. What would Eva do in her games room?

8 Write a description of your ideal or fantasy home. Include:
- what type of building it would be, and the location
- what rooms you would have
- what would be less important for you.

Include at least one sentence using *si*.

Je voudrais habiter dans	un grand appartement au centre-ville. une vieille maison à la campagne.
Si j'étais riche, je voudrais acheter un château ancien.	
Je voudrais	avoir	un cinéma privé. un joli jardin.
Je rêve C'est essentiel pour moi C'est moins important pour moi	d'avoir	ma propre chambre. une piscine. une salle de jeux. de grandes fenêtres.

cent-soixante-sept 167

5 As-tu déjà visité Paris?

- Talking about visiting another town or city
- Translating questions in different tenses
- Spotting different tenses from verb endings

1 Read the questions. Then write the tense: present, perfect, near future or conditional. Translate each question into English.

a Quand est-ce que tu vas aller à Londres?

b As-tu déjà visité le Royaume-Uni ou un autre pays d'Europe?

c Pourquoi veux-tu visiter ce pays?

d Comment est-ce que tu vas voyager et avec qui?

e Quel pays ou quelle ville voudrais-tu visiter un jour?

f Qu'est-ce que tu vas faire pendant ta visite?

> To spot tenses, look at the verb endings:
> - *-e, -es, -e, -ons, -ez, -ent* = present tense
> - *aller* + infinitive = near future: *je vais visiter, nous allons visiter*
> - *je voudrais, tu voudrais, il/elle voudrait* = conditional.
>
> The perfect tense is in two parts: *tu as visité*; *tu es allé(e)*

2 Read the interview. Write the letter of the correct question from exercise 1 for each gap.

Le voyage de mes rêves!

Bonjour, Raphaël. Je crois que tu as reçu de bonnes nouvelles?

Oui, j'ai gagné une compétition et je vais bientôt aller à Londres!

1

Non, je ne suis jamais allé à Londres, mais j'ai toujours rêvé de visiter le Royaume-Uni.

2

Je veux aller à Londres parce que c'est une belle ville historique et culturelle. Je voudrais voir tous les monuments célèbres et visiter quelques musées.

3

Je vais aller à Londres le week-end prochain!

4

Je vais voyager en bateau. Ensuite, je vais aller à la capitale en train. Je vais faire le voyage avec mon père.

5

Je vais visiter la Tour de Londres et le musée de Madame Tussaud. Je vais faire un tour de la capitale en bus de tourisme.

6

Si j'avais de l'argent, je voudrais visiter New York.

> The word 'tour' has two meanings, depending on the gender:
> **le** tour   tour
> **la** tour   tower

les nouvelles (f)	news
avoir toujours rêvé de	to have always dreamed of

3 Listen and check. In pairs, take turns to read Raphaël's answers. Give feedback on each other's pronunciation.

4 Re-read the interview. Is each statement below true or false?

1. Raphaël received bad news.
2. He has never been to London before.
3. He wants to go to London for its history and culture.
4. He is going to London next month.
5. He is flying to London.
6. If he had money, he'd like to go to New York.

5 Listen to the questions and note down the tense. (1–6) Listen again and choose the correct answer (a or b) for each question.

1. a Je voudrais aller en France.
   b Je ne suis jamais allé en France.
2. a Je veux visiter la tour Eiffel.
   b J'ai visité la tour Eiffel.
3. a Je vais aller à Paris le week-end prochain.
   b Je suis parti avec mes parents.
4. a J'ai visité des musées.
   b Je vais faire un tour en bateau.
5. a Je suis allé en Angleterre.
   b Je vais voyager en avion.
6. a J'ai visité New York.
   b Un jour, je voudrais aller à Montréal.

6 Translate the questions into French. There may be more than one way of writing some of the questions.

1. Have you ever been to France?
2. Why do you want to visit Paris?
3. When are you going to go to Paris?
4. What are you going to do in Paris?

> **G**
>
> The simplest way to ask a question in any tense is to use *est-ce que*…?
> *Est-ce que* tu es déjà allé(e) en Angleterre?
>
> Or you can use inversion:
> *Es-tu* déjà allé(e) en Angleterre?
>
> The following question words can be used with *est-ce que*… or with inversion:
> *Avec qui? Comment? Quand? Où? Pourquoi?*
> e.g. Où est-ce que tu es allé(e)? / Où es-tu allé(e)?
>
> *Qu'est-ce que*…? **cannot** be used with inversion.
> *Quel/Quelle/Quels/Quelles* is an adjective and must agree with the noun.
>
> Page 173

7 Read the advert with your partner. Imagine that one of you has won the competition. Do an interview like the one in exercise 2.

- Je crois que tu as reçu de bonnes nouvelles?
- Oui! J'ai gagné une compétiton et je vais bientôt aller à Paris!
- Quand est-ce que … ?

Tu as gagné un week-end à Paris!	Oui, je suis …
Quand est-ce que tu vas aller à Paris?	Je vais aller …
Es-tu déjà allé(e) à Paris?	Oui, je suis déjà allé(e) à Paris. Non, je ne suis jamais allé(e) à Paris.
Pourquoi veux-tu visiter Paris?	Je veux visiter Paris parce que …
Comment est-ce que tu vas voyager et avec qui?	Je vais aller à Paris en …
Qu'est-ce que tu vas faire pendant ta visite?	Je vais faire … Je vais visiter …
Ça va être comment?	Cela va être génial!

- Use information from the advert and make up any additional information (e.g. time, place).
- Make sure you answer in the correct tense!

Gagnez un week-end à Paris!

▶ Deux nuits (pour deux personnes) dans un hôtel
▶ Voyage aller-retour en avion ou en train (première classe)
▶ Tour de la ville en bateau
▶ Visite de la tour Eiffel et du musée du Louvre
▶ Samedi soir: spectacle devant la cathédrale Notre-Dame de Paris

Grammaire 1

Demonstrative adjectives (Culture, page 159)

1 **Re-read the grammar box on page 159. Copy and complete the sentences, filling in the gaps with the correct form of the demonstrative adjective (ce/cet/cette/ces).**

1 Qu'est-ce que tu penses de ___ chaussures?
2 J'ai acheté une robe bleue pour aller à la fête ___ soir.
3 ___ week-end, je vais porter ___ chemise.
4 J'ai trouvé ___ baskets sur Vinted.
5 ___ maison est jolie.
6 Tu vas mettre un pantalon pour sortir ___ après-midi?

> If you are not sure which demonstrative adjective to choose, check whether the noun after each gap is masculine or feminine, singular or plural.

2 **In pairs, talk about how to pronounce each c or ç in the sentences. Take turns to read the sentences. Then listen and check.**

1 Dans cet appartement, il y a cinq chambres.
2 Il y a un cinéma dans ce quartier.
3 Mon cousin français, Camille, est très célèbre.
4 - Tu as reçu mon cadeau d'anniversaire?
   - Oui, il est ici, merci.
5 - Comment ça va ce matin?
   - Ça va bien, merci.

> The letter **c** is pronounced as a soft sound ('ss') rather than a hard sound ('k')
> - before e and i – c'est, ici
> - when it has a cedilla (ç) – ça va.
>
> Listen and repeat the words.
> **c**'est   i**c**i   **ç**a va

Indefinite adjectives (Unit 1, page 160)

3 **Copy and complete the sentences using a word from the box.**

> toutes   tous   toute   tout   chaque

1 ___ les bâtiments du centre-ville sont vieux.
2 ___ ma famille habite en Martinique.
3 Je sors avec mes amis ___ le temps.
4 ___ jour, beaucoup de personnes vont à Paris.
5 J'ai visité ___ les grandes villes du nord de la France.

> An article (word for 'a'/'an' or 'the') is needed after *tout* but not after *chaque*.

4 **Copy and complete the parallel translations.**

1 ___ année, nous allons en Algérie.	Every ___, we ___ to Algeria.
2 Tous les habitants ___ au centre-ville.	___ the inhabitants work in the ___.
3 Je suis resté à la maison ___ le mois d'août.	I stayed at ___ the whole ___ of August.
4 ___ la classe aime habiter en ville.	The whole ___ likes ___ in town.

Using *à* and *de* with the definite article (Unit 2, page 162)

5 Select the correct form of *de* to complete each sentence.
1. La banque est à côté **de la / du / de l'** supermarché.
2. Tournez à droite au coin **de la / du / des** rue.
3. Elle joue **de l' / du / de la** piano.
4. Mon frère fait **du / de la / des** cuisine.
5. J'habite en face **du / de la / des** magasins.

6 Copy and complete the sentences, filling in the gaps with the correct form of *à* (*au, à la, à l'* or *aux*).
1. Le week-end, on joue ▂▂ cartes.
2. Pour aller ▂▂ cinéma, s'il vous plaît?
3. Tournez à gauche ▂▂ feux.
4. Je dois aller ▂▂ pharmacie.
5. Vous êtes arrivés ▂▂ hôpital.

7 Translate the sentences into French.
1. I am going to the shops.
2. The bank is opposite the café.
3. Do you want to go to the sports centre?
4. We are going to play basketball.
5. Sometimes, I like to go cycling.

> Remember:
> à + le = **au** à + les = **aux**
> de + le = **du** de + les = **des**
>
> - *à* can mean 'at' or 'to':
>   On va *au* musée. (We go to the museum.)
> - *de* often means 'of' or 'from', but this doesn't always translate into English, e.g.
>   *loin de* = far from; *près de* = near to; *en face de* = opposite.
>
> Remember, *à* and *de* are also used with *jouer* and *faire* to refer to sports, musical instruments and other activities:
> jouer **au** football
> jouer **de la** guitare
> faire **du** vélo
> faire **de la** cuisine
> faire **des** sorties

Negatives (Unit 2, page 163)

8 Look at the gapped sentences. Predict the second part of each negative expression. Then listen and fill in the gaps.
1. Dans ma rue, il n'y a ▂▂ de cafés.
2. Je ne suis ▂▂ allé au Canada.
3. Le soir, dans mon village, il n'y a ▂▂ dans les rues.
4. En ville, il n'y a ▂▂ pour les jeunes.
5. Dans notre quartier, il n'y a ▂▂ de poste.

> The following negatives are in two parts that go **around** the verb:
> ne ... *pas*   not
> ne ... *rien*   nothing
> ne ... *jamais*   never
> ne ... *personne*   nobody
>
> Remember that *ne* shortens to *n'* before a vowel.

9 Translate the sentences into French.
1. I never go food shopping.
2. In my street, there is no bakery.
3. There is no one of my age in my village.
4. In my area, there is nothing for young people.

Grammaire 2

Using *de* to indicate possession (Unit 3, page 164)

Parler 1 Read the tip on the right. Then, in pairs, take turns to ask and answer the questions below using the information in brackets.

> Remember, you cannot say 'my brother's shirt' in French. You have to say, 'the shirt of my brother' ('*la chemise de mon frère*').

Example: 1
- *C'est ton tee-shirt?*
- *Non, c'est <u>le tee-shirt de mon père</u>.*

1 C'est ton tee-shirt? (mon père)
2 C'est ton sac? (ma sœur)
3 Ce sont tes baskets? (mon meilleur ami)
4 C'est ton appartement? (mes grands-parents)
5 C'est ton anniversaire demain? (ma mère)
6 Le gâteau, c'est pour ta fête? (mes voisins)

Adjectives which can go before or after the noun (Unit 4, page 166)

Some adjectives can have different meanings, depending on whether they are before or after the noun.

Adjective	Meaning before the noun	Meaning after the noun
ancien/ancienne	former	ancient/old
cher/chère	dear (beloved)	expensive
grand/grande	big, great	tall
propre	own	clean
seul/seule	only	alone, lonely

Lire 2 Decide whether the adjectives should come before or after the noun in the French translations.

1 We live in the ancient part of town.	1 Nous habitons dans **l'ancien quartier / le quartier ancien** de la ville.
2 Look at the big house on the left.	2 Regarde **la grande maison / la maison grande** à gauche.
3 My dear auntie lives in Switzerland.	3 Ma **chère tante / ma tante chère** habite en Suisse.
4 He's our only neighbour.	4 Il est notre **seul voisin / voisin seul**.

Lire 3 Translate each sentence into English. Refer to the grammar box to make sure you use the correct translation of the <u>underlined</u> adjectives.

1 La maison de gauche est notre <u>ancienne</u> maison.
2 J'aime avoir une chambre <u>propre</u>.
3 Ma sœur a un appartement dans un quartier <u>cher</u>.
4 Tu vois l'homme <u>grand</u> avec les cheveux noirs?

172 cent-soixante-douze

Si clauses (Unit 4, page 167)

4 Copy and complete each sentence using the correct word/words from the box.

> In sentences starting with *si*, the **imperfect** comes first and then the conditional.
> Si j'**étais** riche, je voudrais acheter un château.

1 Si j'étais riche, je ___ un bel appartement.
2 Si j'___ le temps, je voudrais faire de la natation tous les jours.
3 Si j'avais le choix, je ___ dans une vieille maison.
4 Si je ___ une compétition, je voudrais aller en Afrique.
5 Si j'___ célèbre, je voudrais avoir un cinéma dans ma maison.

> étais   voudrais habiter
> avais   gagnais
> voudrais acheter

5 Translate the sentences in exercise 4 into English.

Forming questions in different tenses (Unit 5, page 169)

6 Re-read the grammar box on page 169 about forming questions in different tenses. Then copy and complete the question you would need to ask to get each answer. Make sure you match the tense of each question to the tense in each answer.

Example: 1 *Pourquoi veux-tu aller à Paris?*

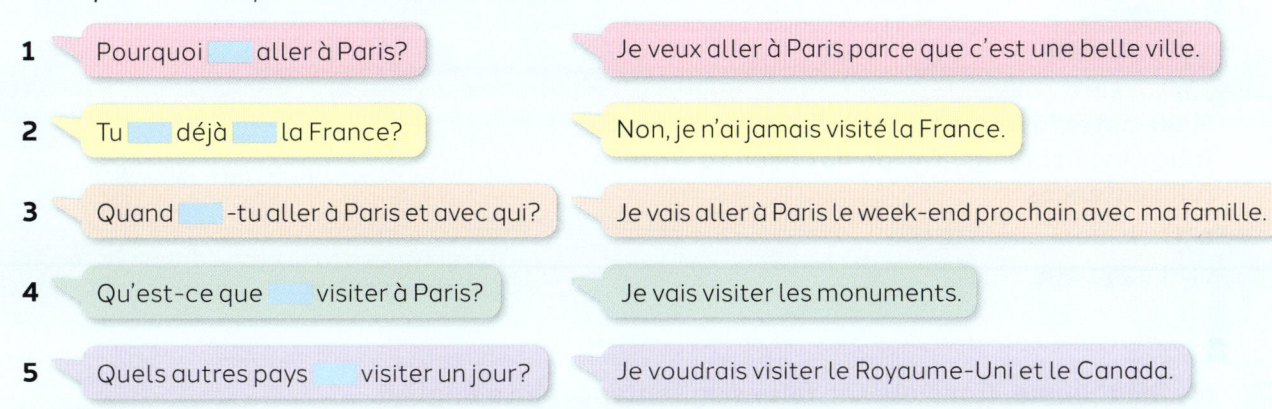

1 Pourquoi ___ aller à Paris? — Je veux aller à Paris parce que c'est une belle ville.
2 Tu ___ déjà ___ la France? — Non, je n'ai jamais visité la France.
3 Quand ___-tu aller à Paris et avec qui? — Je vais aller à Paris le week-end prochain avec ma famille.
4 Qu'est-ce que ___ visiter à Paris? — Je vais visiter les monuments.
5 Quels autres pays ___ visiter un jour? — Je voudrais visiter le Royaume-Uni et le Canada.

7 Translate the questions into French. There may be more than one way of writing some of the questions.

a When did you go to Paris?
b Are you going to visit Canada?
c Why would you like to visit Morocco?
d How do you travel and with whom?
e Which museum did you visit?
f What would you like to do during your visit?

C'est parti!

8 In pairs, take turns to read the text. Give feedback on each other's pronunciation. Then listen and check.

> J'habite dans une vieille ville dans le sud-ouest du pays. J'habite avec ma famille dans un bel appartement. Si j'avais le choix, je voudrais habiter dans une jolie petite maison à la campagne. Dans ma ville, il n'y a rien pour les jeunes. Mais je vais sortir ce soir! Pour aller à la fête d'anniversaire de ma meilleure amie, je vais mettre ces chaussures grises.

Module 7 — Contrôle de lecture et d'écoute

Reading

Lire 1

My ideal place to live. Read these comments from an internet forum.

Maxime:
Je ne sais pas exactement où je voudrais habiter à l'avenir, mais je voudrais habiter en Asie parce que je voudrais connaître une culture complètement différente.

Jade:
Je voudrais habiter près de ma famille en ville, car habiter à la campagne est ennuyeux et il n'y a personne. C'est essentiel pour moi de partager ma vie avec d'autres personnes.

Alessandro:
Si j'étais riche, je voudrais habiter dans un petit village historique. Je ne voudrais jamais acheter une maison moderne parce que j'adore l'histoire, et la tradition est très importante pour moi.

Make notes in English for each person under the following headings. You do not need to write in full sentences.

a Their ideal place to live
b Reason why

> Find all the negatives in the text. They are going to be useful to work out the answers.

> You only need to give one detail. For each question there might be two possible answers.

Lire 2

My ideal home. Translate the following sentences **into English**.

> Don't forget to translate these important words.

> How will you translate this conditional?

a J'habite dans un appartement assez ancien.
b Nous n'aimons pas les logements modernes.
c Je suis très content de mon quartier.
d À l'avenir, je voudrais avoir ma propre piscine.
e Je vais acheter une maison à la campagne avec beaucoup d'espace.

> If you don't know these adjectives yet, can you make an intelligent guess?

> Take extra care translating this word. What do we use in English?

cent-soixante-quatorze

Listening

3 **Buying presents.** Marie, Louis and Alex are talking about buying presents. What do they say? Listen to the recording and complete each sentence by writing down the correct letter (A–C).

1. Marie is likely to get a present on …
   - **A** Sunday.
   - **B** Saturday.
   - **C** Friday.

2. Marie is going to buy her brother …
   - **A** a phone.
   - **B** a book.
   - **C** a game.

3. Louis goes shopping …
   - **A** where he lives.
   - **B** in a shopping centre.
   - **C** in a nearby town.

4. Alex never buys …
   - **A** clothes.
   - **B** bags.
   - **C** pens.

You are going to hear each day mentioned. Concentrate on when she is going to go.

Beware of negatives!

4 **Where I would love to live.** Listen to Fatima talking about where she would love to live. What does she mention? Write the letter (A–F) for each of the three correct options.

A	facilities
B	the local area
C	the building
D	shops
E	the weather
F	neighbours

You may not hear those exact words in French. Think carefully about what Fatima mentions and how it links to one of the options.

5 **My home.** Axel and Léa are talking about where they live. Where do they live and what do they dislike about it? Listen to the recording, then copy and complete the following table **in English**. You do not need to write in full sentences.

	Axel …	Léa …
lives …		
dislikes …		

Listen out for Axel saying something negative about where he lives.

6 **Dictation.** You are going to hear someone talking about their bedroom.

a Sentences 1–3: write down the missing words. For each gap, you will write one word **in French**.

1. J'ai un petit ▢ et un ▢.
2. Je voudrais une ▢ et une ▢.
3. Le ▢ est ▢.

When listening to the full sentences, think about the meaning as well as the sounds.

b Sentences 4–6: write down the full sentences that you hear, **in French**.

cent-soixante-quinze 175

Module 7 Contrôle oral

Read aloud

Parler 1 Look at this task card. With a partner, take turns to read out the five sentences, paying attention to the underlined letters and the highlighted liaisons and cognates.

Jules, your French friend, has emailed you to tell you about his town.

Read out the text below to your teacher.

> J'habite dans une ville.
> Elle est grande et historique.
> Dans ma région, il y a beaucoup de touristes.
> On a plusieurs hôtels et un théâtre moderne.
> J'adore les bâtiments anciens mais la gare n'est pas belle.

Take extra care with how you pronounce the underlined sounds:
- *r* sounds like a raspy sound in the back of your throat.
- *i* and *y* sound the same, similar to the 'ee' in 'bee'.
- *h* is silent.

Remember your liaisons!

Take extra care with how you pronounce cognates.

Écouter 2 Listen and check your pronunciation.

Parler 3 Listen to the teacher asking the two follow-up questions. Translate each question **into English** and prepare your own answers **in French**. Then listen again and respond to the teacher.

These two questions will ask for your opinion on subjects that relate to the text you have just read aloud.

Role play

Parler 4 Look at the role-play card and prepare what you are going to say.

Setting: At the café

Scenario:
- You are at a café in France with a friend and you speak to the waiter.
- The teacher will play the part of the waiter and will speak first.
- The teacher will ask questions **in French**, and you must answer **in French**.
- Say a few words or a short phrase/sentence for each prompt. One-word answers are not sufficient to gain full marks.

Task:
1. Say what you would like to order.
2. Say a type of shop you would like to go to.
3. Ask for directions.
4. Say what you would like to buy.
5. Say why you are in France.

You could say a chemist, shopping centre or supermarket.

You can use *Je voudrais* followed by an infinitive.

Ask for either a drink or some food, e.g. a coffee, an ice cream or some chips.

Start with *Pour aller* or *Où*.

What is the simplest reason to give?

Parler 5 Practise what you have prepared. Then, using your notes, listen and respond to the teacher.

Écouter 6 Now listen to Toni doing the role-play task. **In English**, note down (a) how she **answers** the questions for task prompts 1, 2, 4 and 5, and (b) what question she **asks** for task prompt 3.

cent-soixante-seize

Module 7

Picture task

Écouter 7 Look at the exam card below and read the **first part** of the task. Then listen to Zoë describing the picture. Answer the questions **in English**.

1 What does Zoë say about the people in the picture and where does she say they are? Do you agree?
2 Who does she describe in the most detail and what does she mention?
3 What does she say about the background? Do you agree?

Describe this picture.
Your description must cover:
- people
- location
- activity.

When you have finished your description, you will be asked **two questions** relating to the picture. Say a short phrase/sentence in response to each question. One-word answers will not be sufficient to gain full marks.

You will then move on to a **conversation** on the broader thematic context of **My neighbourhood**.

During the conversation, you will be asked questions in the present, past and future tenses. Your responses should be as **full and detailed** as possible.

> To talk about where people or things are, you can use **prepositions** such as *à gauche* (on the left), *à droite* (on the right) and *derrière* (behind).

Parler 8 Prepare your own description of the picture, mentioning **people**, **location** and **activity**. Then, with a partner, take turns to describe the picture.

> Sur la photo, il y a …

Parler 9 Read the **second part** of the task. Then listen to the two follow-up questions and respond to the teacher. Remember: you only need to give a short answer to each one.

Écouter 10 Read the **third part** of the task. The teacher asks Zoë: *Le week-end, qu'est-ce que tu fais dans ta ville ou ton village?* Listen to her answer. Copy and complete the table below **in English**.

What activity?	Weather

Écouter 11 Listen to Zoë answering the question: *Dans quelle région du monde est-ce que tu voudrais habiter plus tard et pourquoi?* Listen and complete the translation **into English**.

1 I think that I would like …
2 If possible, I would like …

> Try to extend your sentences, using starters such as *si possible* and *je pense que* to improve your answers.

Parler 12 Prepare your own answers to the Module 7 questions on page 227. Your responses should be as **full and detailed** as possible. Then practise with a partner.

cent-soixante-dix-sept 177

Module 7 Contrôle écrit

40–50 word writing task

1 Look at this writing exam task and then, for each bullet point, think about the vocabulary you could include and how you can develop your answer.

> You could start your answer with *Dans mon quartier, il y a un magasin de …* Mention what the shop sells (food, clothes, games, books etc.) and how big it is.

Write a review of a shop for a website.

You **must** include the following points:
- a description of the shop
- your opinion of the shop
- what you are going to buy in the shop this weekend.

Write your answer **in French**. You should aim to write between 40 and 50 words.

> Give one opinion backed up with a reason (*j'aime/ j'adore …, parce que …*).

> Remember to use the near future tense here.

2 Read Nadia's answer to the exam task. Answer questions 1–5 in the coloured shapes.

1 This is an example of **complex language**. What does it mean? Find <u>three</u> more examples of complex language from the text.

2 How could she form an **extended sentence**? What other extended sentences does Nadia include?

Dans ma ville, il y a un magasin de vêtements. C'est assez petit mais j'aime le magasin. Il y a un bon choix de vêtements à la mode. Ce week-end, je vais acheter une nouvelle chemise pour mon beau-père parce que c'est l'anniversaire de mon beau-père. Je pense qu'il va être content!

3 This phrase shows a **variety of vocabulary**. What does it mean? Find <u>two</u> more examples.

4 Which **tense** is this? What other examples of this tense can you find? What other tenses does she use?

5 How could she **avoid repetition** by rephrasing this?

3 Read Nadia's answer again. Write down **in English** <u>five</u> details that she gives.

4 Prepare your own answer to the 40–50 word writing task in exercise 1.

80–90 word writing task

5 Look at this writing exam task and then, <u>for each bullet point</u>:

1 think about what vocabulary you have learned which you could use in your answer. For example:
- **nouns** and **verbs** to talk about where you live
- **verbs of opinion** and **adjectives** to explain your point of view
- language for **narrating a story** about what you did recently in your area
- how to explain where you will live in the future.

2 write down <u>three or four</u> ideas for what you could write about.

3 write down which tense(s) you will need to use in your answer.

> Write to your friend about where you live.
>
> You **must** include the following points:
> - a description of where you live
> - your opinion of facilities in your town
> - something you have done there recently
> - where you will live ideally in the future.
>
> Write your answer **in French**. You should aim to write between 80 and 90 words.

cent-soixante-dix-huit

Module 7

Lire 6 Read Gabriel's answer to the exam task. Answer questions 1–5 in the coloured shapes.

1 This is an example of **complex language**. What does it mean? Find <u>three</u> more examples from the text.

2 This word shows a **variety of vocabulary**. What does it mean? Find <u>two</u> more examples.

3 How could he form an **extended sentence**? What other extended sentences does Gabriel include?

4 Which **tense** is this? What other examples of this tense can you find? What other tenses does he use?

5 How could he **avoid repetition** by using another word or phrase?

> Salut!
>
> J'habite dans une ville qui se trouve dans le sud. Ma ville est vraiment agréable parce qu'il y a des bâtiments anciens.
>
> Malheureusement, je déteste habiter ici car c'est ennuyeux. Il n'y a rien pour les jeunes. Je ne vais pas souvent au centre commercial. Le café a fermé récemment.
>
> Hier, je suis allé en ville pour acheter un pull bleu pour l'école. Ensuite, j'ai décidé d'essayer le nouveau restaurant français. C'était génial!
>
> À l'avenir, je vais habiter dans un endroit calme. Si possible, je vais avoir ma propre maison avec un grand jardin.
>
> Gabriel

Lire 7 Read Gabriel's answer again. Make notes **in English** about the following points:

a where Gabriel lives
b what there is in his town
c <u>one</u> positive aspect of his town and <u>one</u> negative aspect
d what he did yesterday
e where he will live in the future and why.

Écrire 8 Prepare your own answer to the 80–90 word writing task in exercise 5.

- Think about how you can develop your answer for each bullet point.
- Look back at your notes from exercises 5 and 6.
- Look at the 'Challenge checklist' and consider how you can show off your French!
- Write a **brief** plan and organise your answer into paragraphs.
- Write your answer and then carefully check the accuracy of what you have written.

Challenge checklist

🌶️
- ✓ Past, present and future timeframes
- ✓ Connectives, time phrases and sequencers
- ✓ Some extended sentences
- ✓ Different opinion phrases

🌶️🌶️
- ✓ A wide range of tenses
- ✓ Different persons of the verb (e.g. *le café a fermé*)
- ✓ A variety of adjectives
- ✓ A wide range of interesting vocabulary

🌶️🌶️🌶️
- ✓ Phrases with more than one tense
- ✓ Complex language (e.g. *qui se trouve*)
- ✓ More complex negatives (e.g. *ne … rien, ne … jamais*)
- ✓ A variety of connectives

cent-soixante-dix-neuf

Module 7 Vocabulaire

Key:
bold = this word will appear in higher exams only
* = this word is not on the vocabulary list but you may use it in your own sentences

À louer, à vendre (pages 158–159)

Qu'est-ce que tu penses de cet appartement?	What do you think of this apartment?
Il y a …	There is …
un **accès** pour les personnes handicapées.	access for disabled people.
un jardin / une entrée.	a garden / an entrance.
une chambre / une cuisine.	a bedroom / a kitchen.
une *salle de bains.	a bathroom.
Est-ce qu'il y a un jardin / une entrée?	Is there a garden / an entrance?
Oui, il y a un jardin / une entrée.	Yes, there is a garden / an entrance.
Non, il n'y a pas de jardin / d'entrée.	No, there is no garden / entrance.
Qu'est-ce que tu vas acheter?	What are you going to buy?
Qu'est-ce que tu vas acheter / porter pour aller …	What are you going to buy / wear to go …
à la fête de fin d'année?	to the end-of-year party?
à la fête de ton ami(e)?	to your friend's party?
Pour aller à la fête ce week-end, je pense que je vais acheter / porter …	To go to the party this weekend, I think that I am going to buy / wear …
ce *tee-shirt / pantalon.	this t-shirt / these trousers.
cette chemise / robe.	this shirt / dress.
ces baskets / chaussures.	these trainers / shoes.
Je voudrais acheter cette chemise, mais …	I would like to buy this shirt, but …
c'est trop cher pour moi.	it's too expensive for me.
je n'ai pas assez d'argent.	I do not have enough money.
Qu'est-ce que tu penses de …	What do you think of …
ce pantalon noir / blanc / marron?	these black / white / brown trousers?
cette robe noire / blanche / marron?	this black / white / brown dress?
ces chaussures noires / blanches / marron?	these black / white / brown shoes?

Là où j'habite (pages 160–161)

Est-ce que tu habites dans une ville ou un village?	Do you live in a town or a village?
Où se trouve ta ville / ton village?	Where is your town / village?
Comment est ta ville / ton village?	What is your town / village like?
Est-ce que tu aimes habiter dans cette ville / ce village? Pourquoi?	Do you like living in this town / village? Why?
J'habite dans un petit village / une grande ville.	I live in a small village / large town.
Il/Elle se trouve dans …	It is in …
le nord / l'est / le nord-est	the north / the east / the northeast
le sud-est / le sud	the southeast / the south
le sud-ouest / l'ouest	the southwest / the west
le nord-ouest …	the northwest …
de l'Angleterre / de la France / du Canada.	of England / France / Canada.
près de la capitale	near the capital city
Il y a une partie historique / moderne, avec …	There is a historic / modern part, with …
des petites rues.	little streets.
beaucoup de beaux / vieux bâtiments.	lots of beautiful / old buildings.
beaucoup d'entreprises.	lots of businesses.
Habiter à la campagne / en ville est parfait pour moi, car …	Living in the countryside / town is perfect for me, as …
il y a toujours quelque chose à faire.	there is always something to do.
je peux faire tout le temps les magasins.	I can go shopping all the time.
je peux sortir avec tou(te)s mes ami(e)s.	I can go out with all my friends.
Je suis très content(e) d'habiter ici.	I am very happy to live here.
Un jour, je voudrais …	One day, I would like to …
habiter à la campagne / en ville.	live in the countryside / town.
passer plus de temps à *Lyon.	spend more time in Lyon.

Sur la bonne route (pages 162–163)

Pour aller au supermarché / à la boulangerie, s'il vous plaît?	How do you get to the supermarket / bakery, please?
Allez / Continuez tout droit.	Go / Continue straight ahead.
Tournez à gauche / à droite (aux feux).	Turn left / right (at the traffic lights).
Traversez la place / le pont.	Cross the square / bridge.
Prenez la première / la troisième rue à gauche / à droite.	Take the first / third road on the left / right.
C'est à côté / *en face …	It's next to / opposite …
du jardin public.	the public garden.
de la banque.	the bank.
des magasins.	the shops.
C'est devant / derrière …	It's in front of / behind …
le parc.	the park.
la pharmacie.	the pharmacy.
les toilettes.	the toilets.
C'est entre le cinéma et la pâtisserie.	It's between the cinema and the cake shop.
Et voilà, vous êtes arrivé(e)(s)!	And there it is, you've arrived!
C'est loin / près d'ici?	Is it far from / near here?
Ma ville est grande / petite.	My town is large / small.
Ma ville est vieille / belle.	My town is old / beautiful.
Mon village est grand / petit.	My village is large / small.
Mon village est vieux / beau.	My village is old / beautiful.

Il y a …	There is/are …	Malheureusement, / Mais …	Unfortunately, / But …
un hôpital / hôtel / musée.	a hospital / hotel / museum.	il n'y a personne de mon âge.	there is no one of my age.
une banque / gare / poste.	a bank / train station / post office.	il n'y a rien à faire.	there is nothing to do.
beaucoup de/quelques cafés / magasins.	a lot of/some cafés / shops.	il n'y a pas de cinéma.	there is no cinema.
		ce n'est jamais calme.	it is never quiet.
		la pollution est terrible.	the pollution is terrible.

Tendances et shopping (pages 164–165)

Qu'est-ce que vous cherchez?	What are you looking for?	ces chaussures blanches … pour l'anniversaire de mon frère / ma sœur.	these white shoes … for my brother's / sister's birthday.
C'est pour vous?	Is it for you?		
Vous aimez cette chemise?	Do you like this shirt?		
Elle coûte combien, s'il vous plaît?	How much does it cost, please?	J'ai trouvé ça dans un magasin de mode / en ligne.	I found that in a fashion shop / online.
Je peux payer **par** carte?	Can I pay by card?	Il/Elle a coûté …	It cost …
Bonjour. Je peux vous aider?	Hello. Can I help you?	Ils/Elles ont coûté …	They cost …
Quel est le problème?	What is the problem?	quarante euros.	forty euros.
Avez-vous la même chose en noir?	Do you have the same thing in black?	beaucoup d'argent.	a lot of money.
		peu d'argent.	little money. (It/They did not cost much money.)
Ça va comme ça?	How's that?		
Je peux l'essayer, s'il vous plaît?	Can I try it on, please?	Il/Elle n'a pas coûté cher.	It was not expensive.
J'ai acheté …	I bought …	Ils/Elles n'ont pas coûté cher.	They were not expensive.
ce pantalon gris et vert …	these grey and green trousers …	Mais il/elle est trop petit(e) / grand(e).	But it is too small / big.
cette cravate jaune …	this yellow tie …	Malheureusement, ils/elles sont trop petit(e)s / grand(e)s.	Unfortunately, they are too small / big.
cette jupe bleue …	this blue skirt …		
ces chaussettes noires, orange et roses …	these black, orange and pink socks …		

La maison de mes rêves (pages 166–167)

Plus tard, je voudrais habiter dans …	Later, I would like to live in …	de grandes fenêtres.	big windows.
		beaucoup d'espace.	lots of space.
un château ancien à la campagne.	an ancient castle in the countryside.	une salle de sport / jeux.	a sports / games room.
		une salle à manger.	a dining room.
une petite maison en bois à la montagne.	a little wooden house in the mountains.	des chambres d'amis.	guest bedrooms.
		un *joli jardin.	a pretty garden.
un bel appartement neuf.	a beautiful, brand-new apartment.	des voisins sympa.	nice neighbours.
		une télévision à grand **écran** dans ma chambre.	a large-screen TV in my bedroom.
une vieille maison comme dans les films d'horreur!	an old house like in horror films!	un cinéma privé pour regarder les derniers films.	a private cinema to watch the latest films.
Et toi?	And you?	une piscine pour moi tout(e) seul(e).	a swimming pool just for me.
Je voudrais avoir …	I would like to have …		
Je rêve d'avoir …	I dream of having …	Il y a peu d'espace.	There is little space.
C'est essentiel / moins important pour moi d'avoir …	It is essential / less important for me to have …	Je dois partager ma chambre.	I have to share my bedroom.
Si j'étais riche, / Si j'avais le choix, je voudrais avoir …	If I were rich, / If I had the choice, I would like to have …	une maison ancienne / une ancienne amie	an ancient house / a former friend
une cuisine propre et moderne.	a clean, modern kitchen.	une chambre propre / ma propre chambre	a clean bedroom / my own bedroom
un bon **accès** pour les personnes handicapées avec un fauteuil roulant.	good access for disabled people with a wheelchair.	un appartement cher / un cher oncle	an expensive apartment / a dear uncle
ma propre chambre calme et confortable.	my own calm and comfortable bedroom.		

As-tu déjà visité Paris? (pages 168–169)

As-tu déjà visité le Royaume-Uni ou un autre pays d'Europe?	Have you ever visited the UK or another European country?	Qu'est-ce que tu vas faire pendant ta visite?	What are you going to do during your visit?
Pourquoi veux-tu visiter ce pays?	Why do you want to visit this country?	Ça va être comment?	What is it going to be like?
		Quel pays ou quelle ville voudrais-tu visiter un jour?	Which country or town would you like to visit one day?
Quand est-ce que tu vas aller à *Londres?	When are you going to go to London?	Cela va être génial!	That is going to be great!
Comment est-ce que tu vas voyager et avec qui?	How are you going to travel and who with?	Si j'avais de l'argent, je voudrais visiter *New York.	If I had the money, I would like to visit New York.

cent-quatre-vingt-un

Module 8: Mes projets d'avenir

Mon été de rêve
- Talking about summer plans
- Using two different tenses to express the future

1 Parler
Listen and repeat these words. Pay special attention to the pronunciation of *ill/ille* and *ail/aill*.

la fam**ille**   une f**ille**   un b**ill**et

un trav**ail**   trav**aill**er   Vers**aill**es

> The double 'll' in -*ail*/-*aill*- and in -*ill*-/-*ille* sounds like the 'y' sound in English, rather than the English 'l'.

2 Lire
Read the text. Put the images of different summer jobs (a–f) in the order in which they appear in the text.

Quel travail peut-on faire à 16 ans?

Beaucoup d'emplois sont ouverts aux jeunes. Voici quelques idées:

- Vous pouvez travailler dans une ferme: vous pouvez, par exemple, cueillir des fruits.
- Vous pouvez servir les clients. Vous pouvez travailler dans une boulangerie ou dans un supermarché.
- Vous pouvez faire du babysitting ou promener des chiens.
- Vous pouvez devenir animateur de vacances ou aider dans un centre sportif.

l'emploi (m)	job
cueillir	to pick (fruits)
promener	to (take for a) walk

a   b   c
d   e   f

> Summer camps (*des colonies de vacances*) are popular in France. Children go to them to learn new skills, do sports, play games and work in teams. Older teenagers often work as an *animateur* (m) or *animatrice* (f) to look after the children and organise the activities. You can even do a qualification called the BAFA to become an *animateur*.

3 Écouter
Listen to the teenagers talking about potential summer jobs. Then copy and complete the grid in English. (1–5)

	Job	Positive or negative opinion?	Reason
1	Babysitting		

Je voudrais / Je ne voudrais pas	travailler dans	une ferme / une boulangerie / un supermarché	parce que / car	c'est — intéressant. / génial. / dur. / ennuyeux.
	faire du babysitting			j'aime / j'adore / je n'aime pas — les animaux. / les enfants. / le sport.
	promener des chiens			
	être animateur ou animatrice			
	aider dans un centre sportif			

182 *cent-quatre-vingt-deux*

Zone de culture

Module 8

Parler 4 In pairs, take turns to ask and answer questions about the summer jobs suggested in exercise 2.
- Est-ce que tu voudrais <u>travailler dans un supermarché</u>?
- <u>Non, je ne voudrais pas</u> <u>travailler dans un supermarché</u> car <u>c'est dur</u>. Et toi, est-ce que tu voudrais <u>faire du babysitting</u>?

Écouter 5 Listen to and read the text about interrailing. With a partner, work out the significance of each of the numbers below.

Allez partout en Europe avec le Pass Interrail. Explorez en train plus de 30 000 destinations et 33 pays.

Vous avez 27 ans ou moins?
Achetez votre Interrail Pass Jeune!
Réduction de 25% sur vos voyages en train et sur vos activités et vos visites.

Idées de voyage

Je vais visiter l'est de l'Europe – on va visiter la Pologne.

Je vais voir le château de Versailles. On va voyager partout en France!

Ce week-end, je vais à Bruxelles avec ma sœur. Samedi matin, on visite la Grand-Place.

la Pologne	Poland
partout	everywhere
Bruxelles	Brussels

Le château de Versailles

La Grand-Place à Bruxelles

1 25 **2** 27 **3** 33 **4** 30,000

Lire 6 Translate the sentences in the speech bubbles in exercise 5 into English.

Écouter 7 Listen to the statements expressing future plans. (1–5) Which tense is each one in? Write:
- **a** for the near future tense
- **b** for the present tense with a future time adverb.
  Example: 1 a

> **G**
> To express the future, you usually use the **near future tense** (aller + an infinitive), e.g.
> Je <u>vais visiter</u> l'Italie.
> I am going to visit/will visit Italy.
>
> However, sometimes the <u>present tense</u> is used <u>with a time adverb</u> to express the future, e.g.
> <u>Ce week-end</u>, <u>je visite</u> Paris avec mes amis.
> This weekend I am visiting Paris with my friends.
>
> Page 192

cent-quatre-vingt-trois **183**

1 Mes passions et mon avenir

- Talking about future plans and hopes
- Using a range of structures followed by the infinitive
- Using sequencers

Écouter 1 Read the grammar box. Then listen and, for each speaker (1–8), note down:
- the French phrase they use from the grammar box
- the letter of the correct picture.

> **G** You can use any of these phrases, followed by **an infinitive**, to talk about your future plans and wishes:
>
> | Je veux | I want to | Mon ambition est de | My ambition is to |
> | Je voudrais | I would like to | Mon but est de | My aim is to |
> | J'espère | I hope to | | |
>
> Page 192

a avoir des enfants

b réussir mes examens

c voyager et travailler à l'étranger

d aller à l'université

e faire une formation professionnelle

f me marier

g gagner beaucoup d'argent

h avoir ma propre entreprise (le patron)

Écouter 2 Listen and read. Then answer the questions in English.

> Pour commencer, je veux continuer mes études.
> J'espère réussir mes examens l'année prochaine.
> Ensuite, mon but est d'aller à l'université.
> Après, j'espère visiter d'autres pays et être bénévole pour un projet vert à l'étranger.
> Puis je voudrais entrer dans le monde du travail.
> Mon but est de travailler dans les médias.
> Plus tard, mon ambition personnelle est de vivre avec ma copine. Je ne veux pas me marier.
> Un jour, j'espère avoir des enfants.
> **Sophie**

vivre to live

1 What does Sophie hope to do next year?
2 What two things does she want to do between finishing university and finding a job?
3 In which sector is she aiming to work?
4 What is her personal ambition?
5 What does she hope to do one day?

> ★ Use sequencers to extend your sentences and order your ideas.
>
> | pour commencer | first of all, to start with |
> | ensuite | next |
> | puis | then |
> | après | afterwards |
> | plus tard | later |
> | un jour | one day |

184 cent-quatre-vingt-quatre

Module 8

3 In pairs, talk about your future plans.

- *Qu'est-ce que tu veux faire à l'avenir?*
- *Pour commencer, je voudrais …*
  Après, j'espère …
  Puis …
  Et toi?

4 Read the article. Find the French for the phrases below.

Université ou formation professionnelle?

À mon avis, pour trouver un bon travail, il faut aller à l'université.

Moi, je vais certainement aller à l'université pour étudier les maths. Plus tard, je vais choisir une carrière. Après plusieurs années d'études, il y a beaucoup de possibilités!

En plus, à l'université, on peut devenir plus indépendant. On peut aussi se faire de nouveaux amis.

Après l'université, je voudrais être bénévole. Un jour, je voudrais habiter à la campagne avec mon chien!

Anna

Je ne suis pas d'accord. On peut trouver un bon poste sans aller à l'université.

Je voudrais travailler dans le tourisme parce que je veux habiter et travailler à l'étranger.

Mon but est de faire une formation professionnelle pour développer des compétences pratiques.

En plus, je veux gagner de l'argent sans faire de longues études!

Plus tard, j'espère me marier et avoir des enfants.

Habib

la compétence skill

1 You can find a good position without going to university.
2 You can become more independent.
3 I want to earn money without doing long studies.
4 In order to find a good job, you have to go to university.
5 Later, I am going to choose a career.
6 My aim is to do an apprenticeship in order to develop practical skills.
7 After several years of studies, there are lots of possibilities.

> **G**
> *sans* + infinitive means 'without (doing something)',
> e.g. *sans aller à l'université* without going to university
>
> *pour* + infinitive means 'in order to (do something)',
> e.g. *pour gagner de l'argent* in order to earn money
>
> Page 192

5 Listen. Then copy and complete the grid in English. (1–3)

	University or apprenticeship?	Reason	Other plans/details
1			

6 Write a blog post about what you want to do in the future, including whether you want to go to university and why / why not. Include:

- different phrases to introduce future plans
- sequencers
- one sentence using *pour* + an infinitive or *sans* + an infinitive.

cent-quatre-vingt-cinq **185**

2 Express Mondial

- Talking about travelling and earning money
- Using verbs that take *être* in the perfect tense
- Buying tickets at a station

Écouter 1 Listen and read about the *Express Mondial* competition. Find the French for the verbs below, choosing from the underlined words in the text.

Bienvenue à l'Express Mondial!

Le but pour les couples, c'était de traverser le Canada le plus vite possible. Sans avion, sans Internet! Qui a gagné?

Les voyages

<u>On est partis</u> de Vancouver à 14h00 le lundi. <u>On a voyagé</u> en train et <u>on est restés</u> une nuit à l'hôtel à Calgary.

Ensuite, on a pris le bus. Quand on est arrivés à Winnipeg, on est restés deux nuits dans un hôtel. Pour gagner de l'argent, <u>nous avons travaillé</u> dans une boulangerie. On a gagné l'équivalent de douze euros de l'heure.

Finalement, <u>nous avons pris</u> le train et nous sommes arrivés à Québec à 20h00 le vendredi.

Zahida et Ahmed

Voici Zahida et son frère Ahmed. Ils habitent à Paris.

Nous sommes parties de Vancouver à 13h00 le lundi. Pour commencer, nous avons pris la voiture et nous sommes restées une nuit à l'hôtel à Banff.

Après, on a continué le voyage en bus et <u>on a passé</u> une nuit dans un autre hôtel, à Jasper. Nous avons travaillé dans un café et là, <u>nous avons gagné</u> environ quatorze euros de l'heure.

Finalement, on a pris le train, et <u>on est arrivées</u> à Québec à 14h00 le samedi.

Valérie et Nancy

Voici Valérie et sa sœur Nancy. Elles habitent à Biarritz.

1 we took
2 we worked
3 we travelled
4 we arrived
5 we spent
6 we stayed
7 we left
8 we earned

> Both *nous* and *on* can be used to mean 'we'. For some of the verbs, you might see the *nous* form in one text and the *on* form in the other.

Lire 2 Re-read the texts in exercise 1, and look at the maps and the key. Then note down which map corresponds to which couple (Zahida and Ahmed or Valérie and Nancy).

> **G** Remember that some verbs, e.g. *aller*, *partir*, *arriver* and *rester*, form the perfect tense with *être*, not *avoir*. For verbs that take *être*, the past participle must agree with the subject. What difference do you note between the past participles of these verbs in the two texts?
>
> Page 193

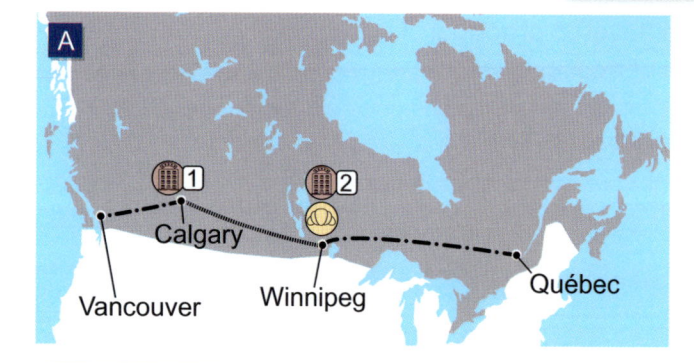

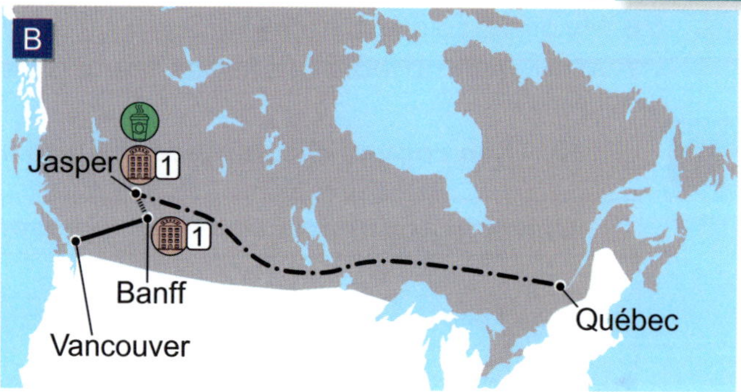

A Vancouver — Calgary — Winnipeg — Québec

B Vancouver — Banff — Jasper — Québec

Key:
- ·–·–· en train
- ———— en bus
- ———— en voiture
- un hôtel
- un terrain de camping
- une boulangerie
- un café
- un magasin

186 *cent-quatre-vingt-six*

Module 8

3 Re-read the text in exercise 1. Copy and complete the grid in English.

	1 Zahida and Ahmed	2 Valérie and Nancy
Left Vancouver at ...	2 p.m. on Monday	
Worked in ...		
Earned ...		14 euros per hour
Arrived in Quebec at ...		

4 Listen to Nicholas and Chloé's account of their journey. Write down the missing words in French. Then answer the question below in English.

1. Nous sommes partis à ▨ heures le lundi.
2. Nous avons pris ▨ et nous sommes restés ▨ sur un terrain de camping à Edmonton.
3. On a travaillé dans ▨ et on a gagné ▨ euros de l'heure.
4. On a continué le voyage en ▨ et on a passé une nuit dans ▨ à Toronto.
5. Finalement, nous avons pris ▨ et nous sommes arrivés à Québec à ▨ le samedi.

Which of the three couples won? (Work out which couple got from Vancouver to Quebec in the shortest time!)

5 Translate the sentences into French. You can use either *on* or *nous* for 'we'.

1. We earned 20 euros per hour.
2. To start with, we took the bus.
3. We stayed for two nights on a campsite.
4. Finally we arrived in Paris at 11 o'clock.

6 Listen to the two conversations. Write down the correct option to complete each sentence. (1–2)

Acheter des billets de train dans une gare en France

- Excusez-moi, à quelle heure part le prochain train pour **(a) Paris / Marseille / Strasbourg**?
- Le train part à **(b) 10h30 / 13h30 / 19h00**.
- Et le train arrive à quelle heure?
- Il arrive à **(c) 13h00 / 21h00 / 15h15**.
- Un aller, ça coûte combien?
- C'est **(d) 18 / 20 / 22** euros.
- Et un aller-retour, c'est combien?
- Un aller-retour, c'est **(e) 28 / 30 / 38** euros.
- Est-ce que je peux avoir **(f) deux allers / quatre allers / deux allers-retours**, s'il vous plaît?
- Ça fait **(g) 76 / 78 / 80 euros**. Merci.

un aller	a single
un aller-retour	a return

7 In pairs, adapt the conversation in exercise 6 to create <u>two</u> new conversations, choosing from the details below.

Destination	Le Mans	Rouen	Nantes
Départ	10:10	11:00	12:30
Arrivée	12:20	13:15	14:00
Aller	30€	15€	20€
Aller-retour	45€	25€	30€

- 2x allers
- 1x aller, 1x aller-retour
- 3x allers-retours

cent-quatre-vingt-sept 187

3 Quelles sont tes compétences?

- Talking about possible future career paths
- Forming feminine nouns
- Looking up words for possible future jobs

Écouter 1 Listen to the careers interviews. Write down the <u>five</u> correct letters for each speaker. (1–4)

Quelles sont tes passions?
- a Ma passion, c'est la mode.
- b Moi, j'adore les sciences.
- c Ma passion, c'est voyager.
- d Aider les autres, c'est ma passion.

Comment es-tu?
- e Je suis travailleur/travailleuse.
- f Je suis sympa et patient(e).
- g Je suis responsable et indépendant(e).
- h Je suis créatif/créative.

Avec qui voudrais-tu travailler?
- i Je voudrais travailler seul(e).
- j Je veux travailler avec des enfants.
- k Je voudrais travailler avec des gens.
- l Je veux travailler avec des animaux.

Qu'est-ce que tu trouves important dans un travail?
- m Être responsable, c'est important pour moi.
- n Avoir un travail intéressant, c'est essentiel.
- o Être actif/active, c'est très important pour moi.
- p Pour moi, un bon salaire est essentiel.

Quelles sont tes compétences?
- q Mon point fort, c'est la communication.
- r Je suis très organisé(e).
- s J'ai une attitude positive.
- t Je m'entends bien avec tout le monde.

G Sometimes we can use <u>infinitives</u> as nouns in French. When they are used this way, we translate them as '-ing' in English. For example:
<u>Aider les autres</u>, c'est ma passion. <u>Helping other people</u> is my passion.
<u>Avoir un travail intéressant</u>, c'est essentiel. <u>Having an interesting job</u> is essential.

Page 194

Parler 2 In pairs, take turns to ask and answer the questions in exercise 1.
- Quelles sont tes passions?
- Ma passion, c'est l'environnement.
- Comment es-tu?
- Je suis travailleuse et gentille.

Ma passion, c'est …	le sport / le théâtre. la lecture / l'environnement. les films / les ordinateurs.
Je suis …	amusant(e) / calme. sérieux/sérieuse. sportif/sportive. gentil/gentille.

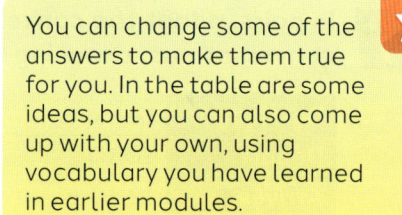

⭐ You can change some of the answers to make them true for you. In the table are some ideas, but you can also come up with your own, using vocabulary you have learned in earlier modules.

⭐ Use connectives to create extended sentences:
et, **donc**, **car** …

Module 8

3 Read the texts. Select the correct job word to complete each one. Then listen and check.

1. Je suis créative et responsable et j'aime travailler en équipe. La cuisine, c'est ma passion. Je voudrais travailler comme ▭. **Camille**

2. Ma passion, c'est la musique. Être créatif, c'est important pour moi. Je m'entends bien avec tout le monde et j'ai une attitude positive. J'espère être célèbre. Je voudrais être ▭. **Jack**

3. Je suis patiente et travailleuse. Un bon salaire est assez important pour moi, mais ma passion, c'est la santé. Je veux aider les autres. Je vais être ▭. **Anna**

> **G**
>
> Job nouns often change according to gender:
>
> -eur → -euse influenceur/influenceuse (influencer)
> -teur → -trice acteur/actrice (actor)
> -en → -enne mécanicien/mécanicienne (mechanic)
> - → -e ingénieur/ingénieure (engineer)
>
> Note that chanteur → chanteuse is an exception.
>
> Some nouns do not change, e.g. médecin (doctor).
>
> People who identify as non-binary may prefer to use the following structures:
> Je suis mécanicien·ne. Je suis ingénieur·e.
>
> When referring to jobs, you do not need the word for 'a' in French:
> Je voudrais être joueuse de basket.
> I would like to be <u>a</u> basketball player.
>
> Page 194

- médecin
- directeur/directrice
- joueur/joueuse de foot
- chef/cheffe
- chanteur/chanteuse

4 In pairs, take turns to choose one text from exercise 3 and read it out.

5 Write a paragraph to explain why you would like to do a particular job and what makes you suitable for it.

Je voudrais être …

Je voudrais être	acteur / joueuse de basket …
parce que ma passion, c'est	le cinéma / le sport.
Je suis	travailleur / active.
Je veux travailler	seule(e) / avec des enfants.
Les films / Être en forme,	c'est important pour moi.
En plus,	je m'entends bien avec tout le monde. le salaire est essentiel.

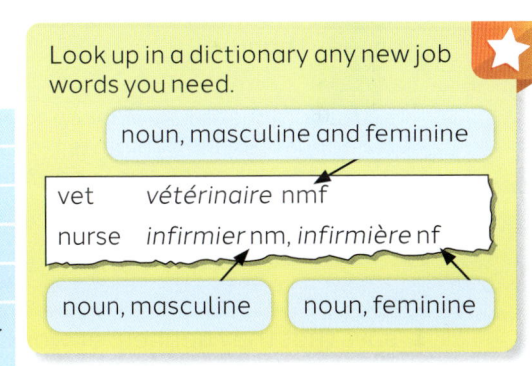

> ⭐ Look up in a dictionary any new job words you need.
>
> noun, masculine and feminine
>
> vet — vétérinaire nmf
> nurse — infirmier nm, infirmière nf
>
> noun, masculine   noun, feminine

6 Listen to Antoine. For each of his family members, write down in English (a) the job, and (b) the <u>two</u> reasons why it's suitable for them.

1. his mum
2. his dad
3. his brother
4. his aunt

7 Imagine that you know these people. Write a few sentences about each person and their job.

- What job do they do? Il/Elle est / travaille comme …
- What is their passion? Il/Elle adore … / Sa passion, c'est …
- What sort of person are they? Il/Elle est …

cent-quatre-vingt-neuf 189

4 Bien payé, mais fatigant!

- Talking about different jobs
- Using verbs followed by *à* or *de*
- Translating into French using a range of timeframes

Écouter 1
Listen and write down the letters of the two correct pictures for each speaker. (1–4)

Les points positifs 😃

- **a** Le travail est bien payé.
- **b** Les gens sont sympa.
- **c** Le travail est intéressant.
- **d** On peut prendre ses propres décisions.

Les points négatifs 😟

- **e** Ça peut être dangereux.
- **f** Les heures sont longues et c'est fatigant.
- **g** La formation est longue.
- **h** On ne gagne pas beaucoup d'argent.

Lire 2
Read the texts and answer the questions.

> Je travaille dans une banque. Un point positif, c'est que mon travail est bien payé. Cependant, c'est fatigant. Il faut travailler dur et les heures sont longues. **Logan**

> Je suis architecte et j'ai ma propre entreprise. Je peux prendre mes propres décisions et j'adore ça. Un point négatif, c'est que la formation est longue. **Lily**

> Je suis journaliste. Le point négatif, c'est que ça peut être dangereux. Mais j'aime le travail parce que c'est passionnant et parce que j'apprends beaucoup. **Harry**

> Je travaille dans un hôtel. Je trouve le travail difficile et je ne gagne pas beaucoup d'argent. Mais je m'entends bien avec les gens qui sont très sympa. Mes collègues m'aident beaucoup. **Joelle**

le/la collègue — colleague

Who …
1 says that they get help at work?
2 has their own business?
3 thinks that they are well paid?
4 thinks that their work is exciting?
5 finds their work hard?
6 says that they learn a lot?

Parler 3
In pairs, talk about what you think the positive and negative aspects are of the jobs pictured below.
- Être *policier ou policière*. Quels sont les points positifs?
- Un point positif, c'est que *le travail est intéressant*.
- Quels sont les points négatifs?
- Un point négatif, c'est que *ça peut être dangereux*.

policier/policière    scientifique    joueur/joueuse de tennis

190 *cent-quatre-vingt-dix*

Module 8

4 Listen and read. Then find the French for the phrases below.

Après l'université, je suis devenu influenceur. Ma passion était la mode, mais en ligne, c'était souvent très négatif.
Il y a deux ans, j'ai décidé de faire quelque chose de différent.
J'ai réussi à créer ma propre entreprise en informatique et maintenant je suis plus heureux.
Les heures sont longues, mais je peux prendre mes propres décisions.
À l'avenir, je vais continuer de travailler dur. **Alexis**

Après le collège, j'ai travaillé comme actrice, mais je n'étais pas très heureuse. Aider les autres, c'est ma passion. Donc, il y a trois ans, j'ai commencé à étudier la politique à l'université.
Maintenant, je suis politicienne! J'essaye de lutter contre le changement climatique.
Le mois prochain, je vais parler à une conférence. Je rêve d'être présidente un jour! **Manon**

1 I decided to do something different.
2 I succeeded in creating my own business.
3 I will continue to work hard.
4 I started to study politics.
5 I try to fight against climate change.
6 I dream of being president one day.

créer — to create
il y a (deux ans) — (two years) ago

Some verbs are followed by *à* or *de* + the infinitive:

commencer à — to start to
réussir à — to succeed in
continuer de — to continue to
décider de — to decide to
essayer de — to try to
rêver de — to dream of

Page 195

5 Re-read the texts in exercise 4. Select the correct option to complete each sentence.

1 Alexis stopped being an influencer because of **bad pay / negativity online**.
2 He changed career **last year / two years ago**.
3 His business is in the **IT / fashion** sector.
4 Manon became an actress after **school / university**.
5 Her passion is **studying / helping others**.
6 Soon, she is going to **attend an event / become a politician**.

6 Listen to the people talking about their careers. Then copy and complete the grid in English. (1–2)

	Job they used to do	What they didn't like about it	Job they do now	What they like about it
1				

7 Translate the sentences into French.

Use the imperfect tense. Take care with the verb endings and remember to put 'ne' and 'pas' around the verbs.

You don't need the French word for 'a'.

Use the perfect tense.

1 After school, I worked in a hotel.
2 I was not very happy and it was not well paid.
3 I decided to go to university.
4 Now I am a scientist. The work is interesting.
5 In the future I will try to do something different.

Do you need *à* or *de* after the verb?

Use the near future tense. Don't forget the *de* after this verb.

cent-quatre-vingt-onze 191

Grammaire 1

Expressing the future using two different tenses (Culture, page 183)

1 Read the grammar box on page 183. Then read the sentences below. Which tense is used? Write 'near future' or 'present + future time adverb'. Then translate the sentences into English.

Example: 1 near future – We are going to work abroad.

1 Nous allons travailler à l'étranger.
2 Elles vont voyager avec leurs parents.
3 Ce week-end, je vais à Paris avec mes amis.
4 À l'avenir, je vais travailler avec des animaux.
5 Demain, elle joue au foot.
6 Il va faire du babysitting.

> Remember that the near future tense is formed using the present tense of *aller* + **an infinitive**.
>
> je *vais* **voyager**
> tu *vas* **travailler**
> il/elle/on *va* **voir**
> nous *allons* **visiter**
> vous *allez* **jouer**
> ils/elles *vont* **faire**
>
> In each sentence in exercise 2, do you hear a part of *aller* + an infinitive, or just a verb in the present tense (e.g. *je travaille, je vais*) **without** an infinitive?

2 Listen and fill in the gaps with the missing verbs. Some are in the near future and some are in the present tense (but express the future). (1–6)

Example: 1 vais visiter

1 Je ___ l'Allemagne avec mes parents.
2 Cet été, Aurélie ___ en Espagne.
3 Demain, je ___ dans une ferme.
4 Il ___ la tour Eiffel.
5 Est-ce que tu ___ en Europe?
6 Ce soir, je ___ au tennis avec ma sœur.

Using different structures followed by the infinitive to talk about future plans and wishes (Unit 1, page 184)

3 Read the grammar box on page 184. Then, in pairs, take turns to choose a letter from each of the boxes. Your partner says the sentence in French.

- b, f
- *Je voudrais avoir ma propre entreprise.* c, j
- *J'espère …*

a I want to …
b I would like to …
c I hope to …
d My ambition is to …
e My aim is to …

f le patron
g
h
i
j

Using *sans* and *pour* followed by an infinitive (Unit 1, page 185)

4 Read the grammar box on page 185. Write out the phrases below in the correct order to form sentences using *sans* or *pour* + an infinitive. Then translate them into English.

1 pour | Je voudrais faire | développer des compétences pratiques | une formation
2 des enfants | sans | On peut avoir | se marier
3 à l'université | Je veux aller | devenir professeur | pour
4 aller à l'université | beaucoup d'argent | On peut gagner | sans

Module 8

The perfect tense (Unit 2, page 186)

5 **Translate these sentences into English. Then look at the underlined perfect-tense verbs. Is the auxiliary verb *avoir* or *être* in each case?**

1 <u>Nous sommes parties</u> à dix heures le vendredi.
2 <u>J'ai pris</u> le train et <u>je suis restée</u> à l'hôtel.
3 <u>On a travaillé</u> dans une boulangerie et <u>on a gagné</u> seize euros de l'heure.
4 <u>Ils ont pris</u> la voiture et <u>ils sont arrivés</u> à Montréal à seize heures le dimanche.

> Remember, the perfect tense is made up of two parts:
> 1 the auxiliary verb (part of **avoir** or **être**)
> 2 the past participle.
>
> Here is a list of some key verbs that form the perfect tense with *être*, and their past participles.
>
> *aller* (to go) → *allé*
> *arriver* (to arrive) → *arrivé*
> *partir* (to leave) → *parti*
> *rester* (to stay) → *resté*
>
> Remember that for verbs which take *être*, the past participle must agree with the subject:
> *Sophie est parti**e** en vacances.*
> *Nous sommes allé**s** en France.*
> *Elles sont arrivé**es** à 10 heures.*

6 **Copy and complete the sentences by selecting the correct auxiliary verb.**

Example: 1 *Ils ont pris le bus.*

1 Ils **ont / sont** pris le bus.
2 Nous **avons / sommes** restés trois nuits dans cet hôtel.
3 Il **a / est** voyagé pendant trois jours.
4 Elles **ont / sont** parties à 20h00.
5 **J'ai / Je suis** arrivée le lundi.
6 Nous **avons / sommes** voyagé en voiture.
7 Est-ce que tu **as / es** resté dans un terrain de camping?
8 Vous **avez / êtes** pris le train?

7 **Imagine that you took part in the *Express Mondial* race around Canada (see Unit 2, page 186). In pairs, take turns to ask and answer the questions below. Use the ideas in the pictures.**

- *Quand est-ce que tu es parti(e)?*
- *Je suis parti(e) à …* 10:00 11:30 13:15

- *Tu as voyagé comment?*
- *J'ai pris …*

- *Où est-ce que tu es resté(e)?*
- *Je suis resté(e) …*

- *Tu as travaillé où?*
- *J'ai travaillé …*

- *Quand est-ce que tu es arrivé(e)?*
- *Je suis arrivé(e) à …* 18:00 19:30 21:00

cent-quatre-vingt-treize 193

Grammaire 2

Using infinitives as nouns (Unit 3, page 188)

Parler 1 Read the grammar box on page 188. In pairs, take turns to make up sentences containing a phrase from each box. Take care with your pronunciation. Your partner then translates your sentence into English.

Aider les autres,
Protéger l'environnement,
Gagner un bon salaire,
Travailler avec des animaux,
Voyager et travailler à l'étranger,

c'est ma passion.
c'est important pour moi.
ce n'est pas important pour moi.
ça ne m'intéresse pas.

Masculine, feminine and plural nouns (Unit 3, page 189)

Lire 2 Read the sentences. Select the correct option to complete each sentence.
1. Mon père est **chanteur / chanteuse**.
2. Ma mère est **acteur / actrice**.
3. Mon frère est **policier / policière**.
4. Ma sœur veut être **président / présidente**.
5. Ma tante est **chef / cheffe**.

> Some nouns have different masculine and feminine forms. The key patterns you need to know are:
> -eur → -euse   influenceur/influenceuse (influencer)
> -teur → -trice   directeur/directrice (director/boss)
> -en → -enne   mécanicien/mécanicienne (mechanic)
> - → -e   président/présidente (president)
>
> There are some other patterns too, e.g.
> che**f**/che**ffe** (chef)
> polic**ier**/polic**ière** (police officer)
>
> Some nouns do not change, e.g. *médecin* (doctor), *artiste* (artist).
>
> People who identify as non-binary may prefer to use the following structures:
> Je suis infirmier·ière.   Je suis influenceur·ceuse.
>
> 💡 Most nouns add *-s* to form the plural. However, there are some exceptions:
> - Masculine nouns ending in *au*, *eau* or *eu* add *-x*:
>   un bâteau, des bâteaux   one boat, (some) boats
>   un jeu, des jeux   one game, (some) games
> - Nouns that already end in *-x* or *-s* do not change:
>   un choix, des choix   one choice, (some) choices
>   un fils, des fils   one son, (some) sons

Écrire 3 Fill in the gaps with the correct form of the noun in bold.

Example: 1 *joueur*

1. Sarah est **joueuse** de foot professionnelle. Son petit frère voudrait aussi être ___ de foot.
2. Mon père était **mécanicien** et ma cousine veut aussi travailler comme ___.
3. Joseph est **médecin**. Sa femme est aussi ___.
4. Ma cousine Zahra est très connue comme **influenceuse**. Mon frère veut aussi être ___.
5. Mon meilleur ami voudrait être **président** un jour. Ma sœur espère aussi être ___ à l'avenir.
6. Ma tante est **professeur** mais mon cousin ne veut pas être ___!

Écrire 4 Write the plural forms of each of the nouns below.

Example: 1 *des châteaux*

1. un château (*a castle*)
2. un ami (*a friend*)
3. un virus (*a virus*)
4. un feu (*a fire*)
5. un joueur (*a player*)
6. un prix (*a price*)
7. un bureau (*an office*)
8. un film (*a film*)
9. un pays (*a country*)
10. un réseau (*a network*)

Verbs followed by à or de + an infinitive (Unit 4, page 191)

Écrire 5 Copy and complete each sentence with à or de/d'. Then translate the sentences into English. Take care with the tenses!

Example: 1 *J'ai réussi à trouver un travail.* I (have) succeeded in finding a job.

> Some verbs are followed by **à** or **de** + the infinitive, e.g.
>
> | | | | |
> |---|---|---|---|
> | arriver à | to manage to | décider de | to decide to |
> | commencer à | to start to | essayer de | to try to |
> | réussir à | to succeed in | finir de | to finish |
> | arrêter de | to stop | rêver de | to dream of |
> | continuer de | to continue to | | |
>
> Je n'arrive pas **à** faire mes devoirs.   I can't manage to do my homework.
> J'arrête **de** travailler le samedi!   I'm stopping working on Saturdays!

1 J'ai réussi ___ trouver un travail.
2 Elle a décidé ___ quitter son poste.
3 Lise a commencé ___ jouer au foot le samedi.
4 Mon père va continuer ___ faire du babysitting pour ma sœur.
5 Je vais essayer ___ aller à l'université.
6 Je rêve ___ devenir mécanicien·ne.
7 Elle n'arrive pas ___ trouver un travail à l'étranger.
8 J'ai fini ___ travailler dans le magasin.

C'est parti!

Écouter 6 Listen and write down the missing words.

J'ai décidé **1** devenir **2**.

3 avoir mon propre restaurant un jour! Je voudrais aussi **4** beaucoup d'argent.

Je pense qu'on peut avoir un bon travail **5** aller à l'université.

L'année prochaine, je **6** faire une formation professionnelle.

7, c'est très important pour moi.

L'été dernier, je **8** allé en Angleterre et j'ai **9** dans un hôtel.

> There are lots of infinitives in this exercise. These often end in -*er*. However, the final sentence is in the perfect tense and, for gap 9, you need a past participle.

Lire 7 Read the text. Look for and note down examples of each of the grammar points below.

> J'ai décidé d'aller à l'université pour continuer mes études.
>
> Mon but est de devenir médecin.
>
> Aider les autres, c'est ma passion!
>
> À l'avenir, je vais me marier mais je ne vais pas avoir d'enfants.
>
> Je voudrais aussi voyager un peu pour apprendre des langues.
>
> L'année dernière, je suis allée en Suisse et j'ai visité des villages traditionnels.

- The near future tense
- Different structures followed by an infinitive to express hopes/plans
- *Pour* + an infinitive
- Using an infinitive as a noun
- The perfect tense with *avoir*
- The perfect tense with *être*
- A verb followed by à or de + the infinitive

Parler 8 In pairs, take turns to read out the text from exercise 7. Give feedback on each other's pronunciation.

cent-quatre-vingt-quinze **195**

Module 8 — Contrôle de lecture et d'écoute

Reading

Lire 1

A gap year. Read this post that Rachid has written on his blog.

> Hier, Clara est venue à son ancien lycée pour parler aux élèves de son **année sabbatique***. Son histoire était vraiment intéressante. Elle a travaillé dans un club de jeunes où elle a lu aux jeunes enfants, et elle a aussi préparé des repas sains pour des familles pauvres. Elle a aimé jouer avec des jeunes handicapés.

**l'année (f) sabbatique* — gap year

a Write down the word for the gap in each sentence, using the words from the box. There are more words than gaps.

> college   youth club   Rachid's family   young   poor   disabled   older

- **(i)** Clara came to her former ___ to talk about her gap year.
- **(ii)** She read to ___ children.
- **(iii)** She liked playing with ___ young people.

Most of the adjectives feature in the text. Look for where Rachid talks about Clara reading to young children and playing with young people.

The blog continues.

> Moi, je voudrais voyager et aider des gens à l'étranger. Clara a gagné de l'argent, mais pour moi, ce n'est pas important si je n'ai pas de salaire. Plus tard, je voudrais être journaliste parce que c'est un travail passionnant et sérieux.

b Complete the sentences below. For each sentence, write the correct letter (A–C).

- **(i)** Rachid is going to …
  - **A** go on holiday.
  - **B** help people abroad.
  - **C** earn money.
- **(ii)** For Rachid, having a salary …
  - **A** isn't important.
  - **B** is important.
  - **C** is more important than travelling.

c Answer the following questions in English. You do not need to write in full sentences.

- **(i)** What job does Rachid want to do?
- **(ii)** Give <u>one</u> reason why he wants to do this job.

Lire 2

My career. Translate the following sentences **into English**.

Think carefully about how to translate these structures.

Think carefully about how to translate both verbs here.

- **a** Je veux continuer mes études.
- **b** Je dois choisir ma carrière.
- **c** Je m'intéresse à beaucoup de choses et il y a trop de choix.
- **d** Je suis allé à un événement qui s'appelle «Mon avenir».
- **e** J'espère voyager et aider des organisations.

These phrases are different ways to express quantities.

What tense is this?

196   cent-quatre-vingt-seize

Listening

3 **Travelling.** Fathia, Ahmed and Morgane are talking about their journeys. What do they say? Listen to the recording and complete each sentence with the correct letter (A–C).

1 Fathia is going to the train station at …
   A 5 p.m.   **B** 6 p.m.   **C** 7 p.m.

2 Ahmed is buying …
   A three tickets.   **B** a single ticket.   **C** a return ticket.

3 Morgane and her sister are travelling by …
   A bus.   **B** car.   **C** train.

4 **My career plans.**

a Marie is talking about her career plans. What does she say? Listen to the podcast and answer the following questions **in English**. You do not need to write in full sentences.

   (i) What career would Marie like to have?
   (ii) What does she like most about this sort of work?

> Marie mentions a necessary quality for this job. Is it relevant?

b Dorian and Ana are also talking about career options. What would they like and not like to do? Listen to the recording, then copy and complete the following table **in English**. You do not need to write in full sentences.

	Dorian …	Ana …
would like …		
would not like …		

5 **Careers advice.** Alex is talking to a career advisor about his future plans. What does he say? Listen to the recording and make notes **in English** under the following headings. You do not need to write in full sentences.

a The industry Alex would like to work in
b What isn't important for him
c What he plans to do after sixth form

6 **Dictation.** You are going to hear someone talking about their dream work.

a Sentences 1–3: write down the missing words. For each gap, you will write one word **in French**.

   1 Je voudrais être ▭ ou ▭.
   2 J'aime bien la ▭ et le ▭.
   3 Mon ▭ travaille dans une ▭.

> These words are very similar to English words, but focus on the French sounds.

b Sentences 4–6: write down the full sentences that you hear, **in French**.

cent-quatre-vingt-dix-sept 197

Module 8 Contrôle oral

Read aloud

Parler 1 Look at this task card. With a partner, take turns to read out the five sentences, paying attention to the underlined letters and the highlighted liaisons and cognates.

Enzo, your French friend, has emailed you to tell you about his future plans.

Read out the text below to your teacher.

> Je trav<u>ail</u>le dan<u>s</u> une b<u>ou</u>langerie.
> J'<u>ai</u>me ga<u>gn</u>er de l'argen<u>t</u> dan<u>s</u> mon temp<u>s</u> libre.
> Plu<u>s</u> tar<u>d</u>, je ne v<u>eu</u>x pa<u>s</u> me marier.
> Je v<u>ai</u>s chercher un poste dan<u>s</u> le tourisme.
> À mon av<u>is</u>, il est important d'av<u>oi</u>r une carrière intéressante.

Take extra care with how you pronounce the underlined sounds:
- *ail*, *gn*
- sounds made of two vowels – *eu*, *ai*, *oi*, *ou*
- final silent consonants.

Remember your liaisons!

Take extra care with how you pronounce cognates.

Écouter 2 Listen and check your pronunciation.

Parler 3 Listen to the teacher asking the two follow-up questions. Translate each question **into English** and prepare your own answers **in French**. Then listen again and respond to the teacher.

Before you listen, can you predict the sort of opinions you might be asked for on the topic of work and future plans?

Role play

Parler 4 Look at the role-play card and prepare what you are going to say.

Setting: At the shopping centre

Scenario:
- You are at a shopping centre in Belgium.
- The teacher will play the part of the employee and will speak first.
- The teacher will ask questions **in French** and you must answer **in French**.
- Say a few words or a short phrase/sentence for each prompt. One-word answers are not sufficient to gain full marks.

Task:
1. Say you are looking for a job.
2. Say the type of job you would like.
3. Say where you work at the moment.
4. Ask a question about the salary.
5. Say what date you finish school.

You can start with *Je veux / Je voudrais / Je cherche …*

Remember, you express a date in French as (*le*) number + month of the year.

You can say you would like to work in a shop, with people, at the till, in an office.

You could ask how much the salary is, using *C'est combien?*

Parler 5 Practise what you have prepared. Then, using your notes, listen and respond to the teacher.

Écouter 6 Now listen to Inès doing the role-play task. **In English**, note down (a) how she **answers** the questions for task prompts 1, 2, 3 and 5, and (b) what question she **asks** for task prompt 4.

198 *cent-quatre-vingt-dix-huit*

Picture task

Écouter 7 Look at the exam card below and read the **first part** of the task. Then listen to Tom describing the picture. Answer the questions **in English**.

1 What does Tom say about the people in the picture? Do you agree?
2 What does he say about what each person is doing?
3 What does he say about the location? Do you agree?

> To talk about the people, you can say that they are standing (*debout*) or sitting (*assis*).

Describe this picture.
Your description must cover:
- people
- location
- activity.

When you have finished your description, you will be asked **two questions** relating to the picture. Say a short phrase/sentence in response to each question. One-word answers will not be sufficient to gain full marks.

You will then move on to a **conversation** on the broader thematic context of **Studying and my future**.

During the conversation, you will be asked questions in the present, past and future tenses. Your responses should be as **full and detailed** as possible.

> If you don't know a particular word, use another one! If you don't know the word for 'nurse', you can say 'doctor'. For 'to push', you can use 'to help' instead.

Parler 8 Prepare your own description of the picture, mentioning **people, location** and **activity**. Then, with a partner, take turns to describe the picture.

> Sur la photo, il y a …

Parler 9 Read the **second part** of the task. Then listen to the two follow-up questions and respond to the teacher. Remember: you only need to give a short answer to each one.

Écouter 10 Read the **third part** of the task. The teacher asks Tom: *Qu'est-ce que tu voudrais faire plus tard dans la vie?* Listen and write down the letters (a–c) in the order you hear the information.

a earn money   b travel   c work

Écouter 11 Listen to Tom answering the question: *Qu'est-ce que tu as déjà fait comme travail?* Write down at least **two** things that he has done and what he thought of these.

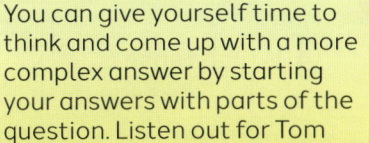

> You can give yourself time to think and come up with a more complex answer by starting your answers with parts of the question. Listen out for Tom doing this.

Parler 12 Prepare your own answers to the Module 8 questions on page 227. Your responses should be as **full and detailed** as possible. Then practise with a partner.

cent-quatre-vingt-dix-neuf **199**

Module 8 Contrôle écrit

Photo description

1 Describe the photo. Write four short sentences **in French**.

Write in full sentences, mentioning things that are relevant to the photo. You could say who and what you can see, where the person in the photo is, what she is wearing and/or what she is doing.

80–90 word writing task

2 Look at this writing exam task and then, <u>for each bullet point</u>:

1 think about what vocabulary you have learned which you could use in your answer. For example:
   - **nouns** and **verbs** to talk about your future plans
   - **verbs of opinion** and **adjectives** to explain your point of view
   - language for **narrating a story** about where you have recently worked
   - how to explain what, ideally, you will do in the future.
2 write down <u>three or four</u> ideas for what you could write about.
3 write down which tense(s) you will need to use in your answer.

> Write to your friend about your future plans.
>
> You **must** include the following points:
> - the type of person that you are
> - your opinion on different types of work
> - where you have recently worked
> - your plans for the future.
>
> Write your answer **in French**. You should aim to write between 80 and 90 words.

Look at the vocabulary you have noted to help you think of ideas of what to write.

3 Read Myriam's answer to the exam task. Answer questions 1–5 in the coloured shapes.

1 This word shows a **variety of vocabulary**. What does it mean? Find <u>two</u> more examples.

2 This is an example of **complex language**. What does it mean? Find <u>three</u> more examples from the text.

3 How could Myriam **avoid repetition** by using another word?

4 Which **tense** is this? Does she use any other tenses?

5 How could she form an **extended sentence**? What other extended sentences does she use?

> Salut!
>
> À mon avis, je suis travailleuse, assez patiente et organisée. Ma mère pense que je suis indépendante aussi.
>
> Je préfère travailler dans une équipe parce que j'aime aider les gens. Mais je ne voudrais pas travailler dans un bureau, devant un ordinateur toute la journée.
>
> L'année dernière, j'ai travaillé avec ma tante. Elle travaille dans une entreprise de médias. C'était très intéressant.
>
> Après le lycée, je vais aller à l'université et ensuite, je vais trouver un poste bien payé. Un jour, je voudrais habiter au bord de la mer.

200 *deux-cents*

Module 8

4 Read Myriam's answer again. Make notes **in English** about the following points:
a how Myriam describes herself
b <u>one</u> thing she likes and <u>one</u> type of job she would not want
c what she did last year
d <u>two</u> things she is going to do after sixth form.

5 Prepare your own answer to the 80–90 word writing task in exercise 2.
- Think about how you can develop your answer for each bullet point.
- Look back at your notes from exercises 2 and 3.
- Look at the 'Challenge checklist' and consider how you can show off your French!
- Write a **brief** plan and organise your answer into paragraphs.
- Write your answer and then carefully check the accuracy of what you have written.

Challenge checklist

🌶
- ✓ Past, present and future timeframes
- ✓ Connectives / time phrases / sequencers
- ✓ Some extended sentences
- ✓ Different opinion phrases

🌶🌶
- ✓ A wide range of tenses
- ✓ Different persons of the verb (e.g. *il/elle*)
- ✓ A variety of adjectives
- ✓ A wide range of interesting vocabulary

🌶🌶🌶
- ✓ Phrases with more than one tense
- ✓ Range of expressions (e.g. *je préfère, j'aime, je voudrais*)
- ✓ Complex language (e.g. negatives, *ma mère pense que je suis*)
- ✓ A variety of connectives (*parce que, ensuite, que*)

Translation

6 Write the correct letter (a–g) to match the English to the French.

1 je trouve
2 je travaille
3 je peux habiter
4 j'aime préparer
5 ils sont
6 j'ai aidé
7 c'est

a I can live
b I find
c it is
d I work
e I helped
f they are
g I like preparing

7 Translate the following five sentences **into French**.

a I work in a café.
b I don't like preparing the lunch.
c The customers are nice but it is tiring.
d Last year, I helped in a shop.
e If I find a good job, I can live alone.

Remember to use dans here.

Don't forget to put the negative around the verb.

Remember to use the perfect tense.

Remember to spot complex grammatical structures such as different tenses, impersonal structures and negatives.

You will need the infinitive form of the verb.

deux-cent-un **201**

Module 8 Vocabulaire

Key:
bold = this word will appear in higher exams only
* = this word is not on the vocabulary list but you may use it in your own sentences

Mon été de rêve (pages 182–183)

Est-ce que tu voudrais …	Would you like to …
travailler dans une boulangerie / une ferme?	work in a bakery / a farm?
faire du *babysitting?	do babysitting?
*promener des chiens?	walk dogs?
être *animateur ou *animatrice de vacances?	be a holiday camp leader?
aider dans un centre sportif?	help in a sports centre?
Je voudrais / Je ne voudrais pas (*promener des chiens) parce que / car …	I would like / I would not like to (walk dogs), because / as …
c'est …	it is …
intéressant / génial.	interesting / great.
dur / ennuyeux.	hard / boring.
j'aime / j'adore / je n'aime pas …	I like / I love / I don't like …
les animaux / les enfants.	animals / children.
Je vais visiter *l'Italie.	I am going to visit Italy.
Ce week-end, je visite Paris.	This weekend, I am visiting Paris.

Mes passions et mon avenir (pages 184–185)

Qu'est-ce que tu veux faire à l'avenir?	What do you want to do in the future?
Pour commencer, …	To start with, …
Ensuite, …	Next, …
Puis …	Then …
Après, …	Afterwards, …
Plus tard, …	Later, …
Un jour, …	One day, …
je veux …	I want to …
je voudrais …	I would like to …
j'espère …	I hope to …
mon ambition est de/d' …	my ambition is to …
mon but est de/d' …	my aim is to …
réussir mes examens.	pass my exams.
voyager à l'étranger et travailler.	travel abroad and work.
être *bénévole.	volunteer.
aller à l'université.	go to university.
continuer mes études.	continue my studies.
choisir une carrière.	choose a career.
entrer dans le monde du travail.	enter the world of work.
faire une formation **professionnelle**.	do professional training.
développer des **compétences** pratiques.	develop practical skills.
gagner beaucoup d'argent.	earn lots of money.
avoir ma propre entreprise.	have my own business.
vivre avec mon **copain** / ma **copine**.	live with my (boy)friend / (girl)friend.
me marier.	get married.
avoir des enfants.	have children.
sans aller à l'université	without going to university
sans faire de longues études	without doing long studies
pour gagner de l'argent	in order to earn money

Express Mondial (pages 186–187)

On est / Nous sommes parti(e)s de *Vancouver à dix heures le lundi.	We left Vancouver at ten o'clock on Monday.
Pour commencer, on a / nous avons voyagé en train / en bus.	To begin with, we travelled by train / bus.
Ensuite, on a / nous avons pris le train / le bus.	Next, we took the train / bus.
On est / Nous sommes resté(e)s deux nuits dans un hôtel.	We stayed two nights in a hotel.
Après, on a / nous avons passé une nuit sur un terrain de camping.	Afterwards, we spent a night in a campsite.
Pour gagner de l'argent, on a / nous avons travaillé dans un café / une boulangerie.	To earn some money, we worked in a café / bakery.
On a / Nous avons gagné **environ** quatorze euros de l'heure.	We earned about fourteen euros per hour.
Finalement, on est / nous sommes arrivé(e)s à *Québec à vingt heures le vendredi.	Finally, we arrived in Quebec at 8 p.m. on the Friday.
Excusez-moi, à quelle heure part le prochain train pour *Le Mans?	Excuse me, what time does the next train for Le Mans leave?
Le train part à …	The train leaves at …
Et le train arrive à quelle heure?	And what time does the train arrive?
Il arrive à …	It arrives at …
Un aller, ça coûte combien?	How much is a single?
C'est dix-huit euros.	It's eighteen euros.
Et un aller-retour, c'est combien?	And how much is a return?
Un aller-retour, c'est vingt-huit euros.	A return is twenty-eight euros.
Est-ce que je peux avoir un aller / deux allers / un aller-retour / trois allers-retours, s'il vous plaît?	Can I have a single / two singles / a return / three returns, please?
Ça fait quatre-vingt-dix euros. Merci.	That's ninety euros. Thank you.

deux-cent-deux

Module 8

Quelles sont tes compétences? (pages 188–189)

Quelles sont tes passions?	What are your passions?
Ma passion, c'est …	My passion is …
le sport / le théâtre.	sport / drama.
la lecture / la mode.	reading / fashion.
les films / les *ordinateurs.	films / computers.
voyager.	travelling.
Moi, j'adore les sciences.	I love science.
Aider les autres, c'est ma passion.	Helping others is my passion.
Comment es-tu?	What are you like?
Je suis …	I am …
amusant(e).	fun.
calme.	calm.
*créatif/créative.	creative.
*gentil/gentille.	kind.
indépendant(e).	independent.
patient(e).	patient.
responsable.	responsible.
sérieux/sérieuse.	serious.
sportif/sportive.	sporty.
travailleur/travailleuse.	hard-working.
Avec qui voudrais-tu travailler?	Who would you like to work with?
Je voudrais travailler …	I would like to work …
seul(e) / avec des gens.	alone / with people.
avec des animaux / des enfants.	with animals / children.

Qu'est-ce que tu trouves important dans un travail?	What do you find important in a job?
Être responsable / actif/active, c'est (très) important pour moi.	Being responsible / active is very important for me.
Avoir un travail intéressant, c'est essentiel.	Having an interesting job is essential.
Pour moi, un bon salaire est essentiel.	For me, a good salary is essential.
Quelles sont tes **compétences**?	What are your skills?
Mon point fort, c'est la communication.	My strong point is communication.
Je suis très organisé(e).	I am very organised.
J'ai une attitude positive.	I have a positive attitude.
Je m'entends bien avec tout le monde.	I get on well with everyone.
*En plus, j'aime travailler en équipe.	In addition, I like working in a team.
Je voudrais être …	I would like to be …
Il/Elle travaille comme …	He/She works as …
acteur/actrice.	an actor.
chanteur/chanteuse.	a singer.
chef/cheffe.	a chef.
directeur/directrice.	a boss.
influenceur/influenceuse.	an influencer.
*ingénieur/ingénieure.	an engineer.
joueur/joueuse de foot.	a football player.
*mécanicien/mécanicienne.	a mechanic.
médecin.	a doctor.

Bien payé, mais fatigant! (pages 190–191)

Être … . Quels sont les points positifs / négatifs?	What are the positive / negative points of being a/an …?
*architecte	architect
*journaliste	journalist
policier/policière	police officer
*politicien/politicienne	politician
*scientifique	scientist
Un point positif / négatif, c'est que/qu' …	A positive / negative point is that …
le travail est bien payé / intéressant.	the work is well paid / interesting.
les gens sont sympa.	the people are nice.
on peut prendre ses propres décisions.	you can make your own decisions.
ça peut être dangereux.	it can be dangerous.
les heures sont longues.	the hours are long.
c'est fatigant.	it's tiring.
la formation est longue.	the training takes a long time.
on ne gagne pas beaucoup d'argent.	you don't earn much money.

Après le collège, …	After school, …
j'ai travaillé comme …	I worked as …
je suis devenu(e) …	I became …
Je n'étais pas très content(e) et ce n'était pas bien payé.	I was not very happy and it was not well paid.
Il y a cinq ans, j'ai décidé d'aller à l'université.	Five years ago, I decided to go to university.
J'ai commencé à étudier …	I started to study …
Maintenant, je suis *scientifique. Le travail est intéressant.	Now, I am a scientist. The work is interesting.
J'ai réussi à **créer** ma propre entreprise.	I succeeded in creating my own business.
À l'avenir, je vais essayer de faire quelque chose de différent.	In the future, I am going to try to do something different.
Je vais continuer de travailler dur.	I am going to continue to work hard.
Je rêve d'être président(e) un jour.	I dream of being president one day.

deux-cent-trois 203

Modules 1–8 Révisions de grammaire 1

Prepositions (Pages 163, 171 and 195)

The prepositions *à* and *de* have several uses:
- *à* often means 'to' and *de* often means 'from'
- *de* can be used to indicate possession
- *à* can be used with places to mean 'in' or 'to'
- *de* features in location prepositions such as *en face de* (opposite), *près de* (near to) and *à côté de* (next to).

Note that *à* changes to *au*, *à la*, *à l'* or *aux* depending on the noun that follows.
Similarly, *de* changes to *du*, *de la*, *de l'* or *des* depending on the noun that follows.

Lire 1
Copy and complete the sentences with *à*, *au*, *à la*, *à l'* or *aux*.

Example: 1 Elle aime aller au musée.

1 Elle aime aller ___ musée.
2 Tu voyageais ___ New York.
3 Nous voulons aller ___ université.
4 Je vais commencer ___ jouer au basket.
5 Il faut aller ___ magasins.
6 Tu veux aller ___ fête de ma sœur?

Lire 2
Copy and complete the sentences with *de*, *du*, *de la*, *de l'* or *des*.

Example: 1 Je suis en face du cinéma.

1 Je suis en face ___ cinéma.
2 C'est la maison ___ mes grands-parents.
3 La poste est à côté ___ banque.
4 Il vient ___ États-Unis.
5 La protection ___ environnement est ma passion.
6 Tu as vu le portable ___ mon ami Louis?

Lire 3
Translate the sentences into English.

1 Mon frère est allé à Paris le week-end dernier.
2 C'est le livre de mon amie Jade.
3 Je vais continuer de travailler dur au collège.
4 Elle vient de Madrid mais elle habite à Barcelone.
5 Le café est en face du grand château.
6 Mon prof a commencé à crier assez souvent!

> When some verbs are followed by an infinitive, the preposition *à* or *de* is required. These include:
> *aider à* — to help to
> *apprendre à* — to learn to
> *arrêter de* — to stop
> *choisir de* — to choose
> *oublier de* — to forget to
> For more verbs followed by the infinitive, see page 191.

Écrire 4
Put the words into the correct order to translate the English sentences.

1 Are you going to learn to sing next year?

| Tu vas | à | apprendre | l'année prochaine | chanter |

2 My uncle continues to go to the cinema every weekend.

| continue | au cinéma | tous les week-ends | d'aller | Mon oncle |

3 Have you seen my friend Alessandro's new tie?

| la nouvelle cravate | mon ami | de | Alessandro | Tu as vu |

4 I forgot to do my English homework last night.

| hier soir | mes devoirs | faire | J'ai oublié | de | d'anglais |

5 The cinema used to be next to the shopping centre.

| centre commercial | à côté du | Le cinéma | était |

6 She comes from Leeds but she lives in Halifax.

| de | mais | Leeds | Halifax | Elle vient | elle habite | à |

204 *deux-cent-quatre*

Révisions de grammaire 1 — Modules 1–8

Demonstrative adjectives (Pages 159 and 170)

Écrire 5 Copy the French nouns, adding *ce*, *cet*, *cette* or *ces*.

1 ___ livre (m)
2 ___ table (f)
3 ___ chaussures (pl)
4 ___ baguette (f)
5 ___ hôtel (m)
6 ___ chien (m)
7 ___ chemise (f)
8 ___ appartement (m)

> Remember that before a masculine noun that starts with a vowel or a silent *h*, you have to use *cet*.

Écrire 6 Copy out the parallel translations, completing the missing words.

Example: 1 This jumper is too big for me. *Ce pull est trop grand pour moi.*

1	This jumper is too ___ for ___.	___ pull est trop grand pour moi.
2	I saw this house ___ ___.	J'ai vu ___ maison hier soir.
3	___ don't ___ this idea.	Je n'aime pas ___ idée.
4	Have ___ these socks?	Tu as vu ___ chaussettes?
5	She doesn't ___ these ___.	Elle n'aime pas ___ voitures.
6	___ ___ these blue trainers.	Je préfère ___ baskets bleues.

Pronouns (Pages 34, 40, 46, 67 and 72)

Lire 7 Read the sentences. Decide which type of pronoun each <u>underlined</u> word in the sentence is: subject, reflexive, direct object or indirect object. Then translate the sentences into English using the sentence starters on the right.

Example: 1 Subject – d – I am going to start buying recycled paper.

1 <u>Je</u> vais commencer à acheter du papier recyclé.
2 Je <u>l'</u>adore depuis trois ans.
3 Elle <u>me</u> donne des fruits et légumes.
4 Il <u>se</u> demande quand sa sœur va arriver.
5 Je vais <u>te</u> parler après les vacances.
6 Nous <u>l'</u>achetons tous les week-ends.
7 <u>Ils</u> n'ont jamais vendu de vêtements sur Vinted.
8 Je <u>m'</u>habille avant le petit-déjeuner.

a She gives me …
b We buy it …
c They have never …
d I am going to start …
e He wonders …
f I have loved him …
g I get dressed …
h I am going to talk …

Écrire 8 Copy and complete the sentences with the correct subject or reflexive pronoun in brackets.

1 ___ suis allée au centre commercial hier. (*subject*)
2 Il ___ entend bien avec tous les profs. (*reflexive*)
3 ___ avons une nouvelle voiture noire. (*subject*)
4 Normalement je ___ lève à huit heures. (*reflexive*)

Écrire 9 Copy and complete the sentences with the correct direct or indirect object pronoun given in brackets.

1 Je ___ ai donné un ordinateur. (*indirect* – 'to her')
2 Je ___ aime depuis deux ans. (*direct* – 'him')
3 Il ne ___ parle pas souvent. (*indirect* – 'to me')
4 Nous allons ___ chercher. (*direct* – 'you')

Modules 1–8 Révisions de grammaire 2

Negatives (Pages 69, 114, 163 and 171)

1 Read the French sentences. Write the letter of the correct English translation for each sentence.

1 Elle n'était pas timide.
2 Je ne suis jamais allé à Nice.
3 Tu n'as vu personne au collège?
4 Il ne va rien acheter au marché.

a I have never been to Nice.
b You didn't see anyone at school?
c She didn't use to be shy.
d He is not going to buy anything at the market.

2 Re-write the sentences in the negative, using the expression given in brackets.

1 J'aime les légumes verts. (ne … pas)
2 Tu es allé au stade de rugby? (ne … jamais)
3 Il jouait de la guitare tous les jours. (ne … pas)
4 J'ai acheté sur Vinted. (ne … rien)
5 Elle est allée au centre commercial. (ne … jamais)
6 Nous aimons regarder la télévision ensemble. (ne … pas)

Remember *ne* shortens to *n'* before a vowel or silent *h*.

3 Put the words into the correct order to make sentences. Then translate them into English.

1 regarder | aime | de films romantiques | n' | je | pas
2 jamais | au centre commercial | elle | n' | allée | est
3 n' | as | au musée | rien | hier? | tu | acheté
4 à la réception | ne | vois | personne | je | de l'hôtel

Asking questions (Pages 12, 18, 111 and 169)

There are several ways of forming questions.

a Intonation (making your voice go up at the end) — Tu es heureux?
b Using *est-ce que* for a yes/no question — **Est-ce que** tu regardes des vidéos sur YouTube?
c Using *est-ce que* after a question word — **Quand est-ce que** tu joues au basket?
d Using *quel, quelle, quels, quelles* (what/which) — **Quelle** est ta matière préférée?
e Inverting the subject and the verb after a question word — Que **fais-tu** pour protéger l'environnement?
f Using *qu'est-ce que* — **Qu'est-ce que** tu as fait le week-end dernier?

The most useful question words are:

combien	how much / how many	quand	when
comment	how	quel(le)(s)	which/what
où	where	qui	who
pourquoi	why	que/quoi	what

4 Read the questions. Write the letter (a–f) of the correct question style from the grammar box for each question. Then translate the sentences into English.

Example: 1 c – Why is he speaking to me?

1 Pourquoi est-ce qu'il me parle?
2 Où vas-tu avec ta famille ce week-end?
3 Quelle est la date de ton anniversaire?
4 Qu'est-ce que tu as mangé au restaurant?
5 Tu veux aller au cinéma demain?
6 Est-ce que ton frère joue au basket?
7 Comment peut-on protéger l'environnement?
8 Qu'est-ce que tu as fait la semaine dernière?

Révisions de grammaire 2 — Modules 1–8

5 Write a question to go with each answer, using a sentence starter from the box.
1 Le week-end prochain, je vais aller au cinéma avec mes amis.
2 Le voyage en train était très long.
3 J'habitais à Reims quand j'étais plus jeune.
4 Parce que c'est mon équipe préférée.
5 Non, je ne veux pas y aller.
6 J'aime aller au bord de la mer.

> Pourquoi est-ce que …?
> Tu vas aller où?
> Tu veux aller …?
> Comment était …?
> Tu habitais où?
> Qu'est-ce que tu aimes faire …?

Infinitive expressions (Pages 62, 87 and 184)

6 Copy and complete the sentences with an infinitive from the box.
1 Un jour, je veux ▬ au Canada.
2 Mon ambition est d' ▬ à l'université.
3 Elle peut ▬ la télé avec ses parents.
4 Je ne peux pas ▬ sans rêver d'argent!
5 Mon but est de ▬ tous les matchs.
6 J'espère ▬ mes examens cette année.

> aller   réussir   habiter   regarder   dormir   gagner

7 Put the words into the correct order to translate the English sentences.
1 I would like to organise a party.   voudrais je une fête organiser
2 She knows how to play the piano.   sait elle du piano jouer
3 My ambition is to open a shop.   un magasin mon ambition d'ouvrir est
4 You must drink lots of water.   beaucoup boire il faut d'eau
5 I hope to study maths at university.   à l'université les maths j'espère étudier
6 You can choose without seeing the cakes.   sans choisir voir tu peux les gâteaux

Past participles (Pages 141, 186 and 193)

8 Match up the correct past participle to each infinitive. Write them out in a list.
1 choisir (*to choose*)
2 rester (*to stay*)
3 mettre (*to put*)
4 partir (*to leave*)
5 écouter (*to listen*)
6 faire (*to do/make*)
7 arriver (*to arrive*)
8 attendre (*to wait*)

> fait   écouté   mis   attendu
> parti   arrivé   resté   choisi

9 Copy and complete the sentences with the past participle of the verb in brackets.
1 Je suis ▬ au lycée hier. (*aller*)
2 Elle a ▬ la porte deux fois. (*ouvrir*)
3 Vous avez ▬ de recycler? (*finir*)
4 Nous n'avons pas ▬ de gâteau. (*faire*)
5 Ils ont ▬ les chaises sur les tables. (*mettre*)
6 Elles n'ont pas ▬ de billets à la gare. (*acheter*)
7 Tu as ▬ le même article que moi? (*lire*)
8 J'ai ▬ à jouer au basket il y a trois ans. (*commencer*)

deux-cent-sept 207

Modules 1–8 Révisions de grammaire 3

Present tense verbs (Pages 8, 10, 20 and 21)

1 Copy and complete the sentences with the correct choice of present tense verb in brackets. Then translate the sentences into English.

Example: 1 habitent – They live in Spain.

1 Ils (*regardent/habitent*) en Espagne.
2 Elle (*va/prend*) au cinéma demain.
3 Je ne (*vends/écoute*) plus mes vêtements.
4 Nous (*portons/attendons*) le bus.
5 Il (*écrit/mange*) un deuxième livre.
6 Je (*joue/bois*) au basket tous les jours.

2 Copy and complete the sentences with the present tense form of the verb in brackets.

1 Elle ___ du lait. (*boire*)
2 Ils n' ___ pas faim? (*avoir*)
3 On ___ à la plage. (*aller*)
4 Je ne ___ jamais le train. (*prendre*)
5 Nous ___ nos devoirs. (*faire*)
6 Elles ___ de Paris. (*venir*)
7 Je ___ en vacances. (*partir*)
8 Vous ___ près de l'hôtel. (*être*)

Past tense verbs (Pages 22, 119, 147 and 148)

3 Read the sentences and match up the correct halves. Then translate them into English.

1 Ce matin, il y avait du soleil et …
2 Je mangeais à la cantine quand …
3 Le week-end dernier, il faisait froid et …
4 Ma mère regardait la télé quand …

a … mon ami a pris mes frites!
b … elle a fait du ski à la montagne.
c … je suis arrivé à la maison.
d … j'ai joué au volley sur la plage.

4 Copy and complete the sentences, putting the verbs in brackets into the perfect or imperfect tense.

Example: 1 J'allais au collège quand j'ai vu la nouvelle prof.

1 J' ___ (*aller*) au collège quand j' ___ (*voir*) la nouvelle prof.
2 Je ___ (*regarder*) un film romantique quand Enzo ___ (*arriver*).
3 J' ___ (*être*) en vacances quand j' ___ (*manger*) au restaurant.
4 Il ___ (*faire*) très froid quand j' ___ (*faire*) du ski à la montagne.

> Remember, for perfect tense verbs, you will need a form of the auxiliary verb (*avoir* or *être*) and then the past participle.

> You will often see the imperfect tense giving some background information before something then happens in the perfect tense:
> *Elle jouait au tennis quand elle est tombée.*   She was playing tennis (imperfect) when she fell over (perfect).

5 Find five perfect tense and four imperfect tense verbs in the text. Write them out, list whether they are perfect or imperfect verbs and then translate them into English.

Example: c'était – imperfect – it was

> Samedi dernier, c'était l'anniversaire de ma mère. Le matin, elle a joué au golf avec ses amies pendant trois heures. Il faisait beau donc elle s'est beaucoup amusée! Ensuite, elle est arrivée à la maison vers midi. Mon frère a fait un grand gâteau, mais nous n'avons pas chanté! L'après-midi, elle a dormi un peu, car elle était assez fatiguée. Moi, pendant l'après-midi, je jouais aux cartes en ligne avec mes amis même s'il faisait beau dehors. Et j'ai gagné!

deux-cent-huit

Révisions de grammaire 3 — Modules 1–8

Talking about the future (Pages 90, 96, 183 and 192)

There are two ways to talk about the future:
a present tense verbs with a future time expression — *Je fais mes devoirs ce soir.*
b near future tense verbs (going to do something) — *Je vais faire mes devoirs ce soir.*

Lire 6 Read the sentences. Find all the verbs used to express the future and note down which form of the future tense is used (**a** or **b** in the grammar box above). Write the verbs out as a list in both French and English.

Example: 1 on va aller – b – we are going to go

1 L'année prochaine, on va aller en France et je vais voir la tour Eiffel.
2 Après les examens, je vais aller au lycée et je vais étudier les sciences.
3 Malheureusement, je ne fais pas de baby-sitting ce soir.
4 Mes parents vont partir en vacances samedi prochain.
5 Tu portes des baskets au festival samedi soir?
6 Il passe le week-end chez un ami et ils font du camping.

Combining tenses with *si* phrases (Pages 92, 108 and 167)

You can use *si* (if) with a verb in the imperfect tense, followed by **je voudrais** (the conditional of *vouloir*), to express your dreams and wishes:
Si j'étais riche, je voudrais avoir une grande maison.   If I were rich, I would like to have a big house.

Écrire 7 Copy out the parallel translations, completing the missing words.

1	Si j'étais ___, je voudrais ___ une belle voiture.	If I ___ rich, I would like to buy a ___ car.
2	Si j'avais le temps, je ___ faire la ___ tous les soirs.	If I had the ___, I would like to cook every ___.
3	Si j'___ célèbre, je voudrais ___ à Londres.	___ I was famous, I ___ like to live in London.
4	Si j'___ le choix, je voudrais ___ moins de devoirs.	If I had the ___, I would like to do less ___.

Using tenses together

Écrire 8 Write an article about your local area for your French friend's school magazine.

You must include the following points:
- what you usually do at the weekend
- the advantages and disadvantages of your town/village
- what you did during the last school holidays
- what you are going to do with your friends next weekend.

Write your answer **in French**. You should aim to write between 80 and 90 words.

- The bullet points prompt you to use a variety of tenses. In this task you will need to use the present tense (first two bullet points), the perfect tense (third bullet point) and the future tense (last bullet point).
- Try to use connective words (but, however, also etc.) to make longer sentences.
- Also include some negative expressions and object pronouns to show your range of language.

deux-cent-neuf 209

Module 1 Révisions

Parler 1
Refresh your memory! In pairs, tell each other what you like to do each day of the week. There are suggested activities in the box below.

- Moi, le lundi, j'aime … Et toi?
- Moi, le lundi, j'adore …
- Le mardi, …

> acheter des vêtements en ligne   aller à des concerts   télécharger des chansons
> aller au cinéma   regarder la télé   suivre des influenceurs

Use a variety of ways to give a positive opinion, such as j'aime, j'adore and je préfère.

Écouter 2
Refresh your memory! Listen to Zoé telling us about a past event. Write down **in English** what you understand. Try to give as many details as possible. Here are some key question words to help you make your notes.

- When (was it)?
- Who (did she go) with?
- Where (did she go)?
- What (did she do)?

Écrire 3
Refresh your memory! Look at the vocabulary list on pages 30–31 and copy and complete these sentences with words that you have not used a lot or at all in your work in this module.

a Je n'aime pas ▇ parce que c'est ▇.
b Je ▇ en ligne.
c À mon avis, Internet est ▇.
d Je vais ▇ avec ▇.
e Je préfère regarder ▇.
f Je joue ▇ dans ▇.

Lire 4
My town. What does Ahmed say about his free time in town?

Ahmed's blog

Il y a plusieurs endroits amusants en ville, comme le stade. Avant, j'aimais passer du temps dans les magasins, mais maintenant, je préfère aller au musée. Il y a aussi une nouvelle **patinoire**. C'est génial car c'est accessible aux personnes en fauteuil roulant comme moi.

Don't jump to conclusions too quickly. Locate where the answer may be and read the sentence to the end.

a For each sentence write down the correct option (A–C).

(i) There are several places that are …
 A fun.   B old.   C pretty.

(ii) Ahmed used to like to spend time at the …
 A stadium.   B shops.   C museum.

b Which of these is the best translation for the word **patinoire**? Write down the correct option (A–C).
 A climbing wall   B horse-riding school   C ice rink

Lire 5
A cultural event. Translate the following sentences **into English**.

a J'aime les musées à Paris.
b En octobre, il y a un grand festival d'art moderne.
c J'adore les activités culturelles dans les rues.
d Je suis allée au festival avec mes amies.
e Je trouve les visites à la capitale très fatigantes.

Watch the word order here.

Think carefully about the tense here.

6. A new app.
Listen to this advert promoting a new app called *Vas-y!* What is mentioned? Write the letter (A–F) for each of the three correct options.

A who it is for	D how you can share info on the app
B date it was started	E number of users
C reductions for tickets	F price of the subscription

7. Read aloud.
With a partner, take turns to read out the five sentences, paying attention to the underlined letters and highlighted liaisons and cognates. Then, listen and check.

Hugo, your Swiss friend, has emailed you to tell you about his free time.

Read out the text below to your partner.

> J'aime être en ligne.
> Je fais beaucoup de choses.
> Je ne m'intéresse pas au sport.
> Je préfère rester chez moi et regarder des concerts sur Internet.
> Je passe des heures sur mon portable à regarder des vidéos.

Remember the liaisons here. Note also that the letter *h* is silent.

Take extra care with how you pronounce cognates.

Take extra care with how you pronounce the underlined sounds:
- *ai* and *è* sound the same
- *é*, *ez* (and *er* when it is at the end of a word) sound the same
- the final consonants *p*, *s* and *t* are silent (unless the next word starts with a vowel). There are exceptions to this rule: the final *t* is pronounced in the word *Internet*.

When you have read out the sentences, take turns to ask and answer the two follow-up questions:
- Qu'est-ce que tu aimes faire sur Internet?
- Qu'est-ce que tu penses des portables?

Remember that you won't see the two questions in your exam. Your teacher will ask you the questions when you have finished reading the text. Short answers are sufficient.

8. Role play.
Prepare your responses to this role-play task. Practise saying them aloud. Then, using your notes, listen and respond to the teacher.

Setting: At the theatre

Scenario:
- You are at a theatre in France.
- The teacher will play the part of the theatre employee and will speak first.
- The teacher will ask questions **in French** and you must answer **in French**.
- Say a few words or a short phrase/sentence for each prompt. One-word answers are not sufficient to gain full marks.

Task:
- Say what type of show you want to watch.
- Say how many people it is for.
- Say whether you would like a programme.
- Say where you are going after the show.
- Ask a question about the show times.

Use *Je voudrais*.

You could use ... *à quelle heure?*

deux-cent-onze 211

Module 2 Révisions

1 *Refresh your memory!* In pairs, play 'adjective tennis'. Take turns to say an adjective that could describe someone and give the English translation.

- *Amusant*
- Fun. *Travailleur*

> Look at the vocabulary lists on pages 54–55 for ideas.

2 *Refresh your memory!* Change the underlined words in the box on the right to write a description of at least three people, real or imaginary.

> Elle s'appelle Myriam.
> Elle a les yeux marron et les cheveux noirs.
> Je pense qu'elle est belle.
> Elle porte des lunettes de soleil.

3 *Refresh your memory!* Write sentences about two famous people, using the information provided.

Name	Sadio Mané
Occupation	footballer
Country of origin	**Sénégal***
Family	no children
Interests	helping others; football

*le Sénégal Senegal

Name	Marion Cotillard
Occupation	actress
Country of origin	France
Family	two children
Interests	cinema; environment

4 *My family.* Read the email that Lucie wrote to her French friend. Write down the word for the gap in each sentence, using a word from the box. There are more words than gaps.

> Coucou Lola! Ça va?
> Alors, qu'est-ce que tu as fait le week-end dernier? Moi, je n'ai pas vu mes amis car c'était l'anniversaire de ma belle-mère. Mon père, ma belle-mère, mes sœurs et moi, nous sommes allés au restaurant. Ma sœur, Jade, est venue avec ses enfants, mais mon frère n'est pas venu car il travaillait. Il donne des cours d'anglais aux étudiants à l'université mais avant, il était chef, donc il a envoyé un énorme gâteau délicieux.

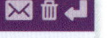

teacher brother student friends family chef children

a Lucie went to the restaurant with her ___.
b Lucie's sister went with her ___.
c Lucie's brother is a ___.

> Read the text and the sentences carefully, paying attention to negatives. What does Lucie say about her friends and her brother? These words appear in the text but it doesn't mean they are the answer.

5 a *Close friends.* What does Enzo say about his friends in his diary? Complete the sentences below. For each question write the correct letter (A–C).

> Je vais te parler de mes deux amis Alex et Louise. Alex est dans la même classe que moi au collège. J'ai quinze ans et Louise a un an de plus. Alex et moi, on s'est rencontrés à l'école **primaire***. Alex est travailleur mais Louise, elle est sportive et active.

*primaire primary

(i) Alex is in the …
 A class below Enzo.
 B class above Enzo.
 C same class as Enzo.

(ii) Louise is …
 A the same age as Enzo.
 B one year older than Enzo.
 C one year younger than Enzo.

b Answer the following questions **in English**. You do not need to write in full sentences.

(i) Where did Enzo meet Alex?
(ii) How does Enzo describe Louise? Give **one** detail.

deux-cent-douze

Module 2

6 *Everybody against racism.* Hugo is talking about *SOS Racisme*, a French organisation that fights racism. What does he say? Listen to the recording and for each sentence write down the correct option (A–C).

1 Hugo says the association *SOS Racisme* …
   A fights for equality.
   B fights against poverty.
   C fights against racism.

2 Its message is that in our society there must be …
   A happiness.
   B demonstrations.
   C respect.

3 According to the association, everyone must …
   A donate money.
   B change things.
   C make posters.

4 Hugo thinks that change must start …
   A at work.
   B at school.
   C in the home.

7 *Dictation.* You are going to hear someone talking about a family member.

a Sentences 1–3: write down the missing words. For each gap, you will write one word **in French**.
   1 Ma ▢ a les cheveux ▢.
   2 Elle ▢ dans une ▢.
   3 Elle ▢ avec son ▢.

   These words are unfamiliar; listen carefully to the sounds.

b Sentences 4–6: write down the full sentences you hear, **in French**.

8 *Picture task.* Look at the picture and prepare what you are going to say. In pairs, practise your descriptions.

To talk about where the people are, you can use a preposition like devant (in front), derrière (behind) or à côté de (next to).

Describe this picture.
Your description must cover:
• people   • location   • activity.

When you have finished your description, you will be asked **two questions** relating to the picture. In pairs, practise saying a short phrase/sentence in response to each question. One-word answers will not be sufficient to gain full marks.

Remember that you won't see the two questions in the exam. Say a short phrase/sentence in response to each question. One-word answers will not be sufficient to gain full marks.

Question 1: *Qu'est-ce que tu aimes faire quand tu as du temps libre?*
Question 2: *Tu préfères passer du temps avec tes amis ou ta famille?*

9 *Everybody is equal.* Translate the following sentences **into French**.

You can't translate this word for word. Look back at your notes to find the fixed expression to say 'there is'/'there are' in French.

Remember to use le/la/l' in front of the noun.

a I am for equality.
b Respect is important.
c There are too many problems in our society.
d Yesterday at school I watched a presentation about racism.
e We must fight against racism and sexism in order to protect our rights.

There are two words for 'our': notre and nos. Which one is needed here?

Think carefully about the form of the verb you are going to use here.

This is an impersonal phrase. You won't be using nous, but il faut.

Use pour …

deux-cent-treize 213

Module 3 Révisions

1 *Refresh your memory!* In pairs, look at the school vocabulary on pages 80–81. Then play 'opinion tennis'. Take turns to say a subject and give an opinion on it.

- Le français
- C'est utile!

> When you give your opinion, start with *C'est ...* or *Je pense que c'est ...*

2 *Refresh your memory!* Write out the jumbled sentences and then translate them **into English**.

a porter / Il faut / uniforme / un
b faut / les / respecter / profs / Il
c manger / en classe / Il ne faut pas
d utiliser / en / son portable / Il ne faut pas / classe
e en retard / arriver / Il / pas / ne / faut

> Look out for each infinitive to follow *il faut* or *il ne faut pas*.

3 *Refresh your memory!* Listen and make notes **in English** on each question below.

a Qu'est-ce que tu penses de ton uniforme?
b Qu'est-ce que tu penses des bâtiments de ton collège?
c Quelle est ta matière préférée?
d Quel est ton avis sur les devoirs?

4 *Future language learning.* Read the comments from an internet forum. Copy and complete the table **in English** for each person.

Clément: L'année prochaine, après le collège, je vais apprendre le **chinois*** au lycée. Si c'est possible, je voudrais travailler à l'étranger. C'est mon rêve.

Ana: Moi, j'adore les langues, mais je préfère l'**espagnol***. À l'avenir, je vais lire des magazines et des journaux espagnols. Je veux voyager en Amérique du Sud parce que j'adore la culture.

Yanis: Si je réussis à mes examens, je vais continuer à améliorer mon anglais. Ma mère est française, mais mon père est anglais et j'aime parler en anglais avec mes tantes.

| His/Her future language plans | |
| Reason why | |

*le chinois — Chinese
*l'espagnol (m) — Spanish

> When looking for reasons why, look for phrases that introduce reasons, such as *je voudrais*, *je veux* and *parce que*.

5 *Learning English.* Translate the following sentences **into English**.

> How will you translate *les* and *à* in English here?

a J'aime les langues au collège.
b Ma sœur est prof d'anglais.
c J'aime répéter et prononcer les mots.
d Aujourd'hui, j'ai répondu à dix questions en classe.
e Les devoirs durent une heure au minimum tous les jours.

> These are 'false friends'. Be careful how you translate them!

> *Devoirs* is plural in French. How do you translate it here?

> Use the rest of the sentence to help you work out the meaning of this word.

Module 3

6 *Against racism.* Jade, Mohamed, Gabrielle and Dorian are talking about what their school is doing to stop racism. What do they say? Write down the word or phrase for the gap in each sentence, using the words or phrases from the box. There are more words or phrases than gaps.

| two | well | in | secondary school | pupils |
| badly | three | rules | five | before | sixth form |

a Jade is in ▭.
b Jade has been helping with the anti-racism project for ▭ years.
c Mohamed thinks that racism starts ▭ secondary school.
d Gabrielle thinks her school is doing ▭ in trying to stop racism.
e Dorian hopes for more ▭ to help with the anti-racism project.

7 *School life.* Do this 80–90 word writing task.

> Write to your friend about school life.
>
> You **must** include the following points:
> - the facilities at your school
> - your opinion on school rules
> - a recent school trip
> - what school work you are going to do tonight.
>
> Write your answer **in French**. You should aim to write between 80 and 90 words.

- Write about what there is in your school.
- You could write about school uniform, for example.
- Talk about where you went and give your opinion.

8 *Read aloud.* With a partner, take turns to read out the five sentences, paying attention to the underlined letters and highlighted liaisons. Then, listen and check.

Take extra care with how you pronounce the underlined sounds:
- i, y
- nasal sounds
- u
- oi.

> Louis, your Swiss friend, has emailed you to tell you about his school's website.
>
> Read out the text below to your partner.
>
> J'aime le site Internet de mon collège.
> C'est très utile et pratique.
> Il y a des liens vers les exercices.
> Je préfère étudier l'histoire en ligne chez moi.
> Demain, je vais utiliser la page sur l'anglais.

- Remember the liaisons here.
- Remember that letters like *t*, *s* and *z* are usually silent at the end of words (with the exception of *Internet*).

When you have read out the sentences, take turns to ask and answer the two follow-up questions:
- Qu'est-ce que tu aimes étudier en ligne?
- Qu'est-ce que tu penses des devoirs?

Adapt the questions to help start your answers, e.g.
J'aime étudier … / Je pense que les devoirs sont …

deux-cent-quinze 215

Module 4 Révisions

Parler 1

Refresh your memory! Spend five minutes looking back at the vocabulary on pages 104–105. Then, in pairs, take turns to say as many French words as possible related to:
- eating and drinking
- parts of the body
- health and wellbeing.

Lire 2

Refresh your memory! Copy and complete the following sentences with the correct translation of the English word or phrase in brackets. Then translate the sentences **into English**.

a J'ai quelquefois mal au ▭ (*arm*).
b Je me coupe souvent au ▭ (*finger*) quand je prépare les repas.
c Je prends des ▭ (*medicine*) quand j'ai mal à la ▭ (*head*).
d Quand je ▭ (*watch*) la télé, j'ai mal aux ▭ (*eyes*).

Lire 3

Refresh your memory! Complete each sentence with one of these words: *chaud/froid/faim/soif*. Then translate the sentences **into English**.

a La température monte et j'ai ▭ !
b Je voudrais boire quelque chose car j'ai ▭.
c Il n'a pas fini son petit-déjeuner, alors maintenant il a ▭.
d Nous avons ▭ car il neige.

> Remember that for these expressions the verb *avoir* translates as 'to be' in English, e.g. *j'ai chaud* = 'I am hot'.

Lire 4

Mental health. Read Gabrielle's report based on her research about mental health.

> Pour étudier les effets de la technologie sur la santé mentale, j'ai posé des questions à des adolescents seulement et pas à des adultes. Les téléphones sont très utiles mais il y a des effets négatifs aussi. Les portables causent des problèmes pour tout le monde, mais les adolescents ont plus de difficultés avec les relations.

a Write down the word for the gap in each sentence, using the words from the box. There are more words than gaps.

(i) Gabrielle studied the effects of ▭ on mental health.
(ii) She asked questions to ▭.
(iii) She found that mobile phones cause teenagers more problems with ▭.

> technology   relationships
> everybody   adults   teenagers
> young children   old people

Gabrielle's report continues.

> Au début, je voulais étudier les effets des réseaux sociaux mais j'ai changé d'avis. J'ai fait des recherches sur les portables avec mes amis. Malheureusement, les adolescents sont souvent victimes de crimes en ville. Et ce n'est pas seulement le temps qu'on passe sur les portables qui a un impact négatif, mais aussi les **applis*** qu'on utilise.

les applis apps

b Complete the sentences below. For each sentence, write the correct letter (A–C).

(i) In the beginning, Gabrielle wanted to study the effects of …
   A social media.   B phones.   C friends.
(ii) She did the research with …
   A people at school.   B her friends.   C people in town.

> Watch out for words that completely change the meaning of a sentence, such as *seulement* and *ne … pas*.

c Answer the following questions **in English**. You do not need to write in full sentences.

(i) What issue do teenagers encounter a lot in towns?
(ii) Name <u>one</u> thing that has a negative impact, according to Gabrielle's research.

deux-cent-seize

Module 4

5 *Écouter*

Healthy school. Charlie is talking about what their school does to promote healthy living. What do they say? Listen to the recording and make notes **in English** under the following headings. You do not need to write in full sentences.

a What Charlie's school's special week is
b Charlie's opinion of this special week
c What Charlie usually does during that week

6 *Écouter*

Dictation. You are going to hear someone talking about what they do to feel good.

a Sentences 1–3: write down the missing words. For each gap, you will write one word **in French**.

1 Je ___ du ___.
2 Avec mes ___, on ___.
3 Mes sœurs ___ faire des ___.

> When deciding how to spell each verb, look carefully at the rest of the sentence. Remember that different spellings can often sound the same: *fais/fait, adore/adores/adorent, mangé/manger, va/vas*.

b Sentences 4–6: write down the full sentences that you hear, **in French**.

7 *Parler*

Picture task. Look at the picture and prepare what you are going to say. In pairs, practise your descriptions.

Describe this picture.

Your description must cover:
• people   • location   • activity.

When you have finished your description, you will be asked **two questions** relating to the picture. In pairs, practise saying a short phrase/sentence in response to each question. One-word answers will not be sufficient to gain full marks.

> As well as answering each question with an activity or food, try to give reasons for your choice or extra details such as when or who with.

Question 1: *Qu'est-ce que tu aimes faire pendant ton temps libre?*
Question 2: *Qu'est-ce que tu manges normalement?*

8 *Écrire*

Healthy choices. Translate the following sentences **into French**.

> Think carefully about whether you need a preposition between the two verbs. Do you need *de* or not?

> Remember to use the correct definite article here: *le, la, l'* or *les*.

a I love breakfast.
b I like to eat two eggs every day.
c Normally, I don't eat unhealthy meals.
d Last weekend, I ate some vegetables.
e When I am thirsty, I drink lots of water because it is healthy.

> What tense will you need here?

> Remember the word order here!

> Use *beaucoup de*, but how will the French for 'water' change the spelling of *de*?

> What is the word for 'some' with a plural noun?

deux-cent-dix-sept **217**

Module 5 Révisions

Parler 1 — *Refresh your memory!* In pairs, take turns to name a means of transport using the words and phrases below. Give one reason why you like travelling that way and one reason why you don't.
- *La voiture*
- *Pratique mais cher*

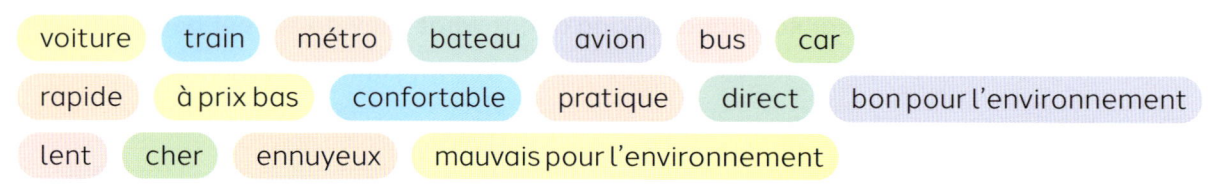

voiture · train · métro · bateau · avion · bus · car

rapide · à prix bas · confortable · pratique · direct · bon pour l'environnement

lent · cher · ennuyeux · mauvais pour l'environnement

Écouter 2 — *Refresh your memory!* Listen, then copy and complete the grid **in English**. (1–6)

	what they complain about	what's wrong
1	room	too small

Listen out for adjectives.

Écrire 3 — *Refresh your memory!* Write a sentence **in French** about each holiday feature in the first column below.

| Le logement / L'hôtel La ville / La plage | était | agréable / cher/chère. beau/belle. |
| Les touristes / Les activités | étaient | sympa / intéressant(e)s. |

Use intensifiers like très and assez to modify your adjectives and remember to make the adjectives agree with the noun. Can you think of any different adjectives to use?

Lire 4 — *Technology and booking holidays.* Read these comments from an internet forum. Answer each question with the name of the correct person.

> Je réserve mes vacances sur les sites, avec mon portable. Je lis les avis des autres personnes. **Toni**

> Je laisse toujours des commentaires sur mes vacances en ligne. Je cherche aussi des offres spéciales. **Lucas**

> Je compare les équipements des hôtels, comme la piscine ou la vue, et j'aime voir les prix pour réserver un hôtel moins cher. **Clara**

Who …
a reads other people's opinions?
b compares facilities online?
c books their holidays with their phone?
d writes comments about their holiday online?
e looks for special offers?
f looks at the prices?

Read the forum comments carefully and don't rush your answer. Remember that the questions will probably not be in the same order as the text.

Lire 5 — *Relaxing holidays.* Translate the following sentences **into English**.

Do you remember this impersonal phrase?

a En vacances, il faut se reposer.
b Ma sœur aime faire beaucoup d'activités.
c C'est fou! Je ne suis pas d'accord.
d En juillet, on a passé deux semaines au bord de la piscine.
e J'espère retourner en France cet été!

How are you going to translate on?

218 *deux-cent-dix-huit*

Module 5

6 **Camping Beau Séjour.** Listen to this advert promoting a new campsite called the *Beau Séjour*. What is mentioned? Listen to the recording and write the letter (A–F) for each one of the <u>three</u> correct options.

A transport	D shopping for clothes
B prices	E evening entertainment
C activities	F entertainment for children

> You won't necessarily hear the French for the words in the table. Before you listen, quickly brainstorm some words that you might hear for each topic.

7 **At the hotel.** Maria, Luis and Fathia are talking to a hotel receptionist. What do they say? Listen to the recording and complete the sentences below. For each sentence, write the correct letter (A–C).

(i) Maria would like to reserve …
   A two rooms.   B three rooms.   C four rooms.

(ii) On 16 September, Luis is going to …
   A leave.   B arrive.   C go to an event.

(iii) Fathia would like a room with …
   A a cooking area.   B three single beds.   C easy access for a wheelchair.

8 **My holiday activities.** Do this 80–90 word writing task.

> Here you can talk about active holidays or cultural holidays, for example, or holidays by the beach or abroad.

> Give details about particular activities you did.

Write about your favourite holiday activities.

You **must** include the following points:
- the type of holiday you enjoy
- your opinion of different holiday activities with reasons
- what you did during your last school holiday
- what activity you would like to try in the future.

Write your answer **in French**. You should aim to write between 80 and 90 words.

> Don't forget to give reasons.

> Set out your answer using a separate paragraph for each bullet point. This shows clearly that you have answered each one.

9 **Read aloud.** With a partner, take turns to read out the five sentences, paying attention to the highlighted liaisons. Then, listen and check.

Camille, your Belgian friend, has texted you to tell you about her summer plans. Read out the text below to your partner.

> Je regarde le Tour de France.
> C'est un événement sportif et familial.
> Je reste chez ma tante dans l'est.
> Elle habite dans un endroit agréable.
> Je vais bientôt aller à la montagne.

> Before you read aloud:
> - look for silent letters
> - look for liaisons between words
> - identify the easiest words to say
> - check any tricky words with your partner.

> Remember the liaisons here.

When you have read out the sentences, take turns to ask and answer the two follow-up questions:
- Qu'est-ce que tu aimes faire en été?
- Qu'est-ce que tu penses des vacances en famille?

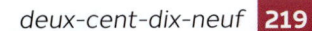

deux-cent-dix-neuf **219**

Module 6 Révisions

1. Parler — *Refresh your memory!* In pairs, take turns to ask about the weather for next week. Use as many different weather words as you can.

- Il va faire quel temps lundi matin?
- Lundi matin, il va faire beau et il y aura du soleil.

> When talking about the weather in the future, use: *il va faire* or *il y aura*.

	lundi	mardi	mercredi	jeudi	vendredi
matin	☀️	☀️	☀️🌡️	🌬️☁️	🌬️☁️🌡️
après-midi	☀️	🌧️	🌧️🌡️	🌬️☀️	☀️🌡️

2. Écrire — *Refresh your memory!* For each word listed below, note down an adjective. Write the adjective in its masculine and feminine forms. Then use these adjectives to write sentences in French.

Example: beau/belle **La rivière** est belle.

- le marché
- les rues
- la ville
- le cinéma
- la piscine
- les transports en commun

> Make sure your adjectives agree with the nouns they describe.

3. Écouter — *A new holiday village.* Yohan is talking to the owner of a new holiday resort. What do they say? Write down the word for the gap in each sentence, using a word from the box. There are more words than gaps.

a The holiday village is near a ▭.
b The village has activities for ▭.
c This year to help the environment, they are going to ▭.

> lake   everyone   respect nature
> beach   adults   stop selling meat
> children   recycle paper

4. Lire — *A summer fire.* Read this online article about a fire that Lola witnessed.

Je passe beaucoup de temps au collège, alors le week-end, j'adore le calme du grand air. Mais un jour, l'été dernier, j'ai eu un choc terrible.

Le ciel était bleu mais il faisait trop chaud. On descendait de la montagne quand, au loin, j'ai vu un grand feu près de la forêt. Les **sapeurs-pompiers** sont bientôt arrivés de la ville et ils ont jeté rapidement de l'eau. Heureusement, la crise s'est vite **terminée***.

On doit arrêter le changement climatique. Je vais organiser une manifestation des élèves et écrire au président.

se terminer — to come to an end

> There are two places in the first paragraph, but which is where she prefers being?

> Each one is mentioned, but where was the fire?

> All three verbs are used, but read the full sentence to work out is the correct answer.

a Complete the sentences below. For each sentence, write the correct letter (A–C).

(i) Lola prefers being …
   A in the open air.   B at home.   C at school.

(ii) The fire was …
   A in the mountains.   B by the town.   C near the forest.

(iii) Lola is going to …
   A stop climate change.   B write a blog.   C organise a demonstration.

b Which of these is the best translation for **sapeurs-pompiers**? Write down the correct letter.
   A paramedics   B rangers   C firefighters

Module 6

Parler 5

Picture task. Look at the picture and prepare what you are going to say. In pairs, practise your descriptions.

You can say that there is a family. Say who is in the foreground (*au premier plan*) and who is in the background (*à l'arrière plan*). Describe what they are wearing and what they look like. You can use prepositions to describe where people are: *devant, à côté, derrière, à gauche, à droite.*

Describe this picture.
Your description must cover:
- people
- location
- activity.

When you have finished your description, you will be asked **two questions** relating to the picture. Remember that you won't see the two questions. In pairs, practise saying a short phrase/sentence in response to each question.

You can say that they are in the countryside and that there are trees in the background. Don't forget to mention the weather.

Try to mention a few activities. Who is running? Who is walking? Who is talking?

Question 1: *Tu aimes ta région?*

Give your opinion on your region. You can also mention what you like doing and why. You can say what there is, and what you can do, using *on peut* + infinitive.

Question 2: *Où est-ce que tu aimes aller avec ta famille ou tes amis?*

Say where you like going and why. Try to use a complex sentence with *si* ('if'). For example, you can say 'If the weather is nice, I like …'.

Lire 6

Where I live. Translate the following sentences **into English**.

You can use 'you' or 'we'.

What tense is this?

a J'habite dans un appartement à la campagne.
b Ici, **on peut** faire beaucoup de choses.
c En été, le lac est idéal pour les familles.
d Hier, je suis allé en ville à vélo.
e **On doit** travailler ensemble pour protéger l'environnement.

Écouter 7

Dictation. You are going to hear someone talking about living in a town.

a Sentences 1–3: write down the missing words. For each gap, you will write one word **in French**.

1 Ma ville est ▬ et ▬.
2 Il y a ▬ de ▬.
3 On voit ▬ de ▬.

You might have never come across these two words so use your knowledge of French sounds.

b Sentences 4–6: write down the full sentences that you hear, **in French**.

For each adjective, use the noun and the verb to help you decide if the adjective is singular or plural.

deux-cent-vingt-et-un **221**

Module 7 Révisions

1 *Refresh your memory!* In pairs, take turns to practise pronouncing the following words. Then listen and check your pronunciation.

une maison   un appartement   un jardin   un bâtiment   un pont
un endroit   un coin   une station de métro   un magasin   l'argent

> Remember your silent final consonants and your nasal sounds.

2 *Refresh your memory!* Write out the jumbled sentences and then translate them **into English**.

a Je pas n' en France habite
b village jamais Mon calme est n'
c personne Je ne ici connais
d pour les Il y jeunes a rien n'
e Il centre pas commercial y a de n'

> Remember that the negative goes around the verb and that *ne* shortens to *n'* before a vowel, a *y*, or a mute *h*.

3 *Refresh your memory!* Listen. Then copy and complete the grid **in English**. (1–4)

	Where they want to go	Directions	Distance/time
1			

4 *Shopping trip.* Rachid is talking about a recent trip to the shops. What does he say? Write down the word for the gap in each sentence, using a word from the box. There are more words than gaps.

a Rachid went shopping with his ▢.
b He bought ▢ for his friend.
c He bought ▢ for himself.

> Listen out for who Rachid is buying for as well as what he is buying.

friend   sister   books   socks   a tie   games   shoes

5 *My bedroom.* Read these comments from Clément and Eva on an internet forum. Make notes **in English** under the following headings. You do not need to write in full sentences.

#Clément#
Dans ma chambre j'ai un lit, une table et mes vêtements. Il n'y a pas d'ordinateur mais je voudrais avoir un bureau et une chambre plus grande car ma chambre est trop petite.

#Eva#
Ma famille et moi, nous aimons notre appartement car c'est confortable. J'habite au centre-ville car c'est près de mon école. Mon frère voudrait habiter dans une maison mais moi, je voudrais habiter dans un grand château dans un autre pays.

a Clément
  (i) One thing in his bedroom
  (ii) Something he would like to have

b Eva
  (i) One reason why she lives where she does
  (ii) Somewhere she would like to live

> You only have to mention *one* detail per question.

222 *deux-cent-vingt-deux*

Module 7

Parler 6 — *Picture task.* Look at the picture and prepare what you are going to say. In pairs, practise your descriptions.

Note down things that you know how to say. You could say who is in the photo, where they are and what they are doing. Remember to use the *il/elle* or *ils/elles* form of present tense verbs.

Describe this picture.

Your description must cover:
- people
- location
- activity.

When you have finished your description, you will be asked **two questions** relating to the picture. In pairs, practise saying a short phrase/sentence in response to each question. One-word answers will not be sufficient to gain full marks.

Question 1: *Que penses-tu du shopping en ligne?*

Question 2: *Qu'est-ce qu'il y a pour les touristes dans ta région?*

Écrire 7 — *My town.* Translate the following sentences **into French**.

Remember to use the correct word for 'my': *mon, ma* or *mes*.

a I like my town.
b It is near Paris.
c My uncle lives in the town centre.
d Recently, I visited a village in the north.
e One day, I am going to live in a modern building.

You can use *près de*.

Remember that the word for 'in' depends on the context.

Think about the word order here.

Make sure you use the correct tenses.

Parler 8 — *Read aloud.* With a partner, take turns to read out the five sentences, paying attention to the underlined letters and the highlighted liaisons and cognates. Then, listen and check.

J'habite dans un village.
C'est petit et traditionnel.
Mes voisins sont très sympa.
Il y a un théâtre et un hôtel qui sont populaires.
Ici, il n'y a pas de grandes chaînes de restaurants.

Remember the liaisons here.

Take extra care with how you pronounce cognates.

Take extra care with how you pronounce the underlined sounds:
- *r* sounds like a raspy sound in the back of your throat.
- *i* and *y* sound the same, similar to the 'ee' in 'bee'.
- *h* is silent.

When you have read out the sentences, take turns to ask and answer the two follow-up questions:
- *Qu'est-ce que tu aimes faire dans ton quartier?*
- *Qu'est-ce que tu penses du tourisme?*

Adapt the questions to help start your answers, e.g. *J'aime … / Je pense que le tourisme est …*

deux-cent-vingt-trois 223

Module 8 Révisions

Parler 1

Refresh your memory! In pairs, look at the career options below. Take turns to express whether you would like that type of career or not.

- *Tu voudrais travailler dans le monde des affaires?*
- *Oui, je voudrais travailler dans le monde des affaires. Et toi, tu voudrais aider les gens?*

Make sure you use structures such as *je voudrais, je ne voudrais pas* and *j'espère*.

- travailler dans le monde des affaires
- travailler avec des enfants
- devenir professeur
- être médecin
- travailler dans un hôpital
- aider les gens
- être bien payé
- avoir ma propre entreprise

Écouter 2

Refresh your memory! Listen. Then copy and complete the grid **in English**. (1–4)

	Type of ticket	Number of tickets	Departure time	Cost
1				

Écrire 3

Refresh your memory! Write at least <u>six</u> sentences **in French** about your future plans. You can use the ideas below to help you or use your own.

Example: *J'espère voyager.*

You can use different verbs here such as 'I hope', 'I want', 'I would like to', or the near future tense 'I am going to'.

- voyager
- travailler sans être payé
- trouver un poste
- acheter une maison
- avoir des enfants
- aller à l'étranger
- étudier à l'université
- me marier

Écouter 4

My future.

a Yasmina is talking about her future. What does she say? Listen to the recording and answer the following questions in English. You do not need to write in full sentences.

(i) Which sector would Yasmina like to work in?
(ii) <u>Why in particular</u> would Yasmina like this sort of work?

Make sure you identify a reason for her chosen career.

b Jules and Chloé are also talking about their futures. What would they like and not like to do? Listen to the recording, then copy and complete the following table **in English**. You do not need to write in full sentences.

	Jules …	Chloé …
would like …		
would not like …		

Module 8

5 **Travelling to town.** Nathan is talking about a journey. What does he say? Listen to the recording and complete the sentences below. For each sentence, write the correct letter (A–C).

1 To start with, Nathan took the bus …
  A at the train station.   B at the tube station.   C at the bus station.

2 When they arrived at the town, they …
  A found a hotel.   B chose a restaurant.   C bought a ticket.

3 On Sunday morning, they travelled …
  A by train.   B by bus.   C on foot.

6 **A recent experience.** Read Théo's school blog. Write the letter (A–F) for each of the **three** correct statements.

Théo …

| A wants to travel. |
| B would like to work in an office. |
| C is interested in working for the police. |
| D thinks he will have a career in tourism. |
| E speaks three languages. |
| F doesn't like meeting people. |

Dans la vie, mon ambition est de voyager. Mon frère travaille dans un bureau et ma sœur est policière. Je pense que je vais avoir une carrière dans le tourisme car je parle trois langues et j'aime le contact avec les gens.

All these things are mentioned, but you need to find the three options that match the full meaning in the text.

7 **A part-time job.** Do this 40–50 word writing task.

You could start your answer with Pour gagner de l'argent … You could mention where you work, what you do and how often you work.

Remember to use the near future tense.

Write a review of a part-time job for a website.

You **must** include the following points:
- what you do to earn money
- your opinion of the job
- when you will work next.

Write your answer **in French**. You should aim to write between 40 and 50 words.

8 **Interests and ambitions.** Translate the following sentences **into English**.

These two verbs need to be translated into their '-ing' form.

a J'adore la musique classique.
b Chanter et danser sont mes passions.
c Je veux travailler pour une entreprise de médias.
d L'été dernier, j'ai aidé une amie dans un théâtre.
e Après le lycée, je voudrais voyager et ensuite je vais continuer mes études.

These verbs are translated into their 'to …' form.

What tense is this and how will you translate it?

9 **Dictation.** You are going to hear someone talking about their future plans.

a Sentences 1–3: write down the missing words. For each gap, you will write one word **in French**.

1 Je ___ ma ___.
2 Je veux être ___ dans un ___.
3 C'est un travail ___ et ___.

These words contain an accented sound.

b Sentences 4–6: write down the full sentences that you hear, **in French**.

deux-cent-vingt-cinq 225

Conversation questions

You can use these questions to help you prepare for two different sections of the speaking exam:
- the questions which follow on from the **read aloud task**
- the questions that you will be asked during the **picture task**.

In the **read aloud task**, there are two follow-up questions. For each of these, a few words or a short phrase/sentence is required in answer to questions about likes, dislikes, preferences and opinion.

In the **picture task**, there are two follow-up questions relating to the theme of the picture, followed by a more general conversation in which you have the opportunity to show the examiner that you know a range of structures and tenses in French.

Module 1 (pages 6–31)

Thematic context: Media and technology
1. Qu'est-ce que tu fais en ligne?
2. Est-ce que tu fais ça souvent?
3. Quels sont les dangers d'Internet? Et les points positifs?
4. Quel est ton avis sur la musique?
5. Qu'est-ce que tu aimes regarder?
6. Tu vas souvent au cinéma? Pourquoi / Pourquoi pas?

Thematic context: My personal world
7. Est-ce que tu as une vie active?
8. Pourquoi aimes-tu ces activités?
9. Qu'est-ce que tu vas faire le week-end prochain?
10. Qu'est-ce que tu as fait récemment avec tes amis? C'était comment?

Module 2 (pages 32–55)

Thematic context: My personal world
1. Qu'est-ce qui fait ton identité?
2. Décris ta famille.
3. Qu'est-ce que tu fais le week-end, en famille?
4. Tu t'entends bien avec tes amis? Pourquoi / Pourquoi pas?
5. Qu'est-ce que c'est, un bon ami, pour toi?
6. Qui est ton modèle dans la vie? Pourquoi?
7. Tu as un chanteur préféré ou une chanteuse préférée?
8. Qu'est-ce que tu as fait pour ton dernier anniversaire?
9. Comment vas-tu fêter ton anniversaire l'année prochaine?
10. Parle-moi d'une occasion spéciale avec ta famille ou tes amis.

Module 3 (pages 58–81)

Thematic context: Studying and my future
1. Quelle est ta matière préférée? Pourquoi?
2. Tu n'aimes pas quelle matière? Pourquoi?
3. Quel est ton avis sur les langues?
4. Comment sont tes profs?
5. Quelles matières voudrais-tu étudier à l'avenir?
6. Parle-moi de ton collège et de ta routine scolaire.
7. Qu'est-ce que tu penses des règles du collège?
8. Quel est ton avis sur l'uniforme scolaire?
9. Qu'est-ce que tu as fait au collège récemment?
10. L'école primaire, c'était comment pour toi?

Module 4 (pages 82–105)

Thematic context: Lifestyle and wellbeing
1. Qu'est-ce qu'il faut faire pour être en bonne santé?
2. Qu'est-ce que tu manges et bois pour le petit-déjeuner? le midi? après les cours? le soir?
3. Qu'est-ce que tu as mangé pour le dîner hier soir?
4. Qu'est-ce que tu vas manger demain et pourquoi?
5. Quelle nourriture est-ce que tu aimes bien acheter?
6. Quel est ton avis sur les restaurants fastfood?
7. Qu'est-ce que tu fais pour être en forme?
8. À l'avenir, qu'est-ce que tu vas faire pour avoir une vie plus saine?
9. Quand tu étais plus jeune, ta vie était comment?
10. Décris ta vie maintenant.

deux-cent-vingt-six

Speaking exam revision

How to prepare:
- Read through the questions to check you understand them. Focus on the question words, such as *Quel …?, Comment …?, Quand …?* etc.
- Check the verbs and time phrases to understand which timeframe the question is about.
- Then practise answering the questions using full sentences.
- Think about how you could extend your answers using more complex structures, particularly for answering questions during the **picture task** conversation.

Ways to extend your answers:
- Join together ideas with connectives: *et, mais, aussi …*
- Add in opinions and justify them: *J'aime / Je déteste … parce que …*
- Use opposing arguments: *D'un côté … d'un autre côté … / Cependant …*
- Add in examples of recent activities in the past tenses.
- Add in examples of future plans using a future tense.

Module 5 (pages 106–129)

Thematic context: Travel and tourism
1. Est-ce que tu penses que les vacances sont importantes? Pourquoi / Pourquoi pas?
2. Tu voudrais voyager? Pourquoi?
3. Parle-moi de tes vacances de rêve.
4. Qu'est-ce qu'on peut visiter dans ta région?
5. Tu es déjà allé(e) à un festival?
6. Décris-moi tes dernières vacances.
7. Parle-moi d'un problème que tu as eu en vacances.
8. Tu préfères rester chez toi ou partir en vacances? Pourquoi?
9. Quels sont les points positifs et négatifs des vacances entre amis?
10. Qu'est-ce que tu vas faire cet été, pendant les vacances?

Module 6 (pages 134–157)

Thematic context: My neighbourhood
1. Que penses-tu du recyclage?
2. Parle-moi d'un grand problème dans ta région.
3. Qu'est-ce qu'il faut faire pour protéger l'environnement?
4. Qu'est-ce que tu fais pour protéger l'environnement?
5. Quand tu étais plus jeune, qu'est-ce que tu faisais pour protéger l'environnement?
6. À l'avenir, qu'est-ce que tu vas faire pour protéger l'environnement?
7. Quel transport en commun préfères-tu et pourquoi?
8. Quels moyens de transport as-tu utilisés récemment?
9. Qu'est-ce que tu penses des voitures?
10. Qu'est-ce que le gouvernement doit faire pour encourager les gens à faire plus pour protéger l'environnement?

Module 7 (pages 158–181)

Thematic context: My neighbourhood
1. Parle-moi de ta ville.
2. Qu'est-ce qu'il faut visiter dans ta ville?
3. Quels sont les points positifs et négatifs de ta région?
4. Quelle est l'importance du tourisme pour une région, à ton avis?
5. Qu'est-ce que tu veux changer dans ta ville pour l'améliorer et pourquoi?
6. Décris-moi ta maison idéale.
7. Est-ce que tu es déjà allé(e) en France?
8. Dans quel pays est-ce que tu voudrais habiter plus tard et pourquoi?

Thematic context: My personal world
9. Qu'est-ce que tu as acheté la dernière fois que tu es sorti(e) dans ta ville?
10. Qu'est-ce que tu vas acheter comme vêtements bientôt?
11. Où préfères-tu acheter tes vêtements et pourquoi?

Module 8 (pages 182–203)

Thematic context: Studying and my future
1. Est-ce que tu voudrais un job d'été?
2. Quels sont tes projets pour le futur?
3. Quel métier voudrais-tu faire à l'avenir?
4. Quelles sont tes passions?
5. Quelle sorte de personne es-tu?
6. Avec qui voudrais-tu travailler?
7. Qu'est-ce que tu trouves important dans un emploi?
8. Quelles sont tes compétences?
9. Qu'est-ce que tu as fait récemment pour t'aider à choisir ton métier idéal?
10. Est-ce qu'il est important de faire de longues études pour avoir une bonne carrière?

deux-cent-vingt-sept 227

French phonics

Here is a list of all the sounds that you need to understand and produce.
The **SSCs** (Sound Symbol Correspondences) will be assessed in the **Read aloud** and **Dictation** tasks.

The **Read aloud** task will be the first task in your oral exam. You will have **14** minutes' preparation time for the whole oral including this task and one further minute in the exam room. The task will contain **five sentences** (35–40 words) from a specific thematic context.

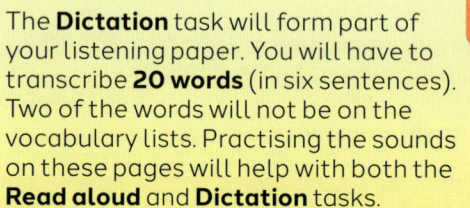

The **Dictation** task will form part of your listening paper. You will have to transcribe **20 words** (in six sentences). Two of the words will not be on the vocabulary lists. Practising the sounds on these pages will help with both the **Read aloud** and **Dictation** tasks.

Sounds	Key word and other examples	Pages with a focus on this sound	Further examples to practise
1 silent final consonant	tout dans, est, deux, trop, tard	pages 7, 9, 47	Il est trop tard. Le magasin est fermé. J'ai trois frères.
2 a	aller table, magasin, social	page 158	Il y a un centre social. Le voyage était confortable. Le festival est génial.
3 i/y	il/stylo idéal, utile, système	i page 20	C'est mon style idéal. Il y a le wifi ici? Ce site est très utile.
4 eu	peu bleu, feu, mieux	pages 87, 95	Il a les yeux bleus. Il est un peu sérieux. Je veux deux jeux.
5 e	je le, me, te, se	pages 20, 23	Je le préfère en rouge. Je me change.
6 au/eau/ closed o/ô	autre/eau/nos/tôt au, beau, vidéos, bientôt	page 107	Je vais voir le beau château. La vidéo est mauvaise. Nos autres amis sont au restaurant.
7 ou	vous ou, rouge, trouver	pages 20, 95	Où se trouve la cour? Je voudrais jouer dans un groupe.
8 u	tu bus, plus, sur	page 20	Le bus est plus utile. Le début est dans une minute. La vue est unique.
9 silent final e	elle petite, belle, groupe	page 9	Elle achète une nouvelle voiture.
10 é/-er/-ez	été/parler/avez mangé, danser, chez	é only – page 7 Revisited: é/-er/-ez page 16	Le week-end dernier, j'ai mangé chez mes amis. Pouvez-vous répéter? Vous avez regardé la télé.
11 en/an/em/am	entendre/dans/temps/jambe comment, ans, exemple, chambre	pages 84, 115	Il porte un pantalon blanc. Elle a trente ans. L'environnement est vraiment en danger.
12 on/om	mon/combien ton, opinion, nombre	page 110	C'est mon opinion. Il y a combien de ponts? Le nombre est bon.
13 ain/in/aim/im	pain/fin/faim/important certain, matin, impossible	page 84	Le matin, je prends le train. Quand mon lapin a faim, il mange du pain. La fin est impossible.
14 è/ê/ai	collège/être/faire très, fête, rêve, maison	page 34	C'est la maison de mes rêves. J'aime faire la fête. Mon collège est très moderne.
15 oi/oy	moi/moyen trois, boire, employer, envoyer	page 64 Revisited: oi page 95	J'ai envoyé trois messages. Boire de l'eau est un bon moyen d'être en forme. Moi, je bois beaucoup.

deux-cent-vingt-huit

Speaking exam revision

Sounds	Key word and other examples	Pages with a focus on this sound	Further examples to practise
16 ch	**cher** gau**ch**e, **ch**anter, blan**ch**e	page 38	Je **ch**ante **ch**aque diman**ch**e. J'aime mar**ch**er avec mon **ch**ien. Mes **ch**aussures sont blan**ch**es.
17 ç/soft 'c'	**reçu/cette** fran**ç**ais, **ç**a, **c**inq, pla**c**e	page 170	Le fran**ç**ais est fa**c**ile. J'ai re**ç**u **c**inq lettres. **Ç**a va bien.
18 qu	**qui** **qu**atre, **qu**and, pour**qu**oi	page 12	**Qu**'est-ce **qu**'on peut faire? J'ai **qu**atre chats. Mon **qu**artier est tran**qu**ille.
19 j	**jouer** **j**aune, **j**eudi, **j**anvier	pages 20, 23	Je **j**oue au tennis chaque **j**eudi. J'aime le mois de **j**anvier. Je n'aime pas le **j**aune.
20 -tion	**pollution** ac**tion**, inten**tion**, rela**tion**	page 135	Il y a des solu**tion**s pour lutter contre la pollu**tion**. J'ai l'inten**tion** de commencer la nata**tion**. J'aime les films d'ac**tion**.
21 -ien	**bien** ch**ien**, r**ien**, b**ien**tôt	page 69	Mon ch**ien** aime b**ien** manger végétar**ien**. Je n'ai r**ien** acheté. Je vais b**ien**tôt partir.
22 s-liaison	**vous avez** troi**s** ans, me**s** amis, de**s** heures	page 7	Mes ami**s** sont trè**s** actifs. J'aime les petit**s** animaux. J'ai passé de**s** heures au centre commercial.
23 t-liaison	**il faut aller** ce**t** été, tou**t** est bien	page 7	Ce**t** été, je vais en France. À l'hôtel, tou**t** était bien. Le film es**t** amusant.
24 n-liaison	**on a** mo**n** amie, so**n** école	page 7	À mo**n** avis, so**n** animal est cool. Mo**n** école est grande.
25 x-liaison	**deux heures** di**x** amis, deu**x** ans	page 7	J'ai deu**x** amis. Il est di**x** heures.
26 h	**hôtel** **h**eure, **h**eureux, **h**istoire	page 107	Je suis **h**eureux où j'**h**abite. Il est **h**uit **h**eures. L'**h**istoire de l'**h**ôtel est intéressante.
27 un	**un** l**un**di, empr**un**ter	page 115	Je cours **un** l**un**di par semaine. Il y a quelqu'**un** ici? Les transports en comm**un** sont bien.
28 -gn-	**gagner** monta**gn**e, campa**gn**e, li**gn**e	page 108	J'habite à la campa**gn**e, près de la monta**gn**e. J'ai ga**gn**é à un jeu en li**gn**e.
29 r	**rien** **r**ester, fév**r**ier, pa**r**c	page 162	Je **r**este ici pendant deux heu**r**es. J'ado**r**e ma**r**cher dans le pa**r**c avec mes pa**r**ents. Il n'est pas trop ta**r**d pour a**rr**êter les p**r**oblèmes.
30 open eu/œu	**leur/sœur** s**eu**l, j**eu**ne, c**œu**r	page 34	L**eu**r s**œu**r est j**eu**ne. C'est la s**eu**le err**eu**r. Il y a n**eu**f jou**eu**rs.
31 open o	**notre** dr**o**gue, sp**o**rt	page 138	Le sp**o**rt est n**o**tre passion. La dr**o**gue est un danger.
32 -s-	**faisons** amu**s**ant, cho**s**e, rai**s**on	page 67	C'est une cho**s**e amu**s**ante. Nous fai**s**ons de la mu**s**ique. Ils ont rai**s**on.
33 th	**théâtre** **th**ème, ma**th**s	page 162	J'adore les ma**th**s et le **th**éâtre. Je bois du **th**é. Le ry**th**me est passionnant.
34 -ill-/-ille	**billet/famille** f**ill**e, s'hab**ill**er	page 182	La f**ill**e s'hab**ill**e pour la fête de fam**ill**e. Je voudrais un b**ill**et pour le mois de ju**ill**et.
35 -aill-/-ail	**travailler** trav**aill**eur, trav**ail**, t**aill**e	page 182	C'est ma t**aill**e. Il trav**aill**e. Je suis très trav**aill**euse.

Écouter 1 Listen to each key sound or key word and repeat the sounds or words. Make a list of the sounds or words you find most challenging and keep practising them. Then, find other words for each key sound to test your pronunciation skills.

deux-cent-vingt-neuf

Role-play skills

What do I need to know about the role play?
- It is the <u>second</u> part of the speaking exam (after **Read aloud**).
- There are **10** possible settings.
- The teacher speaks first.
- You will say something for each of the **five** numbered items.
- Speak in the present tense, or use a conditional like *je voudrais*.
- You will need to ask **one** question.
- You do not need to use *vous*. You can use the informal *tu* form to ask your questions.

Settings

There are ten possible role-play settings. Look back at the modules for some role-play or conversation examples. There are also role-play cards on the exam pages at the end of each module, and in the revision module.

Setting	Module
Cinema / Theatre / Concert hall	M1 U3, M1 Révisions, M2 Exam
Café or restaurant	M7 Exam
Hotel	M5 U4
Campsite	M5 Exam
Doctor's surgery / Hospital	M4 U3, M4 Exam
In town	M7 U2
Tourist office	M5 U2, M6 Exam
Sport / Leisure centre	M1 Exam
Shop / Market / Shopping centre	M7 U3, M8 Exam
Train station	M3 Exam, M8 U2

> Although there are **10** possible settings, many of them require similar vocabulary. Use some of the speaking exam preparation time to look at each numbered item and work out what <u>you know you can</u> say. Look at the example numbered item below and a suggested answer.
>
> **Setting: At the tourist information office**
> **1** Say what activites you would like to book.
>
> In English, you might think of a reply such as: 'I want to book ...'. However, you might not remember how to say 'I want', or 'to book'. Therefore, keep it simple.
>
> Use 'I would like to do / visit / go ...':
> **Je voudrais faire / visiter / aller ...**

Useful vocabulary

Je voudrais ...	I'd like ...
Je veux ...	I want (to) ...
Je peux ... / Je peux ... ? / On peut ...	I can ... / Can I/May I ...? / One/We can ...
Il y a ... / Il y a ...?	There is/are ... / Is/Are there ...?
Je vais (+ *infinitive verb*)	I am going (to) ... (+ *infinitive verb*)
près d'ici / ici	near here / here
Vous pouvez/Tu peux répéter la question?	Can you repeat the question?
Vous avez ...?	Do you have ...?
Il y a ...?	Is/Are there ...?
C'est combien ...?	How much is/are ...?
À quelle heure ouvre ...?	At what time does ... open?
À quelle heure ferme ...?	At what what does ... close?

> Remember that you can ask the teacher to repeat if you have not understood.

deux-cent-trente

Speaking exam revision

Questions

These are a key part of role plays. You will need to ask **one question**. When it comes to your numbered item telling you to ask a question, your teacher will say: *Vous avez une question?* Here are some examples of role-play questions.

> Learn these key question words and phrases:
>
> | | | | |
> |---|---|---|---|
> | À quelle heure? | At what time? | Qui? | Who? |
> | Comment? | How? | Quel(le)(s)? | Which? |
> | Quand? | When? | Combien? | How many/ much? |
> | Où? | Where? | | |
> | Que? | What? | | |

Settings	Role-play example numbered items	Example questions
Tourist office	Ask a question about transport	Il y a des bus ici? Où est la gare? À quelle heure part le train?
	Ask a question about other activities	Qu'est-ce qu'on peut faire ici? Il y a un château près d'ici?
Cinema	Ask a question about cost	C'est combien? Ça coûte combien?
	Ask the employee about food/drinks	Est-ce qu'il y a de l'eau? Où est-ce que je peux acheter des fruits?
Shopping centre	Ask a question about something else you want to buy	Il y a une autre couleur? Vous avez une autre taille?
	Ask a question about places to eat and drink	Il y a un restaurant près d'ici? Où est-ce que je peux manger ici?
Sports centre	Ask the employee about buying a drink	Est-ce que je peux acheter de l'eau ici? L'eau, c'est combien?
	Ask the employee about opening times	À quelle heure ouvre le centre? À quelle heure est-ce que la piscine ferme?
Doctor's surgery	Ask a question about seeing the doctor	Je peux parler à un médecin? Quand est-ce que je peux voir un médecin?
	Ask a question about opening times	À quelle heure est-ce que vous ouvrez? Quand est-ce que vous fermez?
Hotel	Ask about sport facilities in the hotel	Il y a une piscine ici? On peut jouer au tennis à l'hôtel?
	Ask about other facilities	Il y a un restaurant dans l'hôtel? Est-ce qu'il y a un magasin?

> Remember that you can add **est-ce que** to ask a question in French:
> *Est-ce qu'il y a …?*
> Are/Is there …?
> *Est-ce que vous avez …?*
> Do you have …?

Example role play

Look at the example role-play card and the model conversation next to it.

Setting: At the theatre

Scenario:
- You are at a theatre and want to see a play.
- Your teacher will play the part of the employee and will speak first.
- Your teacher will ask questions **in French** and you must answer **in French.**
- You are expected to say a few words or a short phrase/sentence in response to each prompt. One-word answers will not be sufficient to gain full marks.

Task:
1 Say how many tickets you want.
2 Say how old you are.
3 Say what day you would like to see it.
4 Say at what time you would like to see it.
5 Ask the employee a question about cost.

Teacher: Bonjour. Je peux vous aider?
Student: Je voudrais quatre billets.
Teacher: D'accord. Vous avez quel âge?
Student: J'ai quinze ans.
Teacher: D'accord. Et c'est pour quel jour?
Student: Je voudrais venir dimanche.
Teacher: D'accord. Et à quelle heure?
Student: À vingt heures.
Teacher: D'accord. Vous avez une question?
Student: C'est combien?
Teacher: Dix euros.

deux-cent-trente-et-un 231

Picture task

The **picture task** is the final part of your speaking exam and is made up of **three** parts. Before your speaking assessment, you will select **one** thematic context from a choice of two of the six thematic contexts.

Thematic contexts:
- My personal world
- Lifestyle and wellbeing
- My neighbourhood
- Media and technology
- Studying and my future
- Travel and tourism

1 Picture description → **2** Two unprepared follow-up questions relating to the photo. → **3** A broader conversation (3 to 3 and a half minutes) covering the wider thematic context.

Picture description

During your preparation time, **PLAN** how you are going to describe the picture you have selected.

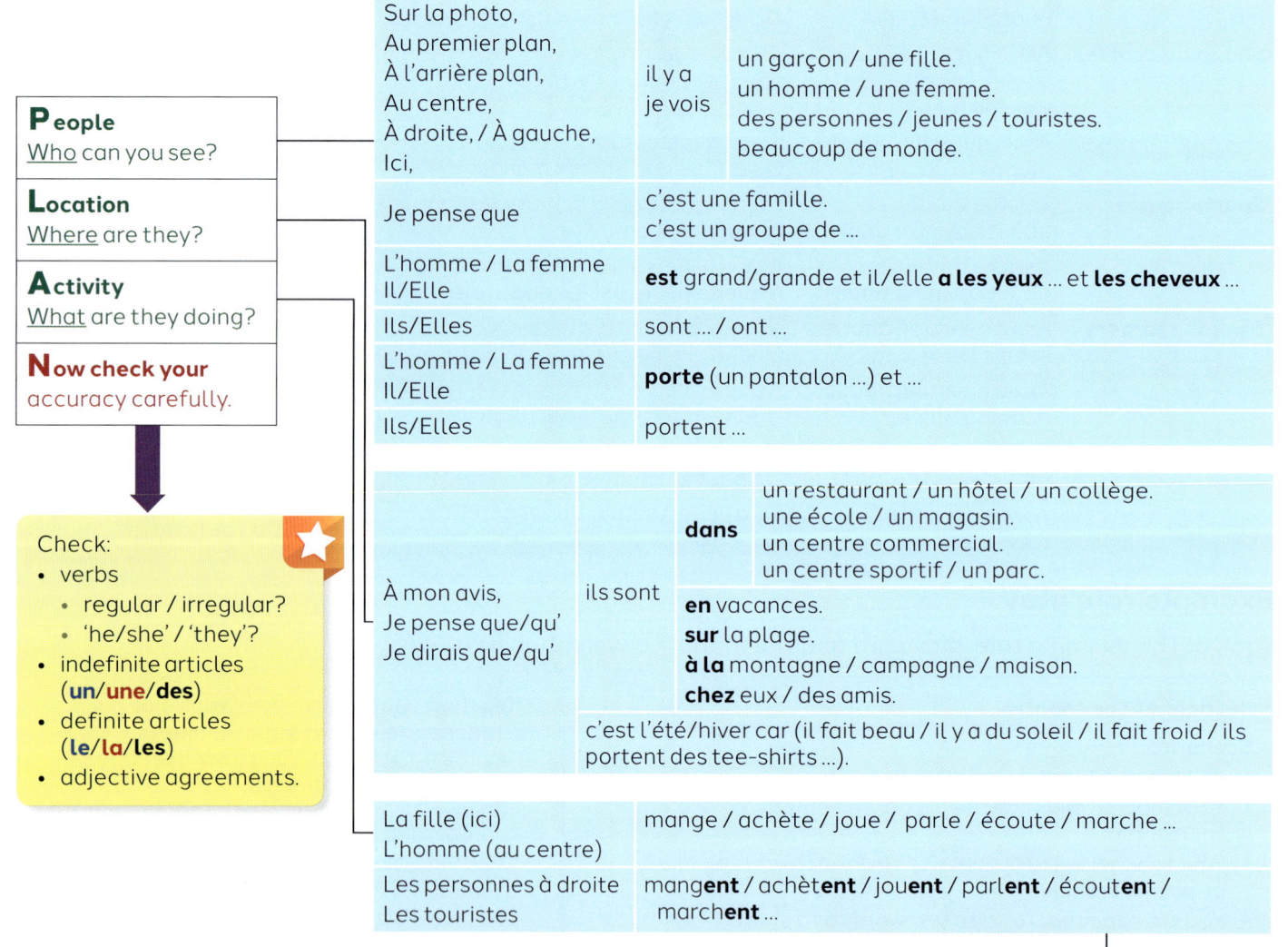

People — Who can you see?
Location — Where are they?
Activity — What are they doing?
Now check your accuracy carefully.

Check:
- verbs
  - regular / irregular?
  - 'he/she' / 'they'?
- indefinite articles (**un**/**une**/**des**)
- definite articles (**le**/**la**/**les**)
- adjective agreements.

Sur la photo, Au premier plan, À l'arrière plan, Au centre, À droite, / À gauche, Ici,	il y a je vois	un garçon / une fille. un homme / une femme. des personnes / jeunes / touristes. beaucoup de monde.
Je pense que		c'est une famille. c'est un groupe de …
L'homme / La femme Il/Elle		**est** grand/grande et il/elle **a les yeux** … et **les cheveux** …
Ils/Elles		sont … / ont …
L'homme / La femme Il/Elle		**porte** (un pantalon …) et …
Ils/Elles		portent …

À mon avis, Je pense que/qu' Je dirais que/qu'	ils sont	**dans**	un restaurant / un hôtel / un collège. une école / un magasin. un centre commercial. un centre sportif / un parc.
		en vacances. **sur** la plage. **à la** montagne / campagne / maison. **chez** eux / des amis.	
	c'est l'été/hiver car (il fait beau / il y a du soleil / il fait froid / ils portent des tee-shirts …).		

La fille (ici) L'homme (au centre)	mange / achète / joue / parle / écoute / marche …
Les personnes à droite Les touristes	mang**ent** / achèt**ent** / jou**ent** / parl**ent** / écout**ent** / march**ent** …

To say what people **are** doing, use the present tense. Remember that *ils mangent* means both 'they eat' and 'they are eating'.

Remember that the **-ent** verb ending is silent.

232 deux-cent-trente-deux

Speaking exam revision

Example picture task (Thematic context: Travel and tourism)

Picture 1

Picture 2

Describe **ONE** of these pictures. Your description must cover:
- people
- location
- activity.

When you have finished your description, your teacher will ask you **two questions** relating to your chosen picture. You are expected to say a **few words** or a **short phrase/sentence** in response to each question. One-word answers will not be sufficient to gain full marks.

You will then move on to a **conversation** on the broader thematic context of **Travel and tourism**.

During the conversation, your teacher will ask you questions in the present, past and future tenses. Your responses should be as **full and detailed** as possible.

Follow-up questions

Keep answers **simple**. For this part of the exam there are no marks for using complex language or extended answers. Your priority is to produce **accurate** language.
Pay attention to question words.

The **two follow-up questions** will be in the present tense and often (but not always) ask for your opinion. You may also be asked about what you would like to do. The questions will be about things such as likes, preferences and everyday routines. What do these question starters mean? How would you begin your answer?

Qu'est-ce qu'il y a …?
Qu'est-ce que tu fais …?
Qu'est-ce que tu aimes faire …?
Qu'est-ce que tu penses de …?
Qu'est-ce que tu préfères …?
Quel est ton … préféré?
Quelle est ta … préférée?

Qu'est-ce que tu fais pour …?
Quelle est ton opinion sur …?
Quelle(s) sorte(s) de …?
Tu préfères … ou …?
Qu'est-ce qu'il y a …?
Qu'est-ce que tu voudrais …?

Conversation

How can I do my best in the conversation?

Listen to the questions and take care with how you start each answer. Are you using the correct tense?

If you make a mistake, just correct yourself. If you want the teacher to repeat a question, ask *Vous pouvez répéter, s'il vous plaît?*

Use the example questions on pages 226–227 to practise answers to questions you might be asked.

- Keep answers relevant.
- Use accurate past, present and future tenses.
- Avoid grammar mistakes.
- Use complex language where appropriate.
- Use a range of grammar and structures.
- Develop and extend answers.
- Give clear answers.

deux-cent-trente-trois 233

Derivational morphology

In the reading exam, you may need to understand and use variations of words which you have learned, for example:

participer (to participate) → *la participation* (participation)   *cinq* (five) → *cinquième* (fifth)

Prefixes

Écrire 1 **Write words which have the opposite meaning to the ones below, adding the prefix *in-* or *im-*.**

1 égal (*equal*)
2 connu (*known*)
3 possible (*possible*)
4 moral (*moral*)

> Adding **in-** or **im-** to a word can give it the opposite meaning:
> *actif* (active) → **in***actif* (inactive)
> *l'égalité* (equality) → *l'***in***égalité* (inequality)
> *parfait* (perfect) → **im***parfait* (imperfect)

Lire 2 **Translate the underlined words into English.**

1 Elle est incapable de choisir une nouvelle voiture.
2 Les règles scolaires sont injustes!
3 L'ordinateur que tu veux acheter est indisponible.
4 Mon portable est inutile pour prendre des photos.

Suffixes

Écrire 3 **Write the ordinal numbers in words in French.**

1 5th   3 20th
2 14th   4 100th

> Cardinal numbers (1, 2, 3 etc.) become ordinal numbers (1st, 2nd, 3rd etc.) by adding *-ième* (or by dropping *-e* and adding *-ième*).
> *deux* (two) → *deux***ième** (second)   *quinze* (fifteen) → *quinz***ième** (fifteenth)
> There are two exceptions:
> *un* (one) → **premier/première** (first)   *cinq* (five) → *cinq***uième**

Lire 4 **Translate the adjectives into English.**

1 comparable   3 jouable
2 aimable   4 mangeable

> Some verbs can become adjectives by adding *-able* or *-eable* to the verb stem.
> *accepter* (to accept) → *accept***able** (acceptable)
> *télécharger* (to download) → *télécharg***eable** (downloadable)

Lire 5 **Translate these adverbs into English.**

1 exactement   3 traditionnellement
2 premièrement   4 uniquement

> Some adjectives can become adverbs by adding *-ment*, or by dropping *-ant/-ent* and adding *-amment/-emment*.
> *libre* (free) → *libre***ment** (freely)
> *patient* (patient) → *pati***emment** (patiently)

Écrire 6 **Write nouns using the stem of the verbs below and adding the suffix *-ation* or *-ion*.**

1 accepter   3 participer
2 organiser   4 réserver

> Some verbs can become nouns by adding *-ation* to the verb stem.
> *préparer* (to prepare) → *prépar***ation** (preparation)
> Some verbs ending in *-ser* can become nouns by adding *-ion* to the verb stem.
> *réviser* (to revise) → *révis***ion** (revision)

Lire 7 **Translate the sentences into English.**

1 Les chiens ne sont pas tous adorables.
2 La participation est importante en classe de musique.
3 Mon père lave la voiture quotidiennement.
4 Son portable est vraiment introuvable!
5 La huitième page du livre est intéressante.
6 La vieille maison n'est pas habitable.

Useful verb tables

Key:
* = this verb form won't appear in exams, but you may use it in your own work

Regular verbs

INFINITIVE	PRESENT TENSE (stem + present tense endings)	PERFECT TENSE (auxiliary + past participle)	FUTURE TENSE (*aller* + infinitive)	IMPERFECT TENSE (stem + imperfect endings)
regarder *to watch*	je regard**e** tu regard**es** il regard**e** nous regard**ons** vous regard**ez** ils regard**ent**	j'ai regard**é** tu as regardé il a regardé nous avons regardé vous avez regardé ils ont regardé	je vais regarder tu vas regarder il va regarder nous allons regarder vous allez regarder ils vont regarder	je regard**ais** tu regard**ais** il regard**ait** *nous regard**ions** *vous regard**iez** *ils regard**aient**
finir *to finish*	je fin**is** tu fin**is** il fin**it** nous fin**issons** vous fin**issez** ils fin**issent**	j'ai fin**i** tu as fini il a fini nous avons fini vous avez fini ils ont fini	je vais finir tu vas finir il va finir nous allons finir vous allez finir ils vont finir	je finissais tu finissais il finissait *nous finissions *vous finissiez *ils finissaient
entendre *to hear*	j'entend**s** tu entend**s** il entend nous entend**ons** vous entend**ez** ils entend**ent**	j'ai entend**u** tu as entendu il a entendu nous avons entendu vous avez entendu ils ont entendu	je vais entendre tu vas entendre il va entendre nous allons entendre vous allez entendre ils vont entendre	j'entendais tu entendais il entendait *nous entendions *vous entendiez *ils entendaient
s'amuser *to have fun*	je **m'**amuse tu **t'**amuses il **s'**amuse *nous **nous** amusons *vous **vous** amusez *ils **s'**amusent	je me **suis** amusé(e) tu **t'es** amusé(e) il **s'est** amusé *nous nous **sommes** amusé(e)s *vous vous **êtes** amusé(e)(s) *ils se **sont** amusés	je vais m'amuser tu vas t'amuser il va s'amuser *nous allons nous amuser *vous allez vous amuser *ils vont s'amuser	je m'amusais tu t'amusais il s'amusait *nous nous amusions *vous vous amusiez *ils s'amusaient

These verbs have a spelling change in the *je, tu, il* (and *ils*) forms that affects the pronunciation. They otherwise behave as regular *-er* verbs.

INFINITIVE	PRESENT TENSE (watch out for the change of stem)	PERFECT TENSE (auxiliary + past participle)	FUTURE TENSE (*aller* + infinitive)	IMPERFECT TENSE (stem + imperfect endings)
se lever *to get up*	je me l**è**ve tu te l**è**ves il se l**è**ve	je me suis levé(e) tu t'es levé(e) il s'est levé	je vais me lever tu vas te lever il va se lever	je me levais tu te levais il se levait
acheter *to buy*	j'ach**è**te tu ach**è**tes il ach**è**te	j'ai acheté tu as acheté il a acheté	je vais acheter tu vas acheter il va acheter	j'achetais tu achetais il achetait
préférer *to prefer*	je préf**è**re tu préf**è**res il préf**è**re	j'ai préféré tu as préféré il a préféré	je vais préférer tu vas préférer il va préférer	je préférais tu préférais il préférait

deux-cent-trente-cinq **235**

Useful verb tables

Key:
* = this verb form won't appear in exams, but you may use it in your own work

Key irregular verbs

INFINITIVE	PRESENT TENSE (watch out for the change of stem)	PERFECT TENSE (auxiliary + past participle)	FUTURE TENSE (*aller* + infinitive)	IMPERFECT TENSE (stem + imperfect endings)
aller *to go*	je **vais** tu **vas** il **va** nous **allons** vous **allez** ils **vont**	je suis **allé**(e) tu es allé(e) il est allé nous sommes allé(e)s vous êtes allé(e)(s) ils sont allés	je vais aller tu vas aller il va aller nous allons aller vous allez aller ils vont aller	j'allais tu allais il allait *nous allions *vous alliez *ils allaient
avoir *to have*	j'**ai** tu **as** il **a** nous **avons** vous **avez** ils **ont**	j'ai **eu** tu as eu il a eu nous avons eu vous avez eu ils ont eu	je vais avoir tu vas avoir il va avoir nous allons avoir vous allez avoir ils vont avoir	j'avais tu avais il avait *nous avions *vous aviez *ils avaient
être *to be*	je **suis** tu **es** il **est** nous **sommes** vous **êtes** ils **sont**	j'ai **été** tu as été il a été nous avons été vous avez été ils ont été	je vais être tu vas être il va être nous allons être vous allez être ils vont être	j'**ét**ais tu étais il était *nous étions *vous étiez *ils étaient
faire *to do/make*	je **fais** tu **fais** il **fait** nous **faisons** vous **faites** ils **font**	j'ai **fait** tu as fait il a fait nous avons fait vous avez fait ils ont fait	je vais faire tu vas faire il va faire nous allons faire vous allez faire ils vont faire	je faisais tu faisais il faisait *nous faisions *vous faisiez *ils faisaient
prendre *to take* (**apprendre**, **comprendre** *follow the same pattern*)	je **prends** tu **prends** il **prend** nous **prenons** vous **prenez** ils **prennent**	j'ai **pris** tu as pris il a pris nous avons pris vous avez pris ils ont pris	je vais prendre tu vas prendre il va prendre nous allons prendre vous allez prendre ils vont prendre	je prenais tu prenais il prenait *nous prenions *vous preniez *ils prenaient

Modal verbs

INFINITIVE	PRESENT TENSE (watch out for the change of stem)	PERFECT TENSE (auxiliary + past participle)	FUTURE TENSE (*aller* + infinitive)	IMPERFECT TENSE (stem + imperfect endings)
devoir *to have to (must)*	je **dois** tu **dois** il **doit** nous **devons** vous **devez** ils **doivent**	*j'ai **dû** *tu as dû *il a dû *nous avons dû *vous avez dû *ils ont dû	je vais devoir tu vas devoir il va devoir nous allons devoir vous allez devoir ils vont devoir	*je devais *tu devais *il devait *nous devions *vous deviez *ils devaient
pouvoir *to be able to (can)*	je **peux** tu **peux** il **peut** nous **pouvons** vous **pouvez** ils **peuvent**	*j'ai **pu** *tu as pu *il a pu *nous avons pu *vous avez pu *ils ont pu	je vais pouvoir tu vas pouvoir il va pouvoir nous allons pouvoir vous allez pouvoir ils vont pouvoir	*je pouvais *tu pouvais *il pouvait *nous pouvions *vous pouviez *ils pouvaient

Useful verb tables

INFINITIVE	PRESENT TENSE (watch out for the change of stem)	PERFECT TENSE (auxiliary + past participle)	FUTURE TENSE (*aller* + infinitive)	IMPERFECT TENSE (stem + imperfect endings)
savoir *to know (how to)*	je **sais** tu **sais** il **sait** nous **savons** vous **savez** ils **savent**	*j'ai **su** *tu as su *il a su *nous avons su *vous avez su *ils ont su	je vais savoir tu vas savoir il va savoir nous allons savoir vous allez savoir ils vont savoir	*je savais *tu savais *il savait *nous savions *vous saviez *ils savaient
vouloir *to want (to)*	je **veux** tu **veux** il **veut** nous **voulons** vous **voulez** ils **veulent**	*j'ai **voulu** *tu as voulu *il a voulu *nous avons voulu *vous avez voulu *ils ont voulu	je vais vouloir tu vas vouloir il va vouloir nous allons vouloir vous allez vouloir ils vont vouloir	*je voulais *tu voulais *il voulait *nous voulions *vous vouliez *ils voulaient

Other useful irregular verbs

INFINITIVE	PRESENT TENSE (watch out for the change of stem)	PERFECT TENSE (auxiliary + past participle)	FUTURE TENSE (*aller* + infinitive)	IMPERFECT TENSE (stem + imperfect endings)
boire *to drink*	je **boi**s tu **boi**s il **boi**t *nous **buv**ons *vous **buv**ez *ils **boiv**ent	j'ai **bu** tu as bu il a bu nous avons bu vous avez bu ils ont bu	je vais boire tu vas boire il va boire nous allons boire vous allez boire ils vont boire	*je **buv**ais *tu buvais *il buvait *nous buvions *vous buviez *ils buvaient
connaître *to know* (**reconnaître** *(to recognise)* follows the same pattern)	je **connai**s tu **connai**s il connaît *nous **connaiss**ons *vous **connaiss**ez *ils **connaiss**ent	j'ai **connu** tu as connu il a connu nous avons connu vous avez connu ils ont connu	je vais connaître tu vas connaître il va connaître nous allons connaître vous allez connaître ils vont connaître	*je **connaiss**ais *tu connaissais *il connaissait *nous connaissions *vous connaissiez *ils connaissaient
courir *to run*	je cours tu cours il court *nous courons *vous courez *ils courent	j'ai **couru** tu as couru il a couru nous avons couru vous avez couru ils ont couru	je vais courir tu vas courir il va courir nous allons courir vous allez courir ils vont courir	*je courais *tu courais *il courait *nous courions *vous couriez *ils couraient
croire *to believe*	je crois tu crois il croit *nous **croy**ons *vous **croy**ez *ils **croi**ent	j'ai **cru** tu as cru il a cru nous avons cru vous avez cru ils ont cru	je vais croire tu vas croire il va croire nous allons croire vous allez croire ils vont croire	*je **croy**ais *tu croyais *il croyait *nous croyions *vous croyiez *ils croyaient
dire *to say*	je dis tu dis il dit *nous **dis**ons *vous **dites** *ils **dis**ent	j'ai **dit** tu as dit il a dit nous avons dit vous avez dit ils ont dit	je vais dire tu vas dire il va dire nous allons dire vous allez dire ils vont dire	*je **dis**ais *tu disais *il disait *nous disions *vous disiez *ils disaient

deux-cent-trente-sept

Useful verb tables

Key:
* = this verb form won't appear in exams, but you may use it in your own work

INFINITIVE	PRESENT TENSE (watch out for the change of stem)	PERFECT TENSE (auxiliary + past participle)	FUTURE TENSE (*aller* + infinitive)	IMPERFECT TENSE (stem + imperfect endings)
écrire to write	j'**écris** tu **écris** il **écrit** *nous **écriv**ons *vous **écriv**ez *ils **écriv**ent	j'ai **écrit** tu as écrit il a écrit nous avons écrit vous avez écrit ils ont écrit	je vais écrire tu vas écrire il va écrire nous allons écrire vous allez écrire ils vont écrire	*j'écrivais *tu écrivais *il écrivait *nous écrivions *vous écriviez *ils écrivaient
lire to read	je lis tu lis il lit *nous **lis**ons *vous **lis**ez *ils **lis**ent	j'ai **lu** tu as lu il a lu nous avons lu vous avez lu ils ont lu	je vais lire tu vas lire il va lire nous allons lire vous allez lire ils vont lire	*je lisais *tu lisais *il lisait *nous lisions *vous lisiez *ils lisaient
mettre to put (in, on)	je **met**s tu **met**s il **met** nous mettons vous mettez ils mettent	j'ai **mis** tu as mis il a mis nous avons mis vous avez mis ils ont mis	je vais mettre tu vas mettre il va mettre nous allons mettre vous allez mettre ils vont mettre	*je mettais *tu mettais *il mettait *nous mettions *vous mettiez *ils mettaient
ouvrir to open	j'ouvre tu ouvres il ouvre nous ouvrons vous ouvrez ils ouvrent	j'ai **ouvert** tu as ouvert il a ouvert nous avons ouvert vous avez ouvert ils ont ouvert	je vais ouvrir tu vas ouvrir il va ouvrir nous allons ouvrir vous allez ouvrir ils vont ouvrir	j'ouvrais tu ouvrais il ouvrait *nous ouvrions *vous ouvriez *ils ouvraient
partir to leave	je **par**s tu **par**s il **par**t nous **par**tons vous **par**tez ils **par**tent	je **suis** parti(e) tu **es** parti(e) il **est** parti nous **sommes** parti(e)s vous **êtes** parti(e)(s) ils **sont** partis	je vais partir tu vas partir il va partir nous allons partir vous allez partir ils vont partir	je partais tu partais il partait *nous partions *vous partiez *ils partaient
recevoir to receive	je **reçoi**s tu **reçoi**s il **reçoi**t *nous **recev**ons *vous **recev**ez *ils **reçoi**vent	j'ai **reçu** tu as reçu il a reçu nous avons reçu vous avez reçu ils ont reçu	je vais recevoir tu vas recevoir il va recevoir nous allons recevoir vous allez recevoir ils vont recevoir	*je recevais *tu recevais *il recevait *nous recevions *vous receviez *ils recevaient
rire to laugh	je ris tu ris il rit *nous rions *vous riez *ils rient	j'ai **ri** tu as ri il a ri nous avons ri vous avez ri ils ont ri	je vais rire tu vas rire il va rire nous allons rire vous allez rire ils vont rire	*je riais *tu riais *il riait *nous riions *vous riiez *ils riaient
sortir to go out, leave	je **sor**s tu **sor**s il **sor**t nous **sor**tons vous **sor**tez ils **sor**tent	je **suis** sorti(e) tu **es** sorti(e) il **est** sorti nous **sommes** sorti(e)s vous **êtes** sorti(e)(s) ils **sont** sortis	je vais sortir tu vas sortir il va sortir nous allons sortir vous allez sortir ils vont sortir	je sortais tu sortais il sortait *nous sortions *vous sortiez *ils sortaient

Useful verb tables

INFINITIVE	PRESENT TENSE (watch out for the change of stem)	PERFECT TENSE (auxiliary + past participle)	FUTURE TENSE (*aller* + infinitive)	IMPERFECT TENSE (stem + imperfect endings)
suivre *to follow*	je **sui**s tu **sui**s il **sui**t *nous **suiv**ons *vous **suiv**ez *ils **suiv**ent	j'ai **suivi** tu as suivi il a suivi nous avons suivi vous avez suivi ils ont suivi	je vais suivre tu vas suivre il va suivre nous allons suivre vous allez suivre ils vont suivre	*je suivais *tu suivais *il suivait *nous suivions *vous suiviez *ils suivaient
traduire *to translate*	je traduis tu traduis il traduit nous **traduis**ons vous **traduis**ez ils **traduis**ent	j'ai **traduit** tu as traduit il a traduit nous avons traduit vous avez traduit ils ont traduit	je vais traduire tu vas traduire il va traduire nous allons traduire vous allez traduire ils vont traduire	je traduisais tu traduisais il traduisait *nous traduisions *vous traduisiez *ils traduisaient
venir *to come* (**devenir** (*to become*) follows the same pattern)	je **vien**s tu **vien**s il **vien**t nous **ven**ons vous **ven**ez ils **vienn**ent	je **suis venu**(e) tu **es** venu(e) il **est** venu nous **sommes** venu(e)s vous **êtes** venu(e)(s) ils **sont** venus	je vais venir tu vas venir il va venir nous allons venir vous allez venir ils vont venir	je venais tu venais il venait *nous venions *vous veniez *ils venaient
voir *to see*	je vois tu vois il voit *nous **voy**ons *vous **voy**ez *ils **voi**ent	j'ai **vu** tu as vu il a vu nous avons vu vous avez vu ils ont vu	je vais voir tu vas voir il va voir nous allons voir vous allez voir ils vont voir	*je voyais *tu voyais *il voyait *nous voyions *vous voyiez *ils voyaient

The verb **pleuvoir** (to rain) is only used in the *il* form.

INFINITIVE	PRESENT TENSE	PERFECT TENSE	FUTURE TENSE	IMPERFECT TENSE
*****pleuvoir** *to rain*	il **pleu**t	*il a **plu**	*il va pleuvoir	*il pleuvait

deux-cent-trente-neuf **239**